With Kindest Wishes

Yours Aye

Duncan L Reid

The Last Miners of Ayrshire's Doon Valley

Donald L Reid **BA FSA Scot**

Foreword by
Kenneth J Gibson MSP

He's done it again! Another rich and warm history from the pen of author Donald L Reid
The Ayrshire Post

The Last Miners of Ayrshire's Doon Valley

Hardback: ISBN 978-0-9566343-5-1

Compiled and edited
By
Donald L Reid BA FSA Scot
Author of
The Lost Mining Villages of Doon Valley
Doon Valley Memories
Robert Burns' Valley of Doon
Matthew Anderson: Policeman-Poet of Ayrshire
and other Ayrshire local interest books
(see page 246 for full list)

A royalty which might arise as a result of this book will benefit:
Dalmellington Band,
Dalmellington Scout Group (33rd Ayrshire)
Patna Primary School
Dalmellington Local History Group
and
Barrmill Jolly Beggars Burns Club

Photos curtesy of East Ayrshire Council, Doon Valley Museum unless otherwise indicated.

This book is respectfully dedicated to all those hardy miners in Ayrshire's Doon Valley who were accidentally killed in the mining industry.

Behold the hour, the boat arrive!
Thou goest, the darling of my heart!
Sever'd from thee, can I survive?
But fate has will'd and we must part

Behold the Hour. The Boat Arrive
Robert Burns

First Published 2016 by
Donald L Reid BA FSA Scot
and
Barrmill Jolly Beggars Burns Club
7 Manuel Avenue
Beith, North Ayrshire, Scotland KA15 1BJ
Tel: 01505-503801
E: *donaldleesreid@hotmail.com*
Web: *www.jollybeggars.org*
Facebook: www.facebook.com/donald.reid.1401

Layout by
Delta Mac Artwork
deltamacartwork@btinternet.com

The publishers gratefully acknowledge financial support from:
The Heritage Lottery Fund;
Scottish Coal Industry Special Welfare Fund
Barrmill Jolly Beggars Burns Club and
Donald L Reid

Printed and bound in Great Britain by
Kestrel Press (Irvine) Ltd
25 Whittle Place, Irvine, Ayrshire, KA11 4HR
Tel: 01294 222222
action@kestrelpress.com

Contents

Lost Villages o' Doon – Poem by Rowena M Love 4
Foreword by Kenneth J Gibson MSP 5
Author's Preface 6
Acknowledgements 8
Introduction 10
Chapters
1 Ayrshire's Doon Valley 16
2 Doon Valley Industrial Past 32
3 Death-Knell of Doon Valley Deep Mining 38
4 Clawfin to Pennyvenie – A Life in Mining (Tom Hutchison) 42
5 Tam o' Dunaskin Glen (Tom McKnight) 48
6 What's in a Name (Edgar Ierland) 55
7 Accident at Pennyvenie (Malcolm Graham) 64
8 Bygone Lethanhill (James McFadzean) 69
9 Benwhat – Random Reflections (James 'Jimsy' McPhail) 73
10 Big-hearted Beoch (Andrew Knox Bone) 79
11 Beoch – A Caring Community (Tom Reid) 83
12 Reflections on Beoch (James L Reid) 92
13 Cairntable Capers (Tom Smith) 98
14 Coalface of Life – Home Was a Hut (Bill Bakkom) 103
15 Miner's Wife – Miner's Daughter (Jeannie Mowatt or McCreath) .109
16 After Benwhat – What? (Stuart Williamson) 119
17 Miner's Tale of a Lost Village (Neil Dempsey) 122
18 Beoch Birthday Blethers (James Chalmers) 131
19 Childhood Memories of Lethanhill (Ann MacLean) 134
20 A Lethanhill Lad in the Mines (Hugh Hainey) 139
21 Cairntable Miner – Poacher Turned Gamekeeper (Jimmy Dunn) .146
22 Lethanhill – A Deserted Mining Village (William Murphy) 151
23 Donaghadee to New Zealand – via Doon Valley (David Boyce) . .156
24 The Human Cost of Coal Extraction (David Scobie) 159
25 Colliery Tradesman (John Collins) 163
26 Benwhat – The Music Plays On (Tom Filson) 168
27 Happy Years at Pennyvenie Colliery (George Brown) 173
28 Mining to Music (Hugh Johnstone MBE) 180
29 Alexander Sloan MP – His Family of the First World War (Esther Clark) 188
30 Houldsworth, Glenburn and Littlemill (Alex Green) 196
31 Days Doon the Pit (Sammy Ballantyne) 200
32 Random Memories of the Pits (Arthur McCrail) 205
33 Working Pennyvenie Coal Face (Harry Kennedy) 210
34 Memories of Waterside (Alexander Mackenzie) 216
35 Doon Valley Mining – Press Reports 220
36 Shared Mining Memories 233
Robert Wallace 233
Margaret Dale 235
Vance Harvey 237
Dennis McQuillan 238
Andrew Galloway 240
Doon Valley Miners at War 242
Epilogue 243
Poem: Ghaists (Rab Wilson) 244
Bibliography 245
Books by Donald L Reid 246
Picture Gallery – Additional Photographs 247
Appendices
List of Fatal Accidents in Doon Valley National Coal Board (NCB) pits/mines 1951 – 1971 261
and List of Fatal Accidents in Doon Valley Opencast Mining Operations 2000 - 2008 263
List of players/officials of Dalmellington Band who worked in Doon Valley pits 264

The author is indebted to Rowena M Love for kindly writing a small poem reflecting the spirit of the Lost Mining Villages of Doon Valley, appropriately titled 'Lost Villages o' Doon'. Great-granddaughter of an Ayrshire miner, Rowena is a writer and poet formerly based in the West of Scotland. She is married with a daughter and is an experienced tutor and performer. Her poetry collection *The Chameleon of Happiness* was published in March 2004 by Makar Press. The reader can find out more about Rowena and her writing on her website:
www.rowenamlove.co.uk

Lost Villages o' Doon

Rowena M Love

teem = empty, echoing, unoccupied
scartin = scraping
plowterin = splashing
lowes = flames, fires

At Corbie Craigs
hoose nor hut are staunin still,
the space whaur they were
teem,
brick an beam as broken
as the mines that fed them.
Benwhat near at haun,
higher up Lethanhill, Burnfoothill,
or Craigmark ablow
are jist as empty.
Beoch, tae, is a lang five mile
frae Da'mellin't'n tae history.

Wreaths are laid
fur the hames that were razed
as if ilka hoose itsel had deed.
Bit bide a wee
in the space whaur they were
and the echoes come real
shapes and sounds mair solid an sure
nor all yer trees an birdsang.

Mither at the mangle, her hauns red raw,
first o her sheets aready snappin wi a guid blaw;
faither scartin last o the coal dust fae his face
wi his well-stropped cut-throat;
a footie gemm, lads efter scuil wi jerseys fur goals
or a sairious team, wi village pride their prod to gie their all;
weans plowterin in the burn, squealin or greetin,
wee Jeannie's ribbon aye at the droop;
windaes flickerin bright wi lowes,
the fires' reek as saft an grey as stags' velvet.

The villages arnae lost,
fur memories o they days
are mortared strang intae that hillside
far above the Doon.

Foreword

Kenneth J Gibson MSP

North Ayrshire and Arran

Like brethren in a common cause,
We'd on each other smile, man;
And equal rights and equal laws
Wad gladden every isle, man.

The Tree of Liberty
Robert Burns

The mining stories in this book are compelling and humbling and remind the reader that in the not too distant past, daily life was a real challenge for those living and working in the remote mining villages of Ayrshire's historic Doon Valley. The fact that deep mining has ceased, not only in Ayrshire but the whole of Scotland, makes this book all the more timely. It also shows how dramatic changes can occur in just a few short years.

What shines through strongly about the mining communities of the Doon Valley is the importance of community spirit, with folk knowing everyone else – their strengths and weaknesses – and the willingness to interact with care, consideration and compassion for neighbours. This is just one example we can all learn from.

These important interviews record the stories of miners who experienced life at the coalface and in the industry generally. The stories will ensure that many of the influences which have shaped the Doon Valley communities will be more widely known and recognised by each new generation.

Donald L Reid recalls that when speaking to a class at Bellsbank Primary School in 2011, one wee boy said: "Whit's coal Mr?" This demonstrates how quickly our social history can be forgotten if it is not recorded in book form, spoken about by those who were miners and kept alive in our schools.

Anyone reading this book will gain a better understanding of what coal is and the cost of extraction in human terms – men killed and injured and health blighted by the working in the coal mines.

Donald L Reid and fellow Burnsians from Barrmill Jolly Beggars Burns Club are to be heartily congratulated in providing all of us with the opportunity of remembering a forgotten Doon Valley mining past.

These moving stories, from the voices of miners who worked at the coal face of life, are an enduring record of an industry which was so important in Ayrshire and especially so in the Doon Valley. It is hoped that in years to come, when readers dip into this book, they will be rather proud of this valuable Doon Valley mining heritage. Enjoy a great read!

A' this and mair I never heard of,
And, but for you, I might despair'd of
So gratefu', back your news I send you,
And pray a' guid things may attend you!

To a Gentleman
Robert Burns

Author's Preface

The charms o the min', the langer they shine
The mair admiration they draw, man;
While peaches and cherries, and roses and lilies,
They fade and they wither awa, man.

The Ronalds of the Bennals
Robert Burns

These precious shared memories are recorded with spontaneity and imperfection, and with the inevitable overlapping of topics, but they will, nevertheless, stir fascinating memories of times past, so special to those in whose footsteps we now walk.

One objective of this project was to allow the miners to speak about their experiences and tell their stories straight from the heart to help preserve part of the social and industrial history of Doon Valley.

These stories will pull the heart strings, not least because of the tragedies which resulted in miners being fatally injured at work which impacted so dramatically on family life. Selected newspaper reports also highlight the appalling frequency of mining accidents.

I was fortunate and privileged to be able to interview many retired Doon Valley miners all with their own special stories to tell. They did so with great spontaneity and pride. These stories now form part of an important social record. Their stories are the kernel of this book.

With the passage of time there are fewer miners who can recall life as it was in the pits and mines of Doon Valley. Without a deep knowledge of the past it is almost impossible to understand and make sense of the present and consequently more difficult to mould the future in a positive way.

The older generation of former miners who experienced life working at Beoch, Pennyvenie, Chalmerston, Minnivey and Houldsworth, possessed a largely untapped but enormous fund of knowledge and wisdom, through the shared adversity of working in dangerous places underground to recover coal for industrial and domestic use.

Miners were generally proud assertive men who would speak their mind. My father often said: "No pupil ever left Beoch School without being able to read and write." And they also possessed a level of confidence in their skills and ability and aspired to have their place in society, knowing that with a good work ethic and dedication, the world was indeed their oyster.

There are many stories still waiting to be told, if only we have the sense to seek them out while the people are still there to tell them. That is a task the reader can address. Older folk have a special life story to tell. Make sure you record their memories of yesteryear before it is too late!

Scotland's national Bard, Robert Burns, immortalised the River Doon, and famously extolled the merits of being able to 'see oursels as ithers see us.' The voices of the past help us to see how others lived and the reader may wish to compare our lifestyle today to that of yesteryear.

It may prove very sobering and humbling and can never be better illustrated than remembering that a wee boy, aged thirteen years, died underground at Pennyvenie in July 1905.

I like to think that in a hundred years time, someone will pick up this book and enjoy a happy look-back in time and wonder a little about the kindly and talented folk who worked in the mining industry of Ayrshire's Doon Valley.

Whilst I have recorded the names of many who assisted in this project in various different ways in the acknowledgements, it would be remiss not to make special mention of Laurence Macintyre, MBE, of Erskine and my wife Kathleen Reid for working above and beyond on the manuscript; thanks also to Archibald Chalmers of Stewarton, Bert Richie of Dalmellington and Roger Griffiths of Stewarton for their assistance in reading and commenting on the manuscript as it evolved. All were extremely helpful and encouraging.

It would also be remiss not to make special mention of the Heritage Lottery Fund for their support of this project, particularly Bobbi Campbell, Gillian Harrison and Lucy Casot.

The real joy for me in compiling this work is that so much more of an almost forgotten past will be preserved and that is, in my opinion, rather special.

Anyone reading this book will gain a better understanding of what coal is and the cost of extraction in human terms – men killed or injured or blighted by working in the coal industry.

Finally, I am very grateful that so many remarkable mining men and their families willingly and enthusiastically shared their precious memories of those challenging days of yesteryear. Happy reading and remembering!

O'Age has weary days,
And nights o' sleepless pain
Thou golden time o youthful prime,
Why comest thou not again?

The Winter of Life
Robert Burns

Donald L Reid
Beith, Ayrshire
2016

Acknowledgements

I am taking the old road again;
By the dyke-side, down to the green glen;
And the breezes in the rowans red,
Whisper in trees of my childhood,
'Come you this way again.'

The Old Road
Maureen Henderson

I am indebted to all the interviewees who shared precious memories with me and others. A similar debt of gratitude is owed to those who provided photographs and information. I should like to express my heartfelt thanks to everyone in the Doon Valley and further afield who gave so much help during my research. What shone through strongly was the great affinity so many folk, from home and abroad, have for the Doon Valley.

This book just seemed to grow and grow, but it was never going to be possible to include extracts of interviews from everyone. There was also a deluge of fascinating photographs; identifying the names of those shown in them was a monumental task with a mixed level of success.

I am grateful to the following for their kind assistance in so many different ways. All reside in the Doon Valley unless otherwise indicated. Ayrshire newspaper archives: *Ardrossan and Saltcoats Herald*; *Ayr Advertiser*; *Ayrshire Post*; *Cumnock Chronicle and Kilmarnock Standard*; hon presidents, president, past presidents and cronies of Barrmill Jolly Beggars Burns Club, Beith, North Ayrshire; Patna Primary School, with a special mention to head teacher, Mrs Sharon Yorkston, and all the pupils of P6 and P7; Christine MacLellan née Ballantyne (Prestwick); John Bennett (Patna); Adrian Booth, railway photographer; David Boyce (New Zealand); Anthony Collins (Ayr); Esther Clark (Ayr); Katy Clark, MP for North Ayrshire & Arran 2005 – 15); Doon Valley Local History Group based at Doon Valley Museum, Dalmellington; Jeanie Cullen nee Gault; Neil 'Neilly' Dempsey; Brian Donohoe, formerly MP for Central Ayrshire 1992 – 2015; Robert Douglas (Prestwick); Louise Dunn, née Scott (Ayr);

Special thanks to the enthusiastic Kennedy Ferguson, a Lethanhill lad, for his wonderful detective work in creating a superb general plan of the 'lost mining villages of Doon Valley' and one of Benquhat (Benwhat), Lethanhill and Waterside; Scott Filson; Elizabeth Forsyth née Hutchinson (Ayr); Libby Gibson of Ayr Road Garage, Dalmellington for her fantastic support in marketing this and previous Doon Valley books; Kenneth Gibson MSP, North Ayrshire and Arran; Mark Gibson of Craigengillan; Dot Graham (Barrmill) for her support and amazing typesetting skills; Morag Halliday and Heather Baillie (Age Scotland); Vance Harvey, Tarbolton; Maureen Henderson (Ayr) for permission to quote from her poem, *The Old Road*; Archie Hutchison of Dalmellington Band; Anne Johnstone; David Johnstone (Patna), Hugh Johnstone MBE of Dalmellington Band for help in supplying photographs and assisting with research; Anne Joss, MBE; Dane Love FSA Scot (Auchinleck); Edwin Lawrence (Ayrshire Post);

Rowena M Love (Scottish poet); Councillor Nan McFarlane, South Ayrshire Council.

John McGee of Wheech Scottish Ancestry Services; Willie McHendry (Ayr); Frank McHugh & David Brown of 33rd Ayrshire Dalmellington Scouts; Laurence Macintyre, MBE, of Erskine; Tom McKnight; Helen McQuater née Armour; Stanley Sarsfield and Elaine Mackie of EAC, Doon Valley Museum for encouragement and kind assistance with archive material from the museum; Anne and Middleton Park of Dalmellington for their support and encourgement; Jan Murray née Hutchison; Sandra Osborne (former MP Ayr 1997 – 2015); Elizabeth Pearce (Fergus, Ontario, Canada).

David and Margaret Rarity (Patna), very good friends, for their usual fantastic support and encouragement; Ian Riggins (Ayr); Bert and Elizabeth Ritchie for their usual outstanding support; good friends Iain and Colette Shaw of Ardrossan for their usual support; John and Noreen Steele, Ardrossan-based authors and good friends; William Stevenson; Quintin and Margaret Stirrit; James Treversh, (Police Memorabilia Collectors Club (PMCC) magazine); Alice and Tom Wallace; Robert (Bobby) Wallace; Hugh Wilkie (Paisley); Rab Wilson, poet (New Cumnock); David Young.

My fellow cronies at Barrmill Jolly Beggars Burns Club also deserve a special mention for their positive help and support of this reminiscence project. In particular, thanks must go to regular companions on visits to the Doon Valley, assistance with the educational element of the project and interviews and research – Norrie and Rose Brown, Norman M Henderson, Warnock Longridge, Iain and Colette Shaw, and Harry Young. Special thanks to all the cronies of the club for their support – Archie Brodie, Marshall Carmichael, Archie Chalmers, John Craig, Willie Edmunds, Maurice Hughes, Bobby Irvine, Tom Irvine, Willie MacDougall, David MacLeod, David McMillan, Gordon Mabbott, Willie Monahan, John Moses, David Pettigrew, R Allan Richardson, Iain Skene, James R Waite, John Waite, Bob Wark, Duncan Winning OBE, Gordon Wilson and Ronnie Yuille.

A very special word of thanks goes to my dear wife, Kathleen Reid; son, Fraser Reid and his wife, Heather; my daughter Elaine Walker and her husband Mark; my delightful grandchildren, Taylor James Reid and Owen James Reid. Above all, I have to thank Kathleen for her unstinting support and patience working on various drafts of the manuscript over countless hours and being so encouraging.

I take this opportunity to sincerely thank everyone who helped in any way in what was a massive project carried out in a relatively short timescale. It was indeed humbling to learn about many of the happy and sad events which touched the lives of those who were interviewed.

I just hope that for those who lived in the lost mining villages of Doon Valley or have local mining connections, it helps to awaken long-forgotten memories. And for those too young to have even heard of these lost villages and coal mining, I trust they will enjoy learning about the past and endeavour to understand and make sense of what was so special about the small isolated Doon Valley mining communities where their forefathers lived and worked as miners.

This project would not have been possible without the financial assistance provided by the Heritage Lottery Fund and their encouraging staff; Barrmill Jolly Beggars Club; Barrmill Lads and Lasses and the Scottish Coal Industry Special Welfare Fund. It is my hope that this book will be seen as being rather special and timely in capturing the social and industrial history, not only of mining, but of the Doon Valley area in general.

Blessings on the old road again,
By the dykeside, down to the green glen;
And the beauty of rowans red,
And the carefree days of my childhood,
Which will not come again

The Old Road
Maureen Henderson

Introduction

From scenes like these, old Scotia's grandeur springs,
That makes her lov'd at home, rever'd abroad;
Princes and lords are but the breath of kings,
'An honest man's the noblest work of God.'

The Cotter's Saturday Night
Robert Burns

Human cost of mining
In the Glasgow Herald of 13 July 1905, headed: Pit Fatality at Dalmellington, the sobering human cost of coal mining was well illustrated in the following brief report.

> *"James Bell, 13, son of William Bell, pit fireman, was run over by a loaded hutch at No. 2 Pennyvenie, yesterday morning and was so severely injured that he died within half an hour. He had only started work the day previous and this was his first trip to the pit bottom."*

It really is important to remember the many men and boys who lost their lives as they worked to earn a living in Doon Valley pits. Those who died as a result of accidents in Doon Valley pits, within the recent past, are highlighted in an appendix to this book

What is coal?
What is coal? In a local interest book, which I hope young people will read, to learn more about their mining heritage, a key question I was once asked by a wee boy at Bellsbank School was: "What is coal." Coal comes from the Old English term col, which means "mineral of fossilized carbon." Since the 13th century this combustible black or brownish-black sedimentary rock has generally occurred in layers or veins called coal beds or coal seams. Coal is composed primarily of carbon along with variable quantities of other elements such as hydrogen, sulphur, oxygen and nitrogen.

From time immemorial coal has been used as an energy resource, primarily burned for the production of heat and later used in the production of electricity across the globe or for heating homes in open fires. It is also used widely for industrial purposes, such as refining metals.

Coal is a fossil fuel that occurs through complex biological processes that takes place over thousands of years. It is the largest source of energy for the generation of electricity worldwide. The downside is that coal is also one of the largest sources of carbon dioxide release one of the great contributors to greenhouse gases attributed to the melt of the ice fields and dramatic changes in global temperatures.

The history of coal mining goes back thousands of years. Despite moves to develop other forms of power generation, coal mining continues as an important economic activity today across the globe. Indeed there have been suggestions that deep mining should be re-introduced in the UK to tap the huge seams for our fuel-hungry country. However, this is unlikely to happen as it would go against the current world-wide aim of reducing green house gas emissions.

The Ayrshire coalfield was located close to the industrial hub around Glasgow. Importantly, the Doon Valley mines were able to boast excellent rail-links for moving vast amounts of coal on a daily basis to Ayr harbour to fuel power stations in the West of Scotland and onward transport to Ireland and elsewhere.

Coal mining was a way of life for over 150 years and most men, followed by their sons, worked in the industry. With the end of Doon Valley deep mining in 1978, there is a real danger that this special way of life will be forgotten with the passage of time. This book will help future generations remember their special mining past.

In Ayrshire's Doon Valley the demise of deep coal mining came earlier than elsewhere. Around Dalmellington the first mine to close was at Bogton in the west side of the village sitting above the Muck Burn. It was opened in 1931 and closed in 1954. It had an average workforce of around 76. It also had the distinction of having an aerial ropeway that transferred coal from Bogton to the railway coal loading point at Minnivey, a distance of 1.5 miles.

Chalmerston 4/5 was a surface mine located high on the hill above Burnton, overlooking Dalmellington. It began production around 1925 and closed in 1959. The average workforce was 256. Chalmerston No. 7 was sunk in 1934 and survived until 1952. This was a surface mine and coal screening took place at nearby Chalmerston No 4/5.

Humans are capable of constructing huge buildings, railway tracks and mansions but once we abandon our creations, nature quickly claims her own back. A good example is Pennyvenie bing (coal spoil heap), the dominant backdrop to Dalmellington. This huge coal bing and the area of the former pithead at Pennyvenie is now completely covered in trees and bushes.

Idea for book

The idea for compiling this book was probably inspired when several members of Barrmill Jolly Beggars Burns Club attended the re-dedication of a lonely, weather-beaten war memorial high up on the side of steep Benwhat Hill on Sunday 12 June 2011. That memorable event attracted many former residents of Benwhat and their families. Most of the Benwhatonians had worked most of their lives as coal miners. The initial idea stemming from that event resulted in a popular book, *The Lost Mining Villages of Doon Valley*. The current book is in some ways a natural sequel looking at the stories of Doon Valley miners.

Benwhat

The remnants of Benwhat village can still be found high on the lonely moors high above Dalmellington in Ayrshire's Doon Valley, where the famous River Doon was immortalised in poetry by Scotland's Bard, Robert Burns. Deserted around 1952, all that remains today of Benwhat, are ruins of the 'new school', the foundations of the rows of miners' cottages and the restored war memorial sitting sentinel above this lost village on the face of Benwhat Hill.

War Memorial Service

Erected in 1921, this war memorial was restored and re-dedicated on Sunday 12 June 2011, when around a hundred former villagers, their families and local folk attended a special and very emotional ceremony led in praise by Muriel Wilson, then the popular Deaconess at Dalmellington Parish Church. They had gathered to remember those villagers who died in two world wars, and more generally, the proud folk who were villagers of Benwhat. At that event the 'Last Post' was played by Dalmellington Junior Band conductor Ian Taylor.

Had we never lov'd sae kindly,
Had we never lov'd sae blindly,
Never met or never parted,
We had ne'er been broken-hearted.

Ae Fond Kiss
Robert Burns

Dalmellington Higher Grade School in 1954/55 showing all the staff members of that time.
Back row (l to r): Hugh Dunn, Andrew Glen, Robert Brown, Mr Douglas, Mr Inglis, unknown, John McChesney.
Second back row: Miss Moddie, unknown, Alex Scott, Mr Wylie, George Miller, Ian Tyre, Mr Maxwell, Mrs Wotherspoon
Second front row: Miss Ida Hodgson, Miss Nan Kennedy, Miss McCreadie, Miss Agnes Wilson (secretary), Miss Robertson (PE), Miss M Smith, Miss Anne Kellock, Miss Grace Park, Mrs Douglas.
Front row: Mrs Agnes Campbell, Miss Drysdale, Arthur Wilson, Miss Cissie Murray, William Irvine (headmaster), Miss Guthrie, William Shankland, Miss Mary Hill, Miss Morrison.

Some junior members of Dalmellington Band played wonderfully well in the packed marquee and this was especially fitting because brass band music was a central feature of village life, the Benwhat Band producing some fine musicians over a hundred years of music making.

Village Activities

The villagers of Benwhat enjoyed working together to make their own entertainment and they regularly held concerts and cantatas and enjoyed many outdoor activities. The majority of the men were proud miners. Wives worked hard to keep the home and look after the needs of their large families. Benwhat had football teams, a silver band, athletics (Doon Harriers), pigeon racing, and lots of evening classes, concerts, cantatas and dances. In short, it was a really happy and lively community, one which it is often said, the villagers were loath to leave, even for much improved housing conditions in the valley below.

Neighbourliness

There was great community spirit and neighbourliness, perhaps not always evident in 21st-century communities. Much of that special community spirit, many villagers said, was left behind in those hills when they left.

Farewell, thou fair day, thou green earth and ye skies,
Now gay with the broad setting sun!
Farewell, loves and friendships, ye dear tender ties –
Our race of existence is run!

The Song of Death
Robert Burns

Benwhat's Spirit Lingers on

The re-dedication ceremony of the war memorial was organised by Drew Filson, who arranged the refurbishment of the war memorial with East Ayrshire Council. For this special event the council and others had a large marquee located on the site of the village at the foot of Benwhat Hill. It was nicely decorated with flowers, and there was an intricately decorated cake showing Benwhat, with the words: 'Bricks and mortar may be gone, but Benwhat's spirit lingers on.'

Memorial restored

Everyone present agreed that this was a very appropriate sentiment indeed. The council had also arranged for the railings of the war memorial to be replaced, the memorial cleaned and the inscriptions restored, and this was greatly appreciated by all the former residents and their families who came to remember past times, family ties and a former village that was still close to the heart.

Shared Memories

Many of those who attended this ceremony were elderly and former villagers of Benwhat or relations of those who lived there. The event brought together folk who had in some cases not met for many years and it was a poignant event with folk exchanging memories of yesteryear. Despite infirmities, many were able to walk up the steep hill to the memorial and simply reflect and remember, many with a tear in the eye, probably realising that this would be their last visit. Sadly, Robert 'Robin' Farrell, who loved Benwhat dearly and had written a small booklet about the village, was one who made his very last visit on that June day, passing away a few weeks later.

The cruel fate should bid us part
Far as the pole and line,

The Cruel Fate
Robert Burns

Lost Villages

Benwhat and its sister villages of the Doon Valley such as Lethanhill, Corbie Craigs, Tongue Row, Cairntable, Pennyvenie and Beoch no longer exist, but they were real family communities, occupied by larger-than-life characters, mainly miners and their families.

Came to Benwhat

Benwhat, built between the early 1860s and 1875 with 130 houses in several straight rows, a village school, reading room and pub, was one of several villages or rows of houses created in the Doon Valley of Ayrshire by the Dalmellington Iron Company in the mid to late 19th century. The villagers came to the area, in common with families from Ireland, England and elsewhere in Scotland, for work in the rapidly expanding iron workings and the iron and coal mining which supported it.

Isolation

With the exception perhaps of Beoch, Benwhat was the most isolated

Hugh Johnstone MBE supplied this photo of the three Torbet brothers. Jimmy, Bill and David outside their house in Broomknowe, Dalmellington. The Torbet family had a long association with Dalmellington Band. All three were also miners.

community in Ayrshire, yet it was able to boast a brass band, a Burns Club, an excellent harriers club that was well known across Ayrshire and beyond, and Benwhat Heatherbell and Rising Star, noted Ayrshire football teams that won many honours.

This community was close knit and independent. The villagers, of necessity in the difficult circumstances of isolated life, were very hardy, especially in the several periods of decline of the iron industry, when work was scarce. In addition, being situated so high in the hills, the weather in winter was often dire, but this was compensated for by some of the most stunning views across Ayrshire and Galloway.

Tied houses

The miners living in the tied houses of these villages were very much beholden to their employer, because if they lost their job, that invariably meant losing their home. These living quarters were generally cramped and lacking, even what today would be described as the most basic facilities. Indeed, the living conditions tolerated by mining families came under severe criticism in reports even before the First World War.

Over the years action was gradually taken to provide more satisfactory housing, but inevitably the poor overall condition of these houses and their remote and inaccessible locations meant that the miners and their families had to be rehoused in more modern dwellings. These were invariably in large council estates or schemes in the Doon Valley built after 1945. The villagers of Benwhat were rehoused mainly in Dalmellington and Patna.

Villages Abandoned

Beoch was the first village to be abandoned, around 1938, and after the Second World War depopulation gathered speed, so that by 1954 all the remote Doon Valley villages had been abandoned, with the exception of Cairntable, which survived until 1963.

Industrial Past

The days of a bustling industrial past in the Doon Valley, with ironstone and coal mining and brick making, are now over. The opencast sites in the Doon Valley have also been abandoned and time will tell whether they can again be worked, hopefully in a manner which ensures that all the areas where coal is extracted are immediately reinstated to an acceptable standard.

Monument to Ironmaking

The monument to ironmaking is the large slag bing at Waterside which still dominates the landscape on the A713, this despite the fact that the last iron ore slag was tipped there around 1922. Another prominent landmark at Waterside is the tall twin chimneys, known locally as the lums, which dominate the landscape for miles around. These were an integral part of iron making and brick production.

Then oh, it was a glorious sight
To see those ironworks so bright
Illuminating darkest night
For miles around Dalmellington.

Dalmellington
Matthew Anderson (Policeman-poet of Ayrshire)

The miner's lamp or Glennie lamp with a pick handle which had a special place in St. Barbara's RC Church on the edge of the motte in Dalmellington. The church was the subject of extensive and repetitive vandalism and had to close. The building was demolished in July 2003.

Brickmaking

At Waterside, clay was taken from the quarry at Dunaskin Glen, and brought to the main factory. The clay was crushed and mixed with water and other additives, which included breeze, a very fine anthracite that aided firing. This process, which is also known as pugmilling, improved the consistency, firing qualities, texture, and colour of the brick.

When the bricks were dried, they were then fired or 'burnt' in a kiln, to give them their final hardness and appearance.

Brick making at Waterside became the staple industry alongside coal production but the last Dalmellington Iron Company bricks were taken from the kilns in 1976. Bricks from Dunaskin were sent to many places and today you can still find these fine bricks with their DICo mark, treasured by Doon Valley folk and displayed in gardens around the area as a reminder of times past.

Yet sometimes, when a wind sighs through the sedge,
Ghosts of my buried years, and friends come back,
My heart goes sighing after swallows flown
On sometime summer's unreturning track.

From Sunset to Star Rise
Christina Rossetti

End of Industrial Doon Valley

The closure of Pennyvenie Colliery in July 1978 nicely pinpoints the end of industrial Doon Valley in which large numbers of local men were gainfully employed in the local coal mines. Subsequently opencast mining took place in the Doon Valley from around 1983 until the demise of Scottish Coal in April 2013. A huge amount of coal was extracted from the hills above Dalmellington right through from Lethanhill to Cairntable by opencast working on the east side of the A713. However, the opencast mines employed very few local men. In essence the giant earth-moving machines largely replaced the need for manual labour.

Lunar Landscape

Sadly, with the demise of Scottish Coal in 2013, the high moors above Patna have been abandoned and left like a lunar landscape with deep craters and mountains created by moving earth to extract coal by the opencast method. Whether this can ever be returned to wild moorland is questionable. However, it would seem that attempts will indeed be made and large earth-moving vehicles were back on site at Dunstonhill in September 2015 as this book was about to go to print. What is certain though, is that any attempt to backfill and return the moorland to anywhere near its former glory, will be extremely expensive. The local community in the Doon Valley were appalled at this sad legacy left by opencast mining. Future coal extraction will have to be very closely supervised to ensure that backfilling takes place immediately after extraction to avoid a repeat of the current disaster.

The Doon Valley is now firmly in a post-industrial period, bringing new challenges and social change. However, local folk wisely remember their roots and are proud of their rich industrial heritage centred on coal production. It is important to nurture heritage because with the passage of time the social and industrial history of any area can be all too quickly forgotten.

Remembering the Lost Mining Villages

So much of the industrial past has already disappeared almost without physical trace. This is evidenced in the former mining communities of the Doon Valley which no longer exist, other than on old Ordnance Survey maps. With the passing of each generation there is a real danger that these small, vibrant communities – lost villages – will be totally forgotten.

Recording some of their social history will help those who follow in our footsteps to remember and better understand how their community of today was shaped by the lives and work activity of those who lived at the sharp end of life, doubtless dreaming of a better tomorrow.

Stories of the past

Across the wild moors and quiet valleys, the ghosts of several long-forgotten villages haunt the Doon Valley in habitations deserted and left to ruin before being hastily demolished. This book allows proud miners and their families, many of whom lived in the lost mining villages, to tell their personal stories of yesteryear as miners.

For a' that, an a' that,
It's coming yet for a' that
That man to man, the world o'er
Shall brithers be for a' that.

A Man's a Man for A' That
Robert Burns

Dunstonhill Opencast Site in 2013 shortly before it closed. The huge mountains of waste are evident in the background. In September 2015 these mountains and craters were being worked on to return them to open moorland.
(Photo: Donald L Reid)

Chapter 1

Ayrshire's Doon Valley

Here dwell the lads who do and dare,
And lasses sweet beyond compare,
And kindly wives who tend with care
The miners of Dalmellington.

Craigmark, Benquhat and Burnfoothill,
All give my heart a glorious thrill,
While memories cloud my eyes until
I scarce can see Dalmellington.

Hills over hills lure waves arise
Beneath these health-inspiring skies.
God bless this earthly paradise
My own, my dear Dalmellington.

Dalmellington
Matthew Anderson (1864–1948)
Policeman-poet of the Ayrshire Constabulary

Origins

The upper section of Ayrshire's Doon Valley is an intriguing area with a fascinating industrial and social history stretching far back in time. The village of Dalmellington lies at a height of 600 feet above sea level and some 15 miles south-east of Ayr. It is situated about one mile east of the romantic River Doon, made famous by the world-renowned Bard, Robert Burns, who certainly knew this welcoming corner of Ayrshire.

The origins of the village name can be read in two ways, either as Dal Muilean Tuin, 'the fort on the plain of the mills', or Dal Meallan Tuin, 'the fort on the plain of the hills'. The *New Statistical Account of Scotland* (vol. 5), written in 1837, says that the name can be traced to its Gaelic origin, *Dail*, signifying a field or valley, and *Muileann*, which means a mill, and the common suffix *ton*. It therefore signifies a mill field. There is evidence for all the explanations of the name, as there are castles, hills, valleys, fields and mills. The noteworthy village motte located at the east end of the village is a large smooth eminence proudly rising above the town, where the ancient Pictish inhabitants perhaps met to settle matters of law and custom. At such places matters of concern to all were raised, or 'mooted', for discussion.

The early church

According to William Douglas (*In Ayrshire – 1872*) the history of Dalmellington can be traced as far back as 1003 when it existed in some form at its present location. Mention is also made of the little church in Dalmellington in the records of the Diocese of Glasgow towards the end of the 13th century. It is known that this original church was situated in the old graveyard below the motte in the village, although all traces of it have long ago ceased to exist.

Galloway persecution times

Dalmellington was strategically located on an ancient route from the south which linked up with the Old Edinburgh Road to Galloway and the pilgrim way to Whithorn. The years 1681–85 are known as the Killing Time because of the atrocities committed, by James Graham, Earl of Claverhouse, Viscount Dundee, among others. He earned his nickname 'Bloody Clavers' by his brutal suppression of the covenanters.

He was regularly in Galloway and indeed is said to have been billeted for a time with Grierson of Lagg and his moss-troopers at Garryhorn Farm at Carsphairn. Accordingly Dalmellington was caught between the royalist presence at Carsphairn and a very active covenanting one in Cumnock, which saw the military in large numbers in this part of the county.

In Extracts from "Woodrow's Manuscript Reprint Relating to the Covananters Who fell In Dalmellington Parish 1666 – 1686," prepared by Hugh Gibson, he asserts that 600 troops armed with cannon, ammunition, iron shackles and fetters, were quartered in the parish in 1685, living off the land.

They caused considerable upset to the local population, then numbering only a few hundred, with whom the soldiers would have been billeted. Fines were levied for worship in the open air, people were imprisoned, families dispersed and houses plundered all because local men stood out against Episcopacy.

Quintin Dick, an elder in the parish church, said to have been a wise, well-educated and caring man, suffered terribly during these years. His house was turned into a guardhouse for soldiers in transit to and from Galloway, where many of them served under the notorious Grierson of Lagg, whose local residence was the house of Garryhorn, Carsphairn. Dick was forced to billet twenty of the soldiers, and eventually was sentenced at Ayr to a fine of £1,000 and banished to the plantations of America. He was imprisoned in 1684 and a year later he was taken from Edinburgh to be detained in Dunottar Castle. He would have been deported to America, but was left behind because it was believed he was dying. He recovered and returned to Dalmellington, where he endeavoured to heal the differences that had separated the presbyterian adherents of the parish.

Another elder of the parish church, Roger Dunne (or Dunn) of Benquhat, was on his way home from Carsphairn Fair in June 1689 when he was ambushed and killed by some rogues who were involved in a local feud of which Dunne had absolutely no part. His grave can still be seen in Carsphairn Kirkyard.

Many other young men, especially those from the farming community, became involved with the covenanters and the names of Sloss, McAdam, McWhirter and Paterson appear in the covenanting records.

Dalmellington Band in February 1952 on the evening of the annual Slow Melody Competition in Dalmellington Church Hall. Most of these men worked in the coal mining industry and the band was supported by subscriptions from local miners.
Back row (l to r): John Tyson, William Hainey, William Hill, David Torbet, William Parker, William Currie.
Second back row: John Smith, David Smith, Edward Kerr, Duncan Wells, Archie Hutchison, Peter Scobie, Jimmy Dick, Robert Boyd, Robert Hill, Andrew Parker (father of William Parker in back row) and Tom 'TP' Park.
2nd front row: Jimmy Ireland, Jimmy Graham, James McPhail, Tom Wilson, Gordon Hunter, William Oughton (bandmaster), John Paulin, John McLeod, Tom Paulin (brother of John Paulin) and William Greig.
Front row: William Kennedy, James Hose, Robert Peters, Bert McRoberts.
(Photo: Dalmellington Band archive)

The Reverend George S Hendrie

Dalmellington is especially precious to its many sons, none more so than those who have left the district. One of the most ardent supporters of the village was the Reverend George S Hendrie, Minister of Dalmellington 1880–1925, chairman of the Parochial Board (1885–95) and a member of the Parish Council (1889–98), who in 1889 penned *The Parish of Dalmellington: History, Antiquities and Objects of Interest*. This booklet was reprinted in 1902 by William Murdoch, a general merchant in Dalmellington, and is still regarded by many as the outstanding historical account of the town and district. In his summing up of Dalmellington he writes:

> *Here in Dalmellington we have our own share of legend. There is scarcely an epoch in our history that is not represented by some story touched on in this history of the parish. It is an old historic land that lies round our door, a land that has seen brave, and oft-times fierce, contendings for liberty, a land in which industrial peace has had its victories, no less than war. Men have here literally 'beat their swords into ploughshares, and their spears into pruning hooks'. Let us not forget its past, and the lessons we may learn therefrom.*

Lord Cockburn

The visitor to the upper reaches of the Doon Valley should take time to explore the village and surrounding area, particularly Loch Doon. One particular visitor was not especially impressed by the village and its environs. Lord Cockburn (1779–1854), the Scottish lawyer, judge and literary figure, visited in 1844, when he had a vision of how Dalmellington could be improved by adapting many of the reforms evident in English villages.

> *I grieve for Dalmellington. The time will come when English neatness shall be introduced into Scotland, what a village Dalmellington may be. A few trees, irregular ground, tumbling burns, a spire, and a mill – what more is wanted?*

Some time later, the noble lord, annoyed at the lack of progress, seems to have damned it with faint praise and was singularly critical of coal miners, describing them as 'black scoundrels.'

> *"It has the appearance, and the reputation of being a singularly virtuous and happy village; and I am told is perhaps the last place in Ayrshire where, with a good deal of old primitive manufacture, rural simplicity and contentment still linger. But the village is now to taste manufacture in an improved state.*
>
> *The devil has disclosed his iron and speculation has begun to work it. There seems to be about a dozen pits sinking within half a mile of the village, and before another year is out those now solitary and peaceful hills will be blazing with furnaces, and blighted by the presence of the vices of a new population of black scoundrels. They were already lying snoring and, I presume, drunk, on many indignant knolls."*

Of course the ironworks and coal mines have long since made their special mark on the valley and its people of yesteryear and sadly are now part of folklore. What would Lord Cockburn make of Dalmellington today?

Robert Hettrick (1769–1849)

The old cemetery contains a covenanting memorial and a plaque to the blacksmith-poet of the village, Robert Hettrick. The plaque was placed over his grave in 1888, partly at the expense of a relative, and partly by public subscription, a mural tablet with the following inscription:

ROBERT HETTRICK, Blacksmith,
Author of 'Poems and Songs'
Born at Dalmellington, 1769 – Died, December, 1849.

Sadly, the old cemetery has been neglected and extensively vandalised over the years and many interesting headstones have been lost.

Similarly, St Barbara's RC Church (built 1959–61), octagonal in shape and copper-roofed, used to sit aloft on the edge of the medieval village motte, but was the subject of ongoing and extensive vandalism from its earliest days. The chapel was closed for several years and demolished in July 2003, a sad legacy to the power of mindless vandals.

The parish church

Dalmellington Parish Church sits on a commanding position overlooking the village. Designed by Patrick Wilson of Edinburgh and built by McCandlish of New Galloway in 1846, the building is of neo-Norman style with a distinctive tower. Nearby is the 1766 harled church hall, formerly the old church built by James Armour. Recent renovations have been effectively carried out by a dedicated and enthusiastic small band of older church members at a time when the national church is struggling with falling membership.

The parish church has a very valuable collection of Covenanting silver. The small cups dating from 1637 and 1650 are reputed to have been taken into the nearby hills around Benbeoch Craig, where they were used to give communion, by the Reverend Alexander Stevenson. In 1869 communion cards were introduced at the church in place of metal tokens. In the parish magazine of November 1909 a Dalmellington exile, Thomas H Wallace of Brisbane, Australia wrote:

Like a Sentinel guarding the little town,
Stands the old grey church on the hill
Though it's many a year since I saw it last,
It is dear to memory still.

There are many who have played within its shade,
Now scattered the world o'er
Who have made their homes in other lands
To return again no more.

The former Lamloch Church (1851) in Low Main Street built by David Millar, is also a notable building and is now the headquarters of the 33rd Ayrshire Dalmellington Scouts, who celebrated their centenary in 2010. The Doon Valley Museum at Cathcartston, which boasts a date

Staff at Glebe Hostel, Dalmellington in 1948. This hostel provided accommodation for men and women working in the pits and as labourers building the housing schemes in the village. Dalmellington had a large influx of Irish navvies around this time. It was said that many Irishmen arriving at Glasgow by boat would immediately ask the way to Dalmellington.
(l to r): May Waugh, Agnes Smith, Mrs J Barclay, Mary Hastie and Jessie Baird.
Middle row: Janet McGarvie, Peggy McGarvie, May Timmins and Margaret Killin
Front row: Miss Jess (head woman), Archie Clark (manager) and Margaret McKnight.

stone of 1744 and was formerly weavers' cottages, also reveals much of the extensive industrial and social history of the village.

Craigengillan

The house of Craigengillan (*c.* 1780) is seen at its best looking across the valley from the road to Loch Doon which leaves the A713 at Mossdale. John McAdam of Craigengillan, who made his fortune as a drover, enlarged or built the house in what has been described as 'an unadventurous Georgian manner'. About 1820 a manorial entrance was added to the east wing. There is also a spectacular domed tower and a square tower with impressive Georgian stables.

The house and its extensive grounds are private and the current owner is the indefatigable Mr Mark Gibson, who has dedicated himself to maintaining and improving Craigengillan and its extensive and beautiful policies, including upgrading the pathway in Ness Glen, building bridges over streams and creating new pathways around the magnificent Dalcairney Linn. A more recent innovation was building a night observatory to enable visitors to enjoy the night skies of Ayrshire.

Quintin McAdam

An earlier laird of Craigengillan, Quintin McAdam, was remarkable in that his widow, Elizabeth Walker, raised a famous action for declarator of marriage, which was based on the following (very brief) circumstances that occurred at Craigengillan on 22 March 1805. He is said to have called three menservants into the hall one day, and holding the hand of Elizabeth Walker, who in 1800 he 'took into keeping', said, 'I take you three to witness that this is my lawful married wife, and the children by her are my lawful children.' He then immediately left the hall and shot himself dead. It is of his forebear, John, a celebrated agricultural improver, that Burns wrote in 1786/87:

An God bless young Dunaskin's Laird,
The blossom of our gentry,
An may he wear an auld man's beard,
A credit to his country!

The old laird's son, also Quintin McAdam, with whom Elizabeth Walker was pregnant at the time of the demise of his father, was responsible for building the romantic walk up the Ness Glen which today has been given a new lease of life and once again attracts visitors interested in walking or canoeing. He would doubtless have been very proud of the work carried out in the glen in recent years through the unstinting efforts of Mark Gibson, Laird of Craigengillan.

Perkelly Burn and trips

In boyhood days when life seemed so happy and simple, the writer has many happy memories of walks through Ness Glen to Loch Doon and trudging down the 'Hungry Brae' to enjoy picnics at Perkelly Burn, often thronged with local folk and happy children paddling in the sunlit summer stream. This was a regular feature of the summer months in the 1950s and early 1960s for folk who lived in Bellsbank. Others will recall, with a twinkle in the eye, the bus trips organised from Bellsbank by John 'Shigs' Coughtrie, taking locals on outings to the seaside at Girvan and Prestwick. These are indeed happy memories.

Local scenes

Those with time to spare would enjoy a walk to the Pickan's Dyke, located above the new cemetery. About 1 mile south of the Straiton Road at the Doon Brig, there is the dramatic waterfall at Dalcairnie (OS77: 466 043) which can be seen at its best when the Dalcairnie Burn is in spate. In recent years it has regularly frozen over with dramatic effect, providing challenges for brave-hearted ice-climbers.

On the Cumnock Road two miles from the village, Ben Beoch Craig (OS77: 498 084), at a height of 1,522 feet above sea level, is seen in spectacular fashion from above Pennyvenie. It has been described as a miniature Giant's Causeway and one can easily picture it as a place of sanctuary for the covenanters, with many caves on its lower slopes. However, due to opencast working in the area and the danger of ongoing surface mining operations it is best not to approach this hill without permission.

Loch Muck

The Muck Water streams through Dalmellington and on many occasions, particularly 17 July 1927 and again in 1934, the centre of the village had been brought to a standstill by severe floods, vividly remembered by a diminishing number of the oldest residents. Interestingly, the commonly held view that the Muck Water rises in Loch Muck (OS77: 514 007) on the borders of Ayrshire and the Stewartry of Kirkcudbright is in fact spurious.

This water actually rises to the north of Campbell's Hill (OS77: 530 027) just over 1.5 miles from the loch. Loch Muck, which sits in a basin some 300 yards above sea level, is good for trout fishing. It has only one exit and drains into nearby Loch Doon, and marks the boundary between Ayrshire and the Stewartry of Kirkcudbright. In recent times it has become a popular fishing ground for the Ospreys nesting at Loch Doon on the east side of the loch opposite the dam.

The Co-op

Formed in 1879, the Dalmellington Co-operative Society became one of the largest employers in the village. By 1950 it had a workforce of seventy-one, with a membership of 1,455 and an annual turnover of £144,000. Forty-eight were employed in shop retailing and it had one mobile shop and eight horse-drawn vans. The bakehouse employed ten bakers and the butchers did their own killing in the slaughterhouse at the Crofts every Wednesday, which was also a half-day shop holiday.

Dunaskin Lads football team in 1931 showing a number of trophies they had won. All were involved in the mining industry in some capacity. This photograph was taken at Holm Park, Waterside. Back row (l to r): James Rowan (committee), Tom Kelly, John Burgess (committee), A Park, George Dunn, Hugh 'Hammy' Frew, Tom Anderson, Hugh Borland, Hugh Reid and Bob Ferguson. Front row: Wull Kerr, J Stewart, H Murray, Joe Mooney, Phil Dunn, Hugh Dunn, S Reddix, Jimmy McDowall and William Muir.

The drapery department supplied all goods in clothing, including ladies' and gents' outfits as well as carpets and furniture. The grocery department was particularly busy and supplied all home provisions as well as selling mining tools such as picks, shovels, hammers and boring equipment. In every respect Dalmellington Co-operative was able to fulfil all the material needs of the villagers.

Loch Doon – molten granite and ice cap

For many people Dalmellington is synonymous with the six-mile-long Loch Doon, the largest of all the Southern Upland lochs, located three miles south of the village. Geological studies reveal that it was some forty million years ago that the Loch Doon hills were created. The Galloway hill group to the south was then being formed by the molten granite, dramatically erupting through the sandstone rocks of the land. The hot liquid granite baked the surrounding rocks to form a ring of hills, a ring we now call the Rhinns of Kells and the Merrick – Galloway's highest hill. But it was up to two million years ago that Loch Doon was formed.

As the climate gradually grew colder, an ice cap developed on top of the Merrick. This ice cap swelled over the land around it. The monstrous glacier gouged out the rock beneath it and carried massive boulders far away. For how else could boulders of Loch Doon granite have been found as far away as North Wales and Northern Ireland? What you see now, the forests, the plants, the remains of homes where people once lived, even the valley itself, is less than the blink of an eye in the life of this land. One can only speculate, in fourteen thousand years from now, how this beautiful land will have changed, but much depends on the way the people of today treat our fragile environment.

Macnabstone

Several hundred years ago the area around Loch Doon was not as deserted as it now seems. For instance, a few minutes' walk from Loch Doon an ancient farmstead is situated on the west side of the loch, 930 yards north of Beoch, in the area named 'Macnabstone' (OS: NS 475 008). It comprises what would probably have been two rectangular buildings (16.7 metres and 8.5 metres respectively in length within stone wall-footings) adjacent to an enclosure and a possible kiln.

What may be another building (3.3 metres by 2.3 metres within stone wall-footings) lies in the north-west corner of the enclosure. Pont's map depicts the farmstead of 'Macknabston' and Armstrong's map records 'McNabbs', but on Thomson's map 'Beoch and McNabston' are recorded as a single farmstead.

Archaeologists speculate that this was once the home of a large family living close to the shores of the loch. They would have lived an almost entirely self-sufficient lifestyle. If you think that no one could ever have grown crops like wheat and rye, barley and oats on the wild moors above this ancient loch, then why did they have a kiln?

Hunter-gatherers

But these hardy folk were not the first to settle on the shores of Loch Doon, not by at least 8,000 years. The earliest inhabitants of Loch Doon were small groups of Mesolithic hunter-gatherers, who lived off the rich wild resources – the plants, fish and animals – of the valley around them.

All they left behind as evidence of their presence were the flint blades, scrapers and arrow points that have been found by the loch over the years. Today the land around the loch is suitable only for forestry and rough grazing, but the tourists who flock to Loch Doon would be wise to remember that it was not always so and the fragile ecology of the area has to be guarded jealously to preserve it for future generations.

Site of Special Scientific Interest

Loch Doon, surrounded by rivers, mountains, forests and moors, is recognised as an area of exceptionally high landscape value. In 1993 the Scottish Office included the loch in the designation of the wider Western Southern Uplands Environmentally Sensitive Area (ESA), in recognition of its landscape, natural history and historical features. It supports a wide range of wildlife, including several important species. Loch Doon is scientifically important for its indigenous population of Arctic char, a relative of the salmon. In 1986 the loch, the only location in southern Scotland where the Arctic char is still found, was recognised as a Site of Special Scientific Interest (SSSI). The naturally occurring char share the loch with brown trout and Atlantic salmon that spawn in the shallow gravel beds on the water's edge. The char are threatened by the increasing acidification of the water due to land use practices and Scottish Natural Heritage have put in place a management plan for the fish, which includes the monitoring of numbers and health of the species and checks on the condition of the water in Loch Doon.

Birds of Loch Doon

Loch Doon is also home to a wide range of bird and plant life. The loch is the largest and best example of an oligotrophic (nutrient-poor) standing water body in south Strathclyde. It supports a number of rare plant species, including slender parsley-piert, round-leaved crowfoot and osier.

The incessant trilling and fluty song that can be heard along the length of the loch belongs to skylarks. Listen out also for the distinctive and haunting 'coor-lee' of the curlew, which abound in the hinterland of the loch on the wild moorland leading from Doon to Girvan Valley. There is something haunting and memorable about the call of the curlew.

Look carefully and catch a glimpse of the common sandpiper, mainly between April and August, as they fly in groups a few feet above the surface of the loch. Circling high above the southern end of

William Hainey, who lives in Dalmellington, on Waterside Pug No. 17 at Waterside in the 1960s with Michael Rooney in the background.

the loch, buzzards float on the thermals.

A few miles further south is the stronghold of the peregrine falcon and the elusive red kites, recently re-introduced into Galloway from Wales. In fact they are absolutely thriving, to the extent that they are already regularly to be seen at Loch Doon. Whooper swans visit the loch's waters in winter and the surrounding area is also home to black grouse, stonechat, meadow pipit, and reed bunting.

Deer are plentiful, and entering the Galloway hills you may encounter wild goats, the mountain fox or perhaps even a golden eagle. At Loch Doon from May until September you are likely to see the delightful ospreys, their giant tree-top nest clearly seen on the west side of the loch opposite the dam, the birds often seen carrying fish to the nest.

Dramatic Scenery

The loch is surrounded by some of the most dramatic and beautiful scenery in Scotland, with the Kells Range on its eastern flank, the Dungeon Range on its southern edge and all of these dominated by the majestic Merrick (2,764 ft) and neighbouring hills to the south-west. This area now abounds with visitors. The tea room and visitor centre at the dam has been a very positive addition for the past ten years and a good place to view the nesting ospreys on the west side of the loch.

Loch Doon was in the past, unfortunately, often littered with caravans all year round, many of them simply abandoned, burned out and a blight on the outstanding scenic beauty of the area. These have now been removed, restoring to the area its natural beauty and a consequent increase in wildlife. A caravan park was created near the dam, but at the time of writing (August 2015) was still unfinished, albeit it was operating.

The narrow road to Loch Doon Castle can be busy with traffic, especially when the weather is good, but because of its historic, scenic beauty and biodiversity, it perhaps does need to be 'light-touch' regulated and protected for future generations to enjoy.

Ness Glen

At the Loch Doon dam the River Doon descends dramatically into Ness Glen, with its sheer rocky sides making it a somewhat inhospitable area, and thunders for about a mile before it settles into 'the bonny banks and braes' through the lower Craigengillan lands. The first mile of the River Doon is arguably the finest and most picturesque of its course, but sadly the overgrown glen makes access challenging for the casual visitor. Robert Hettrick, the blacksmith poet of Dalmellington describes it thus in his poem 'Craigs of Ness':

Where from the Doon her silver torrents pour;
With wonder and surprise we here behold
The yawning glen its dizzy steeps unfold;
And art and nature here we see combined.

Loch Doon's Past

Castles in Scotland were built and strategically placed as symbols of power and authority. However, they were also places of refuge to protect those who lived in fear through years of invasion, raids, wars and political intrigue and treachery. Scotland's history is littered with reminders of our uncivilised past, so most castles have an interesting history.

Loch Doon Castle, the ancient seat of the Lords of Carrick, was built after 1275 on an island at the southern end of the loch. David Wilson MacArthur, in his book on the River Doon (1951), states that the Galloway Picts had used Castle Island to fight off invasion by the Cambrian Celts in the fourth century.

1823 nine ancient Pictish canoes, of hollowed oak 23 feet long, two feet six inches deep and three feet nine inches broad, were discovered.

Three of the canoes were recovered, and one was sent to the Hunterian Museum in Glasgow, while the other two were placed in shallow water at the foot of the loch.

The castle's shape followed that of the islet, which gave it eleven sides. It was a formidable fortress – surrounded by deep water and outwith the range of siege engines. The castle was besieged at least three times, changed hands and was destroyed and rebuilt in its turbulent history. Legend has it that Robert the Bruce took shelter from the English army within its walls during the Wars of Independence.

In 1306 Sir Christopher Seaton, a follower and brother-in-law of Bruce, fled here after the defeat of Bruce at the Battle of Methven. The castle was held by the hereditary governor, Sir Gilbert de Carrick, who fearing Bruce to be a lost cause, surrendered to the English without apparently even trying to fight. Sir Christopher was taken prisoner to Dumfries and hanged as a traitor, while Sir Gilbert escaped with his life. In 1319 the castle was besieged by the English, who periodically invaded southern Scotland for some time after Bannockburn. However, it was said that the castle remained impregnable.

Around 1446 Loch Doon was again besieged and eventually surrendered to a force sent by William, 8th Earl of Douglas, whose power in the region was clashing with that of the infamous Kennedy clan. On this occasion the castle appears to have been seized by the MacLellans of Dumfries, who opposed the Douglas attempts to gain control of Carrick. By 1510 Loch Doon Castle was in Kennedy hands, when it was besieged a third time, by William Crawford of Lochmores. These were indeed dark days at Loch Doon.

During the reign of James V, who endeavoured to curb the powers of the Barons, the castle was burned down and the immense oak roof was thrown into the loch.

Galloway Hydro-Electric Scheme

In the mid-1930s when the Galloway Hydro-Electric Scheme was being created, the loch was used as a reservoir and a tunnel was created, requiring the level of the loch to be raised, with the building of the Loch Doon dam. The castle would have been submerged and it was decided to remove it stone by stone to the western fringe of the loch, where it stands today. The remains of the castle on its island location can still be seen when the water level of the loch is low.

Creating a dam at the northern end of Loch Doon resulted in the loch's water level rising by almost 10 metres, expanding its size and changing its shape. The 1.9 km Doon–Deugh Tunnel running through Culledoch Hill on the east side of the loch was built to divert water from the loch to the River Dee to power the stations that make up the hydro scheme.

The Galloway Hydro-Electric Scheme consists of six stations and eight dams, plus tunnels, aqueducts and pipelines. Drumjohn power station was built in 1986 to capture power output from the water released from the needle valve at Carsphairn Lane. In 2009 the scheme generated 260 GW-h of clean, renewable electricity to power homes and businesses. None of this could have happened without the water supplied from Loch Doon.

School of Aerial Gunnery

In August 1916, in support of the war effort, the War Department authorised the spending of £150,000 to build a specialist School of Aerial Gunnery at Loch Doon, using flying boats to shoot at rail-mounted targets in an effort to replicate dogfights. Despite the warnings and concerns of local people, the planners went ahead with this ill-advised scheme. Hangars, roads and jetties were built and the level of the loch was raised 6 feet by building a dam. The School of Aerial Gunnery was the brainchild of Colonel W S Brancker, later to become Air Vice-Marshal Sir Sefton Brancker; he died in the R101 disaster, when it crashed in France on its maiden voyage on 5 October 1930.

As part of the scheme, a railway line was laid from the Bogton Airfield on the northern edge of Dalmellington, running through Craigengillan Estate to Dalfarson about one mile from Loch Doon. All the materials required for the construction were brought to Dalfarson by rail, and were then transferred by lorry for the short journey to the loch. Constructing the rail link right to Loch Doon would have been very expensive as the physical features of the land would have necessitated digging a large tunnel from Dalfarson southwards, hence the decision to use a combination of rail and road transport.

Meanwhile at Loch Doon the concrete piers along the eastern side of the loch had been built to carry the monorail. Buildings erected included a sewage plant to meet the needs of the population of 1,500 and – strangely enough – a 400-seat cinema, complete with rising seats and a pay-box. This clearly indicated that it was intended that the military presence would be long-term. By May 1917 more than £350,000 had reportedly been spent at Loch Doon, but the real figure must have been substantially more.

Following an inspection visit to Loch Doon by the Duke of Connaught on 1 October 1917, the expenditure on this project began to raise serious questions from the Director of Fortifications and Works, and this was exacerbated by a request from McAlpine, the main contractor, for more funds to blast a 1,150-foot tunnel through the solid granite in order to extend the light railway from the railhead at Dalfarson to the southern end of the loch.

In January 1918 the Parliamentary Under-Secretary of State, Major J L Baird, was sent to Loch Doon to inspect the works, accompanied by Sir John Hunter, the Administrator of Works and Buildings. On receipt of their report the government halted all further work and instituted an inquiry.

And so, after much work with some 1,500 navvies and 500 German prisoners of war involved and a huge amount of money being expended, it was finally realised that Loch Doon was not a suitable location for this enterprise and their plans were indeed fatally flawed.

The subsequent Parliamentary Inquiry concluded that 'Loch Doon will be remembered as the scene of one of the most striking instances of wasted expenditure (in excess of £3m) that our records can show.' The report continued: 'Loch Doon and the country around it will soon return to the solitude and silence from which it was aroused by the introduction of thousands of men over a period of 15 months on an enterprise which was misconceived from the beginning, and which, even if once begun ought never to have been continued.'

The local airfield, covering some 88 acres, constructed at Bogton on the north-western edge of Dalmellington remained an operational airfield until the end of the war. It had two centrally heated hangars, stores and eighteen brick-built barrack blocks to accommodate 500 men. The remains of the hangars and extensive foundations can still be seen on this site.

As with most things in public life, cost is always a key factor. In his book, *Ayrshire 1745–1950*, James E Shaw reveals that more than £3 million had passed from the small bank in Dalmellington during the building period at Loch Doon. The many fine buildings constructed at Loch Doon were simply abandoned and after the war they were demolished. Much evidence remains today of these massive construction works. The track of the light railway can still be followed all the way from the Craigengillan entrance at Bogton Airfield to Dalfarson. This was indeed a folly of monumental proportions, but the visitor today can still enjoy the wonderful scenery of Loch Doon and be intrigued by its industrial past in the dark days of the Great War.

Weaving

As in many other Ayrshire towns in the 17th and 18th centuries, handloom weaving was one of the staple cottage industries and the current Doon Valley Museum was actually occupied by local weavers. However, as the 19th century progressed, this trade went into a long and gradual decline, to be replaced by the growth of the mining industry, with which the Doon Valley villages are proudly associated.

Mining

From the late 1840s the Dalmellington Iron Company and its successors operated dozens of pits and drift mines in the Doon Valley extracting coal and ironstone. Pits such as Bowhill, Polnessan, Dalharco, Houldsworth, Jelliston, Burnfoot, Drumgrange, Dunaskin, Corbie Craigs, Craigmark, Minnivey, Bogton, Sillyhole, Chalmerston, Pennyvenie, Clawfin, Benbain and Beoch had many underground workings until deep mining ceased in 1978 with the closure of Pennyvenie.

The records of the Dalmellington Iron Company and its successor, Bairds and Dalmellington Ltd, show a total of forty-three pits were in the area from 1845 until the present day. All that remains today are the extensive Chalmerston opencast mining operations overlooking and to the north-east of the village. This began production in 1987 with the first coal extracted in June of that year. Incredibly, since then some 8 million tons of coal have been extracted by this method and regularly two trains per day, pulling up to forty wagons, remove this mountain of coal from Chalmerston. In June 2001 a total of ninety-two men were employed on this site and some 16,000 tons of coal are extracted every week.

The Dalmellington Iron Company

Dalmellington's ironworks came into being in 1845, and totally changed the character of this section of the upper Doon Valley. The ironworks quickly flourished and increased. Sometimes as many as seven furnaces were in blast at one time, the blast engine requiring to be doubled in 1866. A hardworking and poorly paid workforce varied from 900 to almost 2,000.

Besides miners, the Dalmellington Iron Company employed all sorts of craftsmen who cast hundreds of tons of metal in a day, and sent the name Dalmellington stamped upon its bars to all parts of the world where pig iron was used. The blast engine house still stands today and bears the date 1847. David L Smith, in *The Dalmellington Iron*

Company: Its Engines and Men, records that when the great beam for the blast engine house was brought by road from Ayr, twenty-four pairs of horses were provided to haul it up the Asylum Brae.

Waterside and the ironworks

Three miles north of Dalmellington, Waterside sits on the edge of Green Hill and was once a thriving industrial village. There was a dramatic growth in the workforce of the Dalmellington Iron Company and by the end of the 1850s Waterside had grown dramatically, with 237 houses and a local economy which was booming.

As the visitor approaches, the view is dominated by two massive chimneys, at 143 and 160 feet. These 'lums', as they are known locally, dominate the surroundings. They dwarf the massive ironstone bing and bear testimony to the extensive mining and iron producing activities of the Dalmellington Iron Company.

The *Ayr Advertiser* of 15 May 1847 issued a word of caution: 'The proprietors of Dalmellington Ironworks intend erecting houses for their workers adjacent to their mines. We hope that the causes of disease, especially smallpox and measles, reported in the newspapers, will cause the proprietors to see that the site chosen is properly drained and the houses, when built, of sufficient size and well ventilated.'

In a report of 17 June 1847 it was highlighted that smallpox and measles were prevalent in Dalmellington and district, although few deaths had occurred. However, it did go on to explain that 'general complaints are on the increase and are considered by many to arise from the poor diet used by the poor, who are unable to purchase suitable food at such high prices that prevail.'

Dunaskin

The ironworks village had a singular confusion of names. It was called Waterside after the name of the nearby farm and this was the name adopted by the Glasgow and South Western Railway for their station. However, the postal authorities called it Dunaskin, after the address of the Dalmellington Iron Works, although Dalmellington was actually three miles further up the valley. Hence even today Waterside and Dunaskin are interchangeable terms for the village. The fascinating history of Waterside is recorded in considerable detail by David L Smith in his book about the Dalmellington Iron Company mentioned above. This excellent and rare book is a factual and entertaining account of the industrial development of the area and is recommended to the reader.

Benwhat Football and Sports Committee circa 1920s. Remote villages like Benwhat were organised for sports and athletics. This high moorland village had excellent football teams and harriers and could even boast a fine brass band.
Back row (l to r): J Adam, J Givens, Joe Dougan, Scott Hannah, Simpson Allan, Joe McKinstry, Alex McHattie (Waterside) and John Filson.
Front row: W Torbet, R Hill, D McBride, George Cook, Alex McHattie, John Allan, J B Galloway, Hugh Murray and ?
(John Relly collection)

Today only two rows of houses remain at Waterside, one at either end of the village. However, anyone passing this way might enjoy learning about the industrial heritage of the area at the open-air museum which aims to preserve the industrial and social history of Waterside.

Nearby, high above Dunaskin Burn, is the site of Laight Castle. David Wilson MacArthur, in his book on the River Doon, tells us that according to tradition it was here that Alpin, King of Scots, after landing at Ayr, met the men of Strathclyde, in a fierce and bloody battle which ended with the death of the Scots king. Whilst this may be somewhat fanciful, it certainly has been part of local tradition.

Dalmellington Band

Dalmellington is proud to be able to boast one of the finest brass bands in the United Kingdom. Formed in 1864 and having won the Scottish Championships on three occasions, 1969, 1976 and 1978, they now boast a first-class youth band which will feed into the senior band, providing continuity of players for the future. Hugh Johnstone MBE and Ian Taylor, with support from other band members, have played a key role in mentoring the youth band, in the process delivering regular competition success at Scottish and UK level.

After tremendous efforts by the band committee, under the outstanding leadership of its President, Bert Ritchie, a new band hall was opened on Ayr Road within the grounds of Dalmellington Community Centre on 2 November 2005.

New Cumnock-based poet Rab Wilson, who mainly writes in Scots, penned a poem after visiting the band hall and enjoying the many photo exhibits of banding down through the years. It is appropriately titled 'Dalmellington Baun'.

Dalmellington Baun

This room, lik a works canteen; stark, functional,
brichtly lit, austere, fit fir ae purpose –
tae fix these players minds anely oan music.
Nae clock hings oan the wa, there's nae distraction,
juist the muckle banners; 'Scottish Champions',
clear mindin o their pridefou pedigree.
The piece they're warkin oan's bi Gilbert Vinter,
bound fir the 'Nationals', comin up in Mairch,
(a wit declares 'a swatch o Arban's Tutor'!).
'Salute to Youth' is technically demandin,
fierce chromatic rins o semi-quavers,
pushin principle players tae their leemits;
concentration etcht upon their faces.
While Airchie, their baun-maister, teases oot
abeelities they thocht they nevir hud;
'A braw wee trio – when ye hear the pairts!'
'Gin thon judge hus goat lugs – best bet, he's listenin!'
an repetition o some fykie pairt
draws frae thaim honed an purposefou perfection.
Ae meenit, saftly, pianissimo,
Syne, stabbin fiercely his conductor's wand,
A snarlin Sforzando, thunderous in its micht!
Oan Airchie's score, 'Eroico' unnerlined,
'Heroically'! juist listen, an ye'll hear,
that smeddum wrocht frae ither generations.
Likesay, the bluid o heroes' in their veins;
whaes faither's faithers wrocht at Pennyvenie,
in Minnivey, at Burnton, an the Beoch,
the huddlet group in thon auld photiegraph,
wi miners cap-laumps, playin Christmas carols,
a history that's leevin, breathin yet.
The Silver Baun, a muckle great machine,
whaes pairts must wark in harmony thegaither,
lik some vast Winding Engine, cast frae bress,
raisin tae the licht its praicious cargo.

Hugh Johnstone MBE

For many folk with Doon Valley origins, the Dalmellington Band is synonymous with the village and many of the leading players have travelled throughout the UK and abroad to play in bands. Importantly, they have always remembered with pride their roots in the Doon Valley. Literally hundreds of players over the years will have fond memories of Hugh Johnstone, MBE, the best-known former player, conductor and stalwart worker and trainer of young players. His contribution to Dalmellington Band and the brass band movement in Scotland is legendary.

Other Dalmellington institutions

The Dalmellington Curling Club is believed to be the oldest surviving organisation in the village, having been established in 1841. Several villagers are office-bearers in the club, which remains active and healthy.

Lodge St Thomas (Kilwinning) Dalmellington No. 433 was formed following a meeting on 1 April 1864 in David McBlane's pub (at the end of the close between Dalmellington Inn and Dale's Butcher shop). The lodge now has its own premises in Low Main Street.

Matthew Anderson, policeman-poet

Like Dalmellington with Robert Hettrick, Waterside also boasts a poet of note. Matthew Anderson, the policeman-poet of the Ayrshire Constabulary, was born in Waterside on 7 June 1864 at 60 Truffhill Row. Like his world-renowned counterpart, Anderson began his working life as a farm hand. He abandoned this work at an early age, however, and put his energies to good use in the Royal Marines where he spent three years as a gunner. He later joined the ranks of the Ayrshire Constabulary, where he served in such far-flung places as Dalmellington, Symington, Barrmill, Kilwinning, Coylton, Drongan and Irvine.

Matthew Anderson, like many of his peers, was well educated and held strong views which did not always make him popular with higher ranking officers in the constabulary. Anderson had a great knowledge and understanding of people and a strong interest in nature which is reflected in his poems. His output was prolific and includes *Poems and Songs* (1891) and *Poems of a Policeman* (1898) which were very popular in the county of Ayr. In retirement he lived in Kilmarnock and died there on 14 November 1948 aged eighty-four. He often wrote poems about the villages where he worked. Of Waterside, his birthplace, he wrote:

This happened a' at Waterside,
As braw a place as ony, O,
Where dark, and deep, and smooth, and wide
The river Doon rins bonnie, O;
Where nicht is no like nicht ava,
For aye sae cheerie; aye sae braw,
The furnaces they bleeze awa'
An' licht up every crannie, O
Oh, 'tis a lovely countryside
When flowers are a' in blossom, O;
An' kindness there is beautified
In mony a manly bosom, O;
'Twas there I grew to be a boy,
An' felt my first, my purest joy
At Muckleholm when herdin' kye
'Mang broomy knows sae bonnie, O.

Lethanhill

On the hill to the east of Patna, 900 feet above sea level, there was also a minor miracle at work. The new mining communities of Lethanhill and Burnfoothill – known simply as the Hill – were born in this harsh environment in the mid-1800s at the behest of the Dalmellington Iron Company (sometimes shortened to DICo), who wanted their workers to live close to the ironstone and coal pits where they would work.

The mining folk on this plateau developed a strong sense of community, exemplified by a willingness to help each other, despite the grimness of life and occupation and the hostility of the environment. This shared sense of community and togetherness was greatly valued and indeed is today often found lacking.

The Hill

By the end of the 1860s, 190 houses had been erected a mile above and east of Patna. There was some confusion about the name of the village. The larger part was known officially as Lethanhill on the Ordnance Survey maps and all the amenities were located there. However, the row to the north and slightly apart from the others and ultimately comprising over ninety houses, was called Burnfoothill, and the whole village was more commonly called by this name. After a time, however, the folk of the district shortened the title to the simpler one of 'the Hill.'

At its peak, the Hill consisted of ten rows of cottages in the Lethanhill part and three rows forming a long front at Burnfoothill looking down on Patna. The village was built by the Dalmellington Iron Company to house the miners who would work the numerous ironstone pits all over the Knockkippen Plateau between 1849 and 1919. These ironstone pits generally went under the names of the farms whose land they were on, or that of a nearby landmark. The prominent ironstone mines, normally not very deep, included Bowhill, Kerse, Polnessan, Downieston, Burnfoot, Drumgrange and Corbie Craigs.

The immediate area around the Hill was saturated with ironstone pits and in seven cases, namely Burnfoot pits Nos. 1, 2, 3, 6 and 8 and Drumgrange Nos. 2 and 4, the pits were actually sunk in the middle of the village between 1847 and 1860. Later additions to the village were built over these expired workings.

Access to the Hill seems to have been a secondary consideration for the Dalmellington Iron Company, for it was only in 1923, and only after a long campaign of lobbying and tireless letter-writing, that the village got its proper metalled road, replacing what had been little more than a heavily potholed dirt track, which was well-nigh impossible at certain times for motor vehicles or horse-drawn carts to climb or descend safely.

By 1954 Burnfoothill was totally deserted, all the families having moved out, mainly to Patna. However, the village school remained intact and children were bussed up from Patna until 1959, when the school too was demolished.

All that remains of the Hill is the plantation which hides the foundations of many of the cottages, the drumhead at the top of the Drumgrange incline, the war memorial and a concrete memorial to the Hill village.

The Drumgrange incline

The remains of the immense double-track Drumgrange incline can still be seen just north of Waterside, east of the A713. This Dalmellington Iron Company line took the railway from Waterside up to the high-level iron ore lines running between Benwhat and the Hill and out to Houldsworth Pit, Benbranigan Pit and the extensive Corbie Craigs pit networks high above the valley of the River Doon.

This incline had a double track, with pulleys set between each pair of rails for the support of the wire rope. At the top, supported by two large brick-built buttresses, was an iron drum, some 5 feet in diameter. This was fitted with a handbrake, operating large wooden blocks set round the perimeter of the drum. The buttresses are still extant and known as the drumhead. This also included a brick-built shelter for the brakeman. The shelter was important because of the wild weather often experienced on the face of this west-aspect which could be operating day and night. Rail wagon traffic moving up and down the incline was removed and shunted into sidings.

The standard wagons using the incline were of 8, 10, 12 and finally 15 ton capacity. Local historian David L Smith (*The Dalmellington Iron Company: Its Engines and Men*) records that on many occasions, despite the braking system, there were wild runaways even in the days of the small wagons. Although he says there was no record of the wire ropes breaking, couplings on the wagons broke from time to time. The runaway was a dramatic event, the wagon contents scattered widely and on one occasion the wagon actually took to the air on its thrilling descent from top to bottom. Fortunately, there are no records of anyone being hurt.

The Corbie Craigs incline operated on a similar basis to its close neighbour at Drumgrange. It ran from the south end of Waterside from the extensive railway sidings there, across a dramatic and impressive wooden viaduct (no longer in existence) which carried it across Dunaskin Glen and upwards along the southern edge of Dunaskin Burn until joining the Hill rail network on the plateau at Corbie Craigs.

The war memorial

The Lethanhill war memorial is a fine obelisk of grey polished granite, approximately 15 feet tall. The monument now stands high on the deserted hillside where the village once stood. The dedication reads:

Erected
by Public Subscription
and
dedicated by the inhabitants
To the revered memory
Of their glorious dead who
In making the supreme sacrifice
During the Great War
1914–1918
Nobly sustained freedom's cause
WWI ROLL OF HONOUR
Blain: John, Private
Ferguson: William, Private
Finlay: Robert, Private
Hynds: Hugh, Private
Lafferty: Ivy, Private
Lafferty: Thomas, Private
McClelland: David, Private
McClymont: Robert, Private
McCormick: John, Private
Miller: Robert, Private
Muir: Robert, Private
Nugent: Charles, Sergeant
Nugent: Dennis, Private
Pyper: Samuel, Private
Talman: James McG, Sergeant
Talman: William, Private

WWII ROLL OF HONOUR:
Finlay: William J, Corporal
Gilmour: James, Private
Stevenson: Alexander, Trooper

The concrete foundations of the vanished buildings can be seen in the grass around the monument and on a visit in 2012 the opencast workings had just began moving mountains of earth, extracting rich seams of coal that the miners of yesteryear could only dream of. This operation was to go so badly wrong in 2014, when the operating company went into administration leaving a huge blight on the wild moors around Lethanhill which is unlikely ever to be fully reinstated, albeit attempts were beginning in July 2015 with workers and machinery based at Dunstonhill.

Benwhat

A mile to the east yet another mining village was constructed by the Dalmellington Iron Company and quickly grew from forty houses to eighty-four. It was called Benwhat. Built on the 1,000-foot contour line, it was ranked as one of the highest and most remote villages in Scotland. Strangely, although both Lethanhill and Benwhat had roads leading down to the valley, there was no road connecting these hill villages. However, they were connected by railway, which also acted as a path for locals travelling between them.

The dominant feature of Benwhat remains the war memorial located on the side of Benwhat Hill. Erected in 1921, it is a grey granite obelisk approximately 15 feet high and standing on three rustic sandstone steps. The monument is surrounded by a wrought iron fence and was fully refurbished in 2011. The dedication reads:

BENWHAT 1921
Erected by the people
Of this village with
Pride and affection
To the memory of
Gallant sons who laid
Down their lives for
Their King and Country
In the Great War 1914–1919
'Greater love
hath no man than this'

WWI ROLL OF HONOUR:
Bryant W. Royal Scots Fusiliers Private
Hill W. Royal Scots Fusiliers Private
Hodgson D. Royal Scots Fusiliers Private
Millar E. Royal Scots Fusiliers Private
Morrison R. Royal Scots Fusiliers Private
Nevile G. Argyll & Sutherland Highlanders Private
Neville W. Royal Scots Private
Parker G. Royal Scots Fusiliers Sergeant
Parker T. Royal Scots Fusiliers Private
Scally B. Seaforth Highlanders Private
Wilson A. Royal Scots Fusiliers Private
Wilson W. Royal Scots Fusiliers Private

WWII ROLL OF HONOUR:
Bunyan T. Gordon Highlanders Private
McMahon R. Gordon Highlanders Private
Robertson J. Black Watch Private

Readers wishing to explore more about these villages are referred to local books by T Courtney McQuillan, Robert Farrell and Donald L Reid listed in the bibliography.

Pennyvenie

In 1912 the last of the Dalmellington Iron Company villages was built in the Doon Valley, called Pennyvenie. This village, no longer extant, was located some 1.5 miles north-east of Dalmellington on the B741 road to New Cumnock. The village was built to house miners, at the same time as the Dalmellington Iron Company was developing what was called locally the Big Mine, or more formally, Pennyvenie No. 4.

An earlier colliery had been opened by the Company in 1872 and finally closed in 1978. At its peak there were 725 men working here and it comprised seven separate pit shafts, the last sunk in 1945.

There were around seventy single and double apartment houses in Pennyvenie, stretched out in small rows ranging from four to ten houses per row along the New Cumnock Road (B741). Although the village had a small primary school, it had no store, church, institute or any form of shopping facility. Villagers had to walk almost two miles on foot into Dalmellington for their provisions and entertainment. They did, however, have regular vans from Dalmellington Co-op, which provided a range of foods.

The closure of Pennyvenie No. 4 in 1961 considerably reduced the nearby employment prospects for men from the village, and many of the mining families left to live in nearby Dalmellington, eventually leaving only a few houses which had not been vacated or demolished. The last remaining row of houses was known as Sighthill and for many years it sat forlornly on the north side of the B741. It was abandoned in 2011 and demolished in early 2012.

The railhead for the Big Mine ran behind what was known as High Pennyvenie and it, too, was swallowed up by massive opencast mining that took place between Beoch and Pennyvenie. Today the playground for the old Pennyvenie school, which closed in the 1960s, having in later years been used as a school for children with learning difficulties, is just about all that remains, except for the massive coal spoil bing that dominates and stands sentinel over Dalmellington, the one highly visible remnant of coal mining in the upper Doon Valley.

The Pennyvenie site was subsequently reworked for extraction of opencast coal, opening in 1987 and operated by Scottish Resources Group, at that time said to be the largest surface mining group in the UK. Scottish Coal was responsible for developing and managing the Group's surface mining interests, providing over 4 million tonnes of coal to the UK's major power generators in the 2011 financial year.

Death in opencast mining

The opencast site at Pennyvenie employed around 130 workers and produced 750,000 tonnes of coal a year and until 2014 when the operating company went into administration, was a 24-hour operation. Tragically, the price of winning coal was still high: on 26 February 2007 at 1pm. Brian French, a 48-year-old foreman fitter, and Colin Ferguson, a 37-year-old tyre fitter, were fatally injured when a Terex TR100 dump truck collided with their Land Rover on a working site at Pennyvenie. Both vehicles were the same colour and the driver of the huge Terex was making a manoeuvre and apparently failed to see the Land Rover, leading to this tragic industrial accident.

Tourism

Patna, Waterside and Dalmellington, on the upper reaches of the River Doon, so proud of their rich social and industrial past, now lack any local employment of significance. Most people travel to Ayr or further afield to find work. Attracting tourists has been helped with the creation of the Scottish Industrial Railway Centre, where some excellent industrial locomotives have been preserved.

They were originally at Minnivey and now they are headquartered at Waterside, where steam train specials are regularly run on Sundays during the summer months. One can only think that the Reverend G S Hendrie of Dalmellington would have been rather proud of the volunteers who have worked tirelessly to preserve steam in the Doon Valley, drawing tourists from far and wide, meeting Hendrie's dream of visitors flocking to his beloved Doon Valley.

Unfortunately, the museum at Waterside, which had the aim of developing Europe's best example of a Victorian ironworks, closed in 2005 due to a lack of funding. However, Doon Valley Museum at Cathcartston, Dalmellington, is a real gem and preserves a great deal of local heritage in its archives.

Employment

Developing tourism to enjoy the natural surroundings such as Loch Doon and Ness Glen must be high on the local agenda. However, attracting a large employer of local labour is undoubtedly the greatest need to help regenerate an area of historical significance and outstanding natural beauty. This is indeed a recurring theme and was well illustrated by the Dalmellington blacksmith-poet, Robert Hettrick, in 1823 when he penned fine words about his vision of prosperity for Dalmellington in his poem 'The Petition of the River Doon'. He saw Dalmellington as a busy manufacturing base where full employment would ensure prosperity for the town and its people.

Let party strife be set aside,
The public good your councils guide;
Let commerce round my windings ride,
Triumphant there,
Then will I be the flower and pride
Of a' this shire.

Dr E S Lee – Sweat of Miners

Perhaps the lure of the upper valley of the River Doon and its people is best summed up by the late Dr E S Lee, a General Practitioner in Dalmellington for over forty years. Born in Singapore in 1906, he studied medicine at Edinburgh and came to the village in 1933 following a short spell in Alloa.

At his retiral presentation in 1973 he said: 'If I could live my life again I would come to Dalmellington. This is predominantly a mining area and most of my patients over the years have been miners. I do not know of anyone who works harder than the mineworker. Although the price of coal is high to the consumer, the reward for producing coal will never be sufficient. I realised long ago that coal could not be won by machines alone, but only by the sweat of miners. And I remember with sadness the early deaths and chronic ill-health of some of your colleagues due to their work in the pits. Some of my most poignant memories are of having to knock on doors to inform local folk of the deaths of husbands and sons in mining accidents.'

Education and heritage

The author is someone who is proud of the education provided at Dalmellington High School, demolished, rebuilt and renamed Doon Academy. The words of a much-loved former English teacher, Arthur

These stones commemorate the large numbers of unemployed folk in the Doon Valley in the years shown. The stones and surrounding ground are regularly maintained in good condition by Wilson Ireland of Patna, the grandson of Joe Ireland who carved the inscription. Photo: Donald L Reid)

W Wilson, are therefore a fitting conclusion to this brief overview of aspects of life in the upper reaches of the Doon Valley. In three short verses he manages to capture the very essence of the history and heritage of the area, in a way that is sure to strike a chord with former pupils.

The High School of Dalmellington
It stands beneath the hills,
Where rushing rivers mingle,
And the wind blows as it wills.
These hills hid ancient dwellings,
Crannogs were in the mere,
Then marching feet of Romans
'Neath the eagle wings of fear.

Our steadfast Covenanters
Put God before the King,
Upholding their religion
Whatever fate might bring.
Skilled were our village weavers,
Thoughtful and studious men,
Now stout courageous miners
Dare death beneath the Ben.

These were the folk before us,
Be proud of them, be proud,
These Scottish folk who bred us
We sing their praises loud.
With all of our endeavours
The future will abide,
May the sons of our sons remember
Dalmellington with pride.

Arthur W Wilson
January 1963
(Set to music by Stuart M Robertson)

This song was sung with vigour and pride at Dalmellington High School's weekly assembly.

Chapter 2

Doon Valley Industrial Past

We labour soon, we labour late,
To feed the titled knave, man;
And a' the comfort we're to get
Is that ayont the grave, man.

The Tree of Liberty
Robert Burns

Mining begins

The Doon Valley owes its industrial development to the existence of prolific amounts of coal and ironstone. Into this quiet rural land of the mid 19th century, dominated by wonderful scenery on either side of the iconic River Doon, came the industrial Houldsworth family in 1845 to found the Dalmellington Iron Works at Waterside.

At Waterside the ironworks soon had five roaring furnaces which later increased to seven and many small iron-stone and coal pits were dug littering the hills of the Doon Valley. A railway line was laid which soon radiated across the high plateau at Lethanhill to Benwhat and around Waterside with lines leading to furnaces, quarries and the myriad of coal and iron-stone mines.

Of course coal had been mined for centuries in the Doon Valley, albeit in small amounts in drift mines where the coal was located near to the surface. This fact is well documented in the *Statistical Account* of 1793, where the Minister of Dalmellington, the Reverend Duncan McMyne reported that 'the parish is full of fine coal, and freestone, in almost every corner of it' and recorded that coal was transported 30 miles away into Galloway. 'There is also iron-stone to be found in the parish, and lead in some of the hills.'

Nearly fifty years later this was still the case, but deeper mining was now evident, as revealed in the *Statistical Account* of 1837, when the Parish Minister of Dalmellington, the Reverend Robert Houston wrote: 'The coal pits have been many, especially in low situations, where till lately the coal was worked at less than 3 fathoms from the surface.'

And it was from these beginnings that a small industrial revolution was to take the valley by storm. In the 1840s the entrepreneurial Houldsworth family, originally from Yorkshire, and with established ironworks in Coltness, Lanarkshire, formed the Dalmellington Iron Company. The following extract from the *Glasgow Herald* of 27 September 1848 highlights the anticipation of the arrival of the new industry.

> *The Dalmellington Iron Works, belonging to Messrs Houldsworth, Glasgow, were blown in for the first time on Monday week, and the first casting took place on Wednesday. The machinery was found to work smoothly and everything went off well. Ayrshire is nearly now girded round with ironworks.*

Houldsworth influence

Henry Houldsworth was the founding father of the Dalmellington Iron Company at Dunaskin. He was seventy-four years of age when he began this project in the 1840s. His life illustrates well the tremendous energy and technological change of the 19th century which transformed the once pastoral south-west of Scotland, a land of quiet hills and valleys, into a booming industrial heart of Empire.

Ironworks

After three years of hectic major construction operations at Waterside, by 1848 the results of this mini industrial revolution were evident to all. The first furnaces were in blast, belching out smoke and dust in this quiet unspoiled land of hills and valleys. New villages were hurriedly constructed to house the large workforce required to mine the coal and ironstone and to carry out all the operations at the ironworks, and by the end of the 1860s most were in place.

New villages

Whilst the industrial conditions were far from ideal, the local population were pleased that many jobs were created. Indeed there was a scarcity of local workers, and outsiders, keen to gain employment, flocked in from the Highlands of Scotland, Ireland, Lanarkshire and elsewhere and took up residence in the new villages, with the appealing names of Lethanhill, Benwhat, Corbie Craigs, Craigmark, Pennyvenie, Kerse, Tongue Row, Cairntable, Beoch and Waterside, also known as Dunaskin.

The influence of railways

The twin villages of Lethanhill and Burnfoothill (the Hill) were built

Dunaskin Power station in the earlier part of the 20th century showing three workers in the turbine room which produced power for all operations at Dunaskin. The turbine was built by the British Thomson-Houston Company of Rugby. The workers are (l to r): Tom Campbell, Albert Smith and Angus McLeod.

Dunaskin Brickwork which was located in Dunaskin Glen in1905. 4th from the left in the back row is David Colquhoun. He later worked at Dunaskin Brickwork on the Waterside site which started production around 1926. His son David was killed during the Second World War. The men are holding brick moulds, being hand made at that time. It was reckoned that David Colquhoun was so proficient at brick making that he was faster than many of the machines subsequently used in this process.

between 1849 and the 1860s on the Knockkippen Plateau at 900 feet above sea level and one mile above Patna and the River Doon. The villages were a series of miners' rows built by the Dalmellington Iron Company close to the iron pits where the men worked converting iron ore extracted from surface workings into pig iron in open hearths.

The fast-moving industrial development meant that transport links were vital to ensure that the coal, ironstone and finished pig iron could be readily transported to the harbour at Ayr. This was accomplished in 1856 with the completion of the Ayr – Dalmellington railway, by which time frenetic local activity resulted in a spider's web of railway lines running along the plateau above the Upper Doon Valley and from Pennyvenie to Houldsworth, the remnants of which can still be clearly seen and followed today. This was an amazing feat of industrial construction and many navvies must have been engaged in the extensive engineering operations which led to these many lines being laid along the 900-foot to 1000-foot contour high above the Valley of Doon.

Wage boom and social life

The 1870s can be regarded as a period of great prosperity for the Dalmellington Iron Company and its workforce. Industry was booming across Britain and the wages of local miners rose to an incredible £7 to £8 per week. In later years the miners and their families were to look back nostalgically on this period, which they referred to as 'the time o' the big money'.

It was around this period that many of the miners in these villages acquired the status symbol of that era – an American organ. The miners valued education for their children in the hope of guaranteeing them a better future. There was a well-organised social and recreational calendar of events which included football teams, quoits, athletics, choir, pipe band, Burns Club, brass band, bazaars, educational improvement classes, cantatas and concerts.

There was the annual sports event, a day never to be missed, with great athletes competing from near and far. Indeed, modern-day communities would have difficulty replicating the range and variety of social and recreational facilities available in the Doon Valley's lost mining villages. All of this was not only self-created but self-supported. There were no grants available in those times to support a range of community activities.

Community spirit

The villages were new, but the workers were all of the same social background and were determined to make the best of the circumstances in which they found themselves. Indeed, most of them probably considered themselves fortunate to have a job, because losing it also held the prospect of losing a home, a real fear for any miner with a large family to support.

They were, nevertheless, proud people and the sense of community spirit was evident from the earliest days of these newly created mining communities, with neighbours being friendly and helpful to each other. There was a sort of shared sense and understanding of living life in difficult circumstances in relatively remote areas which helped everyone to pull together. This facet of life in the lost mining villages was always commented upon by former residents and was apparent right up until the final days of depopulation. When former villagers held reunions, this period was always dwelt on.

> *The spirit of 'Esprit de Corps' or the 'one for all' and 'all for one' spirit was strongly emphasised by Mr John Relly, principal speaker at the seventh annual Benquhat Re-union which took place on Saturday in Dalmellington Community Centre. Special reference was made to togetherness of the homely folks of Benquhat with happy smiles in evidence when he made reference to the 'Hill Line' and the many courtships and ultimate marriages between the Hill (Lethanhill) and Benquhat couples. He spoke of how a serious illness was the concern of the whole village and how physical help was provided and how on one occasion after a great snowstorm the villagers banded themselves together hurriedly, to clear away the snow and so allow an ambulance to quickly remove a very sick man to hospital.*
>
> *Ayrshire Post*, 13 March 1970

Changing times

The pendulum quickly swung back from the good days of high wages and by the 1880s wages were back to around 25 shillings per week. Times were again pretty grim for the miners and furnacemen in the Doon Valley, as they were often laid off for weeks at a time with no wages. To help the family survive these difficult times, they would sell off possessions. The second-hand shops in Ayr were reported to be full of American organs, sold off by struggling miners, putting food on the table being more important than making music.

There was overcapacity in the mining industry and English firms were doing much better than their counterparts in the Doon Valley, the remoteness of the local ironworks at Dunaskin being a distinct disadvantage for the once highly regarded Dalmellington iron ore. Times were changing and sadly not for the better.

Mining population

By 1911 the section of the Ayrshire population representing the mining industry numbered around 40,000 people. Of this number roughly 30,000 lived in miners' rows or villages owned by the local mining companies. The remaining 10,000 lived in towns and other villages. By 1913 the period of mining expansion had come to an end and no more rows of houses were built, whilst little or no maintenance was carried out on the existing housing stock.

Steam crane at Pennyvennie Colliery with Waterside's popular character, Tom Bruce, who from boyhood days until his death, was an enthusiastic member of Dunaskin Band where he played the double bass. The winding wheels for raising and lowering the pit cage can be seen in the background. Pennyvenie No. 7 opened for coal production in 1947 and closed in 1978.

A group of Carters who transported goods and industrial items at Dalmellington Iron Works. The works opened at Dunaskin in September 1848. This was probably taken in late 1890s.

End of iron production

Waterside, which consisted of some eighty-nine houses in 1851, grew around the original ironworks, which were built between 1846 and 1856. The Dalmellington Iron Works ceased production of pig iron in 1921, but the size of the dominant slag bing at Waterside, which has been reduced immeasurably since then for road bottoming, testifies to the huge amounts of iron which must have been produced at Waterside between 1848 and 1921, a period of only seventy-three years.

In the early 20th century, the industrial development of Britain was firmly based on steel making, another nail in the coffin of iron production. Moreover, with the ever increasing levels of imported iron ore from Spain, to replace the worked out Doon Valley iron ore, the end of iron production in the Valley of Doon was inevitable. Only the outbreak of the Great War gave it a stay of execution.

After the war the demand for iron and coal fell. Local production costs soared, wages began to fall and this was a period of increasing industrial strife. Dalmellington Iron Company miners took part in the three-week strike in October 1920. With the threat of another such strike looming in March 1921, the board of the Company took the decision to close the ironworks and move away from the Doon Valley. The famous Dunaskin furnaces were blown out, never again to produce the world-famous Dalmellington iron, and no further tipping of molten slag on the famous Waterside bing occurred after 1921.

Mr Robert McCall, a former headmaster at Dreghorn speaking at the 1969 Hill Reunion, remembered his boyhood days and touched on the impact of the iron production.

> *Many a time I walked and often ran from the Hill down to Waterside to catch the train. Down there in the valley was Jimmy's burn where we dooked (swam) and guddled. In the distance was the road up past High Keirs. Many a time I have walked that way to Straiton. In the middle distance was the enormous slag bing, dominating the valley, which used to glow and brighten the night sky in my boyhood days.*

So 1921 was indeed a defining moment in the history of industrial Doon Valley, with the end of iron production, but old King Coal would still reign supreme until the last Doon Valley colliery at Pennyvenie closed in 1978. Strangely enough, within a few years of the end of deep mining, opencast mining came on stream in the Doon Valley, surface mining producing amounts of coal that underground miners could only dream of.

Bairds and Dalmellington

William Baird & Co. Ltd, coal and iron masters, had been founded in 1830 with their industrial base centred in Lanarkshire. They also had interests in Ayrshire related mainly to various coal and ironstone pits and the Muirkirk and Eglinton ironworks. However, as we have just seen, by the early 1920s the winds of change were blowing through

The furnacemen at the Dalmellington Iron Company works at Waterside were a hardy breed. All these men would have lived at Waterside or the surrounding villages, but unfortunately their identities are unknown today. Some quite young boys worked at the furnaces as shown in the front row circa 1910.

Last shift at Pennyvenie Colliery. All would have mixed emotions. Some pleased to be finishing working down the coal mines; others concerned about what the future held for them, but all proud miners. Several commemorative photos were taken that day when different shifts finished.

industrial Scotland and there was a gradual downturn in mining and iron production caused primarily by a drop in demand for iron, closely linked to an inability to compete against cheaper foreign imports of ironstone.

Market Price

Unfortunately, the blackband ironstone seams in the Ayrshire and Lanarkshire coalfields became more difficult to work and consequently they were unable to produce ironstone in the quantities and at a price demanded by the market. This culminated in the closure of ironworks at Muirkirk, Dalmellington and Kilwinning in the 1920s and the coal owners then concentrated on coal production in the rich, if difficult to work, Ayrshire and Lanarkshire seams.

Two Main Companies

The two principal companies involved in coal mining were William Baird & Company and their competitors, the Dalmellington Iron Company, the latter being in poor financial shape due to the Depression, whereas Bairds seem to have been more financially resilient. In 1931 the two companies amalgamated: the new company was rebranded as Bairds and Dalmellington and concentrated its efforts in coal production for the home market and diversified into brick making.

The new company, 75% owned by William Baird & Co. Ltd, controlled some 70% of the Ayrshire coalfields. In 1933 they employed around 7,244 miners in over twenty collieries in the county. This number included pits in the Doon Valley: Beoch, 150 miners; Bogton No. 1, 90 miners; Houldsworth, 260 miners; Pennyvenie No. 4, 160 miners; and Pennyvenie Nos. 2, 3 and 6, 440 miners.

By 1938, despite the years of depression, Bairds and Dalmellington's gross profit stood at 17.5% and this was not only sustained but rose to 20% during the war years and peaked at 27.5% in the year before the nationalisation of the coal industry.

1947 Important Year

The year 1947 was a key year for industry in Scotland, with the majority of coal mines being taken under government control under the auspices of the National Coal Board. At the time of the nationalisation of the coal mines in 1947, the Doon Valley pits taken into the national fold were: Beoch Nos. 3 and 4, 369 miners; Bogton, 96 miners; Chalmerston, 262 miners; Bowhill, 37 miners; Houldsworth, 248 miners; Pennyvenie No. 4, 216 miners; Pennyvenie Nos. 2, 3 and 7, 417 miners. But nationalisation sounded the death knell for many small mining companies, including Bairds and Dalmellington Ltd, which was finally wound up in 1953.

The NCB later used the ironworks site at Waterside for administrative purposes and coal-related storage and movement. The brickworks and kilns at Waterside finally closed in 1976. The Scottish mining story continued until the closure of the longest-serving colliery during the National Coal Board era in Ayrshire, a proud record which goes to Barony Colliery near Auchinleck, which maintained production from 1947 until it was closed as the last Ayrshire deep mine in 1989. However, the last deep mine in Scotland was Longannet in Fife, which closed in 2002, leaving only opencast sites in the Scottish coalfields.

Capturing the industrial past

Through the efforts of hard-working local volunteers led by Miss Anne Joss, MBE, of Dalmellington and District Conservation Trust, Dunaskin was given a new lease of life as a significant outdoor heritage museum in 1983. There had been many years of diligent preparatory work before the opening stage was even reached.

Dunaskin was a visitor attraction for all the family, taking them on a historical journey through time looking at the industrial past in terms of iron production, coal mining, working steam engines and brick-making. Indeed, the history of the Doon Valley is in many ways a microcosm of the history of Scotland, making this museum one of exceptional importance. The 'Dunaskin Experience' allowed the visitor to explore the past as it was actually lived by Ayrshire folk.

Museum site

An open-air, living museum set amidst beautiful rolling countryside, it followed the story of the people and places of the Doon Valley through the industrial revolution, two world wars and right up to modern times. The 'Mary Gallagher Experience' was an audio-visual presentation which recreated Ayrshire life in the 19th and early 20th centuries.

Classed as a Scheduled Ancient Monument, the museum's 110-acre site had historic buildings and walks, including nearby Dunaskin Glen, which is a designated Site of Special Scientific Interest. There was also a period cottage and industrial machinery as well as a restaurant and shop, all aimed at making the visitor experience as pleasant and interesting as possible.

Sadly, the museum was forced to close in 2005 due to a lack of financial support and perhaps a lack of vision by key decision makers who controlled the purse-strings, not perhaps fully realising the importance of this exceptional industrial site, not only at Ayrshire level, but as a national gem.

In 2010 Ayrshire Railway Preservation Group moved their many industrial railway locomotives from Minnivey, near Dalmellington, to Dunaskin. They have given the site a new lease of life, with even more steam trains available to tempt visitors to once again recall the days of an industrial steam railway and wonder at the magnificent heritage of ironmaking, coal mining and brick production.

We cam na here to view your warks
In hopes to be mair wise,
But only, lest we gang to Hell,
It may be nae surprise.
But when we tirl'd at your door
The porter dought na bear us:
Sae may, should we to Hell's yetts come,
Your billie Satan sair us.

At Carron Ironworks
Robert Burns

Chapter 3

Death-Knell of Doon Valley Deep Mining

I remember well, those scars of blue,
That covered my Granddad's hands.
Hands that were gnarled and wrinkled,
The hands of a working man.
Many a man bears the scars,
From the work they had to do,
But only the working miner's hands,
Have the scars forever blue.

Scars
Ian Winstanley

A difficult and dangerous occupation

Coal mining has always been and will always be a dangerous occupation wherever it is carried out and no matter how stringent the safety rules. One only has to look back to 1950 when the country was holding its breath and praying fervently as 129 miners were trapped in the Knockshinnoch Mine at New Cumnock. Amazingly, 116 were rescued in dramatic fashion, whilst tragically 13 men lost their lives.

More than half a century later it is a commonly held view, especially in former mining communities, that Prime Minister Margaret Thatcher's Plan for Coal destroyed the industry across the nation. Jobs were lost and entire communities were rocked to their very foundations as coal mines closed and populations began to dwindle, close family ties being cut, as families moved away in search of work. However, what could not be so easily destroyed was that spirit of caring that marked out mining communities.

Thatcher's Plan for Coal

Deep mining in the UK was seen as being increasingly expensive when compared to cheaper imports from South Africa and Australia, where opencast operations won coal at a fraction of the cost. This, too, was later to be proved true in Cumnock and Doon Valley. With conflict between the National Union of Mineworkers and the Thatcher-led Tory government in 1984–85, the writing was on the wall for deep mining in Scotland and the UK. It was indeed the beginning of the end with pit closures rolling in quickly like the unstoppable tide.

One of the things that depressed many folk in the 1980s in Britain was that society seemed to be so divided. Because of the miners' strike and the Falklands War of 1982, people either really didn't like Thatcher at all, or they really loved her, marking her down as one of the truly great British prime ministers. She was something of an enigma – loved and hated in equal measure. Her legacy will certainly show her strengths and leadership skills, but mining communities across the UK will doubtless still have little time for her because of her role in the demise of deep mining in the UK.

1984-85 Strike in Ayrshire

The great strike has been over for more than a quarter of a century, but certain memories – as rock-hard as the coal itself – endure. In Ayrshire and other mining communities, a few of the men and their families who endured the hardships of a strike that lasted from 5 March 1984 for one difficult year, regrettably cannot bring themselves to forgive those who 'scabbed' – crossed the picket lines and continued to work. It should also be remembered that those who worked on had their own reasons for doing so and they were primarily linked to supporting their families and perhaps having the foresight to know that a prolonged strike would hasten pit closure. Indeed, they were proved right.

No Victory

However, it was certainly true that the strikes in the mines in the 1984–85 period heralded the death knell for deep mining in the UK. The Ayrshire miners of Barony and Killoch were a proud and determined lot and with solid support for the strike from family and friends, they were prepared for a long stoppage, perhaps hoping that it would end quickly in victory. But victory is not a word that can be used on either side of that momentous dispute.

These were difficult times with real financial consequences for many families. Inevitably there was conflict between the strikers and those who chose to work on – so-called scabs – and sadly folk still talk of that schism, apparently still live in Cumnock and Auchinleck communities.

From personal experience, I recall the typical scenes of conflict vividly. At that time I was a police inspector in charge of contingents of men who

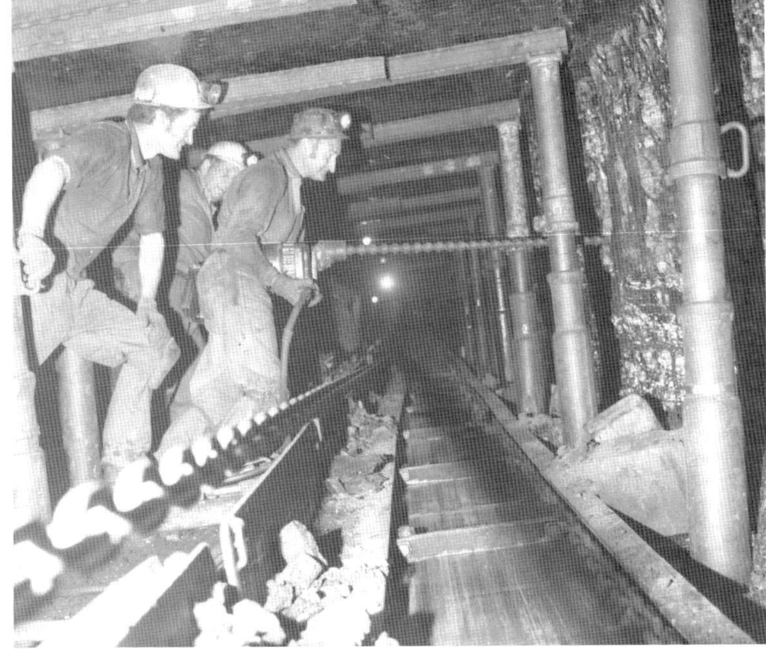

The man operating the boring machine at Pennyvenie is Hugh Uriarte and the nearest man is Alex Millar with the furthest away miner, Jock Kennedy.
(Photo: EAC DVM)

Coming up from the pit the day war broke out, 3 September, 1939. Dalmellington miners left to right, Matthew Dempsey, Jimmy Whalen, John Dick. At the time of this picture Matthew would be 51 years of age, having been born in Benwhat. He died in 1966. In WW1 he had been a Royal Engineer and was gassed and taken prisoner in May 1918. The outbreak of another war in September 1939 would have been a matter of concern for him, like many others, who by then had sons who would become involved.
(Photo: Tony Collins collection)

Pennyvenie Mines Rescue Brigade on a training exercise with Jimmy Smith (first left), George Sturgeon (2nd left), Jimmy Baird (third from left), Alastair McWhiter (4th from left), John 'Tubby' Boyd (6th from left), Douglas Drysdale (7th from left), Ken Murdoch (9th from left).

carried out policing operations at Barony Colliery, where large numbers of pickets endeavoured to stop non-striking miners and lorries loaded with coal entering and leaving the pit. It was a difficult period for strikers and working miners and their families, of that there can be no doubt.

Miners' remember

Here are a few of the views expressed at the time by miners involved, giving a brief insight into the impact on them and families of the strike.

> *'We need to keep fighting. Don't forget, we have gained more than we lost – friendship and pride.'*
>
> *'I took my seven-year-old son to the doctor, who said he was suffering from anxiety. He was worried about me because I was on strike.'*
>
> *'My attitude has changed. I thought I was a socialist all my life, but now I know what socialism really is. It's a whole way of life and we're living it now during this strike.'*
>
> *'You're not allowed to stop the lorries. The police won't allow peaceful picketing and that aggravates the men.'*
>
> *'I lived through the 1972 and '74 strikes, but it was a picnic compared to this strike.'*
>
> *'We were fighting for our jobs, our children and our communities. It was a hard few months, but I'm proud of it.'*

Pennyvenie closes

The following is an excerpt from the *Ayr Advertiser* of July 1978 highlighting the closure of the last pit in the Doon Valley, pre-dating the 1984 strike by six years. Whilst there were no coal pits operating in the Doon Valley at that time, many of the Doon Valley miners worked at Barony and Killoch and so they, too, suffered during that major strike.

A service of Remembrance following one of the early Hill Reunions. This was led by the Rev Ritchie of Symington. The Dunaskin Band was conducted by John Robertson. Everyone is standing within the remains of the old schoolhouse. Perhaps the reader can recognise someone.
(Courtesy of John Relly collection)

Underground at Pennyvenie showing the diesel locomotive used for moving hutches full of coal between the loading point near the face and the lie where it was stored until taken to the pithead.

Thursday, July 6th 1978 was an historic and in many ways a sad day for Dalmellington and the Doon Valley. It marked the end of an era with the closure of the last pit in the area, Pennyvenie Colliery. With the setting up of the Dalmellington Iron Company in the early 1840s coal has been produced commercially throughout the valley for upwards of 130 years.

The closure of Pennyvenie in July 1978 meant 450 job losses in an area already severely hit economically and socially by earlier pit closures. In 1960, thirteen years after nationalisation, some 2,500 men were employed in the industry throughout the Doon Valley. In 2012 there are none, except for a few who worked for a time on the Chalmerston and Benbain opencast sites, where huge machines have been substituted for manual labour.

Pit families

Pennyvenie was a colliery employing whole families over many years. Family names with long service include Calderwood, Dempsey, Kennedy, Paterson, Semple, Brown, Ritchie, Reid and Wallace. A proud tradition of deep mining in the Doon Valley had come to an end, but it has to be said that many miners were rather relieved that their own sons would no longer have to work in the small, dark, damp and dangerous bowels of the earth. Ironically, within a further twenty years there would be no deep mines left anywhere in Scotland. The closure programme had indeed been an unstoppable tide of change and the view of many is that strikes simply hastened the end.

End of Ayrshire deep mining

Killoch Collier closed in 1986, only one year after the strike ended. Not far from the Doon Valley, the Barony Pit near Auchinleck had been originally sunk in 1907, enlarged by Bairds and Dalmellington Ltd in 1938, and further developed by the NCB after 1950, with a new shaft 2,052 feet deep sunk. It, too, suffered economic problems and was finally shut down in 1989, when it had the honour of being the last NCB pit in Ayrshire.

A further twist of irony was that by 2012 more coal was being extracted from the Doon Valley than there ever was in the days of deep mining. Opencast mining began in the Doon Valley a few years after the closure of Pennyvenie. A railhead was developed at Minnivey, just beyond Craigmark, and two trainloads of coal were removed almost every day, to the sorting facility at Killoch.

However, regular coal movements by train from Minnivey ceased in 2011 except for the occasional coal movement. Since the demise of the opencast coal operating company in 2014 there have been no regular coal movements and site at Minnivey has been abandoned. Whether this will change in future is unknown.

It was common to look up towards Benbeoch Craig from Dalmellington and see towering industrial haulage vehicles from the opencast wending their way over the hill delivering coal to the Chalmerston loading point for removal by rail. The miners of the early 20th century would simply be staggered to see how coal is won in the second decade of the 21st century.

With the end of deep mining in Ayrshire at Barony Colliery in 1989, no other miners would be killed or maimed in the old-style deep mining – all too often the price of winning coal. However, tragedies still occur in surface mining with fatalities still part of the cost of gaining coal.

Winds of change

Now, with its deep coal mines gone and opencast also stopped in the Doon Valley, a new model of power generation looms ominously upon the horizon of the Doon Valley, and the local community does not like it. The next few years will reveal if they have been successful in fighting off the winds of change, as industrial windfarms, which already mark much of Scotland's countryside, present a real threat to scenic Doon Valley. At the time of writing (September 2015) the signs were ominous. A large windfarm on the Dalmellington – Straiton Road was well under construction and likely to spread to other sites in Doon Valley. The winds of change were indeed blowing strongly.

With future hope I oft would gaze
Fond, on thy little early ways:
Thy rudely caroll'd, chiming phrase,
In uncouth rhymes;
Fir'd at the the simply, artless lays
Of other times.

The Vision
Robert Burns

Chapter 4

Clawfin to Pennyvenie – A Life in Mining

Tom Hutchison

Of a' the Airts the wind can blaw
I dearly like the west,
For there the bonie lassie lives,
The lassie I lo'e best.
There wild woods grow, and rivers row,
And monie a hill between,
But day and night my fancy's flight
Is ever wi' my Jean.

Of a The Airts
Robert Burns

Tom Hutchison then aged ninety-one, a retired miner, was interviewed by Donald L Reid at his home in Hopes Avenue, Dalmellington, on 14 March 2005. He was married to Jane (born 15 February 1917 - 3 January 2005), better known to all the family as Jean, and they had a long and very happy marriage. It was a joy to journey down memory lane with Tom as he recounted special memories of his life and times as a coal miner and family man. Tom died on 3 May 2006.

Sad Start to Life

I was born on 12 March 1914 in Old Cumnock. I was raised by Mrs Elizabeth 'Lisa' Yates and her husband Ben. Lisa was my father's sister. It was a wee bit sad, because my mother Margaret Hutchison had a hard time at the birth and she died on 19 March.

So I was brought to 1 Broomknowe Dalmellington when I was one week old and lived there very happily and was raised by my Aunt Lisa and Uncle Ben. They just became my parents and I will always be grateful to them.

They were kindly folk, but I often wondered what my own mother would have been like, but you can't ponder too much on these things as life goes on and you have to face it head on.

School

I attended Dalmellington School and the headmaster was James Smith. He was the father of famous Dalmellington man and railway historian, David L Smith. Smith was a great man for local history, especially the rail systems and the men who worked them in the upper reaches of the Doon Valley

I enjoyed my time at school. I had a lot of pals, Alan McCreath, Sanny Findlay, Tommy Prendergast, but we just called him Pinner. Most folk had nicknames at school and these followed them into the pits. I wasn't bad at school and worked hard, but I suppose I was glad to leave at Easter when I became 14.

First Job

My first job was at the Washer at Craigmark. In those days you got a job right away and most of them were connected to coal mining. The hutches came straight down the hill from Chalmerston, a mine sitting high on the hill above Craigmark, and into what we called the Tumbler. My job was to take the hutches into the tumbler which then tipped their contents - coal - onto a moving conveyor belt.

This was called the screes which basically was a system for checking the coal and removing any stones or dirt. At that time there were a lot of old boys who previously worked down the mine, but through age and infirmity were unfit to work and given a job on the screes.

They picked out the stones and dirt leaving only the good coal which then went along the belt line and tipped into railway wagons which were then taken away for further processing. This was a continuous process and some of the young lads who just started in coal mining worked with the older men to learn how to do things safely.

On the Tumbler

The job that I did at that time was keeping the hutches going forward towards the tumbler. I had to take the hutches forward and make sure it got into the tumbler. This was a continuous process. It was repetitive work and after a couple of months you knew all the moves, so it became a bit boring for a young lad aged 14.

I suppose nowadays folk would probably be shocked that someone so young was working in what was potentially a dangerous job, because you always had to be on your guard. A trip or stumble could land you under the wagons. The old boys were always warning the young lads to be very careful.

Wage Slave

The wage I earned at that time (1928) was 2/1d a shift and because we worked a quarter hour longer than our fellow workers along the line at Pennyvenie, they only got 1/11d, so we were on the big money. I was only about four months at the washer at Craigmark when I got a job working underground at Pennyvenie No 2. This was definitely exciting but bewildering because it was new and dangerous.

I'll never forget going down in the cage to the pit bottom and I was totally bewildered because I was only 14 and just a boy entering a man's world. This was me for the next 48 years of my life – a long journey in coal mining.

I worked in the various Pennyvenie pits such as Nos 2, 3 and No. 5 mine (an ingaunee – shallow drift mine) and then there was Pennyvenie No. 6 which was developed further up the hill. You were sent to the various mines as the gaffer dictated and you simply knuckled down and got on with it.

Working Coal

The conditions in the mines and pits over the years were pretty bad and to be honest they didn't really improve that much after nationalisation. My first job was working at the foot of a causie (pit jargon for an underground roadway). There was another lad, 'Buller' Dalziel from Burnfoothill working with me underground.

We worked at the foot of the causie and the hutches came from the pit bottom. We had to rope and couple the hutches and then we would "chap away" which was simply to ring a bell and the lad at the top of the causie would start it moving. That was when you had to be careful and keep out of the way.

We had to operate the brake by leaning on a wheel to slow it down if that was required. You had to be careful because there were usually six hutches roped together and they could run away if you didn't take care. By that time I was on real big money because I was earning 3/3d per shift. This would be the start of 1930 and the government was realising the importance of coal for industry to keep the country running efficiently.

Tom Hutchison was in good form that day and about to attend a family wedding.
(Photo: Hutchison family)

Drawing Off

In 1931 I was asked by big Tam Hunter if I would come and draw off for him. That was basically removing the coal that had been hewn at the face and barrow them back to the loading point where I put them on the hutches.

Tam worked at the coal face of Pennyvenie No 5 so my job was supporting him by filling the hutches with coal and bringing them to a gathering area known as the lie. This was where the hutches were stored before being taken to the surface.

You would then bring an empty hutch back from the lie back to the face. This was very hard physical work and you had to be very fit. Mind you, the rewards were better because by that time I was earning

5/6d a shift which was good money in those days.

I had to hand this money over to my mother every week and I got pocket money. It wasn't much but enough to get by and this continued right up until I got married. This was the way of things for my generation of miners.

Black Damp

We called No 5 Pennyvenie 'Black Damp' and there was a crust which formed over your light after working a shift. Most of the miners thought there was gas in the mine at times which didn't do anything for our health. But you had to work to earn money and the gaffers didn't take kindly to complaints.

Some of the older miners didn't have the carbide lamp and still used tallow which was like a grease substance covering a wick and they kenneled (lit) up the wick. This caused a lot of reek and was potentially very dangerous if there was gas about.

The conditions were really bad with lots of water and low seams. At that time I worked with wee Charlie 'Chuck' Baird, a wee rotund man and drew for him and we got on famously. I recall that I tended to sleep a lot when I got home and that was due in part to hard work, but may also have been partly due to the noxious gases and foul air in the workings.

Pennyvenie No. 2

I then returned to work at Pennyvenie No 2. I remember on one occasion I was waiting to go up on the hutches to leave work slightly early. The bottomer was Wull McGraw, a good billiard player and he was responsible for chapping the men up and down.

Wull would chap one for a hutch and three if there were men on the hutches. I was waiting to leave because I was due to play football for Craigmark, a juvenile team at that time, against Dunaskin Lads. The hutches, filled with coal, had gone along the line when I suddenly heard a loud whishing noise and I dived for cover and the hutches came flying back down and crashed and the air was filled with black debris.

It was one of those moments that frighten the life out of you and brings home just how dangerous mining was in those days. I had been due to go up on the next rake of hutches and that could have been the end of me. No one should ever underestimate how dangerous it could be in the coal mines. Needless to say I didn't get to the match that day as there was a hellish mess to sort out to get the hutches back on the rails and continue coal production.

Danger Lurks

I remember that the water was very bad in that mine. They had driven a road in the mine into what we called Young's mine and the water was just terrible and that too, made the roof conditions dangerous.

It was always damp and cold. There were never any serious accidents that I can recall, but a lot of minor accidents and quite a few near-misses. You had to watch constantly and be very alert because dangers lurked everywhere.

When Pennyvenie No 7 mine was sunk I went there next. We had to drive two mines as one was needed to suck out the air from the other to make conditions tolerable, as good ventilation was essential for safety to avoid potentially disastrous build up of gas.

Mine Driver

I was chosen as a mine driver and this involved working in shaping the face, drilling holes and firing shots to remove it and make progress towards the coal. Some of the seams were very narrow and you would be lying down and it was hard, hard work for all the miners.

Some of the coal seams were only 1 foot and we called them wild coals because they weren't workable, but the quality of the coal was good. The open cast today – (2005) will have taken all that coal out in the last few years because they miss nothing and go down deeper in some cases than we did with deep mining. The old miners of my early years would be amazed at the technology and machinery used today in opencast mining.

Cameraderie

The men I worked with were the best. They were just great. There was a wonderful cameraderie. Some great characters, too. In fact when I retired on 29 November 1975 the one thing I missed was the great blethers we had down the pit.

Tam Hastie and Dennis Scalley were two amazing larger-than-life characters. They tell the story of them going up the cemetery brae in Dalmellington. Half way up they had to stop for a blether and Tam said, "Well, maybe we'll come up a wee bit easier the next time."

One wee man from Annbank came up to Pennyvenie when the pits closed in his area. He didn't have a permanent job, and when he came up he was what was known by us as being on the skite. He would say: "I know I can't do much, but I'm definitely good company."

Pennyvenie Mine First Aid team circa 1952.The members were very proficient in the first aid skills required to ensure that any accidents happening at the colliery were dealt with quickly and professionally before the arrival of medical aid.
Back row (l to r): Tom Filson, William Dryborough (Colliery Manager), James Armour.
Front row (l to r): Tom Gillespie, George Wallace BEM, William Wallace and Andrew Hare.
(Photo: Bobby Wallace collection)

Times Past

Dalmellington was a nice place to grow up in. There was a genuine village feel about it. Everyone knew each other because most of the men worked together in the pits and the women were known to each other.

There wasn't television in those days and entertainment was self made. When I was a wee boy I used to caddy at Dalmellington golf course. Not many folk today will even know that we had a golf course in our village down opposite Broomknowe.

In 1926 it was lovely weather and all the miners were out during the miners' strike. I was only 12 and was taking the cattle from the Promised Land where the aerodrome was on the north-west side of village opposite the playing field.

The miners I passed on the way would be out walking and talking in groups because they were all on strike. They would be kidding me about the cows and making mooing noises as I helped herd the cattle up to Gateside Farm at the top of Broomknowe where old John Ireland had the farm. So, although the miners were on strike and having difficult times with no money coming in, they were still full of fun. I probably didn't realise then that I would soon be one of them working down the pits.

Marriage & Family

I married Jean Kennedy in 1937. Jean was 20 and I was 23. We married in the Black Bull Hotel. That was what happened in those days. We had four of a family, two sons and two daughters and I was married for 67 wonderful years. My wife died on 3 January 2005. My family were Tommy and Archie, Janet and Elizabeth.

Shops & Businesses

The Co-op was the mainstay of Dalmellington. I deplore the fact that it met such a terrible demise. Maisie Kerr had the dress shop. Geordie Cron had the hardware shop. If he didn't have something you were looking for in stock he would say: "Sorry, out of stock, but it's coming on the 5 o'clock train."

And most of the time he was dead right. In fact, it was a wonderful service we got from shops such as George Cron. It would be difficult to match today (September 2015). Murdoch the butcher was located where Dale's shop is now. I used to watch him carry a full cow into the shop over his shoulder. Malcolm Ross was the butcher just off the Square. Ebenezer had an old dilapidated chip van and came round the street with fritters and they were lovely and popular with locals.

I used to go to the matinee in the old picture house near where Craigmark play. There was an old lady who stayed with us and she used to play the piano and it was quite a task and hard work as she had to follow the film and play appropriate music to suit. Her own name was Mrs Dickson, but her professional name was Margaret St Barb. She lodged with us at 1 Broomknowe for many years. She was a converted Roman Catholic and eventually she went to live at Nazareth House in Kilmarnock. I remember visiting her and I took our Archie with us when he was a wee lad.

Home Guard

I was in the Home Guard during the Second World War I remember that the signal for an invasion was the sounding of the church bell. One night the bell rang and we all went to the police station in Ayr Road, Dalmellington, which was our HQ. I was sent to guard the Moss Brig and others went to the Iron Brig on the Straiton Road.

One of the men hadn't been properly trained and he put a bullet in his rifle but took the safety catch off. We heard the gun going off and our Commanding Officer, Robert Stewart, said: "Right lads, this is it," and we thought we were under attack.

Mind you, I don't know what we would have done, because we had all drunk a few pints before being called out. On another occasion we were all on the roof of the Picture House and we linked hands and although the roof was not flat, we could run the length of the roof with our hands linked. It was quite amazing, really, when I think back to those daft days during the years of the Second World War.

Mechanisation

In 1975 I was still working at Pennyvenie No 7 and decided to retire. The mines had changed immeasurably between me starting work in 1928 and finishing in 1975. The biggest difference was mechanisation. In my early days most things were done by manual labour. It was back-

Pennyvenie electricians gather for a photo in their workshop around 1976/77.
(l to r): Tom 'Tucker' Steele, workshop electrician; Parker Cullen, apprentice electrician; John 'Winkie' Wilson, shift electrician; Alex Stark, shift electrician; Tom 'Tammy' Calderwood, chief electrician; Tom Wilson, shift supervisor and Tommy Winning, assistant chief electrician.
(Courtesy of Ian McPhail),

Chalmerston No 6 pit in 1937 with John Armour looking after the pit horse, Rattler. This was a scene replicated in many pits right up into the 1950s. All the miners had a great affection for pit ponies and they were always treated very well.

breaking work, but by the time I finished most of the hard work was done by machinery such as coal cutting machines and conveyor belts. I was elated to be finished.

Retirement

I had had enough. The last shift was a backshift and I actually thought that we wouldn't need to go down the pit at all that day, but I was wrong. However, we had to go and get changed and go down. We came up later on and there were a few of us finishing that day including big Jock Chalmers and a few men from Annbank.

We were all aged sixty and a deputy said a few words of farewell and that was it. Away we went, not a lot to show for 48 years service to the coal mining industry, but that was the way things were. I suppose it was a sort of emotional experience knowing that it was our last time working underground at Pennyvenie.

Strike Free

You hear folk talk about the militancy of the miners. Well, I can tell you that I never took part in one official strike from 1928 until 1972 but that was a big strike when many of the Ayrshire miners were picketing the power station in Kilmarnock to stop coal supplies going in.

There was another in 1974, the year before I retired. The miners were a great bunch and I have many happy memories and am very proud to say that I worked in the pits of the Doon Valley.

I would say that I had a very happy and enjoyable life. Every spare moment was spent in the outdoors because working down the pit was not conducive to good health. Most miners enjoyed the outdoors such as fishing and walking because of the working conditions they endured.

Wonderful Life

I can honestly say that I have been very fortunate with my wife, Jean, and wonderful family. I suppose reaching this stage in life, I am even more fortunate. There was a lot of talent lost because many of the men in the coal mines could have done much better if the opportunities had been available to them.

Doon Valley men had to go to the mines because that was all there was for them in those days. However, I can tell you that so many of them were well educated, thoughtful, caring and considerate family men of great talent and yet they were proud of their work in the coal mines of the Doon Valley. And of course, I was too, because coal mining was my life.

Till a' the seas gang dry, my dear,
And the rocks melt wi' the sun!
And I will luve thee still, my dear,
While the sands o' life shall run.

My Luve is Like a Red Red Rose
Robert Burns

Chapter 5

Tam o' Dunaskin Glen

Tom McKnight

Away far doon within the dreary mine,
Where neither light of day nor sun doth shine,
Where darkness in its dreadest mood does reign,
There, all unseen, without the slightest sign,
The treacherous roof is running through a vein,
Till, crash! It falls – a collier's life again

Only A Collier
Matthew Anderson
(Policeman Poet of Ayrshire)

Tom McKnight is a man who loves the Doon Valley, especially Waterside. On a daily basis, even in challenging weather conditions, he drives from Patna to Waterside and parks opposite the chapel. He then makes his way up Dunaskin Glen, his eyes concentrating on the peregrine, buzzard, foxes and deer which he enjoys watching in the glen.

Some days he walks up the Corbies incline to the remains of Corbie Craigs where his father spent his formative years. Tom feels a close bond with Corbies and the steep-sided Dunaskin glen.

He has been doing this walk most of his life. Since he retired it has become a daily ritual which he relishes. Every new day he sees the flora and fauna, changing colours, water levels rising and falling and ever-changing scenes. He has been present in the glen on several occasions when dramatic landslides have occurred.

In an interview with Donald L Reid in May 2015, he recalls some of his memories of working at Broomhill Mine near Kerse; tells of his love of Dunaskin Glen and Corbie Craigs and reminisces on pearl fishing on the River Doon.

First Twins

I was born in Doonbank, Patna on 29 September 1944. I was a twin. I always remember my mother saying that my brother, William, and I were the first twins born in Doonbank.

I attended Patna Primary School which was then located opposite the Doon Hotel, no longer extant, on Main Street, Patna.

Life at Corbies

My mother was Agnes Boag who originally hailed from Maybole. My father was William McKnight. He was born in Ayr before moving to the Corbies (Corbie Craigs). The ruins of Corbies, sits on the south side of, and near the top of Dunaskin Glen. It was remote and lonely. I regularly visit because it's close to my heart.

My father would be about seven years old when his family moved to No. 6 Corbie Craigs. He was fond of the Corbies, a single row of only ten houses, all occupied by miners and their families and he often talked about his life there.

I remember my mother telling me that my father, as a wee boy, used to walk from Corbie Craigs to the Cutler Farm to get milk. The Cutler Farm was located on the south side of Waterside just off the A713 road. This farm has been lying derelict, probably since the early 1970s.

After getting the milk at Cutler he would then walk to the far end of Waterside to the store and get wool for his mother for her knitting. Women were great knitters in those days, and all the weans had wonderful hand-knitted garments.

On one occasion he came back with the wrong colour of wool and was sent back down the incline at the side of Dunaskin Glen into the valley below to return to Waterside store to change the wool. Weans were dearly loved, but were rarely pampered like today.

Nowadays, young folk seem to go everywhere by car and they are missing out on sheer freedom and the learning experience of growing up and being self-sufficient. Well, I might be wrong, but that's what I think. I'm so grateful that being like my father in his boyhood days, I enjoyed being independent, fit, willing to work for the benefit of the family and getting to know the local area including its fascinating hills and glens.

That for me was very special and I'll always be grateful that I loved that type of upbringing. My generation enjoyed the great outdoors and I'm very grateful for that. I will always get out and about around Waterside and especially Dunaskin Glen and the Corbies as long as I am able.

Tom McKnight features in: Tam o' Dunaskin Glen.

Pennyvenie Mines No. 1 Rescue Brigade circa 1920. This team are displaying some of the equipment used in mine rescue. The equipment is clearly of early vintage.
Back row (l to r): T Chambers (manager), H Kerr, J Hunter, M McCormack (Instructor).
Front row: G English, T Gault (Captain), and J Brown.

Clawfin & Minnivey

My father was a miner all his days. He was a right grafter, but proud to be a miner. As a boy when he left school at 15, he worked first of all at a private mine called Clawfin which was located near to Benwhat. Later on he spent the rest of his coalmining life at Minnivey Colliery, Dalmellington, before he retired aged 64. He died aged 78 in the early 1980s.

My father worked at the coal face – the drawing he called it. They used to send several hutches full of coal from the face along to the loading point to get up to the surface. That was in the private mine at Clawfin, before nationalisation. He told me that when they filled the hutch, they used to chalk the miner's number on the wooden cart, so at the surface they knew which miner had filled the hutch. This would be to keep a record of the production by the team and for payment purposes.

Flying Start at Prestwick

Leaving school aged fifteen in 1959 I started work as a mechanic at Dalblair motors in Ayr where I served my time. Afterwards I went to Prestwick Airport where I worked building the wings on the Handley Page Jetstream aircraft.

I remained there for about two years but there were so many redundancies.The future was so uncertain that I applied for and got a job at the Stamp Works in Ayr. I worked on producing the forge stamping axles for lorries and stayed there for around nine years.

Broomhill Mine

In the early 1980s I went into a private coal mine, located near Kerse, which was called Broomhill. I understand that the mine was privately owned by Tom Cook from Maybole. It was strange how I got the job. I was cycling past Cairntable at the top of the brae, when I met Tom Cook coming out of the mine road and I stopped to blether to him.

He mentioned the mine and because I was unemployed at that time, I asked him if he was looking for workers. Mind you, I had never been down a pit in my life. He started me right away as a watchman and within a few weeks I was working down at the coalface.

Auld Tug

There were two us working there at the coal face. Arthur Paton from Patna was the clerk at the pithead and I worked with a man who was simply called 'Auld Tug' from Rankinston. He was a carnaptious man

The Mine Rescue Team probably taken at a course in Kilmarnock in the 1960s.
Back row: George Sturgeon, Sanny Baird, Pat McKay, John 'Tubby' Boyd.
Front row: Jimmy 'Patsy' Murphy, Terry Morran, Willie Dick, 'Jocker' Black (played football with Airdrie) and Jimmy Baird.

Dunaskin Glen showing the gorge-like formation. The upper reaches of the glen are steep and not recommended for the casual walker. The substantial remains of the houses at Corbie Craigs can still be found at the top of the glen.
(Scott J Rarity collection)

and he was the oversman, but he could be so crabbit at times. I don't think he was keen on working underground at Broomhill because it was a dangerous place to be in.

I quickly realised speaking to other more experienced miners, that working in a small private mine was very different from working in the NCB mines. Of course I had never experienced the NCB mines, so I just got on with the working conditions at Broomhill, because it was all I knew.

Broomhill was just a small mine and everyone had to be able to do all the jobs including working the haulage ropes and taking the filled tubs from near the face to the surface and then bring the empties back down to the coal loading point near the face. There was no hiding place for anyone and the gaffers made sure everyone pulled their weight. Production of coal was their top priority at all times.

Danger in Mine

What struck me from day one was that it was a dangerous place to work and the rules were very lax, especially around safety. You weren't supposed to ride on the top of the hutches with the coal. However because it was a steep mine and a long walk from the coal loading point to the surface, we took the easy way sometimes which on one occasion nearly cost me my life.

I used to ride on top of the coal hutch to get back to the surface, lying face down on the hutch. When the hutches were filled it was near the roof and there was little space once you lay on top of the loaded hutch.

Little did I know on one occasion that the roof had dropped slightly along the main roadway. There was movement at Broomhill because it was sinking all the time and I regularly heard strange noises which was probably the pressure on the supports and props.

Accident

As I travelled along on top of the loaded hutch I came into contact with the roof of the mine and the force ripped off my safety helmet, tore my vest and the buckle of my belt was torn off and the force also ripped my trousers off

My back was badly bruised, too. I managed to roll off the hutch and I was shaking like a leaf. That shows just how close I was to being killed that day. It was my own fault. I shouldn't have been riding the filled hutch, but these were the daft things that went on that could have so easily been fatal. That was the nearest I've ever been to being killed. It gave me one fright that I'll never forget. I never rode on the hutches after that and was quite content to walk the long distance to the surface.

On another occasion, when the pit went into liquidation, I was kept on and employed as a watcher on nightshift. One of the duties was to go down the mine on my own at night and start the pumps to keep the mine from flooding.

Later on I had to go back down to switch them off after they'd cleared the water, otherwise the pump would have burned out. When I think about it now, it was crazy to go down that mine on your own, but that was how things were then. You just got on with it. There could so easily have been an accident whilst I was down there alone.

Flooding in the Mine

On another occasion when I was on duty myself, I went down the mine and walked right along to the coal face. They had sumps in these mines where all the water gathered at the lowest point. If the pumps were not running it would have flooded the mine and that would have closed it for good. When I went down to check the water situation, I was down at the face and it was full of water.

There was only one way up and I heard a whooshing noise away above me. I had the most hellish sinking feeling in my stomach and I thought: I'm dead, because I was trapped at the face. I thought it was a roof fall further along the road.

I managed to get into a man hole at the side of the mine, and the water came whooshing past me. I can tell you, I'm not religious, but I was praying it would stop. It did stop because I'm here today. What had caused it? There had been a break in one of the main pipes allowing the water to run. I got the fright of my life.

Barrow-load of Fun

I often worked with a wheelbarrow to do different jobs down the mine. Tam Cook was a hard yin. He wouldn't spend a penny on the mine if he could avoid it. It was allegedly in liquidation and I was doing maintenance with another miner, Jim Eccles, who lived in Dalmellington.

We had to keep the mine free of flooding on different shifts. I told Tam Cook that the barrow was hopeless as each night I had to pump up the front tyre. He said he'd fix it. The next night when I went out he left me – not a spare tube – but a John Bull repair kit, so I'd to fix the puncture myself. Tam Cook was some man to work for, but I can laugh about it now!

Fainting Down the Mine

I worked about seven years at the pit, but I can tell you I was a fit man when I finished. I remember one time I went down the pit and I was filling bags of coal. Tam wouldn't allow us to run the fans and I was filling two bags a week for my own use.

I remember it was so warm and there was no air circulation because the fans were off and the sweat was pouring off me. I actually felt a bit strange and fainted. I came to lying on the ground and after sitting a wee while went back up the mine. Of course there was no one there. These times were very scary.

Blizzard Conditions

On one wintry Saturday night in the early 1980s I was out at the mine and I was alone. I had an old triumph motor bike and I managed to get through the snow drifts from Patna. The A713 between Patna and Polnessan was infamous for snowdrifts.

The wind was howling and it was driving snow. It was quite simply a blizzard. The snow was drifting on the road between Patna and Kerse and it was difficult to get through to the mine on the motorbike.

In fact I could hardly see. When I thought about it the next day I realised how stupid I was to even go to the mine that night. These were things you did and I knew that I had to keep the pumps running, or the mine would flood, and we'd all be out of a job. On arrival at Broomhill I relieved Jim Eckles, and went down the mine and did my work.

When I got back to the pithead the phones were down. I later learned that the blizzard had brought the telephone lines down.

Phone Down

That same night Tom Cook had phoned the mine. He regularly did this to check things were okay, but the phone was down, so he couldn't get hold of me. He then phoned Eckles and got him out of his bed at his home. Eckles was able to tell him that when he handed over to me at Broomhill, I was going down the mine to check the pumps. Cook must have suspected I had been trapped at the mine as they couldn't make contact, so he probably panicked and called out the police, who went to his home and picked him up.

McKnight Found

Later on at the end of the shift at 3am, I was going out the road end through the snow drifts and moving very slowly on my motor bike when I saw blue flashing lights at Polnessan. It was the polis with landrovers and Tom Cook was with them. The polis waved me down and asked me who I was. I told him I was Tam McKnight. He said that they were all out looking for me. I hadn't a clue that anything was wrong and all I wanted to do was get back home safely to Patna.

The polisman looked at me with a big smile. He was probably relieved that he wouldn't have to spend any longer out in the blizzard. He said: "You're supposed to be deid, Mr McKnight, trapped down a mine at Broomhill." Auld Cook was sitting in the Land Rover. The big polisman said to Cook that it was illegal to have a man working down a mine on his own. I remember Cook's reply: "It's our bread and butter. We've got to do these things to make it work or the men would be out of a job."

When you went down the mine you could be there all night. There was a lot of coal going out, but there is no doubt that safety wasn't top of the agenda at Broomhill. I remember on one occasion I was working with young Cook and we were howking out lots of coal, but the packing and support wasn't going in to keep the face safe. I said: "This place is going to come down about us and we'll be trapped and killed." He just said it would be fine.

Mine Collapse

One day I felt it was getting really dangerous at the face, so I moved away from what they called the ballroom – that was a wide place at the face. We were taking coal out everywhere because we knew the mine was going to be closing down. I moved up to the pit head.

Seamus Cook asked me to go back down to the face and get the borer. I was walking along the hutch tracks towards the face when I heard a whoosh and the place we had been working in less than an hour before collapsed. It was non-existent. When I got back to the surface I was feeling really frustrated and said to Seamus: "See your borer, you'll never see it again because it's buried at the face."

I could write a book about that mine. I worked there for a few bags of coal and pennies and it nearly cost me my life more than once. This mine closed probably around 1986 or thereabouts. Mind you, it was the best of coal. Great stuff, but my nerves couldn't have stood it much longer. The mice used to run about your feet while working the haulage.

In a strange sort of way I had a love-hate relationship with that mine. I worked very hard and was always reliable, but it could never be described as a safe place to work. There again I suppose miners working in modern pits might say the same too. There were too many gaps in the safety for my liking and it's just as well that it closed when it did.

Dunaskin Glen

My father, William, was a Corbie Craigs man and a harrier. Corbies sat above Dunaskin Glen and my father was always about the glen. He used to take me when we lived in Doonbank and he loved going up the glen.

He showed me all the various bits of the glen and where the birds nested. So, my own interest in Dunaskin Glen started when I was a wee boy. All my life I've just loved going up there or going round the Corbies.

William Watson Stone

There is a stone in the glen which is marked: "William Watson, 1909." I was told this was in memory of a wee boy who died when he fell off the side of the glen. Perhaps he stayed at Corbie Craig or Benwhat. The stone is located in the Dunaskin Burn just opposite the site of Laigh Castle.

I've been visiting the glen on at least a weekly basis for over 60 years now. The fact is that on every single visit I see or hear something different depending on the season and I find it very uplifting to go there. I think the attachment takes me back to my father and to Corbie Craigs.

Glen Wildlife

The amount of wildlife is amazing in and around the glen. There are deer which hide around the trees at Dunaskin. There are dippers in the Glen. Cuckoos lay their eggs in the nests of other birds in May and June. There is at least one peregrine falcon and a buzzard nesting there.

Another view of Waterside showing the Chapel Row and the slag bing. The little pug is working hard as demonstrated by the amount of steam being thrown out. All the engines at Waterside were tank engines, generally 0-4-0 and 0-6-0T and the greatest number to be stationed at Waterside at one time was believed to be eleven.

Workers underground in Clawfin Mine which was situated near to Benbeoch Craig in 1931. This photo clearly illustrates the conditions in which the miners had to operate. Health and safety was not high on the agenda of the coal owners prior to nationalization of the mines in 1947. The supporting wooden prop looks very suspect according to miners who have examined this photograph.
(l to r): Tommy Knox (father) and his three sons, Tom, Matthew and Frank of Patna.

An early view of Waterside Works taken from the slag bing with the works office dominating the centre and, of course, the ever-present chimneys which dominate the scene.

In fact I've been in the glen on several occasions when there have been landslides which can be quite dramatic, so it can be a very dangerous place to be. The glen is changing all the time and you have to be very careful where you walk as it's a dangerous place if you don't know your way around.

As you probably appreciate Dunaskin glen is very special to me. It's the connection with my father and the sheer beauty of it at different times of the year which pulls me back so often. I've seen foxes and badgers in the glen. There are three large ponds in the burn which have good wild fish in them

Salmon go up the Dunaskin Burn at the back end of the year when the water is running high. They come up to spawn and I've seen several salmon in pools. I've also found dead salmon well up the glen.

Doon Pearl Fishers

The Doon was historically renowned for its pearl mussel fishery. Long ago, especially when the miners were on strike, a few of the older hands would go to the River Doon with a glass-bottomed-box to seek out the famous Doon fresh water pearls. If they found any pearls they would be taken to a jeweller in Ayr and sold, or perhaps kept as local keepsakes

My father used to have a go at getting the pearls in the Doon with some success. Later on in the late 1950s I also had a go at fishing for pearls. I used a snorkel and mask as you could get down to the bottom and identify the mussel beds. I would go with my older brother, Jim. We got to know where the best mussel beds were located.

I still know the best places today for mussel beds. I monitor them, nowadays, to make sure they are not interfered with. Thankfully very few folk go after pearls now, as it has been illegal to interfere with the mussel beds since 1981.

In 1967 I was swimming in the River Doon near Netherhill. I felt a mussel with my toe. I swam down and brought it up. I threw it to Bill, my twin brother, who was at the other side of the river. He opened it and shouted that it contained a cracker of a pearl. I got this Doon pearl and put it in a ring for my wife and it adorns her finger to this day.

Since then I've long appreciated the importance of freshwater mussel beds and the role they play in the health of the river. What folk need to understand is that very few mussels contain a pearl, but the belief that they might, have led to many beds being pillaged.

Freshwater pearl mussels are very important to the bio-diversity of the River Doon. They can actually survive for over 100 years which is incredible. Hopefully, as folk become more environmentally aware, the River Doon mussel beds will remain intact in the future. And that can be achieved by folk leaving them well alone.

Looking Back

I have to say that like my father before me, I was proud to have had the experience of working down a mine. Father probably worked in conditions which were equally dangerous at times and perhaps even more so. It's a good thing that there are no longer deep mines in Scotland, because no matter how good safety procedures are, they are never guaranteed in the bowels of the earth.

The site of Broomhill mine was later taken over for opencast mining. I often wonder if they ever came across that boring machine which was lost at the mine face. Memories of days past are precious. I often think of my seven years working underground in that coal mine.

I get a shiver down my back, sometimes, when I think of the working conditions I had to endure down the mine. They nearly cost me dearly more than once. But that was a long time ago and I can honestly say that I have thoroughly enjoyed my lifelong love affair with dear lonely Dunaskin Glen and its near neighbour, Corbie Craigs.

Looking down Dunaskin Glen towards Waterside showing the dramatic features of this narrow gorge.
Photo: Donald L Reid

Aye when my daily darg is done
My heart gets light and gay,
An frae the bowels o' earth again
I went my homeward way:
Hoo nice it is to ken a spot
My weary limbs to bring;
Oh, welcome then my ain wee cot,
Where sweet affections cling.

A Miner's Fireside Song
Matthew Anderson (Policeman Poet of Ayrshire)

Chapter 6

What's in a Name
Edgar Ierland

I lang hae thought, my youthful friend,
A something to have sent you,
Tho' it should serve nae ither end
Than just a kind memento.

Epistle to a Young Friend
Robert Burns

Edgar Ierland features in the chapter: What's in a Name?

Edgar Ierland (80) was interviewed in May 2015 about his memories of mining in the Doon Valley as well as highlighting some personal reflections on life's journey. He was born in 1934, at No. 28 Truffhill Row, Waterside, no longer extant. All that remains today are the foundations of the rows.

Truffhill was a row of cottages mainly occupied by coal miners and their families sitting facing the A713 and looking across to the River Doon made famous by Scotland's Bard, Robert Burns. Today Edgar lives in Patna with his wife, Jean, where they thoroughly enjoy tending a large garden.

Family Background

I am the son of Wilson Ierland, who was born at No. 18 Drumgrange Row, Waterside, on 7 November 1912. I was born in the next row, known as Truffhill on 16 November 1934. This was the row which was burned down in a fire in August 1943. There were four rows, but none now remain. My father, Wilson Ierland, was the youngest of ten children. Sadly his mother died when he was only ten days old. He was reared by his father and sisters.

It must have been very difficult for such a large family in such a small house, but that was the way of things in those days. Young people today would probably be appalled, but we were surprisingly contented, because we also had the great outdoors and a freedom not available to young folk today.

Happy Days

If anyone cares to search the ground immediately behind the memorial to the unemployed at the side of the A713 just north of Waterside, they will come across the foundations of Drumgrange and Truffhill. That was my boyhood home and a happy place it was, too.

We had the route of the incline leading up to Lethanhill right behind us and the river Doon in front. In those days the road (A713) was very quiet, so everyone played outside. There was no television in any of the rows, so we simply made our own entertainment.

Big families were commonplace in Waterside. My surname is a strange spelling - Ierland. I know that my grandfather, Joseph Ireland, when he got married changed the spelling of the surname to Ierland for what reason I don't know.

What I do know is that the spelling of the surname has caused me and my family a lot of problems over the years. Folk dealing with my family for a variety of reasons, quite understandably think it must be spelt wrongly and that it should be Ireland and not Ierland.

My dear wife, Jean and I have been very happily married now (2015) for fifty-seven years. We have three sons: Jim, Alan and Brian and we are very proud of them and their families.

Spelling Boy

In fact I remember on one occasion I got into trouble at Lethanhill School because my surname was Ierland. The teacher looked at a paper I had written with my name shown clearly on top and he glanced at it a few times. He said sarcastically: "Can't you even spell your name boy."

I tried to explain to him, but he wouldn't listen, so when I got home I told my dad. He got my birth certificate and I took it in the next day to school and showed it to the teacher. He looked at it, folded it and gave it back to me. He never said sorry, but the spelling of my surname has caused many complications for me over the years.

Brickwork and Pits

On leaving school my father worked in the brickwork at Waterside for around fourteen years before becoming a coal miner for the remainder of his working life. He often remarked that it was quite enjoyable in the brickwork, but the work was very repetitive.

I began my coal mining career at Pennyvenie No: 4, known locally as the Big Mine. My grandfather, Joseph Ierland, was also a miner and worked all his days at the Houldsworth Pit just north of Patna. Indeed my mother's father, Robert Edgar, also spent his entire working life at Houldsworth. So mining was deeply ingrained in my family background. Many men in the Doon Valley worked in one of the several pits locally.

I don't think my father, Wilson Ierland, was very keen on me taking up work in the pits, probably because he understood all too clearly how dangerous they could be. My grandfather, Joseph Ierland, originally hailed from Kirkcudbright which I understand he left when he was a wee boy. He was born in 1870 and it would seem that he came to Patna initially. When he married my grandmother, Margaret Maltman, they moved to Drumgrange Row, Waterside, about 1890.

Stone to the Unemployed

The famous landmark stone in memory of the unemployed which sits at the front of the A713 road at what was then Drumgrange Row, was actually carved out by my grandfather, who understood the plight of the miners and the unemployed of his time. I think he wanted folk to remember - not only during his lifetime but thereafter - what being unemployed was actually like because it removed the dignity of work for many men and brought great strain on family life.

Work Ethic

Nowadays it's sad to say that for some folk unemployment just seems to be a lifestyle choice and there is no shame attached to being out of work. In fact, some will tell you that they have no intention of ever working because the state provides for them rather well. Fortunately I was brought up to understand the importance of work and to work hard and be caring of others who were not so fortunate.

This family tradition of maintaining the stone in memory of the unemployed has been carried on by my cousin, Wilson Ireland, (spelt in the common method and differently from my surname) each year. The stone is a real landmark and nicely reflects on and encourages folk to remember the difficult times for many over the years and indeed in our own time in the Doon Valley. Mind you, in my young days it was relatively easy to move from job to job and most of the men did work in the pits.

Fire at Drumgrange

In August 1943 when I lived at Truffhill Row, Waterside, there was a fire which spread through the full length of the row. I remember it so well. I was nine years of age. I was coming back from Kirkmichael that day with my father. We had bought tomatoes for folk in the rows who had ordered and paid for them, something my father did regularly, because there was a kindness about folk which was illustrated by a common bond of sharing which was rarely taken for granted.

I vividly remember as we cycled back between Kirkmichael and Patna at the top of the Smiddy Brae, Patna, father said to me that the smoke billowing high into the sky from Drumgrange rows was probably because a house chimney was on fire. This happened occasionally when there was a build-up of soot in the chimney.

We pedalled faster as we approached and when we got nearer we could see that it was our row that was on fire. You can imagine that was a shock because all the houses in the entire Truffhill row were destroyed, including our house. Our immediate concern was that folk were safe, but it did leave me rather shocked.

I think the fire must have been started by an electrical fault in the loft and spread right along the entire row. Folk didn't have much furniture in those days. Sad to say, all the houses were destroyed, but strangely enough most of the local folk didn't have much furniture because they were poor. This row of houses was destroyed and beyond repair so they were later demolished. We simply went to our grandfather's house in the adjoining row, Drumgrange, and we all simply made do.

Houldsworth pit just at the time of its closure in 1975 showing lots of materials lying around.

Families at Truffhill

I remember that in the row which was burned there was the McKenzie family. John was a clever man and could sculpt things out of coal. Then next door was the Boyle family; Barbour family and an old man, Jimmy Colville and then my Uncle Tom Lyon and Aunt Ruby; George Phillips and family; Coughtrie family and Mrs Drysdale and family; Joe Collins. He was only in the house six weeks when it was burned down.

There was also Sam Coughtrie, Mrs Graham, and then our family; Gillan family, John McCormick and family; and in the next house there were two brothers, but I don't remember their names as they hadn't been there for long. In the end house was a Mrs Thomson.

Folk from the row which was destroyed were re-housed all over the place. Some went up to Lethanhill, others went to Dalmellington and many others went to live with other family members in other towns, because there simply were no council houses available to re-house everyone. These were times when you had to sort things out for yourself and depend very much on the good grace of other family members and friends.

Sent to Clydebank

In my family I had one young sister, Ann and my mother, Mary, was also expecting a baby at the time of the fire – my youngest sister Margaret. My sister Ann and I were sent for two week to live with my Uncle Jim and Aunt Belle in Clydebank.

When I think about it now, this was a strange move because I always remember how bad Clydebank was because of the bombing during the war. Even as a wee boy I could see the devastation suffered in that town. It was all a wee bit strange going from a row of houses in the countryside, all destroyed by fire, to a town which was literally flattened by bombing by the Luftwaffe in March 1941, so that town was still in a state of chaos in terms of building clearance and rebuilding of houses and businesses.

Despite this my sister Ann and I were made very welcome at Clydebank by Aunt Belle and Uncle Jim. They probably felt very sorry for us because our house had been destroyed in such sad circumstances. I also felt sorry for them and the poor folk of Clydebank because so many houses were demolished by bombing and the subsequent fires.

Headmaster's House

The fire at Drumgrange was in August 1943 and my family went to live in what was the headmaster's house at Lethanhill the following February 1944. We were able to take up occupancy of the headmaster's house at Lethanhill on a temporary basis because there was no other house available for our family. Ayr County Council must have been in extreme difficulty getting all the Truffhill folk re-housed. What was supposed to be a short term move carried on for four years at Lethanhill.

There was no electricity in the house, but there was a flushing toilet which was great. What we didn't realise was that every winter the water froze because it came from a nearby spout which always seemed to freeze over near the headmaster's house.

So, I had to go to Polnessan row adjacent to Lethanhill, to get water. I had to carry pails of water down to our house when the water froze and by the time I carried it home, my fingers were frozen stiff.

I remember an old lady, Mrs Annie Mitchell, who would call and invite me into her house to fill the pails with water from her sink. The spoot or spicket which was outside in the middle row, was a distance to walk and she must have felt sorry for me.

It was only years later when I started going out with my wife, Jean, that I discovered that Annie Mitchell, who had been so kind to me when I was a wee boy, was her grandmother.

An aerial view of Houldsworth Pit which operated from 1900 until 1965. After being closed by the NCB it was successfully operated for a number of years by Mr Jim Love, formerly a Scottish cycling champion.

Strange how these things happen and connections are made which you never knew about at the time. I always found most of the mining families very friendly. Perhaps it was because we all had fairly basic living conditions, certainly compared to what we have today.

Headmaster in Ayr

I should also explain that the headmaster of Lethanhill School in my time, Mr McAuley, lived in Ayr and was happy to travel by car each day rather than live in the schoolhouse, so that was why we were allocated that house.

I understand that he did live in the house for a time, but I think the conditions there were apparently too much for him because the weather conditions at Lethanhill could be much worse than in the valley below, especially the wind and rain and of course the snow in winter.

So, Mr McAuley moved back to Ayr and travelled each day. We moved out of the headmaster's house around 1949 and moved down to Doonbank.

Headmaster for Lethanhill

The next occupants of the headmaster's house would be Mr George Donahoe, headmaster of Lethanhill. He took occupancy with his family in late 1951 and lived there until around 1959. It must have been very difficult for them as a family because Lethanhill was abandoned in 1954 and quickly demolished, except for the school, which, strange as it might seem, remained open until 1959. I think Lethanhill must have ranked amongst the loneliest schools in Scotland

The pupils were bussed up from Patna until the new Patna school opened in 1959 when they all transferred there. I attended Lethanhill School from 1944 and for the last few months until late in 1948 I went to Patna School.

The Big Mine

I officially left school in December 1949 on the Friday and started on the Monday in the Big Mine (Pennyvennie No 4). During the war years my father worked at what was known as the fire doors at the Big Mine. I used to go out and visit my father if he was working a long shift on a Saturday. I suspect that he was getting me ready for the day when I would be working in the pits.

Occasionally one of the workers would escort me underground to see what was happening. I loved it and I think that after that my only aim was to work down a pit. Mind you I didn't quite realise what I was letting myself in for, because it takes a bit of getting used to. Anyone who says they have never been scared underground is probably telling a wee white lie.

Screening Work

I worked initially at the screes which involved picking the stones out of the coal from a moving chain belt. Everyone started off doing this at the pits. The belt was made of what I would describe as steel chains with coal on top of it and as it passed along we picked the stones out from the coal.

The screes was manned by the elderly miners, because they were not fit for the coal face or working down the pit and the young men starting in the pit worked with them and learned from their experiences of underground working. Mind you it was a boring repetitive job and bad for the back because you were standing in one place for so long. After a year in the pithead I was then sent underground and that was me for the rest of my mining career.

The pithead gaffer at the Big Mine when I started was Joe Waugh of Dalmellington and the under-manager was John Kennedy, who later became manager of Pennyvenie. I think in fact he went to Beoch before Pennyvenie, so he was very experienced.

The Clipping

I was at what was called the Clipping. The hutches came up the mine in pairs, close-coupled. The diesel engine brought them out in rakes of thirty and they were uncoupled in pairs and I then clipped them onto a rope which drew them up to the surface. At the top there was a 'clipper off' who took the clip off.

The hutches would go over the weigh bridge so the weight of coal could be calculated and the next full hutch pushed them on and they were then clipped back on to return down the mine for the whole process to begin again. It really was a well organised system for getting coal from the face and up to the pithead and returning the empties underground. It was all well done.

Beoch to Big Mine

In fact, the Beoch hutches came down the line to the Big Mine to be unloaded, a distance of perhaps two miles. The coal was then loaded via what was called the tumblers and there were four of them. After screening (picking out the stones from the coal) they were loaded automatically on the coal wagons ready for transport by rail to Waterside for further cleaning in what was called the washer.

Someone down below the tumblers then moved the wagons forward on the slight slope, so that all the wagons were filled with coal in turn. The steam locomotive - we called them pugs - came twice or three

Pennyvenie Mine No. 4 with the houses at High Pennyvenie in the foreground and Benbeoch Craig on the skyline. All the coal from the Beoch and Blackwater (offshoot of Beoch) was brought to No. 4 for loading onto wagons. This photograph of a busy pithead is dated at around 1940. Over the years many local men were killed or injured in the pits.
(Photo: EAC DVM)

times each day to deliver empties up to Pennyvenie and take the wagons laden with coal to Waterside for further processing at what was the large washing facility there.

Underground

After a year at the clipping I did my coal face training at the Big Mine. I trained with a man who lived in my current house before us and we've been living here for 50 years. His name was Bobby Baillie.

You went with a collier and you learned how to strip the coal and put the supports in safely to prevent the roof collapsing. This was vital for safety. When I started at first it was all wooden props that were in use, but not long after that the steel straps and doughty metal props which were pumped up hydraulically, came in and they were much safer.

Getting to Work

We used to go to our work on carriages. There was a rail line from Houldsworth up to Pennyvennie No 4. There was a steam pug which pulled a rake of old carriages. It was run on what we called the high line and we walked up to the line from Doonbank where the train was waiting to transport the workers.

Across the Moors

The Beoch men got off the train at the rail terminus along with Big Mine workers. We simply went to the pithead at the Big Mine to our various jobs, but the Beoch miners had then to walk across to a small gauge line to be transported onwards to Beoch across the high moors. They had a long journey to and from work and they were sorely exposed to the elements, especially in winter.

How they got from the Big Mine to Beoch was in small carriages, not much bigger that the hutches we used for transporting coal and dirt underground, but with seats, so the Beoch men sat in these cramped carriages and a small diesel engine pulled them up to Beoch Mine and returned them back to the Big Mine at the end of their shift.

Later on most folk travelled by bus to Beoch, but the railway was the main transport system when I started out. It must have been quite difficult for the Beoch miners in the winter being driven across the wild windswept moor in the snow, arriving frozen to start a long shift. They must have been chilled through to the bone at times.

Endless Rope

The endless rope from the Big Mine to the Beoch brought full hutches clipped onto the haulage rope, one clip at the front and one at the back and these were called 'smallman clips.' So, it was hard work to get the tubs emptied and the carriages ready to continue back empty.

This was a continuous process and the line between Beoch and the Big Mine was always busy. It would be a couple of miles at least, so you always had to be on your guard.

I remember that when they drove the tunnels at the Big Mine we could hear machinery working at the Beoch. The intention was to bring the ropeway underground from Beoch direct to the Big Mine, but that never came to fruition.

The reason was that, in the winter, there was work lost because of the weather on the moors between the Big Mine and Beoch. It could be very bad in winter and both the bogey line and the small rail link were often closed due to drifting snow. However, soon after that, in 1968, the Beoch also shut and some of the miners came to Minnivey and others to Pennyvenie.

Closure of Big Mine

I worked at the face at the Big Mine (Pennyvenie No. 4) until 1960 when it closed, so I was then sent to Minnivey which was located next to Burnton, Dalmellington in February 1960.

There would be salvage work carried out at the Big Mine until later in 1961 to recover machinery and other items of equipment, but that only involved a few men.

I then worked at the coal face at Minnevey from 1960 – 1975 and when it also closed I moved to Pennyvenie No 7 and later on I went to Smithston (privately owned) mine where I finished my mining career.

Under the Moss Road

Minnivey operated what was called hand-stripping at the coal face in my time there. In the mid 1960s they introduced the 'flighter' which was simply a coal cutter adapted with a plough and flights were fitted to the coal cutter chain. This made life a lot easier as opposed to hand stripping at the coal face.

Mind you, it was still always potentially dangerous, so you had to be careful at all times down the mine. The rope was taken on pulleys over the machine back down the coal face where it was anchored. Shots in the coal face were then fired, the coal cutter was then started and inched forward, the flights pushing the loosened coal onto the bottom load belt.

Because we were driving under the moss and what is still known today as the Moss Road (A713 as you enter Dalmellington from Ayr), four or five teams of miners were put on what was called 'the ham and egg shift' – 10am to 5pm so that the coal and debris could be moved during the day.

As we were working under the moss, we could not remove all the coal as that would have made the roadway unstable perhaps leading to an inrush from above. So what we did was to go through this dangerous area in 30 foot places some fifty to seventy yards apart which reduced the likelihood of the peat and moss dropping down into our working roads.

Eventually the seams got smaller and smaller and it was clear to the miners that the pit was going to close, because coal output was so low and no new quality seams were developed. I then transferred to Pennyvenie in late 1975.

Close Call going to work

During the time a few of us travelled to Minnivey in Gibb McBride's van, including Danny Onions, Johnny Givens, Charlie Tait, Jock Thomson and Harry McGreavey. One very cold frosty morning when the ice was clearly on the road surface we were travelling just past the Dalmellington end of the slag bing at Waterside where the road bends.

Our van skidded and spun around several times and ended up facing the railway embankment. We all got a bit of a fright, but fortunately nothing was coming the other way and none of us was hurt. I remember Johnny Givens saying: "Boys, I saw the slag bing four or five times there."

On asking Gibb McBride, our driver, who was slumped over the wheel if he was alright, he replied: "Aye, but don't tell anyone else at the pit about this or they'll all be wanting a shot the morn." We all had a good laugh about that near miss.

Smithstone Mine

After Pennyvenie closed in 1978 I went to work at Smithston private mine. I remained at Smithston from 1978 until I was made redundant in 1987. However, I understand that it was taken over in the last two years of its life by an English company who then shut it.

I loved working up there despite the fact that the conditions were not great and water was always an issue. The pumps were working away almost constantly to keep the water under control to avoid the mine flooding and perhaps having to close.

I have to say I was in a few accidents myself. In the main it was usually nothing too serious, but I was more seriously injured later working in the private mine, Smithston mine, also known locally as Love's Mine. This mine was located just above Houldsworth and this mine was driven down to access good amounts of coal reasonably near the surface.

Jim Love - Cycle Champion

Jim Love, a former Scottish Cycling champion in his day, had been a manager at Houldsworth, so he would know the geology of the area very well and the prospects for extracting coal reasonably near the surface. So I think that was why the private mine above Houldsworth was driven.

Small Work Force

There were only a few men, probably less than 20, who worked in Smithston mine, but every one of them had to work hard simply because we were few in number and producing coal was the be all and end all.

I liked working at Smithston because you knew everyone very well, whereas the big pits like Killoch and Barony were simply too big and impersonal. You never got to know your workmates like you did in the smaller pits of the Doon Valley.

Changing Facilities at Patna

As I mentioned there was a lot of water in the underground roads in Smithston. In fact it was often steel toe-capped wellingtons we wore rather than pit boots. The changing facilities where we got ready in our pit clothes to go down the mine was located well away from the actual mine. It was in the former McKnight's garage on the A713 in Patna which was about two miles from Smithston mine.

The miners then had to drive or be driven along to Polnesson on the A713 one mile north of Patna and drive up the steep brae to the original Houldsworth Pit. Cars were parked there and everyone then walked further up the hill to the Smithston mine entrance.

At the end of the shift we did the reverse, so you had to drive back when you were covered in muck and coal dust with blackened face and hands. It was far from ideal. Quite often the showers were cold by the time we arrived at Patna because other miners had used all the hot water, but like other things in life, it could be annoying when you were cold, wet and dirty, but we just got on with it.

My Accident

On one occasion I was brushing with Willie McDerment – heightening the roof – and removing the debris from that process – hard, dangerous work. The next thing I knew, part of the roof came crashing down, a very frightening experience, I can tell you. I thought I was a gonner that day.

I was covered in dirt and grime and I was disoriented and wasn't sure what was happening. However, the next thing I knew I had arrived in Ayr County Hospital. The two fingers on my left hand - the middle and ring finger - were facing outwards.

I was kept in hospital and got an emergency operation during which both fingers were pinned. That accident happened not long before Smithston closed and I took redundancy. I was aged fifty-five when I finished which is young by today's standards.

I attended the hospital for around a year for treatment to my two fingers. Even today I am unable to bend those two fingers and that was down to my accident at Smithston mine. It was a near miss and I could so easily have been killed by that roof fall. When I think back to incidents like this it really is sobering to think what a narrow escape I had. Sadly, too many other miners were not so fortunate and far too many lost their lives over the years.

I can honestly say that I really loved the company working with some great neighbours down the pit. We talked about everything under the sun from football, holiday, politics – you name it and we discussed it. I always seemed to land with great neighbours, many of them great characters who always had a story or joke to keep you going and encourage you when the going was tough down the mine.

Fellow Miners

In Minnivey the characters I worked with included Sam McBride and John McCulloch. John was a great Dalmellington brass band player and like so many other miners a talented and well educated man. At Smithston Mine I worked with Willie McDerment and he was a great neighbour to work with and a real hard worker. The work had to be done, because if coal wasn't being produced then the gaffers wanted to know why and there were very few of us, so there was no hiding place.

At Minnivey I worked with Ian Reilly, Willie Calderwood, Ian Happle, Rab Wallace, Sam McBride, Gibb McBride, Johnny Givens, Danny Onions, Tom Anderson, Robert Coughtrie, Davie Coughtrie, John McCulloch, Jock Robert, Wull McHattie, Johnny Walker, Bill Hose, George Graham, Davy Whalen, wee Buddy Dinwoodie, Alex Thomson and the two Filson twins – Andy and Tommy, lifelong bandsmen with Benwhat Band.

You got to know them all well because you worked side by side down the mine. You joked and laughed with them, you played tricks on each other and you argued about everything from football to religion, so you became quite close, but the work got done just the same.

One special friend, John Wharrie, now of Drongan, came to the Big Mine from Mossblown way back in 1952. We worked together and became good friends. And to this day my wife Jean and I still visit John and his wife Pearl. We go on holidays together. That friendship resulted from us both being miners and nowadays we often blether about days down the mine.

Pennyvenie No. 4

At Pennyvenie No. 4 my fellow workers included Billy Graham, Adam Calderwood, Andy Burns, John Wright, Billy Whalen, Sam Toal, Robert McHendrie, Willie Taylor, Billy Ireland, Jim Ferguson, Jim Dempsey, Jim Wallace, 'Tanny' and 'Dykes' Anderson, Alex Baird, Pat Malone, Jackie Jones, Willie Gillespie, Joe Paulin, George 'Churler' Graham, Jock Orr, Willie McMinn, Dave Tait, Wilson Tyson, Jimmy Reid, Jock McLean, Harry Ritchie, Al Geddes and John Wharrie. There were also lots more, but you don't always remember names so far back in time.

Smithston

At Smithston I worked with Willie McDerment, John Fairlie, David Tait, Johnny Wallace, George Graham, Jock Stead, Rab Malone, Billy Carey, Hugh McGarry, Alex Strickland, Buddy Dinwoodie and his son, Wee Budd, Al Geddes and Jimmy Stewart. Three of the men travelled from Muirkirk to Patna to work in this mine.

All the men I worked with at Minnivey, Pennyvenie and Smithston were fine men. I remember once speaking to your father, (James L Reid), about the men we worked with. He mentioned a word that stuck in my mind. The word was 'top notcher.' Many of the fellow workers in the mines I've mentioned and countless more I've failed to remember, were all 'top notchers.'

Hard Graft

Looking back I can say that I really did enjoy my time working underground in the coal mines of the Doon Valley. It was hard graft and danger never lurked far round the corner, but you just got on with it. I don't think you could have worked underground if you were constantly fearful, but you did have to respect the underground workings and be safety conscious. Mining wasn't for everyone and some folk couldn't hack working underground.

I would say that I was really fortunate in my working life. Best of all was working with a group of ordinary men who were really quite extraordinary going under the name of proud coal miners.

Primal Fear

When I think about those days, in the mines the reality is that you were actually living moment by moment with that most haunting primal fear – the prospect of being buried alive or killed by a rock fall or being run over by an out-of-control hutch or something as simple as stumbling and falling. That was all it took for calamity, falling on the ground or not being careful with putting in enough support at the coal face.

Many Doon Valley miners will be able to testify that tragedy almost happened to them or their work mates on more than one occasion. I think we all looked into the abyss at some point underground. I have two useless fingers to remind me that I, too, was lucky not to have been killed in the Smithston mine.

Indomitable Spirit

However, miners dealt with that fear every single working day. They had this indomitable spirit which amounted to what was a truly bravura performance. They were living proof of the extraordinary power of the human spirit to win coal whilst keeping safe and being able to smile and laugh at life.

A group of miners at No. 1 Pennyvenie in the late 1800s or early 1900s. The tall man 5th from right is a Mr Orr of Dalmellington who was a blacksmith.

The former coal miners of Ayrshire's Doon Valley are getting fewer in number with each passing year. But memories of mining, whilst those of us who remain will always speak about it from the heart, will never die until the last of its sons have been gathered unto their father's care.

Even then memories will hopefully live on through the pages of this and other books remembering the cost of winning coal and the men who risked life and limb in that process. I hope so anyway. I have enjoyed my precious days as one of the Doon Valley miners.

Romance still brightly gilds the door
Of bygone days that are no more

(traditional)

Chapter 7

Accident at Pennyvenie

Malcolm Graham

It's my believe that every man
Should do his share of work,
And in our economic plan
No citizen should shirk.

I Believe
Robert W Service

Malcolm Graham, 84, was destined for a career in coal mining until he suffered a serious accident at Pennyvenie Pit when he jumped on and fell from a moving train. He was seriously injured when his right leg was caught by the train wheels.

After a few days in Ayr County Hospital his right leg had to be amputated below the knee to effectively save his life. Here he recounts that dreadful experience together with personal reflections on a varied life which took him away from the coal face of mining.

Craigmark

I was born at 54 Craigmark, Dalmellington, on 26 January 1931. My mother says that I was born on the floor there, so it couldn't have been a very pleasant experience for her as the houses at Craigmark were cold and drafty.

Moving to Dalmellington

I had just started the school in Dalmellington when the family moved in 1936 from Craigmark to 19 Hopes Avenue, Dalmellington. I always remember going back to Craigmark and visiting the old Craigmark Store where all the families got their messages (groceries & other supplies).

Although the family were pleased to get a modern house, there was a sadness at leaving our neighbours and seeing families moving away. The plan was that Craigmark would be abandoned and demolished and by around 1937 that aim had been achieved.

Family connections

My mother was Catherine Johnstone. She was born in Hosiery Street, Tannochside, Lanarkshire. My father was John Graham, who was born and raised at Lethanhill, the old village sitting high on the hill above Patna.

Family

My maternal grandfather, John Johnstone, came through with his family from Lanarkshire, to work in the pits of the Doon Valley. When I was a wee boy, my grandfather worked at the pithead at Chalmerston. He worked until he was aged seventy-six finishing up at Minnivey. He worked in the screening plant there, a job usually left to older miners who were unfit to go underground. I don't remember by maternal grandfather, Henry Graham, but I was told he worked on the pugs at Waterside. His son, who was also Henry, also worked on the pugs.

Father – John Graham

My father, John Graham, was born in 1897 at Lethanhill and my mother was born in 1899. They got married in the manse at Dalmellington by the Rev. George S Hendrie in 1920.
In our family there was my sister Mary, who was born in 1921. My brother Henry was born in 1924 and Sam was born in 1928. I was the youngest born in 1931. All my family predeceased me.

School to Pit

I remained at Dalmellington Higher Grade school where the headmaster was Mr Thomson, until I was fourteen years of age. I left the school at Easter 1945. When the boys were about to leave school, the training officer from the pit came along and the boys were lined up.

Those going to the pit were told to be there at 7am on the Monday morning. I turned up at the required time to begin at the pit training school. The training lasted for just one week and then we had a week down the pit to see what it was like. After that I was sent to Pennyvenie No. 4, which was known locally as the Big Mine.

The tumblers

My job there was to uncouple the hutches coming up the mine. The hutches came up pulled by a rope and my job was to uncouple them

Malcolm Graham memories are recorded in: Accident at Pennyvenie.

Four miners at Pennyvenie Colliery towards the end of its life. It closed in 1978
(Photo: EAC DVM)

and they went onto the tumblers where the hutches were literally tumbled upside down and the coal fell into the wagons below. The process went on until each coal wagon was filled. The wagons below moved along to allow each one to be filled in turn.

End of War

I was only there for a few months and it was the day after VJ day when war finished in August 1945. We all got a one day holiday from the pit. I had been up dancing at Craigmark Institute where there was a special event to mark the end of the Japanese war. There was a great feeling among the locals knowing that war was finally at an end and that perhaps better days lay ahead.

Serious Accident

In the morning I went out to Pennyvenie. I went to the pit baths and after changing I went to get on the carriages to go up to the Big Mine about a mile further on. The railway carriages were used to transport the miners from Pennyvenie to the Big Mine and bring others back at the end of the shift. The railway carriages had just started to move when I arrived, but I was determined not to miss my work.

I ran and jumped on as the train was moving away and my feet slipped off the running board of the carriage and I fell backwards and ended up under the wheels. The carriage ran over my right foot. I still remember that day – Friday 17 August 1945 at 6.30am. I suppose I was lucky because the carriage could have went right over my legs or entire body and I could have been killed instantly.

Strange peacefulness

Tam Shaw was the driver of the pug which ran over me. Adam McGill was the guard. Several men jumped out the carriages to come to my rescue. I always remember holding my leg up with my hands and I could see that my leg had been flattened. There was blood everywhere. Someone put a tourniquet on and someone else gave me a cup of black tea from a flask. I was shaking probably due to the shock. The miners were talking to me and trying to reassure me that everything would be fine. The strange thing was that I didn't seem to feel any pain and there was a strange sense of peacefulness. Perhaps it was my body coping with the injury.

To hospital

An ambulance arrived and I was taken to Dumfries Ward, Ayr County Hospital. My whole foot was covered in stitches and was put in a stookie. There were over fifty stitches in the various wounds to my leg. The doctors were desperately trying to save my foot.

Penicillin was just in its infancy at that time and they had a drip going directly into my leg. I remained in the hospital for some days as the medical team fought to save the leg. However I remember that one day they took me to the theatre. The surgeon asked me if I had any feeling in my toes. I was able to move my toe and he sent me back to the ward.

Leg Amputated

On 5 September 1945 at visiting time in the evening, my leg was in a very bad way. Gangrene had set in and I could see that my leg was smelling and green. I was taken to the theatre that day and had my right leg removed just below the knee. After that I made a quick recovery and was home within a further two weeks.

A couple of months after the accident I was taken up to Soutar Brothers, Sauchiehall Street, Glasgow, and they fitted me up for an artificial leg. They gave me one which was capable of extending

Two miners working underground at Pennyvenie with the metal props showing that it was probably in the 1960s or 70s. However, from the perilous position of the props and undulating ground, it's not difficult to imagine how disaster could easily strike in such tough conditions.

Low Pennyvenie probably in the 1940s when all the houses would have been occupied by local miners and their families. In the background is the Big Mine. None of this exists today, all the houses in High and Low Pennyvenie, a scattered community, having been demolished from 1960s onwards with none of the originals remaining by 2006.

because they said I would need this as I was growing. I received my new leg in January 1946.

Afterwards I was able to go to the dancing at Craigmark and enjoyed a night on the floor and dancing the night away. However, the next day my right leg was in a state with raw flesh where my leg joined the artificial limb. It had been rubbing and it was still not tough enough to weather the friction.

Compensation

There was a court case and I was eventually awarded 8/2d a week compensation for losing my leg in the fall from the train. When I was 21 years of age it went up to £1-2s-4d.

Pal suffers accident

On VE day or just around then, George Kerr, who was a school pal and lived in Park Crescent, Dalmellington, was run over by a set of hutches at Minnivey. He was not so seriously injured and was very fortunate. He suffered a broken leg and bruising. We remained pals for years. In fact I was best man at his wedding.

George now lives in Irvine and we still talk occasionally and exchange Christmas cards. He continued to work in the pit and only left when Monsanto at Dundonald was built and left to go to work there. Quite a few miners left to go and work there at that time.

.

School then railway

After my accident I went back to the school at Dalmellington and stayed there until the summer holidays in 1946. I then got a job at the Food Office in Ayr where I remained for 6 months. In the meantime when I was sixteen I had applied for a job in the railway, so I started in March 1947 at Waterside and remained there until I left aged twenty-four in 1955.

I worked between Waterside and Dalmellington Stations as a clerk in the station office. I would prepare invoices for all the coal going down the line to Ayr. One of the bosses said the Ayr - Dalmellington line was one of the best paying lines in Scotland because of the coal going down. However, the passenger figures were not so good.

I remember that the general manager at NCB Waterside used to say to me that I should really be working with the NCB as my accident had been caused working at the Pennyvenie. His view was that as my accident happened under the Coal Board, I should have been offered a permanent job there. Apparently anyone who was injured at the pit was usually accommodated in some type of suitable job.

Cook and sew

I was a member of the Army Cadets based at that time at the old picture house next to Craigmark Burntonians Park across from Dalmellington School. The army cadets held a dance to help with buying artificial limbs for me. I was very grateful to them for that act of kindness.

My parents were very annoyed that I had suffered this accident. My mother learnt me to sew and bake after the accident. I think she was concerned that I might be on my own in later life and she wanted to prepare me with basic life skills – the sort of things I would be able to do on my own. I remember she bought me two big table covers which I embroidered. I think the skills she taught me did stand me in good stead.

Marriage

I married on 26 June 1953 to Alice Frew who was from Broomhouse near Uddingston. I met Alice at the dancing at the Merrick Hall when I was aged eighteen. What happened was that some of Alice's friends came to live at the Glebe in Dalmellington, where miners and their families coming into the district were initially accommodated.

We married when I was aged 22. We had a son, Malcolm, who now lives in Nottingham and daughter, Eleanor, who lives in Townhead, Dalmellington. I have five grandchildren, all now grown up. They are Peter, Louise, Helen, Finlay and Nell.

Wages and new home

When I married the NCB asked me if I would like a settlement in respect of the accident when I lost my right foot. I settled for £500 which was a fair amount in 1953. When I left the railways in 1955 I was only earning £5 a week. When I worked for the NCB at Waterside I got 8/- more. The £500 set me up.

We rented a single end house in Croft Street, Dalmellington from Willie Newell, the coalman. We were paying 4/- a week rent, but it was good because most young couples at that time would normally have to stay with in-laws or rent a room in a council house until they were allocated their own, council house. Three years later we were allocated a council house in Raecawr Avenue, Bellsbank. They were brand new and good quality, so Alice was absolutely delighted.

NCB Waterside

In 1955 I went to work at NCB Waterside where I worked at the weighbridge. I did this job for around three years and and then transferred into the NCB wages office still at Waterside. The Wages Department manager was Mr Forrester. The chief wages clerk was Gordon Drysdale.

Work Colleagues

At the office in Waterside I worked with Louis Scott, Tom Graham of Patna, Nancy Forrester, daughter of the manager, was working there, too. She married Allan Jackson who tragically was killed working at Beoch Colliery in 1957. Archie Campbell and Bertie Campbell from Patna, Bob Hunter, Billy Carr, Billy Kellock, Sadie Borland, Beth

Auld, Mary Campbell and Rita Rae, also worked in the office. It was a busy place and good to work in and everyone got on well.

Transferred

I worked for the Coal Board for 32 years and retired in 1987 aged fifty-six. By that time I had moved from Waterside after ten years to Lugar where I served for nineteen years and later moved for three years to Killoch Colliery where the wages office was then located. And for the last eight years of my working life I was the wages accountant, so I did work in a job that gave a high level of personal satisfaction

Joys of Work

I enjoyed the job better when everything was done manually rather than with computers. I always felt that there was more satisfaction doing everything manually, but it did put a strain on you as everything had to be ready for Tuesday each week.

When it came to holiday period when miners were looking for holiday pay, we had to work Saturday and Sunday to get things ready so all the miners and other staff could be paid on time.

In those days it was monetary wages which were paid out. For the backshift, nightshift and dayshift we would go to the pits with a driver in the coal board van and pay out the wages as the men finished their shifts. In later years more miners started to have their wages paid into the bank.

Reflection

I always said that if it hadn't been for my accident I would almost certainly have been destined to be a miner all my working life. Indeed when I think about it I could possibly have been killed in the pits, so in some ways my accident at that early age certainly had a strong bearing on my future life. I'm now eighty-four and I have had a good life with a wonderful wife and family and a reasonable pension.

My dear wife Alice spent the last few years of her life in Dalmellington Care Centre before she passed on 13 November 2014. What I've learned in life's uncertain journey is that our time on earth is made up of all types of experiences, good and bad. And what I've come to realise is that the secret of happiness is to accept both with good grace.

Fate

There is a saying that a life without pain and suffering is a life not fully lived. I often think back to that day in 1945 when I fell under the wheel of that railway locomotive at Pennyvenie and subsequently had my right leg amputated. As I lay there on that cold railway track, surrounded by caring miners trying to help and reassure me, and despite my serious injury I was overcome with a most wonderful sense of tranquility. And fate was to dictate that my life was changed forever, but still linked closely to the coal industry.

Let us probe the silent places, let us seek what luck betide us;
Let us journey to a lonely land I know.
There's a whisper on the night-wind, there's a star agleam to guide us,
And the Wild is calling, calling . . . let us go.

The Call of the Wild
Robert W Service

Chapter 8

Bygone Lethanhill

James McFadzean

For a' that, an a' that,
Our toils obscure, an a' that,
The rank is but the guinea's stamp,
The man's the gowd for a' that

A Man's a Man for A' That
Robert Burns

James McFadyean.
(Photo: Donald L Reid)

Donald L Reid interviewed James McFadzean at his home in Rankinston in 2003. He kindly shared his memories of life at lonely Lethanhill where he was born and spent his formative years. He passed away in February 2007 aged ninety-three.

My family

I was born at 57 White Brick Row, Lethanhill on 27 January 1914. It was the year when the whole world seemed to go mad, with the outbreak of the Great War. My father, who was also called James, was a miner at Houldsworth Pit which had opened in 1900 and he worked there all his days. He died on 1 August 1941 during the Second World War.

My mother, Elizabeth Adams, had me baptised by the Minister of Waterside and Lethanhill church, the Reverend William Gracie, on 11 October 1914. I had four sisters, Lizzie, Agnes, Annie and Sadie. Lizzie and Agnes went into farm service when about fourteen years of age. Agnes went to Carnachon Farm, Patna and Lizzie went to Dormaston Farm, Trabboch. Perhaps not surprisingly, they both subsequently married men from the rural community.

Sister Annie had polio when young and was left with a bad leg, so she wore a caliper. She worked for quite a time in service to the Minister at Waterside, the Reverend Anderson. Sadie was the youngest and worked in Ayr for a baker and later worked at Seafield Hospital doing domestic work. The only one surviving today is Sadie. I was the second youngest in the family.

Lost villages

My mother originally belonged to Tongue Row. This was a row of houses on the (B730) road from Rankinston to Kerse, about half a mile from Kerse at the side of the road. Neither Kerse nor Tongue Row nor indeed nearby Cairntable survive, all long gone now, but they were lovely wee places when I was young and everyone was working. The old school with schoolmaster's house at Kerse, which the local children all attended, still stands, although it's really in a very sorry state. However, it's many years since it was operated as a school.

So, Tongue Row, Cairntable and Kerse are all really lost villages with a wonderful past because they were full of characters that faced life at the sharp end with great fortitude. None of these places had anything but very basic facilities that folk today take for granted. But I suppose it was just what they were used to and they wouldn't be any the wiser as there were no TVs in those days. All the folk around them were in the same position.

My family moved from the Hill in 1946 and my mother died a year later in Ayr. She was a great woman and looked after our family very well indeed at the Hill and I can tell you that things weren't easy for her, but she simply got on with doing the very best she could. We were lucky to have such a great lady. Even now as an old man, I remember her with great fondness.

Electricity arrives at the Hill

I can remember one great occasion living at the Hill. That was in 1927 when I was thirteen years of age. The Dalmellington Iron Company (DICo) put electricity into the houses. It was just great to have lamps in the street. I remember the men who put them in. There was John Robertson, another was 'Ooie' Thomson, who belonged to Waterside and the third was John Nixon.

This was a great thing for everyone because before that we had no street lights and the lights we had indoors were paraffin lamps which were smelly and bad on the eyes. The men put one lamp at each end of the rows and this became a gathering point for local folk at night. Mind you, this put a shilling a week on the rent and that didn't please my parents. I remember the date well because it coincided with our move from the old school at Lethanhill to a new school which was built up nearer the war memorial.

Living conditions at the Hill

Living conditions at the Hill in those earlier years, and I remember them clearly, were poor. No other word can describe it. Families had to go out into the street to fill pails from the street pumps and carry them home and then had to boil the water for washing using the coal boiler. Everyone was the same as there was no running water in any of the houses in those early years. The cooking was done on the range stove or over the open fire. It was amazing the wonderful food that mother could produce and her baking was memorable. I can smell the scones and girdle scones as we speak. Mmmhh! She was a real gem and I was so fortunate!

Company store

My mother had to get all our provisions from the DICo. When I was a boy all the provisions for the Hill were brought up the Drumgrange incline from Waterside, loaded onto the pugs (small steam engines) which took them to the Hill store and then on along the railway line to supply Benwhat store. That will seem strange to folk today, but that was just how things were done. The incline was a great system when you think about it. All in all an amazing feat of engineering.

Lethanhill with villagers clearing the remnants of what has been a heavy fall of snow, whilst other villagers go about their business. By 1954 this mining village had been abandoned and later demolished.

In 1930 Bairds and Dalmellington followed on from Dalmellington Iron Company and in 1947 the NCB took over the site. This team was made up of staff who worked in the offices at Waterside. Many of them lived locally in what became known as the lost mining villages.
Back row: (l to r) James Roberts, John Ferguson, Frank McKie, Willie Dougan, John Relly and Louis Scott.
Front row: Tommy Rafferty, Ian Robb, Willie Burns, Billy Thomson and Campbell McMillan.
(John Relly collection)

The rear of Lethanhill School about 1953. David Young, aged three is with his mother Mrs Janet Young and the girl is Janet Foden, visiting the Young family at the Store house, Lethanhill. Jack Young was the last manager of the Lethanhill Store, then operated by John McDonald, the father of popular Doon Valley man, Matt McDonald, fondly remembered as the publican at the Palace Bar, Waterside until the early 1970s.
(Photo: Courtesy of David Young)

Rail network on the Hill

At that time Benbranigan Pit was still working and many of the men from the Hill and Benwhat worked there. The railway on the Hill was crucial for getting supplies to folk as well as for moving the coal and ironstone. Later on vans came up to the Hill from other suppliers such as the Co-op in Patna.

As I recall the rail network on the Hill was lifted about 1929 although lower down the railway lines still ran to Houldsworth Pit where many of the men worked. The Drumgrange incline still operated for several years after that, probably finishing in the early 1930s.

I remember that Alex Beattie was one of the engine drivers and Jimmy Stevenson and John Campbell were fireman and guard in my schooldays. They also operated the incline which ran from the Hill down to the north side of Waterside.

School on the Hill

One teacher at Lethanhill School I can remember was Miss Ward. She belonged to Orkney. She took lodgings at the Hill and was very much involved in the life of the community. In fact she married Tommy Allan. Tommy was the manager of Pennyvenie Pit in those days, but belonged to the Hill. There was also Miss Joanne Campbell. She belonged to Wick. She married Malcolm Ross, who was a Hill man who also trained and became a teacher. There was a Miss Doull. She came from up north too. I can mind them all fine.

Mining

When I started work in 1928 at Pennyvenie No. 4 my mother got me up in the morning and made the fire, boiled the kettle on the open fire and made my breakfast then made my piece (sandwiches) and saw me out to work. All the women on the Hill did this duty for their husbands and sons – it was just how things were done in those days. They knew that working down a pit was dangerous and demanding work and they wanted to make sure that every man was well prepared.

Down the incline

I would then walk across to the drumhead and down the Drumgrange incline to Waterside. There was a pug (steam locomotive) waiting there with five wagons which took the miners from the Hill, Patna and Waterside along the line to Pennyvenie. On arrival there was a small surface hutch (small wagon) mineral line which connected up Clawfin

Nos. 1 and 2, Benbain and Beoch.

The men had to walk from No. 4 Pennyvenie to Clawfin. There was what they called 'an endless haulage' to Beoch. Hutches went one way and the full ones came the other way. Men could use the endless haulage to travel in between Pennyvenie and Beoch. They simply sat down in the empty hutches for the journey. That's how things were done in my days at the pit and there was no such thing as health and safety. By and large we managed fine and watched out for one another.

Happy man

In 1937 I got a job at Houldsworth, working down the mine. I was there for nine years. I then worked in Berbeth Mine at Coalhall for about five years and then when it closed I transferred to Littlemill Pit between Rankinston and Cairntable. I worked there until I retired in 1974. I would say I have been very fortunate in my long life and looking back I don't think I would have wanted to change much. I was very happy with my lot in life and if you can say that, I think you are saying quite a lot, especially as the world is so complex and, at times, very cruel for many folk.

Fare-thee-weel, thou first and fairest!
Fare-thee-weel, thou best and dearest!
Thine be ilka joy and treasure,
Peace, Enjoyment, Love and Pleasure!

Ae Fond Kiss
Robert Burns

Hugh Relly (left) and John 'Jock' Relly visit Benwhat and have a seat in the ruins of the village school on May 31 1954, as they recall special memories of their auld village.
(Courtesy of John Relly collection)

Chapter 9

Benwhat – Random Reflections

James McPhail

These were the folk before us,
Be proud of them, be proud;
These Scottish folk who bred us
We sing their praises loud.

Arthur W Wilson (1963)

The McPhail family were originally from Benwhat. James 'Jimsy' McPhail on the left has his memories recorded in this book, Benwhat – Random Reflections.
(l to r): James 'Jimsy' McPhail, John, McPhail and Calum McPhail.

James 'Jimsy' McPhail, then in his eightieth year, was interviewed by Donald L Reid in 2003. Sadly, Jimsy died in 2011 after a short illness. He was raised in Benwhat in a family of ten, not by any means uncommon in the lost villages. He worked in the mines locally all his working life. A lifelong and very committed member of Dalmellington Band, he served more than sixty-eight years as a player and was a playing member of the band when they became champions of Scotland in 1969 and 1976.

All his life he was a staunch supporter of this wonderful band. Indeed, for many the band is synonymous with the village from which it takes its name. Jimsy was a popular man about Dalmellington and he would be rather pleased that his random thoughts, going back to 1929 when he attended Benwhat School, are a lasting legacy to be enjoyed by those who follow in his footsteps.

Remote Benwhat

I lived at Benwhat with my parents and their eight children in conditions which by standards of today were very, very poor, but I know that we were a happy lot, despite the hardship of living in such a remote place. With ten folk in a small house of two rooms there was no privacy. In my family there was Chrissy, Robert, Catherine, John, Elizabeth, myself, Helen and Calum. My father was Malcolm and my mother Catherine.

School

I remember going to school at Benwhat as a wee boy. My teacher was Miss Kidd in the infants class in 1929. Francis Ferguson was the headmaster, a reasonable and popular man, who came from Dunaskin and travelled via Dalmellington up the hill to Benwhat every day in an old car.

Other well-known teachers at that time were Miss Mary Hill, who later stayed in Ayr Road, Dalmellington; Miss Florence Kerr, who later married Louis Scott, a well-respected man from Waterside; and Miss Munro, who lived in digs in Benwhat with Mrs Galloway. I remember that the school was used for dances, concerts and cantatas which were also called soirees. Weddings were also held in the new school, which opened in 1927, and in many ways it was the hub for special social occasions for the village.

No nonsense store

The store was operating at that time and Sanny Orr was in charge. I remember later that Harry Moore took over running the store. In fact I think his daughter is still living in Prestwick.

We used to queue up for the daily paper to take home, before going to school, but if we talked too loud and got up to nonsense, Harry would order us all outside. He stood no nonsense. The local men enjoyed going for a pint at the store, especially on a Saturday. They worked hard all week in the pits and were keen to enjoy a social drink at the store which opened from 11 a.m. until 3 p.m. and again from 5 p.m. until 9 p.m. in those days. At that time the beer was sixpence a pint and if you wanted to carry out a screw-top (bottle of beer) it was ninepence. No whisky was sold in the store.

Mother's domestic work

As I said, there were ten in my family and we lived in very cramped conditions, but many others were just like us. My mother had a difficult time and had to work very hard to look after us all. She was always on the go – cooking, cleaning, sewing or doing the washing up. The wash house was in the back porch with a built-in boiler to heat the water from a coal fire.

Once or twice a week the boiler fire was lit and a big washing was done by my mother. The houses at Benwhat were mainly one and two bedroom. There was no such thing as central heating, but there were open fires. Quite a few folk used what was called Beatrice Paraffin cookers in the porch to cook on.

Hungry lads

As boys we simply got on with life at Benwhat. We would enjoy running about the moors, playing football, and going to find birds' nests, and we often spent a full day pottering about Dunaskin Glen. I remember that at times we were starving, having been away all day and could hardly walk home, we were so hungry. Happy days, though.

Doon Harriers and Heatherbell

There was the Doon Harriers based in the village. All the older boys were members and everyone was proud of one famous runner, Robert Reid, who was a champion of Scotland. Adam McHattie was also a great harrier in these days.

We also had Benwhat Heatherbell and Rising Star, two amateur teams made up of local men, and between them they were very successful and won many trophies. There was one player, David Murray, who went from junior status to play for Aston Villa, not bad for someone coming from a remote hill village like Benwhat. The folk I recall involved with Rising Star were Jimmy Wilson (manager), Tommy Stewart, Hugh Murray, 'Riddy' Murray, Jimmy Stewart and 'Daidsy' Wilson.

Progress in life

David Relly, better known to us boys by his nickname 'Dykes', was a great Labour supporter and Rangers FC daft into the bargain. I recall him boasting of people born in Benwhat who did well in life. He was very proud that there was a doctor, headmaster, chief accountant and a minister born there. As I recall the minister was Robert Pollock and John Watson was the accountant. A village worthy (character) whom I remember as a boy was 'Sybus Galloway'. His job was to chap all the miners up (wake them up) in the morning to make sure they got to Chalmerston Mine on time for their shift starting.

The reading room

The Institute in Benwhat, better known as the reading room, was enjoyed by most folk and competitions were held every week. Newspapers and periodicals were available for anyone to read. There was a little shop in the Institute and it was under the control of Andrew

Corbie Craigs, a lonely deserted row of ten cottages, was constructed around 1850. Located high above a spur running off Dunaskin Glen, it overlooks the Rough Burn. It housed workers in the local mines. It was abandoned around 1952, but substantial ruins remain. In 1942 living there families including McHendry, McCart, Gardener, Hainey, Ferguson, Riley, Bradley, Kirk, Hodgson and Brown. There was still folk living at Corbie Craigs in 1954. (Photo: Donald L Reid)

Doon Harriers 1938/39. The Doon Valley produced some very fine athletes over the years. In particular Robert Reid, who was a baker with Dalmellington Co-op, won a large number of trophies and competed all over Scotland with great success becoming a Birchfield Harrier. Back row (l to r): A Hannah, R Filson, A McHattie, J S Hannah and J B Galloway. Middle row: J Wallace, S Sturgeon, W Currie, J Lindsay and Lewis Scott. Front row: A Travers, A Gardiner, D Whiteman, Robert Reid, Hugh Uriarte, William McHattie, R Campbell, Jack Dinwoodie and Lewis Uriarte.

Hannah, known locally by the nickname 'Snat'.

Billy Torbet followed on from Hannah and was caretaker for quite a while. One of the jobs that he had to do, which was quite sad, was going round houses and advising everyone when there was a death in the village and giving folk the times and details of the funeral. I remember that he had a bit of a temper and would shout and fling things if the boys misbehaved in the reading room. The membership of the reading room was one penny per week and that later rose to twopence, but it was worth it despite the hefty rise! There was a whist club held twice weekly and it was very popular, too.

Romance

Romance also blossomed at Benwhat and inevitably villagers married. Off the top of my head I think particularly of Jimmy Gordon who married Jeanie Bennet; Will Hodgson and Peggy Murray; Davy Torbet and Matsy McMahon; and Alan Dick and Janet Robertson. There were others, too.

Caring Co-op

At one time the Co-operative based in Dalmellington played a big part in the life of the people of Benwhat. They fed you, cled (clothed) and even buried you. A comprehensive service, you might say. Most of the folk used the Co-op and the service was first-class with vans calling regularly.

From 1929 they came to Benwhat with horse-drawn vans providing services such as the baker, butcher, milk and rolls, paraffin and briquettes, so the villagers were well provided for, although they were remote from the rest of the folk in the valley below and they were subject to the elements to a much greater degree – the weather in winter could be horrendous, the village sitting 1,000 feet above sea level.

Burns and Benwhat

The works of Robert Burns were popular in the village and with miners in general. Benwhat Burns Club was formed in 1940 during the war and affiliated to the Burns Federation in 1944. David Dunsmuir, a Benwhat man and Glasgow policeman, gave the first Immortal Memory and James Hill was the chairman that night. There are only two members of the club alive today (2003) – myself and Johnnie Gray (Jimsy McPhail subsequently passed on in 2011 and Johnnie Gray in 2012). Many good speakers came to Benwhat including John Pollock, a headmaster and his father before him; Major John Weir DSO OBE, Miss Ferguson and David Dunsmuir (junior). I still have possession of the Benwhat Burns Club certificate of membership of the Burns Federation.

Parker brothers killed in Great War

I clearly remember my Granny Hill, she lived at 66 Benwhat, telling me about two brothers she lost in the Great War. They were Jim and Tom Parker. In the 1939–45 war Benwhat lost John Robertson, Tom

Dalmellington Band leads a parade from the school through the village to Pennyvenie Colliery with Councillors and officials of the Mineworkers Union and members of the public to mark the handover of the nation's colliers from private owners to the National Coal Board on January 1 1947.
(Photo: Dalmellington Band)

Bunyan and Bobby McMahon. All these men were known to me and popular in the village. Quite a few others served and thankfully came back, but it's sad to think of the lads from our little community who were killed. What can you say about men like those who never returned? Only that 'we will remember them'. They were our neighbours and friends.

Halloween

At Halloween I remember that a special cart came up from

Dalmellington with all sorts of nuts and apples for the young folk to celebrate Halloween. This was great for the children. Mr John Robertson, somewhat balding on top, came up to sell his wares and was shouting about the good nuts on offer when one of the boys, 'Toy' Bennet, shouted back: 'Aye, they're monkey nuts, hazel nuts and baldy nuts too.' It was all fun and taken in good part.

Rechabites

The Rechabites is a biblical name used by Christian groups in my day keen to promote total abstinence from alcohol. They were organised as the Independent Order of Rechabites. Most of the young folk in Benwhat were members of the Rechabites and went to the regular meetings held in the school hall. You got a bible lesson delivered by one of their members, we played games and then you got a drink of lemonade and a bun to eat. This was run in Benwhat at that time by Robert Bryan, Sunday School Superintendent and Kirk Elder at Dalmellington. He lived next door to us. He was a kindly and well-respected man.

Contrary canary

Alan Dick was another great character. He could talk all day about canary breeding and looking after budgies, which was his passion. He once sold a canary to a Mr Aitken, who told Alan that he wanted one that was a good whistler. A week later Mr Aitken arrived back at Benwhat and told Alan that the canary had a broken leg. 'Well,' replied Alan, 'you said you wanted a good whistler, not a step-dancer.' He was a real character.

Brass band

The village had a good brass band. In fact there were three brass bands within a few miles of one another. They were Benwhat Band (1871), Dalmellington Band (1864) and Waterside Band (1869). Mining areas had a strong brass band tradition. I'm proud to say that I have been a lifelong brass band enthusiast, still playing until a few years ago. Now, I am still fully involved in the committee of Dalmellington Band, formed in 1864, having been treasurer for many years.

Benwhat Band was formed in 1871 when the conductor was Jamie Armour, and the Armour family was always involved in the band thereafter. Benwhat Band was supported by locals in the village and the Currie family had five members who all played. Every year the band played at the memorial which was located on the brae face of nearby Benwhat Hill. Everyone was proud of this small village band. They practised twice a week in the school hall and I can still remember the music floating across the moorland.

Families in Benwhat

Like the other villages and small communities that no longer exist, the families tended to be large. In Benwhat we had McHattie, McEwan, McPhail, Galloway, Gordon, Thomson, Ferguson, Currie, Relly, Wilson and Dunsmuir, all with some wonderful characters who made village life special. The village midwife was Granny Wilson who lived in Stone Row. She delivered most of the babies and many folk who were born there will be grateful for her skill and self-taught expertise.

War planes

I remember that we often heard the planes going over during the war, probably in early 1941. At the time of the Clydebank Blitz there was a social evening being held in the school and we heard many German planes flying over late in the evening. We could hear them clearly but we were not aware of who was catching it. Poor souls! The wardens warned us all not to use torches or light matches. You could hear the blasts and see the sky lit up. Later on, a light bomb was recovered at Kilmein Hill between Benwhat and Lethanhill and it had probably been jettisoned by a German bomber returning home.

Winter of 1947

I think it was in 1947, the winter was incredibly bad and on one memorable occasion we were snowed in for about a week with heavy drifts which made the roads impassable. The vans couldn't get through from Dalmellington, so we had to walk down and carry supplies up by hand to Benwhat. That was just how things were done. The circumstances were difficult and we had to respond accordingly.

I remember that the first van to get through on the Friday was Malcolm Ross, a popular Dalmellington butcher for many years. His shop was located just off the Square at the Burnside and today William Paterson runs the shop. As Malcolm drove up into Benwhat he got a big cheer and everyone was out to greet him.

We don't seem to get such bad winters nowadays, but it was made all the worse because we were living on the high moors at 1,100 feet above sea level, so if the weather was bad in the valley below, we got it even worse. It was not uncommon for the snow to be up to the top of the back door and many a time we had to shovel our way out of the house to get to the coal shed.

Starting work

I left school in 1938/39 and started work at Chalmerston pithead just at the time war was declared. Robert Filson was the shift gaffer and Willie Miller the manager. I worked there until Christmas 1959 when Chalmerston closed. By that time Minnivey was operating and I started there in January 1960 after the New Year holidays. I eventually retired from the pits in 1981 and by that time I was working at Barony Colliery near Auchinleck as all the Dalmellington pits had closed by July 1978.

Leaving Benwhat

I remember that our family was among the first to leave Benwhat and that was a sad occasion indeed. We moved to 103 Park Crescent in 1943. We liked Benwhat and were reluctant to leave, because it was a great wee community and it was what we were used to all our days. For all the lack of amenities, it had been my home all my life up till then, so it was a bit of a wrench to leave all that we knew and cared about. In fact my brother John was so upset that he used to go back to Benwhat several times a week to the reading room to socialise with his auld pals. He found it hard to let go and settle in to the social life in Dalmellington. Benwhat had that sort of pull on you.

I suppose it would be around 1952 or slightly later before the last folk left Benwhat and I think John Thomson, who later became a well-known bookmaker in Dalmellington, would be one of the last to move. Even by 1947–48 folk were moving out steadily and demolition was ongoing in some of the vacant rows even at that time when folk were still in residence in others.

It was, I suppose, a case of happy enough to move to a new modern house, but sad to leave an old home and good neighbours and happy, even joyful, memories. I can say without any fear of contradiction that the McPhail family were all very proud to belong to Benwhat.

Why am I loth to leave this earthly scene?
Have I so found it full of pleasing charms?
Some drops of joy with draughts of ill between;
Some gleams of sunshine 'mid renewing storms?

Stanzas On The Same Occasion
Robert Burns

Malcolm and Catherine McPhail of Dalmellington. His son was James 'Jimsy' McPhail. Malcolm was fatally injured at Pennyvenie on 5 April 1952. There are still several family members living in Dalmellington.
(Photo: Ritchie family)

Benwhat Comforts Fund (Ladies Committee) 1939-1945 war. The ladies are pictured outside Benwhat School after one of their meetings where they made plans to raise funds to support the men serving in the forces during the 1939-1945 war. Many of those in the photograph have relatives still living in the Doon Valley.
(l to r): Mrs Margaret Campbell, Mrs Agnes Gourlay, Mrs Phamie Douglas, Mrs Annie Campbell, Mrs Sarah Filson, Mrs Scott Hannah and Mrs Alex McHattie
(Miss Anna McHattie collection)

Chapter 10

Big-hearted Beoch

Andrew Knox Bone

Andrew Knox Bone

Benbeoch Craig, grim, weird and wild,
That awed me when I was a child,
Where rocks on mighty rocks are piled,
The wonder of Dalmellington.

Dalmellington
Matthew Anderson

Known locally and affectionately in the Dalmellington of his day as 'Knoxy', the late Andrew Knox Bone was a proud miner at Beoch. He had a great interest in the social history of the Doon Valley and recorded his research in several manuscripts. The following consists of edited highlights of Memories of Beoch, written in the mid-1970s. Andrew Knox Bone died on 18 June 1984, aged seventy-seven, and is buried in Dalmellington Cemetery.

Family from Beoch

My grandparents (Bone) lived at North Beoch (off the B741) for some years in the 1890s. During that period my father was Superintendent of Beoch Sunday School. After the passing of his parents and sister, Mrs Findlay Lorimer, he left Beoch and went to live in Ayr. But his heart was always with the Beoch folk. In Ayr he got a job as an agent with the Refuge Assurance Company. He was subsequently transferred to the Dalmellington run and soon had a regular call to the Beoch to collect insurance money. On a Saturday in November 1901, he was just passing Beoch Mine when he was told that his uncle, James Wallace, had been killed in an accident in the mine.

Pennyvenie

In later years when we all lived at Pennyvenie – some three miles from Beoch on the B741 road – my father and my sister restarted Beoch Sunday School. My father seemed to have a nice way with the children. In fact, some of the scholars still remember him with reverence yet, even some who live as far away as London.

My father died in 1932. In the summer he would walk from Pennyvenie to Beoch, a distance of just over two miles. Some of the children who attended the Sunday School used to walk along the road from Beoch to meet him and my sister, and after Sunday School was over they would again escort them part of the way from Beoch to the Main Road which runs from Cumnock to Dalmellington as they walked back home.

Where do sinners go?

One Sunday he was asking the children some questions, one of which was: 'Where do sinners go?' Up shot the hand of a little boy, who said: 'Ma mither pits the big yins in the fire and the wee yins in the ashpan.' This caused great hilarity, especially among the older children who understood that he was mixing up the word sinners for cinders, the various ashes left on the fire after coal and wood is burned. My father must have had a great knack for working with children. He could see the funny side of things, too, which helped him in his work.

Soirees at Beoch

My father and sister were assisted at the Beoch Sunday School by Harry Halliday and Bob Reid. Bob was the father of Bobby Reid, the

Scottish Cross Country Champion who ran with Benwhat Harriers before going on to better things with the famous Birchfield Harriers. The Reverend John A Kinloch (Minister of Lamloch Church, Dalmellington from 1933 to 1944) used to enjoy the social evenings at Beoch, especially the soirees, when the children started singing their favourite choruses. They were great singers and full of such enthusiasm.

Miss Walker of Camlarg

Miss Jean Walker of Camlarg House, Dalmellington, was a very generous and good friend to Beoch Sunday School. When it came near Christmas time Miss Walker would send word for my father to come across from Pennyvenie to Camlarg House. When he went over he was made very welcome and always came away with a very generous donation from her for the Sunday School.

Here is just one instance I have on record: the usual annual gift of a Christmas tree, cut down and delivered to Beoch by James Thompson or John Morgan, both estate workers at Camlarg. Along with this there was £2 in cash, six Bibles, six books, and a bag of sweets and an orange for every child at the Sunday School. And at that time in a little isolated place like Beoch, 5 miles from Dalmellington and over one mile from the main Dalmellington–Cumnock Road, there were fifty-nine children in the Sunday School. Miss Walker was a very generous donor. And it was the same procedure when it came round time for the Sunday School trip. A nice donation in cash was given to ensure that all the children were well fed.

Beoch children of 1926

Here are the names of the children, with ages in brackets, who attended Beoch Sunday School in 1926. This information is gleaned from records in the possession of my father.

David Shearer (10), Douglas Shearer (8), Robert Shearer (2), David Givens (12), Andrew Givens (9), John Givens (7), Mary Givens (3), Willie Givens (1), James McLelland (13), Peter Halbert (5), Thomas Halbert (3), Willie Halbert (2), Samuel Halbert (1), Mary McLarty (4), Samuel McLarty (3), Alese McLarty (1), Elizabeth Chalmers (12), David Chalmers (10), Rachel Chalmers (7), James Chalmers (5), Willie Chalmers (3), Isa Chalmers (1), Paul Chalmers (13), John Chalmers (11), Annie Chalmers (9), Jean Chalmers (7), Margaret Chalmers (5), Nell Chalmers (3), Nan Chalmers (?), Willie Reid (10), George Reid (7), Elizabeth Reid (5), Matthew Reid (3), James Reid (1), Margaret

Rowan (13), Grace Rowan (11), George Rowan (9), John Rowan (6), Adam Rowan (3), Marion Halliday (13), James Halliday (8), Matthew Halliday (3), Henry Halliday (1), Willie Jackson (5), Stewart Jackson (3), Robert Jackson (1), Annie Gavin (7), James Gavin (6), Agnes Gavin (5), Margaret Gavin (3), Marion Gavin (1), Margaret Rodgers (15), Thomas Rodgers (13), John Gray (1), Jean Shedden and Willie Shedden.

Kind and generous folk

Readers will appreciate that the children of entire families were members of the Sunday School and parents saw to it that their children did attend. My father had to give up teaching the Sunday School in 1928; and the good folks of the Beoch, to show their appreciation, gifted him a 'Dennistoun' gold pocket watch, and they gave my mother a silver-mounted umbrella. They were kind and generous people and this was wonderful when you consider that they were very poor themselves. After this my father continued to serve in the Lamloch Church Sunday School in Dalmellington until his death in 1932, which came after a short illness.

Beoch hospitality

The Beoch folk were always famous for their hospitality and friendliness. They used to have some grand nights, especially at the

The tip of the spoil bing at Beoch mine, closed in 1968, shows that work on clearing the site was well underway. It was located on the north side of the Dalmellington – New Cumnock Road some 5 miles from Dalmellington. The sinking of Beoch No. 3 began in 1866 and the houses would have been erected sometime thereafter. Beoch No. 4 was sunk in 1937 and closed in 1968.

The Wren's Nest in the foreground and in the distance is a row of cottages at Pennyvenie called Sighthill. These houses were generally occupied by higher ranking members of the workforce at Pennyvenie Colliery such as managers and oversmen. You can see the rake of coal wagons and the Pennyvenie Farm behind Sighthill. The farm was demolished to make way for opencast working and later re-established on the opposite side of the B741.

ferm (farm) dances. James Paulin used to play the fiddle at these dances. Nancy Smith and Rab Smith played the piano, and fiddle too. Auld Willie Riggins, a real worthy, used to teach the young ones how to dance and took them through each routine. Willie was a fine old man, one whom I highly respected. Tragedy struck in his family twice with two of his sons, Walter and John, both killed in mining accidents. And yet he still had a wonderfully positive outlook, always wishing to be helpful to others.

The schoolmistresses and teachers that come to mind from Beoch, where there was a small school, were Miss Eaglesham, Mistress, and she was a sort of mother to the whole community. Then there was Miss Nicholson, Mrs Keillor, Miss Irwin, Miss Dickson and Mrs Park, who served at different times at Beoch School.

Walking to church

I used to hear my father tell the story of old John Smith, farmer at Beoch Farm, which was very near to the Beoch row. He was a keen Free Churchman, and each Sunday morning he would leave for the church in Dalmellington wearing his working boots, and his fine boots would be slung over his shoulder.

When he came to what was called the Collier Row, later Camlarg Cottages, just past Pennyvenie, he would call in at old Mrs Currie's house, change into his fine boots and continue his journey to the church in Dalmellington. On his return from the service of worship, he would call again and have a meal with Mrs Currie, change into his old boots and continue walking all the way back to Beoch Farm.

Beoch also had its share of pigeon fanciers and names such as Chalmers, Curragh and Findlay come to mind. It also had its share of keen fishermen and those who were prominent included Rowan, Black and Holland to mention but a few.

Beoch families

The folk of Beoch who were household names in my time included Chalmers, Curragh, Carruthers, Paulin, Riggans, Wilson, Findlay, Anderson, Jess, Black, Rowan, Gavin, Halliday, Rodgers, Givens, Reid, Shedden, Hallers, McLarty, not forgetting the Smiths of Beoch Farm. If I hear mention of any of these names, it brings back happy memories of Beoch.

My wife and I kept friendly with the Rodgers family. Mary (Mrs Duncan) lived at Skerrington, Cumnock. Grace (Mrs McCallum) lived in Ayr. Margaret (Mrs Paton) lived in Bexley Heath, Kent and she died in 1962. Tom Rodgers lived in Broadstairs, Kent. This just shows how folk from the Beoch moved to a variety of different places, but every one of them held a special place in their heart for that small isolated community.

My wife, son Edward and his wife and myself have been down to Margaret's on holidays. On one of our visits Margaret got on to talk about the happy days at Beoch and Pennyvenie. Margaret was a frequent visitor to our house in Pennyvenie and she was just like one of

Tom, Jimmy and Willie Reid, all brothers, who lived at Beoch and were local miners. Jimmy and Willie cycled to Dalmellington High Grade School provided by the education authority. The Reid family lived at Beoch from 1930 until 1938 when they moved to Gateside Street, Dalmellington. All three brother have now passed on. (Photo: Donald L Reid)

the family. Margaret veered the conversation round to the Sunday School at Beoch.

Soon we were wandering way down memory's lane,
For there we were engrossed 'twas very plain.
With a proud, and somewhat sentimental rule,
We talked of nought, but Beoch Sunday School.
Of how the classroom always rang,
With the choruses, the children sang.
Or the soirees, when they used to say,
Their pieces are always bright, and gay,
And of the trips they used to have,
And run the races for a laugh,
And oft my father's views were sought,
For he was the Superintendent of the lot.

Andrew K Bone

Those privileged to live at Beoch will, I am certain, retain very happy memories of this lonely place on the wild lonely moors towered over by Benbeoch Craig because it was very special. It was home.

Craigmark, Benquhat and Burnfoothill,
All give my heart a glorious thrill,
While memories cloud my eyes until
I scarce can see Dalmellington.

Hills over hills like waves arise
Beneath these health-inspiring skies.
God bless this earthly paradise –
My own, my dear Dalmellington.

Dalmellington
Matthew Anderson

Chapter 11

Beoch – A Caring Community

Tom Reid

The tender thrill, the pitying tear,
The generous purpose, nobly dear,
The gentle look that rage disarms –
These are all immortal charms.

My Peggy's Charms
Robert Burns

Tom Reid of Beoch, Dalmellington and Barnsley recalls mining days and life at Beoch. (Photo: Reid family)

Tom Reid was eighty-four years of age in 2004 when this interview was carried out. He was the eldest son of Tommy and Catherine Reid who in later years lived in Gateside Street, Dalmellington. The other family members were John (Jock), Jimmy, Bill, Margaret, Donald and Cathy. Tom was born in Tarbolton in 1920. When he was about nine years of age the family moved near to Dailly to what was a row of very basic miners' cottages known simply as the Rumily, no longer in existence. His father, Tommy, worked in Blairquhan Colliery at this time.

Again in pursuit of work, the family moved from Dailly to Beoch, located on the Dalmellington–Cumnock Road (B741), some 5 miles from Dalmellington. After working for a few years at the Beoch Mine after his schooling, Tom married Clarice in 1948 and moved to Barnsley. His only daughter, Moira, is married and lives in Goole with her husband, Mike, and children, Kerstin and Keely. Tom spent the major part of his working life at Barnsley Main Colliery until it closed in 1966. Thereafter he worked at ICI Chemicals in Huddersfield, retiring in 1983. Tom was very artistic and enjoyed painting and drawing, and he often thought back to happy family days at Beoch – a great wee place.

Fortunately, Tom had many vivid memories of his years at Beoch and many of these are highlighted in the following extract from the interview. He painted a wonderful picture of the way life was at Beoch in the 1930s. Tom passed away on 14 February 2008.

Arriving at Beoch

I would be about ten years of age when I came to live at Beoch in 1930. I remember sitting on the back of the lorry with the furniture piled high behind us. My mother and father were in the front with the driver. My mother had my youngest brother, Wee Don, on her lap. I remember that it was a lovely day. What I remember most was coming over the road from Straiton, with long steep hills and the lorry struggling to win the hills.

When we got to the top of the Beoch brae, turning off the Dalmellington–Cumnock Road, I could see the solitary row of houses with the red-top slate roof of the school just beyond down in the valley. I remember that all the lums (chimneys) were reeking, the smoke curling high into the air. The lorry then trundled down the ash-surfaced road, past the coal bing, where men were tipping muck and rubble from the mine, and into Beoch which would be my home for the next eight years. It was just one row of houses with a two-storey building at either end of the row with external wooden steps leading to the top storey.

Moving in

My father, Tommy Reid, got the key to our house from the factor and he removed the wooden shutter from the windows. The neighbours turned out to watch us move in. The men were very neighbourly and offered to help us unload: 'Can we gie ye a haun, Sir?' they asked my father. And soon we were established with the beds set up, a good fire going, kindly neighbours offering broth and bread. 'The wee ones must be starving', was the invitation to a welcome meal, which we gladly accepted. Folk in those days seemed to be genuinely caring and interested in each other.

Blackleading the fireplace

With the place swept out, and a great fire burning and the kettle on the swee, the oil lamp lit and the beds set in their alcoves, we retired snug and happy to sleep on our first night at Beoch, of happy memory. Next day we were scrubbing the floors, putting the valances and the screening curtains around the inset beds and blackleading the fireplace and the ovens, set at both sides of the fire. We all mucked in to help.

Settling in

My father, Tommy, naturally started work immediately at Beoch Mine, because in those days if you didn't work there was no money coming in. He was a skilled machine man, used to all the different types of coal-cutting machines. His work entailed being on nightshift. We settled well at Beoch, getting to know everyone within a few days. The place just felt right for us and we were happy from the outset.

Beoch School

The schoolhouse was quite a modern building of grey painted wood, with a reddish slate tiled roof. It was located about 200 yards from the houses. The teachers of my day, Mrs Park and Miss Taylor, both had their own quarters attached to the school. They came by taxi to Beoch and lived at the schoolhouse till late on Friday then went home for the weekend. Mrs Park, the headmistress, was married to a local man. Her son, George, was about my age and in my class. She had two older daughters, at college, who spent all their free time with her. They were lively sociable girls who greatly added to the social life of the village and were great friends to my mother and others.

Mrs Park took three classes in one classroom (composite classes) while Miss Taylor also took three classes in the other classroom. Mrs Park taught those who were about nine to fourteen years whilst Miss Taylor taught the younger children. Looking back, they really worked wonders with us. It was hands-on education and contact at all time with the parents. I really enjoyed school at Beoch so much and learned a lot.

Local benefactors

In those days many local dignitaries and charitable trusts donated prizes and awarded bursaries to all the local schools. I wish I could remember all their names, but one or two I do recall. Miss Walker of Camlarg House was a benefactor of Beoch School. She gave an annual prize to the best scholar in all grades and toys for every child at Christmas.

The greatest prize was the Gavin Memorial Prize. It was a black japanned watch of real quality. This was gifted each year to the top pupil at Beoch and inscribed to the Dux Medallist. Mr Gavin was connected to Craigengillan Estate at Dalmellington. I wish I could thank the families of these benefactors for the great pleasure their gifts and bequests gave us all, for we really had nothing and these gifts were special to everyone at Beoch.

Summer at Beoch

In the summer holidays we lads and lassies would roam many a mile around Beoch. We would go down to the River Nith where we guddled for trout and bathed in the deeper pools. The Nith begins its journey to the sea on the Solway coast just a mile from our picnic spot. Further downstream was the Pochery, which flowed steeply down from Maneight to join the Nith.

This was a favourite picnic spot for everyone. On nice weekends, and there seemed to be many of these in my boyhood days, families walked over the hill from Beoch and past McLarty's cottage to picnic at the Nith. We were often joined here by folk from the Cumnock area who had travelled to this favourite spot on bicycles and motor bikes. Life just seemed so much simpler in those carefree days.

Sojourn to Benbeoch Craig

We would go out in the morning and not return till dusk. Our parents never worried where we were because they knew we were safe from

Dalmellington men clearing snow on the Dalmellington to Carsphairn Road in 1948 using manual labour only. The snow is some eight feet in depth.

harm other than bruises and bumps. Being hungry on these occasions never worried us. We had only to call at the local farmhouses and the farmer's wife would bring out buckets of buttermilk and piles of scones and cheese and oatcakes. We also made regular sojourns to Benbeoch, simply called the Craig. We would climb up to the cave where, it was said, Paterson and Peden took refuge during the persecution of the Covenanters during what was known as the 'killing times' in the 1680s.

Our water supply

There was a spring of clear water on the Craig below the scree of huge boulders, many bigger than houses. In those days this spring supplied Craigview and Pennyvenie with their drinking water. The Beoch was also supplied by a spring just off the Cumnock Road, 100 yards below the Beoch brae.

Besides fishing and guddling for trout, there was an abundance of rabbits. These were a seasonal addition to our diet along with wild birds' eggs in spring. The ones which were commonly eaten and looked forward to immensely by the folk at Beoch were peewits, stankeys (water hens), grouse and whaup (curlew), and occasionally wild duck.

Sports

When we were not roaming the countryside, there was always some sporting activity going on and we played football just about every night. These games involved both men and boys, the men joining in after coming home from the pit. The girls and women enjoyed skipping and beds (peevers) and many young people today may find this rather strange.

A favourite with everyone was rounders. The whole population turned out for this, including the older folk, grandmothers and grandfathers. There was real community spirit and a willingness by everyone to have good fun and take part. There was always something to do, but it was self-made.

Vans calling

Another aspect of the social life in this remote village was the van men calling with their various wares to sell. Every day, except Sunday, there would be two, three or more van men calling at Beoch. They didn't just come to pay us a passing call. They came for an hour or two. Some in fact came for the whole day. They were all friends. Practically every family had a favoured friend among the van men.

Friday evening was exceptionally busy. This was settling-up day for the grocers, butchers, greengrocers, drapers and bakers, who plied their trade almost always on credit, because money was scarce and the women were always waiting on the weekly pay packet to settle bills. Thinking back, these must have been worrying times for our parents trying to make ends meet, but they must have hidden it well.

On one occasion my father was unable to work for almost a year because he hurt his hand down the mine and had blood poisoning which left him with limited movement. On hard times such as these the traders allowed families to run up bills which families could only partially repay until the breadwinner was fit for work. There seemed to be a genuine compassion towards one another in these times and perhaps it was because it was a very small community and everyone knew the business of the other.

Doctor Lee calls

Bobby Currie was a grocer who owned Craigbank store, New Cumnock. He was a staunch friend to our family, as was Willie Slonimski, who had a small general store in New Cumnock. To these people we owed more than money. Every week, or more often when we needed him, the doctor paid a regular visit. It was essential on the day of the doctor's visit that my mother, Catherine, made a full pot of broth.

Dr Lee was a small lean young man of Chinese extraction. He was a man of good humour and very popular with all his patients. Years later when we had all moved far away, and when I came home to visit the family in Dalmellington, Dr Lee would make his way to visit us and reminisce about the old days at Beoch. He was a lovely man and a doctor of the old school. Many folk of my generation will realise what a special man we had as our doctor and friend.

We also had other people who gave of their time to us at Beoch, which we greatly appreciated. Mr Eddie Bone walked every Sunday from Pennyvenie, almost four miles each way, to hold a Sunday School meeting. And later on, when old Eddie died, this duty was taken on by Dan Wallace, and Dan's son-in-law, John Brown, also from Low Pennyvenie.

The Reverend Ninian Wright

Another man who was very popular, especially with the lads at Beoch, was the Reverend Ninian Wright, at that time Minister at the Kirk o' the Covenant in Dalmellington. He formed a branch of the Scouts at Beoch which we really enjoyed. Scouting was very popular in those days. He spent a great deal of his time on us, besides running the main troop of Scouts in Dalmellington and attending to his many church duties. He had quite a famous brother who was the 'Radio Doctor' for the BBC for many years. Ninian Wright was an impressive, kindly man, who is fondly remembered.

Bus service arrives

The advent of the bus service from New Cumnock to Dalmellington in 1932 was welcomed by the Beoch people. Although it was only one every two hours, it made a tremendous difference to the social life of folk at Beoch. Suddenly we had reasonably easy access to the amenities of Dalmellington such as the picture houses (we had two of them), the pubs and the shops, owned by Italians – the Bertellotti Brothers; and Andersons – both providing supplies of all sorts.

Saturday in Dalmellington

'Callie' Anderson then opened the Merrick Café and Merrick Hall in High Main Street, Dalmellington. This proved to be very popular on Saturday nights with people flocking in from all over the Doon Valley and Cumnock to dance the night away. Many men from New Cumnock were working at the Beoch Mine and the Blackwater which had only recently been opened. Because of this, the late buses back to Beoch and Cumnock were always jam-packed.

A line drawing of North Beoch as remembered by Tom Reid who was a former miner at Beoch and lived there for 8 years. (Donald L Reid collection)

Many of the men were inevitably slightly drunk and in good humour. It is hard for me to describe the happy atmosphere on these late buses, but suffice to say that when I think about it I always smile. There was laughing, singing and some shouting. It had to be experienced.

At the top of the Beoch brae we disembarked, walking down the brae in groups, still laughing and singing; those slightly the worse of drink tailing off to relieve themselves. It was an estimated 1.3 miles from the bus stop down to the village and if it was raining you were totally soaked.

Hunter's Sports

A big occasion for us every year, and indeed all the other pit villages for miles around, was Hunter's Sports, held in Dalmellington. This was a semi-professional event with quite big sums of money to be won. In fact in the five-a-side football competition, teams from Rangers and

Celtic and other professional sides took part. But invariably, the winner of this event was a team consisting of the Scobie brothers and friends, who hailed from Craigmark and Burnton. They were virtually unbeatable, even in their late thirties.

There were also bicycle races, foot races at every distance, as well as weightlifting and highland dancing to entertain the large number of spectators who turned out for this major event. We were especially interested in the tug-of-war as the Beoch Mine team invariably won it. Pipe bands and the Dalmellington Silver Band added greatly to the atmosphere of what was always a very special day.

Wull (William) Hunter, the sponsor of the sports, was a great benefactor to many people in the Dalmellington area. He had been injured in a mining accident at Pennyvenie and with his compensation money he started a bookmaker's business in Dalmellington. Betting was against the law in those days, but many folk enjoyed a bet, especially on the horses, so Wull Hunter prospered.

When we moved to Dalmellington I got to know Wull very well and I believe he was one of the most honest and decent men I ever knew. He occasionally got into hot water with the local police because of the betting laws, but he was a great man for the village and very well thought of by everyone.

Snow

Coming originally from Tarbolton and later Dailly, then moving to Beoch in 1930, we were quite unprepared for the heavy snowfall which we encountered at Beoch. One winter morning we woke up to complete darkness in the back room. When my father opened the back door there was a white solid wall of snow. There had been a blizzard blowing all night and the wind had brought drifts which completely blocked the backside of all the houses, except the larger ones at either end of the row.

Sledging

Every house at Beoch had a sledge. We inherited one which had been left in the coal house by the previous occupants. And over the years we built others, some good and some bad. The good ones invariably had runners of spring steel. The main sources of these were the long suspension springs from perambulators (prams). These were greatly sought after and prized.

The Givens family were experts at building good sledges. They had one long sledge which could take six people and this was very popular with the grown-ups, who also enjoyed sledging, sometimes more so than the children. We had several ready-made sledge runs. The nearby Spring Hill was the most popular, with the run starting some 400 yards above the village, down a gradient of about 1 in 5 using a track, now grassed over, which had been used originally to transport coal tubs down to what we called the 'old line'.

This was an old track which went as far as Dalricket Mill, with a bridge over the River Nith of which only the stone supports remain. At Dalricket Mill attempts had been made to bring locomotives through to the Beoch from the Cumnock direction. Rails had been laid for a considerable distance, but abandoned probably for economic reasons. However, we had great fun, young and old, tobogganing down these slopes.

Foraging for coal

Another very practical use for the sledges was transporting coal. Although concessionary coal was available, it cost 10 shillings (50p) per ton. And for the families who had only one breadwinner, having a ton of coal to pay for was something they could ill afford. And, of course, for those families who had a breadwinner ill or injured and unable to work, it meant having to forage for coal on the bings (coal spoil heaps). In the winter the sledges were ideal for transporting coal from the bings.

There would always be four or five people on the bing in the evenings, when the tipping of spoil had finished. On the better days in the spring, summer and autumn, for transporting the sacks full of coal and dross, we had old bicycles. These were constructed from old bicycle frames and wheels found in the dump at the back of what was known to us as the Stable brae. The stables were, of course, long gone.

Families at Beoch

When my family first arrived at Beoch in 1930, there were some nineteen families in residence. Most of their names I can recall, but some were comparative newcomers like us. Some of the older families had moved out to more modern houses mainly at Craigview and Pennyvenie, on the main bus route and closer to Dalmellington.

These families had spent all their lives at the Beoch. And all the menfolk still worked in the Beoch Mine. Families such as Chalmers, I think there were five families of them, two of whom still lived at Beoch at that time. Others I can recall were Findlay, Curragh, Black, Riggans and Jess. Eddie Jess, though much older than I, was a great friend of

John T Maguire known simply as Tam Maguire was well-known in Dalmellington where he operated a garage and taxi business from 1934 until his death in 1967. He owned the garage at Burnside and in 1957 built and operated the Ayr Road garage. Here Tam is seen with his Austin taxi. He also operated the ambulance in Dalmellington for many years and it was a standing joke that he took local people to be married in his taxi and later took them to the maternity hospital in the ambulance.
(Photo: Courtesy of Kennedy Ferguson)

mine. He was a qualified masseur, having studied for this in the evenings after work. From Eddie Jess I picked up his great appreciation of music. The great tenor of the day was Enrico Caruso. As we worked together he would hum or sing the arias from the operas and other orchestral works of great composers. There were many men with wonderful talents at Beoch.

Gramophone music

Every family at Beoch had a gramophone. Now, you have to understand that Beoch had no electricity, so these were powered by clockwork mechanism. You had to wind the motor up by means of a handle. Popular songs of the day were mainly from the music halls, Irish songs and of course Scottish songs. A great favourite was Arthur Tracy and among the popular songs I still remember were 'Alice Blue Gown', 'Oh I Wonder, Yes I Wonder', 'Silver Threads Among the Gold' and 'I'm Only a Strolling Vagabond'.

And of course there were the wonderful waltz songs sung by the great Richard Tauber. Jack Buchanan was also very popular, with songs such as 'Goodnight Vienna'. Another great favourite was Frank Crumit with 'Abdul Abulbul Amir' and 'Granny's Armchair'. In these days people sang in the home, in the shops and at work. It was wonderful and so natural. Folk in those days seemed to be happier and less self-conscious.

Radios

Radios at that time were few and far between. My father, Tommy Reid, had been a radio enthusiast from the early days. He bought a radio kit advertised in the *Radio Times* magazine. It was a Mullard make with two valves with a black metal case. It could be constructed without the use of solder. There was one instruction on the manual which read: 'Do not omit the spacers.' It puzzled us. What does omit mean? It was a word we had never encountered before. We often laughed about it later. Luckily we hadn't omitted them. The kit cost £2 10s. And in due course almost everyone eventually had one, because it allowed us access to the world news, although the quality was very poor.

Pocket money

Soon I would be working and earning money. My father had promised I would get half-a-crown (2s. 6d.) pocket money when I started working. Up to this I earned 3d. a week from Mrs Stewart for fetching her butter from Maneight Farm, about 1 mile over the hills from Beoch. I also got 3d. a week from Andy Rodgers for feeding his ducks.

More families at Beoch
Among the families at Beoch during our later years there were McArthur, O'Neil, Stewart, Rodgers, Givens, Gavin, Carruthers, Halbert, Reid (our family), Paxton, Halliday, Rowan, Chalmers (James), Chalmers (William) and Clark. Then shortly afterwards, came families of McCabe, Prasher and Standring. A family who could also be included was McLarty, who lived just over the hill in the Shepherd's house near the Nith. Their children attended Beoch School, as did other children from nearby farms. Amazingly, these families had between them some seventy offsprings. There would also be lodgers, usually relatives, living with many of the families, as was common in those days. When you include the parents there would be around 140 people living in twenty houses at Beoch. Our family, at a later date at Beoch, had my uncles Archie and Johnnie Lees to live with us when my grandfather Lees died. They lived with my mother and father for the rest of their lives and moved with the family to Gateside Street, Dalmellington in 1938.

School to Beoch Mine
I left school in 1934 at the beginning of the summer holiday and started work at Beoch Mine almost straight away. My best friends, Jim Halliday (who later was lost at sea in 1940 when the ship he was on, HMS *Esk*, went down with all hands), Colin McArthur (who pulled me out of the River Doon when I fell in up Ness Glen, when I was drowning), Peter Halbert and others of my age, were all working at what we called 'the platform'. This was so named because the coal tubs coming up from the mine came onto a flat section. The tubs, in fours, had a device called a 'smallman clip' which fastened on to the haulage rope. These clips had to be changed from the front of the tubs and put on the rear, because at the end of the platform the haulage ropeway started dropping down again on its way to Pennyvenie No. 4 (known locally as the Big Mine), where it went into wagons.

Tipping at the bing
At the platform there was also the blacksmith's shop, and a hut where we had our 'snap' (something to eat). Another job we had was disengaging the tubs of pit waste, stones, rocks and other debris, which had to be tipped on the bing which ran straight out on to a steep hillside. At that time it went out about 600 yards and had a height at its end of over 100 feet.

It was great working in the summer, earning money and building up our stamina, because the work was hard. The clips were tedious and tiring at first, but this was greatly alleviated by our contact with our fellow workers. In breaks we would help the men who tipped the muck tubs, and help the blacksmiths by pumping the bellows or doing general work about the shop. The roadman, a cheerful chap, muscular and strong, was called Joe Rollo. He had been in the USA, as had the blacksmith, Willie Dempsey. We loved listening to their tales of the Depression in America where, for a time, they had been hobos (tramps).

Wages
Though as young workers we were earning, it wasn't a great deal. My wage was one shilling and eleven pence halfpenny per day. For six days I took home ten shillings and ninepence including stoppages (deductions from wages). Working on the platform in the winter was vastly different. The platform was so exposed to the elements. During periods of heavy frost the haulage cable, a one-inch steel rope, had to be kept moving, so the tubs had to be run off or held unclipped.

Big fires were kept burning to keep the clips warm and frost free. The empty tubs, sent up along the line from Pennyvenie, had to be held at the platform and the wheels locked or snubbed with iron or wood lockers. On one particular morning my father came in off nightshift. A gale was blowing, with ice-laden rain driven almost horizontally. He said to my mother: 'Don't get Tam up this morning. It's not fit for man or beast out there!' I was awake listening in my warm bed, thinking about the poor devils who had to go out.

Up for work
But at 8 o'clock there was a thumping at the door and at the front window. My mother opened the door. It was 'Knoxy' Bone, the pit gaffer, and he said to Mother: 'What's up wae Tam? Get him out now.' And, of course, I had to go. Some other lads from further afield had failed to turn up. They lived as far apart as Waterside and Craigmark. Their mothers no doubt had the same idea as mine had. And all for one and eleven and a halfpenny! That particular morning it was all hands on deck. The blacksmith and his striker, David Gemmell, had been co-opted with Joe Rollo to keep the tubs going. The coal had to be moved at all costs.

Down the mine
We had just over a year of working on the platform when a new set of

lads left school. They came not only from Beoch, but from as far away as Patna, Waterside, Dalmellington and Craigmark. And so it was our turn to go down the mine. We got half a crown a day underground. Big money! Incidentally, the wages of the adult surface worker at this time were six shillings and threepence a day.

On my first day down the Beoch Mine I was quite apprehensive. Although I had played around the pits for years and I had walked quite a distance into the mine at Clawfin, at least as far as natural light would allow, I had never been down a mine. So, my first day down the mine was interesting. I went with men I knew well, down through the two steel doors into the back airway. It took at least two of us to open the door and go through into the return airway. When we were all in and the door had clanged shut behind us, we had to open a second door and go through this.

Roaring fan

There was a roaring noise from the great fan which blows air into the roadways. Looking up at the giant fan through the protective mesh grill, one could see daylight through the massive blades sucking air from all parts of the mine. The sound was really deafening. There was a strong draught of hot air on our faces. We had to walk bent over. My feet were in a ditch created by water running into the mine. On my right side were 6-inch-diameter pipes taking pump water from the lower part of the mine to the surface for disposal.

The mine bottom

I was glad when we got to the mine bottom because I could stand up again under 8-foot arch girders. There was a great hustle and bustle at the mine bottom. The main haulage from the underground workings was at right angles to the haulage taking the coal tubs out to the surface and bringing the empties back. Because of this all the tubs had to be slewed on a large metal plate before being clipped on to the main haulage. The same applied to the empties coming in. I was set on assisting this operation. After a year at this as well as other jobs on transporting closer to the coal faces, I eventually got a job with a collier as one of his two 'drawers' or trammers. This involved filling tubs and fetching them to haulage pick-up points.

Talented miners

In the mines it was surprising just how many well-cultured and knowledgeable people you worked with. One such was Jock McKenzie. He travelled every day from Waterside to work. He was an accomplished artist and sculptor. He was able to sculpt the most beautiful figures in anthracite. Besides this, he made musical instruments such as violins and banjos as a hobby.

I also met mathematicians like old Duncan Gray from New Cumnock, who taught me the basics permutations. Football pools were very popular then. Others who worked with me in the mine were members of brass bands and pipe bands and very skilled in these pursuits. There were many very kindly and talented men in the mines.

Co-op dividend

With being in work, my friends and I would go to Bertellotti's café in Dalmellington on a Saturday night and blow half-a-crown. Well not all! We saved a bit for the pit holidays at Glasgow Fair time. Holidays were not paid in those days. They were just days off. People depended on the Co-op dividends. Of course, families bought just about everything from the Co-op, so if you had a big family, you got a large dividend at the end of the quarter. This was a godsend for most folk in the Doon Valley at holiday times.

Cycle touring

A good touring bicycle cost £4 19s 6d and getting this gave us great freedom. At weekends we toured far and wide. A Sunday run would be to places like Dumfries, Castle Douglas, Barrhill or Girvan. We would go cycle touring during the summer holidays. We would be laden with tents, primus stoves, kettles, pans and blankets as well as spare clothing. We went to Rothesay one year and camped on Canada Hill overlooking Rothesay bay.

Another year we went to Maryport in Cumbria when it rained all week and we had to sleep in a farmer's barn. We usually saved about 30 shillings for the holidays, which was quite sufficient. In fact one year we went to Portobello and I had enough left to buy a few presents for the family. My cycling pals on holiday were Jim Halliday, Colin McArthur and Peter Halbert.

When we went down the Nith or roaming elsewhere near Beoch, practically all the lads of the village went with us. Danny Standring, younger than we were, was a 'slowcoach' and we always had to wait for him to catch up. But we had wonderful times and looking back we were so happy and fortunate being so close to nature.

Home Guard

Years later, during the war, there were a great number of troops around

Dalmellington, engaged in exercises prior to invading North Africa. I was in the Home Guard involved in some of the exercises. We were pursuing some soldiers concealed at the side of the road. One of them shouted to us. It was Dan Standring. He came to the house later to reminisce about the happy days he and his family had spent in the Beoch. Betty, his sister, came after the war from her home in Canada to see us. Other old neighbours also came to visit us when we moved to Gateside Street in Dalmellington. That was the sort of friendships that developed at Beoch.

Leaving Beoch in 1938

When we got to know that we would have to leave the Beoch, this was in 1938, we were all unhappy. I was eighteen years of age and very much a working man by then. We had been such a close-knit little community, in the real sense of the word. Caring and sharing in a very genuine and non-judgemental way. We were to move to much better houses in Dalmellington with hot water laid on and a flushing toilet. We had none of these at Beoch. However, had we been given the choice we would have remained where we were. Well anyway that's how I felt at the time, but I suppose it was inevitable that it had to end.

Looking back

But we would return to the Beoch again and again many years later to reminisce and remember those days, when we hadn't much in terms of possessions, but so much in terms of real friendship and freedom to roam. Years later I'd take my mother and father down to where the houses used to be at Beoch. All that remained were the foundations and the old school toilet block where the farmer at Beoch later used to store materials. All the stones and bricks had gone, but vivid memories of the past remained with us. And we would wander up and down roughly measuring and saying: 'This is where our house must have been. Mrs Chalmers lived up there', and so on.

Precious memories

Wonderful memories came flooding back of special folk and happy boyhood days. My mother would say touchingly: 'I loved this place', and I would notice a tear in her eye. She would no doubt be thinking of the year when my father was unable to work and the family of seven (and later nine when uncles Archie and Johnnie came to live with us at Beoch) all had to survive on 26 shillings a week.

My mother helped to earn more by taking in washing. There were several of the larger families at Beoch who were glad of my mother taking in washing to help them in that way. She would get between 5 shillings and 10 shillings a week. It was 10 shillings for a big washing and half of that for a smaller one. And there was no condescension in this. It was simply 'neebor' helping 'neebor'. Despite these hard times my mother really did love her years at Beoch, because all her family were around her and family was everything to her.

A happy place

I don't think the Beoch was unique in being a happy place to live in, despite the lack of basic amenities. But everyone there was in exactly the same boat and perhaps that was one reason for us being happy – content with our lot – with what was, in retrospect, a very basic existence by today's standards. But everyone was on the same level.

From what I hear from other people who lived in similar small mining villages in the Doon Valley at that time, they all look back to happy memories of growing up. We had what doesn't exist today – and that was a freedom to roam without restriction – in perfect safety. We had a trust in our fellow man and a simple lifestyle which younger folk of today couldn't even begin to understand. The villagers were hardy, down-to-earth folk with great compassion and practical kindness. I am very proud to say that I was one of the folk privileged to live at Beoch and work at Beoch Mine.

Farewell my friends true and leal,
Where'er we stay or restless roam
True-born hearts shall ever feel
We'll always call Beoch home.

Tom Reid

Chapter 12

Reflections on Beoch

James L Reid

When shall I see that honor'd land,
That winding stream I love so dear?
Must wayward Fortune's adverse hand
For ever – ever keep me here?

The Banks of Nith
Robert Burns

James L Reid spent forty-two years of his life working in the coal mines of Ayrshire, including Beoch, Pennyvenie and finally Killoch, rising to become an oversman and deputy manager. He was married for fifty-four years to Mary Hose and they had a daughter, Anne, and sons, Donald, Jim and Hugh; grandchildren Fraser, Mark, Samantha, Elaine, Christie and Shannon; and great-grandchildren, Charlie, Taylor, Owen, Emmy and Amber.

Jimmy was an elder at the Kirk o' the Covenant (now Dalmellington Parish Church) serving as treasurer under three different ministers, beginning with the Reverend John Morton. He was also treasurer of Dalmellington Bowling Club for many years. A keen trout and salmon fisherman, he really enjoyed fly fishing which he saw as a great escape from working in the coal mines. At the time of this interview (2012) Jimmy was aged eighty-eight and living in Dalmellington Care Centre. He passed on 4 November 2013 aged 90.

Looking back

Looking back on life and seeing what progress has been made in your family, work and social life can be an enriching experience. As we all travel through life there is a tendency to become so embroiled in the day-to-day business of living that we sometimes fail to appreciate the value of taking time to reflect on the many and varied experiences which have led us to where we are today and hopefully to see what is really important about life. For me what has been of the essence of my life journey was my wife, Mary and my family and my work in the coal mines.

In my own boyhood days at Beoch, there was only a wireless (radio) to learn about what was happening elsewhere in the world because it was so remote. Reading in the evening was difficult because the only light we had was from a smelly paraffin lamp.

Entertainment and play were self-made. And yet as I think back I did have a very happy time in this remote community situated just over a mile from the B741 Dalmellington to New Cumnock Road. I often marvel at how life has changed so much from the 1930s until today.

In writing this short note of my memories, I can honestly say I have thoroughly enjoyed the journey down the road of my boyhood days and seeing again in my mind's eye the folk who made my own days of youth so interesting. I hope those who shared similar experiences in close-knit communities like the Beoch will enjoy these brief reflections.

Where I was born

I was born the third son of Thomas and Catherine Reid (née Lees) in James Street, Tarbolton on 12 October 1923. It was a row of old dilapidated houses known locally as 'Snail Row'. When I was about five years of age we moved to Westport, Tarbolton. My father worked at nearby Tofts Pit at that time.

Moving to Dailly

I started my schooling at Tarbolton and attended primary school for about one year before our family moved to a small village near Dailly and close to the Maxwell Colliery. This small community was known as the Rumily and although we lived very near to Maxwell Colliery, my father actually worked as a borer at Killochan Pit about three miles away.

Following the long and bitter miners' strike of 1926 most collieries in Ayrshire were on two, three or four days of work per week, hence the reason why there was much movement of miners around Ayrshire in order to get the most beneficial conditions to support their families, so it was the practice for mining families to move about for the best jobs. While we lived at the Rumily I attended Wallacetoun School for about one year. This school, now closed, was approximately two miles from our house, which meant that at the tender age of six or seven years I had to walk four miles each day.

North Beoch

Some time during the early 1930s we flitted (moved house) to a remote village called North Beoch or simply Beoch. The reason for the move was because my father was more or less guaranteed a full week's work at Beoch Mine, which was situated less than a mile from the rows where the miners and their families lived. The community consisted of twenty houses and was situated some 4 miles north-east of Dalmellington on the B741 road and some 2 miles westwards off this road along a rough track. The village consisted of a double-storey block with an open stairway at either end of the row with sixteen single-storey houses between.

My family

When we came to Beoch our family consisted of my father Thomas, my mother Catherine, older brothers Tom and John, myself, Willie, and Donald was the baby. During our years at Beoch my sisters Margaret and Catherine were born. My mother's brother, Uncle Donald Lees, came to live with us because there was no work for him at Tarbolton and he stayed with us and worked at Beoch Mine. Uncle Donald as a young man in his twenties sustained a football injury to his leg which turned poisonous and he died. After that Uncle John and Uncle Archie, also of Tarbolton, got work at Beoch Mine and came to live with us. In fact they spent the rest of their lives with the family, moving to Dalmellington with us around 1938.

Our house

The houses at Beoch were all room-and-kitchen with two set-in beds in the kitchen and two beds in the room. Jutting out at the front of each single-storey house was the scullery which had a cold water tap and sink. Our furniture consisted of a dresser, a table, four chairs in the kitchen, two chests of drawers and two chairs in the room. There was also a cupboard in the scullery.

The lighting in the house was by paraffin lamp and also by the use of candles. There was no electricity. There was a large open fireplace with a side oven. Over the fire there was what was termed a swee, which could be swung in over the fire for baking purposes or boiling the kettle. The swee had a number of chain links which could be used to raise or lower cooking pots over the fire as required. At the front of the fire there was always a fender and wooden footstool. The fender was made of steel and was always gleaming bright due to liberal application of Brasso rubbed in with emery paper.

James L Reid, father of the author, Donald L Reid, who fondly remembers his boyhood days at Beoch, but wasn't overjoyed at cycling three miles each way to attend Dalmellington Higher Grade School in the 1930s in all weather conditions. The bicycle was supplied by the education authority. (Photo: Donald L Reid)

A dirt road ran the full length of the row in front of the sculleries and on the opposite side of the road there were coal houses plus two blocks of four wash houses. The women of the Beoch took turns at using the wash houses and it was normal practice to ensure that the large boiler was always full of hot water to provide washing facilities for the miners returning from work at the nearby mine.

The midden

Needless to say, the sanitary arrangements were extremely primitive. There were three large middens measuring approximately 12 by 6 by 3 feet into which all forms of rubbish were dumped. In those days (the 1930s) we usually had a considerable period of warm summer weather, so you can just imagine how convenient three middens were in providing a perfect breeding ground for all sorts of bugs.

It was little wonder that one year we had an epidemic of scarlet fever and diphtheria which affected every family to some degree. Periodically, Jimmy Bell came with a horse and cart to empty the middens and the contents were taken away and spread on fields around Pennyvenie.

Snowed in

Although we normally had good summers, we also had severe winter weather with considerable falls of snow which nearly always resulted

in heavy drifting. I can remember a number of winters when Beoch was cut off by deep drifts and no form of transport could get through. Villagers had to trudge through the heavy drits to Dalmellington and carry essential foodstuffs back and that was a long and tortuous walk, even in good conditions, but must have been grim in such poor weather.

In the 1930s, Beoch Mine employed a good number of men from the New Cumnock area and it was not unusual for these men to be marooned at the pithead until the road was cleared by manual labour and a bus got through to take them home. The villagers, although they did not have an excess of bread, cheese and other basic foods, always managed to supply food to the stranded men.

Beoch village school

The village school at Beoch had two classrooms with three or four grades in each room. These would be called composite classes today. There were two teachers at the school in my time. Mrs Park took the older pupils and Miss Taylor taught the younger children. The standard of teaching was very good because I don't know anyone from Beoch School who did not receive a good grounding in the three Rs, unlike

Beoch Colliery which was located about 1 mile west of the Dalmellington – Cumnock Road (B741) some 5 miles from Dalmellington. It closed in 1968 when most of the workforce were transferred to Pennyvenie.

Beoch rows, also known as North Beoch, was very remote and built to accommodate miners working at nearby Beoch mine. The sinking of Beoch No. 3 began in 1866 and the houses would have been erected sometime thereafter. Beoch No. 4 was sunk in 1937 and closed in 1968. In 1948 No 4 was producing 330 tons per day, 90,000 tons per annum with a workforce of 169 miners. Beoch rows were abandoned around 1938 when most residents had moved to Dalmellington.

today's education system where we have a large number of pupils leaving school unable to adequately read, write or count.

I spent a very happy three or four years at Beoch School, where I found the three Rs easy to comprehend. I would dearly have liked to remain at Beoch School, but Mrs Park decided my education would be more complete if I went to the Higher Grade School in Dalmellington. In hindsight I don't think either Mrs Park or my parents thought about the difficulties of getting me from Beoch to Dalmellington in order to be there when the bell was rung at 9 a.m.

Getting to Dalmellington

In those days there was no such thing as transport provided for pupils, regardless of the distance from school. I had to walk the one mile from the village up to the main road and get the first bus into Dalmellington at 9.40 a.m., arriving in class about 10.00 a.m., thus missing one hour of teaching each day. I had to borrow notes from another boy and write them up at home by the light of a paraffin lamp, and sometimes they were long. This very unsatisfactory arrangement, which was in place for my first year at Dalmellington, had, I believe, a very detrimental effect on my education.

After that the Education Authority, in their generous wisdom, provided me with a bicycle in order to get me to school in time to start at 9 a.m. In some of the very bad weather days, I managed to get a lift to Dalmellington from Jimmy Currie, the Co-op van driver, who delivered milk and rolls to Beoch about 8 a.m. He was very kind, because the Co-op policy was strictly that no one should be given lifts.

When I look back at my schooldays I feel certain that if I had been able to have had higher education at Beoch instead of all the difficulties involved in getting to Dalmellington, I would have achieved greater educational qualifications.

I was always happy at Beoch School, where I had all my friends and all the joyful out-of-school adventures, whereas the time spent in cycling to and from Dalmellington plus writing up notes when I was unable to get there on time, proved a real headache and I was never quite happy with that arrangement. Nowadays young folk simply wouldn't understand that a young person would be expected to cycle more than five miles each way, in all weather conditions, to attend school. However, that was the way things were and you simply had to get on with it.

Happy boyhood days

Although the Beoch was pretty isolated and had little or no modern facilities, I look back on my boyhood days spent there as some of the happiest days of my life. In the summer time, the boys went in search of all kinds of birds' eggs, including peesies' (lapwings'), which were plentiful and delicious to eat. We also found whaups (curlew), snipe, golden plover, partridge and a whole host of smaller birds – mavis, blackbird, wren, skylark, chaffinch and sand martin.

Swimming and guddling

We used to swim in the River Nith which was about two miles away over the hill. We had no bathing costumes or towels and we used to

Pennyvenie Pit and baths. Pennyvenie Pit closed in 1978 when most of the miners transferred to Killoch Colliery and Barony.

Beoch School in 1935. It seems strange that a small row of miners houses in a remote area warranted a school of its own. However, it also served the farming community in the district. Beoch was depopulated in 1937/8, families moving to Dalmellington.
Back row (l to r): Thomas Halbert, George McLarty, John Reid, Sam McLarty, Adam Rowan, David McLarty and teacher Miss Pattie Ireland.
Second back row (standing 4): teacher Mrs Park with Malcolm McLarty, Georger Park and Henry Halliday.
Row of seven: Mary Given, Margaret McLarty, Ella Armstong, Betty McArthur, Kathy Armstrong, Matt Halliday and Dan Standring.
2nd front row: Donald Reid, Betty Standring, Bessie McLarty, Betty Stewart, Jean McCabe, Robert Paxton and Jim O'Neill.
Front row: Lewis O'Neill, Fred Standring, Willie Reid, David McLarty, Burney Halbert, John Stewart, Willie Given and James McLarty (Photo: Courtesy of John Reid collection).

race each other back home to Beoch. The Nith and Beoch burns both had runs of salmon and sea trout in the autumn, in those days. I used to catch large sea trout by guddling in the burns. This involved lying on a stone, placing your hands around the large stones in the water, and catching the trout in your bare hands. All the boys enjoyed doing this in my day and you could come away with several good-sized fish that were cooked and greatly enjoyed that same night by all the family.

Sledging

In the winter we had home-made sledges. The runners were made with old pram springs which were conveniently shaped, nicely curved upwards at each end. The drill was to pull the sledge with someone sitting on it until the runners were nice and shining, and then take the sledge to the top of a nearby fairly steep gradient. In our case this was an abandoned railway track bed and there we had a miniature Cresta run. Everyone including the adults enjoyed sledging when the weather was right.

Beoch characters

The Beoch had a number of characters among its residents. There was Lewis McArthur (senior), Jimmy Rowan, Sam Paxton, Tom (Tam) Standring and Andy Rogers. All had their own peculiar idiosyncrasies. Lewis McArthur bore a good resemblance to W C Fields, a film star of that period, and for some reason, which I never understood, he used to get very hot under the collar when some mischief-makers called out 'cuckoo' when he passed.

Jimmy Rowan was a big man, over 6 foot, very fond of a drink, but was said to be afraid of being alone in the dark. Sam Paxton was a small man with very little to say, particularly in the presence of his wife. Tam Standring, although very obviously not flush with cash, liked a tanner double on the horses and a game at cards. Tam seemed to be forever on the cadge. If it was not a cup of sugar, dry tea or a loaf, he would find some other item to borrow from neighbours. Andy Rogers' wife and family left him. I don't know the reason, and thereafter he became more or less a recluse.

Demise of Beoch Row

The villagers of Beoch were all rehoused in council houses in Dalmellington in 1937. My family were allocated a four-apartment house at 3 Gateside Street. What a transformation from our previous home. We now had electric light, hot water tap and flushing indoor toilets. Needless to say, we were all delighted, but there was still a degree of sadness at leaving a place where we could wander freely and had many good friends.

My mother in particular was very sad to leave Beoch, despite having such a good house in Dalmellington. I think Beoch Row was demolished probably around 1938 and all that remained was the old school outdoor toilets which the local farmer later used as a storehouse. Today the area where the row was is covered in spruce trees and the only identifiable area is the old toilet block, marking where Beoch row stood.

Beginning work

I left school at Dalmellington in 1938. I was unemployed for a short time, then for a few months worked as an apprentice cobbler with John Kissell, who had a footwear repair plus cycle shop in Croft Street. This was later to become part of Gibson's garage, now also closed. My first wage was 10 shillings (50p) a week. I didn't enjoy this work and managed to get a job at the pithead at Benbain. I was working there when the Second World War began and I progressed from the surface to working underground with my father.

Pit accident

I remember one incident at the pit, when I was about eighteen years of age. I was working in the pit with my father, Phil Dunn and Hugh McCreath. At that particular time we were working down the pit and the only light we had was the carbide lamps. Five holes had been drilled in the seam, using a hand machine – rickety – and gelignite and strum detonators had been inserted in the bore holes. The strum was ignited in each hole in turn and this had to be done fairly quickly in order to allow time to seek shelter before the first shot exploded.

We counted one, two, three, four, explosions, but there was no fifth. After waiting a considerable time and assuming that the fifth strum had not been lit, we all ventured back into the workplace. Hugh McCreath had just bent down when the shot exploded, sending a shower of coal particles and dust into his face and eyes. As far as I can remember, Hugh lost the sight in one eye and his face was left badly marked for the rest of his days. Following that I worked on my own through nearly all the various categories of conventional mining.

Mining education

When I was twenty-seven years of age and had been married for four years, I rather belatedly decided that there was not a great future in working my guts out for a living at the coal face. So I started attending night classes in Glasgow. I worked hard and got a colliery deputy and shotfirer's certificate and after further study at the Royal College of Science and Technology in Glasgow, gained a Colliery Under-Manager's certificate.

I was shotfirer, deputy and finally oversman for about sixteen years at Beoch Colliery, then ten years as dayshift oversman in Pennyvenie, and my final three years in the coal industry were spent as oversman, covering three different shifts at Killoch Colliery. I was very happy to retire from Killoch in August 1981 and have enjoyed many pleasant years since then. But I can say with much understanding and honesty, and I believe any miner would agree, that forty-two years in the coal mines of Ayrshire was more than enough for any man.

Hard-handed stalwarts of labour,
Nurtured to grin and to bear,
Seldom a thought of the danger
That haunts every corner down there,
Praying to Christ it was shift change
But not in the language of prayer.

Cage Load of Men
Joe Corrie

Chapter 13

Cairntable Capers

Tom Smith

And fare thee weel, my only luve!
And fare thee weel, a while!
And I will come again, my luve,
Tho' it were ten thousand mile!

My Luve is Like a Red, Red Rose
Robert Burns

Tom Smith, a retired miner with an artistic skill as a painter, now lives in Drongan. He was interviewed in March 2012 about his memories of life at Cairntable, another of the lost villages. Cairntable, on the B730 Polnessan to Rankinston road, consisted of two rows – forty-eight houses in all – built a few years before the 1914–18 war. The houses were erected for the miners who worked in 'Barr's' mines and at the old pits near Rankinston.

All the villagers over the years knew each other well. 'Auld' Andrew Lindsay was a miners' representative at the colliery and ran the Sunday School. Elspie Knox's shop at the 'Wee Row' and Bob Deans' at the top of the village served the community well. When children would shout 'shop' as they entered, Bob would say: 'You're making some noise, son – can you no' shout without raisin' your voice?'

With the passage of time only a few will remember Jean Watters, who was always present when there was an illness or trouble in the village. She could prescribe a cure for just about anything from a cold to corns.

Other well-known villagers were Jimmy Colvin, who looked after the village hall; David Wilson, a kind and genuine man, who was headmaster of Kerse School; Geordie Irvine, whom everyone admired for his contented nature. Cairntable as a village is no more. The last tenant had moved out by July 1963 and it was demolished shortly thereafter.

My family

I was born at 4 Cairntable on 13 August 1938. I was the fifth youngest in a family of ten. From the oldest to the youngest, my sisters and brothers were Robert, Andrew, Isa, Margaret, George, myself, Mina, John, Marion and Elizabeth. We lived with our parents, Robert and Charlotte. My sister Margaret stayed in Trabboch with our Gran McDonald. My father was born nearby in Tongue Row, a small clachan located just above Cairntable. My mother died at the age of forty-five shortly after we moved to Drongan in 1951.

Kindly mother

Mother was a kind-hearted body and if there were ever any rows in the house, they were caused by my father as my mother had a lovely nature. She worked very hard to look after my father and my brothers and sisters and her life revolved around the home. She was always cheery and mixed among the other folk in Cairntable. They all went on regular walks along the railway line as I suppose there wasn't really an awful lot else to do in such a small community. Cairntable lies about 2 miles from Polnessan and Rankinston on the B730 road.

My father worked first of all in Littlemill No. 3 and then when No. 5 was opened up he worked there. The pit was located about half a mile from the rows. The miners walked along the railway to get to the pit. He worked as a miner all his days.

Our wee village

Cairntable was a small mining village which consisted of forty-eight houses in two rows. There was a row with twenty and then a gap and another twenty houses above that, and across the road there were another eight houses. The forty houses consisted of one room and kitchen and a small scullery. The row of eight houses, we called it the Wee Row, had two rooms and a kitchen.

Although there was electric lighting in the house, there was none in the street. However, when I was young the County Council installed three street lights to cover the entire village. The first was located at the bottom of the rows near the railway bridge. The second was near to No. 21 at what we called the Middle Corner. The third was situated at the small shop at the top of the village.

Earliest memories

My earliest memories of Cairntable were that we ran about with a gir'n' cleek (gird and cleek – a metal hoop and stick) and my mother used to say jocularly to me: 'Are you going to school this morning on the bus or on your gir'n'cleek. She had a smashing sense of humour. As you can imagine, living in a small house with mother, father and eight children was quite crowded.

There was no indoor toilet, but there was a flushing toilet in an outhouse which was shared with the next-door neighbours. In our case we had John and Sadie Colvin and they only had one son. So, it wasn't all big families, but small families were in the minority.

When I think about it now, it must have been very hard for my father and mother, what with such a big family and with poor wages in the pit. My mother never worked, but her time was taken up to the full in looking after us all.

Living conditions

There was what you call inset beds. The house was what we called a room and kitchen. The kitchen was also the living room. In the kitchen there were two inset beds and in the other room there was one inset bed. We also had a bed settee and I remember that it was myself, Robert and Andrew who slept in that at night. My mother and father slept in the inset bed in the kitchen. The girls, Marion, Mina, Elizabeth and Isa, slept in the living room. It was quite chaotic.

At the back of the rows there were five outhouses with four toilets in each. Each toilet was shared by two families. Mind you, and anyone who lived there will tell you this, they were kept spotless. You simply couldn't leave a mess for someone else to clean. That wasn't acceptable and everyone knew it.

Radio entertainment

My grandmother also lived in Cairntable with us. She was a great knitter and I remember that she loved sitting in front of the fire knitting away furiously and listening to the radio. The programme she liked best was called The Man in Black. There was also Dick Barton and later on the whole family enjoyed the McFlannels, and of course Jimmy Shand and his country band was a real toe-tapper. Later on my grandmother moved to Rankinston to live with my Uncle Andrew and Aunt Mary and this gave us a little more room in our house. There was no television in those days unless you were very rich, and no one had a TV that I was aware of in Cairntable.

Railway halt

There was a railway halt next to the village. This line ran from Holehouse Junction on the Ayr–Dalmellington line and it ran right up to the main Kilmarnock–Dumfries line. As boys we would walk along the line down to Kerse Loch and enjoy swimming and bird nesting. There were always lots of plovers' eggs to be found, but funnily enough you hardly see a plover today.

Tom Smith enjoys looking back to happy days in Cairntable Capers.

Bathing at Kerse Loch

I also remember that in those days the summer weather seemed to be brilliant. Folk today will find this strange, but there were no baths (showers) at Littlemill Pit. My father and the other miners would often come home from the pit in the summer, perhaps off early shift, and get some soap and walk along the railway line to Kerse Loch and go in for a swim and a wash, because they were covered in coal dust from working down the pit. The circumstances in which we lived were just accepted by us, but today's generation would find it outrageous, but that was simply the way things were. There were absolutely no luxuries to speak of.

Home cinema memories

My father was a man who in many ways was ahead of his time. He had a cine-projector and some nights he would invite neighbours into the house. He loved his photography. He would set up a big white sheet and the house was bursting at the seams with folk crowded in as he showed a film to the delight of everyone.

The kids would even be trying to peer in the window to see the film. He was also interested in short-wave radio and he would repair radios for local folk. In fact I still have a reel of his cine film which I had put on video and copied for the family. This is now a great record of our early days at Cairntable. I never tire of looking at this magical video and seeing my parents and brothers and sisters as they were in 1946 as youngsters.

It is especially poignant now that Mum, Dad, George, Andrew and Margaret have all passed away and it seems strange watching them in their younger days as happy-go-lucky kids. The fact that my father had the foresight to make these movies is a wonderful gift to us today and it does bring great joy tinged with sadness. The video is a great record of some aspects of life at Cairntable and helps us to enjoy a journey down memory lane.

I remember when my father bought a sound projector and a big screen. He hired films every week and showed them round the village halls in the district with Dick Nisbet of our village. Dick had a car and took my father to the halls and these were a great attraction for local young folk. He started in Cairntable and then showed these films in Tarbolton, Drongan, Rankinston, Lethanhill and Patna in the 1940s. They went down a bomb.

Gala day

There was annual gala day at Kerse Whinny. This was the hill above Kerse School. Every year this went on and there would be sports and stalls and competitions and everyone from Cairntable, Kerse and elsewhere would be there. It was always eagerly awaited by us and was really a big day for us living in a small village.

Games

Games we played were common such as kick the can, hide and seek, football and running about with our girs. Sliding down the railway embankment on old hessian tattie bags was common in the summer. Bogies, made by my father, were also great fun and on the video taken by him is footage of me going down the hill into the village lying face down on my bogie. A bogie was a wooden frame with four wheels which could be steered and it was great fun for a daredevil youngster.

There was also a playground at the back of the rows with four swings and a roundabout which we played on most days. We would go on walks up Ashentree Glen which was located near to the farm by the same name. We would often go up and spend the day there. We'd make a fire and roast tatties, which were always delicious. I remember that we would catch minnows in the burn and have a competition to see who could catch the most.

Picnics at Kerse

We were often in bare feet as the summers seemed to be so good and the tar would often stick to the soles of our feet. Our parents also took us on picnics along to Kerse Loch and we had great fun playing games. Again my father captured these special moments on film and it's grand to look back at them today. As well as filming our family, he also filmed many of our neighbours. Of course, many of them have also passed on, but the memory of these days is all the more special probably because they are no longer with us.

Village shop

There was a small wooden shop at the top end of the village. In my time it was run by Bob Deans and his wife. This was where the villagers shopped, although the likes of Patna Co-op had a mobile shop which called in. At Deans' shop you could buy bread, cheese and lard. I don't recall my mother going to Ayr for her shopping, but she would go on the bus to Patna Co-op.

Dalmellington Band at Carnegie Hall, Dunfermline, in 1969 when they won the Scottish Brass Band Championships with the test piece *Carnival Romaine*. Hugh Johnstone was the conductor and is a lifelong band member.
Back row (l to r): Donald Tyson, John Tyson, Hugh Uriarte, Tom Paulin, Alex Yates, William Cuthbert, Robert Dunn and Archie Hutchison.
Middle row: Edward Kerr, Robert Boyd, Bert Ritchie, Fred Galloway, David Sturgeon, Lewis Uriarte, Tom Paulin (uncle of other Tom Paulin), Ian Boyle and Willie Hainey.
Front row: William Kennedy, Jim 'Jimsy' McPhail, Robert Dunn, John McCulloch, Hugh Johnstone (conductor), Peter Murray, Jim Graham, Tom Wilson and John 'Jubie' McCulloch.
(Courtesy of Dalmellington Band)

Littlemill Colliery which opened in 1860 and closed in 1974. The twin towers of Killoch Colliery can be seen in the background.
(Photo: Tom Smith collection)

The buses serving Kerse were single-deckers because of the railway bridge at the edge of the village and later on I remember seeing the first double-decker bus, which was quite something for a wee boy. In these days there was very little traffic passing through Cairntable.

Steam loco stranded

I remember about 1947 when it was a very severe winter. A steam engine came along and got stuck in one of the railway cuttings near the rows. I remember all the men in the village and Littlemill Pit going onto the line to help dig out the train. Because of the snow the men had to walk from Cairntable to Patna to get bread to feed their families. So, although the summers seemed to be very good the winters were often dreadful.

Pals of yesteryear

My pals of early days in the rows were John Grant (now of Ayr); Dan Easton, now of Dalrymple; Harry McTimpany, who became a policeman and lives in Ayr; David McCulloch, who died a few years ago; Robert Paterson of Dalrymple; Tom Campbell, his sister Irene Campbell; Janette Callaghan and Maureen McKie. All these folk and their families and many others besides, lived in Cairntable when I was growing up.

Kerse School

We all attended the school at Kerse and went up the hill to school on the SMT bus. The teachers I remember were Miss Hynds, Mr Johnstone and the headmaster was David Wilson. He lived in the headmaster's house next door to the school. Later on he moved to Hollybush School. I remember going to Ayr with the school to see the film *Scott of the Antarctic* in the Gaumont Cinema in High Street. It was great as a boy to see that. We also took part in cross-country running at school.

Leaving Cairntable

My family left the village in 1951 to move to Drongan when I was aged thirteen. I remember being quite sad at having to leave Cairntable, because that was all I had ever known. The house we moved to was at 69 Glencraig Street. At the same time other folk moved in to Drongan from such places as Drumsmudden, Trabboch and Skairs, but most came from Cairntable.

They were starting to run Cairntable down with a view to demolition, because the sewerage system was apparently a major problem. Some of the folk from Cairntable also moved to Dalrymple, some to Patna and some to Polnessan. The village remained intact until the early 1960s with a steadily diminishing population and it was eventually emptied completely about 1963 and then demolished.

Littlemill Colliery showing the winding gear and railway line about 1975 after the pit had closed. The man is Robert (Bert) Smith, who originally hailed from Cairntable and used to show films around the local villages in the 1940s and 1950s. The little boy is Brodie Smith, Robert's grandson. The line was closed at that time.
(Photo: Tom Smith collection)

Littlemill Colliery with Robert (Bert) Smith, his grandson, Brodie and Jimmy Kiers, who was formerly a miners' union rep. They are seated at Littlemill Cilliery shorty after it had closed in 1974 and demolition was already underway. The wheel in the background is a winding wheel from No 5 colliery at Littlemill.
(Photo: Tom Smith collection)

Cairntable, a place of very happy memory, was a lovely little community.

The village was rased in 1963
Now nothing's left today.
If you ever travel on that road,
Don't look for such a place,
For mother nature has returned,
Now it's gone without a trace.

Cairntable
Tom Smith

Chapter 14

Coalface of Life – Home Was a Hut

Bill Bakkom

Then catch the moments as they fly,
And use them as ye ought, man!
Believe me, Happiness is shy,
And come not ay when sought, man!

Here's A Bottle
Robert Burns

Bill Bakkom was born in 1934. He has lived for many years at 3528 Hedalen, Norway. However, his formative years from 1935 until 1946 were spent at Corbie Craigs. Affectionately known as the Corbies, it sits high above Waterside on the 900-foot contour. It was a row of ten miners' houses located precariously on the edge of Dunaskin Glen.

Today the visitor will find that there are still substantial ruins at Corbies, with two trees standing guard over this lonely and deserted clachan. Bill suffered genuine hardship as a youngster and his glimpse of life is revealing and humbling. His son, Leif Erik, has visited Corbies several times over the years to 'touch base' with his family roots. This interview by Donald L Reid is a very moving account of a difficult life for a young lad and the chapter title, Coalface of Life, is very appropriate.

Born Canada

I was born in Fort Frances, Ontario, Canada on 29 June 1934. My father was Gilbert Gudbram Bakkom, who was Norwegian. My mother was Robina McKenzie Reid and she was born in Maybole in 1894. Her father, William Reid, was the only chemist in Maybole at that time. Her mother, Margaret McKenzie or Reid came from the Orkney Islands.

Bill Bakkom as a wee boy in 1946. He was brought up in a wooden hut located adjacent to Corbie Craig rows. His boyhood experiences are illuminating and heart-breaking living for years in a garden hut at Corbie Craigs.
(Photo: Bill Bakkom collection)

Bill Bakkom on a visit to Corbie Craigs with Donald L Reid in 2004, a place which still holds dear memories for him, albeit times were very tough.
(Photo: Donald L Reid)

My family

My mother married my father in 1920 in Canada. He had been in the Canadian army stationed at Kilkerran near Maybole where they met. She went to Canada to marry him. I had five sisters, the oldest was Margaret, then Olga, Thora, Lillian and Amelia. I was the youngest. My mother and father separated in 1935. He drank a lot and didn't treat her very well and I think that was why she cried so much. So, my mother came back from Canada with my sister Thora and me, to live in the Doon Valley.

Hut at the Corbies

Folk will find this intriguing and perhaps even difficult to believe, but mother had a basic garden hut built by the local joiner in Dalmellington and it was sited and erected about 50 yards from the row of ten houses at Corbie Craigs. That's how I came to be there and that was home to my mother, my sister Thora and me for the next eleven years. I suppose you could say that we were living in real poverty.

Meeting my family

My sister Thora, who was about seven years of age, came with my mother from Canada, but the rest of the girls, Margaret, Olga, Lillian and Amelia, remained with my father and they were looked after by a Mrs McLeod. In 1956 I met my sisters Margaret, Lillian, Olga and Amelia for the very first time in Canada.

As you can probably imagine, it was a very moving occasion and there were lots of tears. I think they found it unbelievable that mother, Thora and I had been living in a garden hut on a high hillside above Dalmellington for so many years, because it was indeed tough times at Corbie Craigs. Meeting my sisters was a happy time, but sad because of all the years that were lost to us as a family. I met my father the following year in Fort Frances.

Early memories

One of my earliest memories of Corbie Craigs was starting school at Benwhat in 1939. Benwhat was about 1 mile from Corbies along a rough road. My cousins Neil, Hugh, Willie and Mary Hainey also went to Benwhat School, as well as my sister Thora, who was seven years older than me. I hated school from the start and remember crying and not wanting to go.

As this was the start of the war we were all issued with gas masks which were in a little cardboard box with a string so we could carry it on our shoulders. As I recall I wasn't very popular at school, probably because I was different from everyone else, living in a hut at Corbies.

School at Benwhat

My fellow pupils were poor, but my family was even worse off in every possible way because we lived in a garden hut. I remember that I was regularly picked on by other boys at school and I was desperately unhappy.

We used slates with wood frames at that time for our writing. One good thing, however, was that I got meals at school and to be honest without them I think I would have starved to death. Unlike me, my sister Thora loved school. She was very bright and popular. She won the best school prizes every year. She died in America of cancer some

DOON HARRIERS. 1938-39.

years ago, but throughout her life she had fond memories of Corbies and school at Benwhat, despite living in a wooden hut.

Silent films

Meals in our hut at Corbies tended to be tea, bread, treacle or fried oatmeal. Happier times at school included going to the gym to watch silent Charlie Chaplin films and of course enjoying school lunch. I also loved when we got out of school to collect bags of sphagnum moss or work in the school gardens.

Head lice and injury

I remember that there were a lot of head lice at school and my mother always over-reacted. She would wash my hair with paraffin and use a fine comb for the lice. Perhaps that's why today in my seventies I have so much hair! One time I got my annual pair of tackety boots. I had a hole in my socks and I got an infection in my foot which was really bad. Had it not been for the wonderful Dr Lee in Dalmellington I might have lost my foot.

Winter

I had to walk from Corbies to Benwhat every day, which was fine and healthy and enjoyable. Being located so high up on the hills, the weather could be very harsh. In fact I can remember that the winters

Doon Harriers in season 1938/39 with their distinctive club badge. Robert Reid, a top harrier who went on to run with Birchfield Harriers where he remained all his life, is 4th from left front row.
Back row (l to r): A Hannah, R Filson, A McHattie, J S Hannah, J B Galloway
Middle row: J Wallace, S Sturgeon, W Currie, J Lindsay and Louis Scott.
Front row (runners): A Travers, A Gardiner, D Wightman, Robert Reid, Lewis Uriarte, William McHattie, R Campbell, J Dinwoodie and Eddie Uriarte.

Underground at Pennyvenie Pit in the 1960s showing the dress of the miners and the hutches used to move the coal along the underground workings.
(l to r): John Craig, Sam McLarty, George Sturgeon and Hugh Rogers.

were very severe and on many occasions I was unable to go to school because the roads were covered with heavy drifting snow to a deep level.

Cooking and baking in the hut

My mother cooked all our meals in the hut. We had oatmeal, onions and lard which she cooked for dinner. We had a cup of tea without sugar because it was rationed during the war. She sometimes made treacle scones, which was a great treat. At Christmas it was a clootie dumpling, which was wonderful for us and she would put farthings in it and it was great to find one as you enjoyed eating the dumpling. Simple things were precious when you didn't have a lot, and in our case that was an understatement.

We were very poor indeed. The folk in the rows at Corbie Craigs were also poor, but the difference was they lived in proper stone-built houses. They had cold running water, but no electric light and like us had to use a paraffin lamp, but they did have indoor toilets. In our wooden hut we had absolutely no facilities.

Coal

There was a coal stove which my mother used to cook everything on. There was no lighting except that provided by a paraffin lamp. We often had no coal and I had to try to find wood or go looking for coal in the outcrops in the glen, but this could be a dangerous, risky business because the banking was steep and unstable and a rock fall was always a possibility. But, it had to be done and as a wee boy I always felt a responsibility for my mother and sister.

I also went down to Waterside with my mother on a regular basis to try and find some twigs to fire the stove. I remember that the nuns from Waterside used to visit my mother a lot. I was scared of them, but I think they appreciated our precarious situation.

Prejudice

Strange to think we lived in the only wooden hut on the plateau and because I wasn't Scottish I was treated quite badly by the other young folk in the district. I was often knocked about by other youngsters. During the war we could hear the air-raid sirens going off at Dalmellington and Waterside. From our hill location we could see the German planes flying towards Clydebank. We had identity cards which we had to carry and my mother had ration cards which she gave to the shopkeeper to buy her entitlement of scarce food.

Collecting peat and water

I remember Mr Bell, farmer at nearby Burnhead Farm, located just behind Corbie Craigs. He used to cut peat and I would get some to burn on the stove in our hut. He appreciated that we didn't have much and he probably took pity on us. We had no toilet in the hut where we lived. We only had a toilet pail which was used in the hut, especially during

Andrew Galloway and James McKinstry who were mine driving at Chalmerston in 1939. This was a very dangerous part of mining, the danger of roof falls always lurking in the background. Props had to be securely positioned to ensure safe working and these can be clearly seen.

The lady pictured at the Benwhat War Memorial is Agnes Wilson, (nee Pollock). Known as Granny Wilson and midwife to the many born in Benwhat. The photograph dates from the unveiling of the memorial in 1921. She lost two sons in the war. Their names can be seen over her left shoulder. They were Alexander Wilson and William Wilson. Both were in the Royal Scots Fusiliers. Sitting beside Agnes Wilson are William's children, Margaret and Alexander.
(Photo: Courtesy of Tom Wilson collection)

Benwhat School class of 1949 when the village was quickly being depopulated with most moving to Dalmellington and the new housing scheme at Bellsbank.
Back row (7) l to r: Scott Hannah (Janitor), Mrs Campbell (cook), Andrene Campbell (daughter of Mrs Campbell, cook), Betty Brown (Corbie Craigs), Andrew Armour, Susan McLeish, Thomasina Hill
Second back row (10): John Carruthers, Robert Douglas, John Kennedy, John McLean, John Johnstone, Billy McFadzean, David Rowan, Miss Paterson (teacher) and Mr Jeffries (headmaster).
3rd back row: (10): Marion McCreath, Rebecca Ballantyne, John Buchanan, Flora McCulloch, Nancy Currie, Gertrude Auld, Jean Murphy, Susan Cairns, Mora Murphy and Robert Hearton.
Second front row (11): Elizabeth Wightman, Andrew Currie, Francis Kennedy, John Bennet, Tom Wightman, Alec Armour, Kathleen Moore, Billy Douglas, Gwen Millar, Jean McHattie and May Barbour.
Front row (8): Archie Galloway, Alec Ireland, Cairns, Bobby Galloway, Drew Galloway, Jim Murray, Jim Murphy and Cairns. The three Cairns pupils (one girl and two boys) were only briefly Benwhat residents and their first names are unknown.
(Photo: courtesy of Robert Douglas collection)

the night and was emptied well away from our hut in the morning.

I also had to collect pails with drinking water and my mother would put a cloth over the pail to keep the water clean. The hut consisted of one small room – it was just a small garden hut. My mother and Thora slept in the top of the bed and I slept in the bottom. Mind you, some of the families had ten folk living in a room and kitchen at Corbies, so our situation was by no means unique.

When it was windy, and it was often like that, the whole hut would rattle and shake and in winter when the snow was bad and being driven by the winds, it would actually come through the joints in the hut. Mind you, with the stove on, it was actually quite cosy.

I remember that as a boy I was always hungry. I never had a Christmas present as such, other than an apple or orange. My mother didn't work and she depended on the state to keep us going. We simply accepted our lot, but we were very poor indeed and I often wished I could have done more for Mum and Thora.

Coin find

When I was about eight years of age, I found a lot of coins below a large stone on the ruined walls near to the Rough Burn below Corbies. A man came along and I showed him the coins. He gave me sixpence and took them. Later on I wondered if they had perhaps been valuable Roman coins, but I'll never know. However, I'm sure that the plateau area will have been rich in antiquities still to be discovered.

Family feelings

Looking back, the summers seemed to be much better, but the winters were very bad and the hut was draughty. My mother used to cry every day because she had left her other daughters in Canada. She must have had a broken heart. I missed the fact that I didn't have a father and that hurt me quite a bit. I grew up quite unhappy at times and life seemed to have dealt us a very unhappy hand. Part of my sadness, I suppose, was for my mother, and my sisters who were living in Canada, and I think they would have been feeling the same, being separated from us.

My great pal was Robert McCart, who lived at Corbie Craigs. I sometimes played with William Hainey, who was my cousin. I also played with Jimmy McGowan. We used to run about the hills and roads with a gir'n' cleek. The burn below the Corbies was also a popular place to play. We used to go looking for birds' eggs and we'd spend hours down the Dunaskin Glen.

Moving away

I left Corbie Craigs at the age of twelve in 1946 to go to live at Maidens in a house. I was pleased to be leaving our old hut. It was so claustrophobic to live in and as I got older I found it more and more difficult to put up with it. There was simply no privacy whatsoever. Can you imagine any children of today living as a family in a garden hut on a high hill in the middle of nowhere?

Visits to Corbies

I've returned to Corbie Craigs on several occasions over the years and find it very moving and nostalgic. On reflection I am glad that I lived there and have no lasting regrets now, even though there were some very unhappy times. I believe it gave me a greater understanding of life and people. I survived with very little, but I believe that I appreciated better that small things in life are important and sometimes you simply have to get on with things and make the best of the situation in which you find yourself. There are always folk worse off than you.

Greatest regret

I suppose the greatest regret was being separated from my sisters in Canada and there is still a hurt in me that we were brought up separately in different countries. These are the things that unfortunately happen when there is a breakdown in the family unit. I always felt very sorry for my mother because she was constantly grieving for her girls who were in Canada.

As a wee boy I always wished I could have done something to help her, but it was like a death in the family and she was simply heartbroken for her daughters, probably always wondering how they were and what they were doing. I went to live in Canada in 1956 and travelled by boat from Southampton to Quebec.

Jeanie McCreath at Benwhat War Memorial in 1988. Although she lived in Dalmellington for many years, her heart was always in Benwhat.

Mother's visit to Canada

In 1958 I was delighted to be able to bring my mother across to Canada and she stayed for about two months and saw her daughters and her husband. It was a great joy for her being reunited with the girls and there was a real sparkle in her eye that I'd never seen before. However, my mother and father wouldn't talk to each other and there was still great bitterness in that relationship. My mother returned to Scotland and lived in Maybole where she died in 1972. I don't think she ever quite got over losing her daughters, and you can understand that.

I travelled greatly over the years. I went from Canada to Norway and now at the age of seventy-eight I still sometimes think about returning to live in Ayrshire, but I certainly won't be living at Corbies in a hut! One thing, however, is certain: Corbie Craigs – the place of my early years – will doubtless draw me back to glimpse again my days of youth and to quietly remember my mother, dear Olga and my other sisters and shed a tear of sadness and joy.

A grateful, warm adieu;
I with a much indebted tear
Shall still remember you!

The Farewell
Robert Burns

Chapter 15

Miner's Wife – Miner's Daughter

Jeannie McCreath

I'll act with prudence as far as I'm able,
But if success I must never find,
Then come, Misfortune, I bid thee welcome –
I'll meet thee with an undaunted mind!

Fickle Fortune
Robert Burns

With a good memory of the past, 'Auntie' Jeannie McCreath nee Mowatt, who was born in the village of Patna on 29 May 1920, was a weel-kent and much-loved lady. Donald L Reid is indebted to Alice Wallace, a good friend of 'Auntie Jeannie', for her kind assistance in this 2007 interview. Mrs McCreath passed away on 12 January 2009 at the age of eighty-eight, but will be fondly remembered by everyone, to whom she will always be 'Auntie Jeannie'.

Benwhat years

Memories outlined in this reflection of the past cover the period when I lived in Benwhat, from 1926 to 1951. It was a special wee place and we were all proud of it. I suppose with the passage of time as we all get older and tend to look back on our formative years, places like Benwhat become even more precious. It was located high up on the hills above Dalmellington on a flat plateau with hills to the rear and great views out across the Doon Valley to the Galloway Hills and Loch Doon.

Mind you, the weather could be pretty atrocious because of the open location. But it was a friendly and welcoming wee place. I often think back to those special days and the folk of that era, because I am among the last that actually grew up in Benwhat. We didn't have much compared to nowadays, but everyone was in exactly the same situation and perhaps that made it not so bad. I suppose the young folk of today would be appalled at the living conditions with no proper toilets or baths, but we just accepted that was how things were in those days.

Flitting and Mother's passing

I was born on 29 May 1920 in Patna. I remember flitting to Benwhat when I was five years old. The flitting was by horse and cart and I was perched precariously on top of the furniture as the horse made light work of the track which ran from Burnfoothill along the hill (former railway) line to Benwhat. My family had lived in Patna in the old building near the Doon Brig that was later a shop and most recently was Armour's Funeral Parlour.

My family consisted of my mother and father, brother George who was born when we stayed at Brigend in Patna, and wee sister Mary, who sadly died when she was only eleven months old. More sorrow was to visit our family when my mother died at the age of forty-two when I was just nine years of age. From that time on I had to grow up very quickly as I then took on the role of keeping house for my father. I suppose having to do housework every day after mother's passing really did spoil my childhood years, at least a little.

Earliest memories

Among my earliest and happiest memories was my mother coming to school at 11 a.m. with cocoa and toast and she always wore a shawl around her shoulders. The reason for this was that it could be very cold up on the high moors above the Doon Valley and a shawl kept you very warm.

When my sister Mary was born I remember that she wore a plaid with the wee one (child) tucked inside to keep warm. A plaid was a tartan blanket worn across the back with the baby tucked in at one side. Every woman would use a plaid in these days and in fact it was common right up into the 1960s. The plaid allowed the woman to have one hand free to do chores such as stirring pots as the meal was being prepared.

Father's passing

Further sadness came to my family with the passing of my father. He had been a well-respected man in Benwhat. But he was unable to work due to ill health. His joints were all swollen and very painful with arthritis. He was librarian of the village reading room and secretary of the Soldiers' Comfort Fund. However, he had a long life and died aged eighty-three.

On the move

Our family lived in four different houses at Benwhat – Nos. 1, 27, 31 and 105 – at different times over the years. There were usually some empty houses in the village, so if you fancied a move to a better house, you made application and it was normally granted. There were single and double houses in the rows which had been built to house the miners and their families near where they worked. With no wages coming in because father didn't work, I had to go down to the DSS of those days. This was known locally as 'the Parish' and to avoid the stigma attached to this, I chuckled and told children with me that I was going down to see the doctor.

Family income

The family's income was £1 12s. 6d. from the Parish and 7s. 6d. half-benefit from the Miners' Union, making it £2 for the week. Out of this I had to pay 3s. 6d. rent each week, which included electricity. Bob Burgess from Waterside used to come up to Benwhat on a motor bike with sidecar to collect rent from the villagers, but I was resourceful and worked on ways of making a little more money by doing odd jobs, which helped our family a lot.

Earning extra money

For example, when Nurse Gilmour or Nurse Harvey, the district nurses, came up to deliver home births, I used to help by boiling water and laying everything out for them and cleaning up after the delivery. I took the bedcovers and towels home for washing. This had to be followed up for two weeks because at that time the new mother took to bed for at least ten days, a system which young mothers of today would find strange indeed. For these two weeks of hard work I earned 10 shillings.

To get some extra coal for the living-room fire I would help neighbours by carrying in their load of coal, and for doing this I was given four pails of coals. So, as you can imagine, life was not easy.

I remember Sally Reid (Gray) and myself carrying buckets of coal up the incline from Waterside, which was no easy task. I also helped locals with housework, not just for the money, but because I enjoyed socialising. The welfare of friends and neighbours in Benwhat was important as it was a very close-knit community. The villagers were a hardy and independent lot. They had their own way of thinking and dealing with things with strong determination. They had their own culture which was quite remarkable.

Schooldays

I started and completed my schooling at Benwhat, beginning at age five in 1925 and leaving when aged fourteen in 1934. In 1926 the new school was built in Benwhat. I can remember all the pupils walking from the old school to the new school carrying their books. There were classes in the school for all the children, so there were brothers and sisters of different ages sharing the same class and teacher.

In later years Benwhat School was used only as a primary school and when children were eleven years old they went down to the Higher Grade School at Dalmellington. When the headmaster came up to the village in his car, the children had to stop playing and acknowledge him. The boys had to salute and the girls had to bow. I recall some great teachers.

Miss Hose taught infants. Miss Young, Miss Davidson, Miss Kerr, Miss Paterson and Miss Hill I remember well. The headmaster was Mr Frank Ferguson and later a Mr Jeffries, the last headmaster in the village. As well as covering all subjects at school, they taught recreation and gym. During the 1926 strike the old school building was used as a soup kitchen. The school janitor was Scott Hannah and the cook was Mrs Campbell.

My family

I married Allan McCreath when I was aged twenty in 1940. We were well suited as we both had an easy-going nature and enjoyed a good laugh. Our marriage was very happy and we had three children: Marion, George (also known as Pordy) and John. At present there are five generations in the family – Jeannie, Marion, John, Hugh and Lee. I have twenty-seven grandchildren and great-grandchildren and two great-great-grandchildren.

In 1951 after twenty-six years living very happily in Benwhat, Allan, I and the children moved to Bellsbank when I was aged thirty-one. We were allocated a house in Bradon Avenue and I still live there to this day. (Mrs McCreath passed away in 2009.)

Neighbourliness

I believe that living in Benwhat gave me the ability to cope with difficult times assisted by good friends and neighbours. Everyone living in the village had very little and depended on the wage coming in each week, and that just kept us at a basic level with very little to spare. We were all at the same level with no one better off than the other.

In fact if someone was having visitors they could go to a neighbour and borrow rugs for the floor, crockery and cutlery. That's the way it was. Folk would always rally round to help. I suppose young folk today, trying to understand how we lived, would be aghast at this, but that was the reality of living life with not very much. We did share, and yes we did really care.

If the doctor or ambulance came up to Benwhat, folk would wander up to the row wherever it was to enquire who was ill, what was wrong, in the hope that it wasn't too serious, and genuinely offer help. They would hover about to see if they were needed or how they could help. Life was difficult but everyone was in the same position, with most folk having enough to meet basic needs, but not having any luxuries. The villagers shared tough times and good times and lasting friendships resulted. Aye, these friendships carried on long after we all left Benwhat for Bellsbank.

Looking back

Life revolved around work, eating and sleeping, rather like today, but life was harder then with little opportunity for luxuries such as holidays or modern conveniences in the home. Folk were, however, resilient and created their own entertainment in the village institute or school hall. They were generally concerned and looked out for each other and most of the houses were kept clean and tidy. I was friendly with Sadie Douglas, Ethel Thomson and others of that era and we still enjoy talking about happy times at auld Benwhat.

Women's work

The women didn't have it easy. They had to go outside to the water pump in the street to fill pails of water, whether it was for drinking, cooking, cleaning or washing. White enamel pails were used for the drinking and cooking water and zinc pails for anything else. In the house there was a basin used for washing your body. You stripped off your top and gave yourself a good wash as far as possible, and then you stripped off your bottom half and did the same.

Toilet time

There was a zinc pail for use as a toilet, so you had to hurry to use it just in case someone came in. You see, there were no indoor toilets in Benwhat. Some villagers had built a small outside hut for use as a toilet, but the toilet pail had still to be emptied outside well away from the houses. Holes were dug in which this could be deposited and this was just accepted as a part of daily life. When visitors came and asked where they did the toilet, they would be told: 'From here to Rankinston. Pick a spot.'

Visiting sheep

House doors were left unlocked along the rows. Often folk would leave the door off the latch and it was quite common for a sheep to wander in looking for a tattie (potato). One day I remember leaving my dishes sitting on a card table and a sheep came in, knocked it over and broke all the dishes. This was quite a big loss, because they weren't easily replaced, especially during the war years as you just couldn't get replacements.

Reading room

The reading room, also called the Institute, was two houses knocked together at the end of a row of houses. This was used by villagers for reading books, magazines and newspapers. The men also played cards there and they gambled for small amounts of money.

Winters living at Benwhat

The winters were often hard, with snowfall and drifting making life difficult. I remember the snow drifting to roof level at the back of the rows. The men went out the front door, then round the back to dig a way through to the water pumps. Unemployed men were paid 1 shilling per hour to dig a clear path down the road to Dalmellington rail track where the miners got a pug which took them to the pit. Some went to Beoch and others to Pennyvenie.

If the unemployed refused to go out and clear the snow, they were refused their benefit money. There is a photograph showing heavy snow at Benwhat, which meant that the men were unable to get to the pits and that qualified the miners for a Bevan shift – they were paid for the shift.

Drying clothes

The miners had to walk to their work or to the toll road for a lift on railway wagons in all weathers. Their working clothes were often soaked and they had to be dried, ready for the next shift, and that was a real chore for the women because there was no central heating in those days. All we had was a coal fire in a draughty and damp room-and-kitchen. Young folk today wouldn't even begin to understand what it was like, being so used to central heating and modern facilities.

So, the working clothes would be draped on the winterdykes around the fire. Working trousers were made of moleskins, so they took a long time to dry. They were difficult to wash and patch. Dalmellington Iron Company, later Bairds and Dalmellington, owned the pits and the miners' houses. The pits were mined for ironstone in the early days, but later it was mainly for coal. There were also contractors and sub-contractors at the pits. Some of the children collected the wages on a Friday from Archie Kennedy and took them straight to their mothers.

Mother's passing

I mentioned earlier that my mother had died when I was just nine years of age, so I had to learn to cope with housework very quickly. Mrs Florence Thomson was a great help to me and encouraged me greatly. She was always a welcome visitor to our home. I quickly learned how to make soup and I could always go and see Florence to discuss problems.

The Thomson family consisted of Tom and Florence and they had eight children, namely, Nancy (Mrs McCulloch), Ethel (Mrs John Buchanan), Alex (married Cathy Coburn), Jack (married Jean McVey), Jean (Mrs Andrew Gilmour), Helen (Mrs Robert Knox), Flora (Mrs Robin Heaney) and Ena (Mrs David Aitchison). The strong family friendship continues to this day with me, now eighty-six years of age, and surviving members of the Thomson family.

Meet for tea

After moving from Benwhat to Bellsbank, I would meet with Nancy, Ethel, Jean, Cathy and Lizzie Yates for a blether and tea every Wednesday. Each took their turn to host the others and this still continues after fifty years, which must be something of a record. That was the sort of pull Benwhat had on us all.

Wash days

When washing blankets you had to be sure of a good day, because they were needed on the bed again at night, because there were no spares. Everyone was the same. We only had the basics and no more. The washtub was filled and we had to trample the blankets with our feet. This was actually quite enjoyable and after rinsing and wringing them through the big wooden mangle, it took two of us to shake them out.

Some women didn't even have a mangle, so they had to squeeze and wring them by hand, which wasn't easy. The drying greens were up the back of the rows and the clothes would be hung out to dry. This was quite a heavy job and we had all the other household chores to do as well, but it was nice to have the lovely fresh blankets on the bed at night.

Cooking

The open coal fire was used for cooking and the kettle was always on for something. There was also a Dover stove in the kitchen and a primus stove. Most of the women were quite good at making a guess at the heat and time required when baking. Pancakes and tattie scones were made every week and toast was made at the fire which was simply lovely.

Stone floors

The floors of the houses were stone-flagged, but were easily swept out then scrubbed. Carpets were homemade rag rugs. Stookie was used to clean the floor and front doorstep and it was called a rubbing stone. This came from broken ornaments, often in the form of popular items such as Umbrella Twins and Whistling Boy.

Electricity arrives

The same items were used to fill empty polish tins (peevers) by wee girls when playing at beds. Ash from the fire was good for cleaning the fireplace. Electricity came to Benwhat in 1933 from Waterside Power Station, which was previously built to power the ill-fated Loch Doon School of Aerial Gunnery during the First World War.

However, all that the tenants of Benwhat had was a light socket hanging from the ceiling to give them light. There were no sockets on the walls to plug anything in, simply the one from the ceiling to give light. Mind you, we didn't have electrical items to plug in anyway in those days.

When some women eventually got electric irons, they fitted them in the light socket to do their ironing, but if too many used them at the same time, the power went off. There was a Mrs McFadzean who was electrocuted when connecting her iron to the socket. Before the days of electricity the villagers used carbide or paraffin lamps.

Sports

Wull Hunter the bookmaker was a big man who organised and

Benwhat Store after the old school to its rear had been demolished. This photo is probably taken in the early 1940s. The war memorial erected in 1921 on Benwhat Hill can just be seen.

sponsored a sports day once a year. This was held alternately at Benwhat and Dalmellington. This was a great event for the whole community and the whole town turned out for it. It was the highlight of the year. The Benwhat Silver Band played at it when it was held in Dalmellington and everyone marched down behind them from Benwhat.

At the field there was a table set up showing all the event details and the prizes were displayed. A stage was set up for the highland dancers and Jimmy (Squeakie) Telford played the fiddle for them. Adam McHattie was a good runner in the Benwhat Harriers and he generally won all of the men's races. And Jim Hose mostly won the high jump. Robert Reid was also a really good runner for the Harriers and he often went to Edinburgh to enter a Scottish Championship race and later became a famous runner with Birchfield Harriers. There were some wonderful people who belonged to Benwhat.

I remember when I ran in the races I had to borrow sandshoes from Tom Thomson and it was worthwhile. I remember winning a yellow teapot and a stand. There was usually a fancy dress parade at Hunter's Sports, which Beenie Torbet and Lizzy Kirk helped to organise. In later years, Anna Kirk (Willie Macintosh's wife) and Helen McPhail helped to organise it. The kids loved taking part in fancy dress.

Fight at football

The Heatherbell football team played at Benwhat and whenever there was a home game, Beenie Torbet and Lizzy Kirk would sometimes begin fighting with one another. The men did not interfere and stayed clear as they were probably too scared to get involved. But sometimes things got out of control and there was a free-for-all at the finish. Benwhat did have its moments, you know!

My brother George Mowatt was the secretary of the Doon Harriers. They were really good and they entered events competing against other harriers from all over Ayrshire and often with great success.

Memorable folk

Robert Bryan was a really nice, good-living man, who walked down to Dalmellington Church every Sunday. He was a hard-working pit man, just like the rest. But he was so kind and pleasant-natured. He ran a Sunday School class for the weans of Benwhat. I used to look at him, because he was such an inspirational man, and in my childlike way I would think he was just like God.

Georgina Watson was a Sunday School teacher and she only taught the girls. She was very pretty and was also nice-natured. At Christmas she gave all the girls a small gift. They all received the same, a lovely wee handkerchief folded inside a Christmas card. I thought she was like an angel. The hanky was far too good for me to use.

Sunday School trip

The Sunday School trip was another big event in our lives. Benwhat Silver Band led the way with all the children, mums and dads, grannies and family friends all following behind. We walked down the incline to Waterside to get the train to Ayr and then walked to the Low Green. We had the same walk back on the return journey but it was always worth it.

At Benwhat store, there was a wee area sectioned off and used by fly drinkers. It was called the Borehole. It was just a wee corner with a wooden seat. I acquired this wooden seat in later years and got Joe Wilson to use the wood to make me two lamps. One was a standard and the other a matching table lamp. I used them when I moved to Bellsbank and I still have them to this day. They remind me of Benwhat and I simply treasure them.

The war years and food

In Benwhat most people were healthy. They certainly had good fresh air, clean water and good basic food. The views across the valley on good clear days were simply stunning. During and just after the war years, food was rationed and there was a limited amount per person. Our staple diet was porridge, and home-made soup made with whatever vegetable we could find, and using a bone or a stock cube. Boiling beef was also used for stock and then the meat from that was used for dinner or supper. Nothing was wasted. Tatties and mince was also a staple food.

Poaching for rabbits or fish gave a welcome meal, too. Some folks also kept hens which supplied them and others with eggs, and some villagers had vegetables planted in their gardens, which had to be fenced off due to the sheep wandering about freely. Most of the women were good at baking scones and shortbread, clootie dumplings and pancakes or girdle scones. There was a swee at the open fire which the girdle sat on for making things like girdle scones. The orange juice which you got free from the clinic if you had a baby was mixed with dry milk to make lemon curd.

Santa calls

Georgina Dick, when working in the post office, used to run a Christmas club. Someone had ordered a sewing kit for their little girl and was then unable to pay for it. I, being a wee girl at that time, had asked Santa for a sewing set. My mother managed to acquire one at the post office. I remember getting it on Christmas day; I was simply overwhelmed because I believed in Santa at that time.

Wonderful neighbours

Isa McBride had a big family of her own, but she was a good and generous neighbour. When Sadie Douglas, next door, had a baby, Isa came round to see her. She brought round a cup of tea and a slice of bread and butter. All nicely set on a tray and covered with a nice wee tray cloth. Sadie was so grateful and said that her piece and butter was a real treat. Money can't buy the wonderful feeling when getting something like this, when you had very little. These wee things meant a lot to these people when times were hard.

Benwhatonians

Alan Dick used to breed and sell canaries. His son, Alan, married Janet Robertson. Alan became well known as a very good goalkeeper with Craigmark Burntonians. Some of the women were really good knitters. Bella McKinstry was one of the very best.

Jeanie McCreath whose memories can be found in the chapter: Miner's Wife – Miner's Daughter. This will take the reader back to early days living in remote Benwhat. She enjoyed weekly blethers with good friends, Sadie Douglas (back) and Ethel Thomson. (Photo: McCreath family)

Jim Armour was the founder member of the Benwhat Silver Band. He was the father of well-known Benwhat folk Andy, Richard, Jim, Alec and Mary. Ravie Torbet, brother of Beenie, used to say the water from Campbell's Spoot (well) tasted better when it was in whisky. The water was rooted down from the hills by a pipe that fed Campbell's Spoot and this was lovely fresh water which everyone wanted to drink. In later days, after the demise of the village, when folk went back to visit, there was always a request from someone to fill a bottle of water for them.

Mobile merchants' visit

I remember that Jimmy Hair and Jimmy Hopkins were fruit merchants who came to Benwhat with their lorries to sell their produce. The first time as a wee girl I can remember having an apple and an orange was when I pinched them from Jimmy Hopkins' cart. In later years I remember being at a wedding with Jimmy Hopkins' son and I told him what I had done and I bought him a drink. When I think back to these times I still fondly remember Jimmy, who provided a great service to our community in Benwhat and in later years did the same for the people of Bellsbank, where I moved.

The Relly family lived at No. 66 and had six children; two are still living today, albeit they are well into their eighties. John and his wife Ina (Ferguson) were from Waterside and now live at the Braemar Residential Home, Ayr. They have one son, Murray, who actually owns and runs the Residential Home.

Entertainment

There were several annual events held in Benwhat and these were eagerly awaited and well attended. These included social evenings and the Eastern Star dance every year. Tom Hodgson played accordion and Hugh Gourlay played the drums and they were a popular local band in the Doon Valley. I remember I used to have holes in the soles of my shoes so I had to be careful that nobody could see these when I was dancing. Francie News was another well-known man who played accordion and Tommy Carruthers played drums. There was also Hugh Ferguson from the Hill (Lethanhill), another good musician.

Basket whists were popular. One woman would supply sandwiches and cakes for her four guests so that at the end of the card games everyone could have a nice tea. This would raise funds for whatever the purpose would be.

Going to the pictures

A wee treat, especially for the women, was going to the pictures (cinema) in Dalmellington. On Monday nights during wartime they would either walk down or get the bus. There was always a free matinee at New Year and you were given an orange as a treat by the cinema owner.

Cantata

A cantata was a concert or play. The folks of Benwhat were quite imaginative when it came to entertainment and many an enjoyable night was had listening to villagers entertain in style. The Filson twins, Tommy and Andy, were good singers and always keen to help out, especially for any charity event. Jim Armour was a very good organiser and planning plays was his forte and, of course, he was also the bandmaster. He had a nice manner and achieved much success because of this.

I remember when Jean and George Sturgeon were in a play called *Wee Curly*. I was also in it and with Ethel Buchanan (Thomson) we ended it by singing 'After the Ball Was Over'. In *The Creggie* Mattie Ivers was the head of the family, and Freddie Galloway was in *The Face at the Window*. So, a lot of men as well as the women got involved in the life of the community in terms of entertainment and it was always good fun and well supported by villagers.

Boat race in the sheugh

The boat race often took place on a Sunday and caused much noise and hilarity. The men each had their own boats which were modified matchboxes. The race started at a wee tunnel at the end of the Laigh Row. The sheugh (drain) ran through and down beside the row and the men and boys ran alongside their boats to keep track of their progress. They of course had bets on as to who would win and it also gave the villagers a bit of entertainment watching the menfolk running alongside the sheugh.

Sunday jaunt

When the miners would be enjoying a beer in the village store on a Saturday night, they often planned a wee day away for their family. When they returned home they would announce that they were going on a jaunt on Sunday, usually to places such as Ballantrae, Maidens, Croy Shore or Sandyhills. They had already booked a bus and would have organised enough names to fill it.

When they reached their destination there was usually a tattie field nearby and they would collect some Ayrshire tatties and these were boiled in sea water, already salted, using an old pan or a square biscuit tin on a primus stove. And when they were ready they were simply delicious with a blob of margarine over them. Sometimes, too, they would collect whelks from the beach and bring them home.

Granny's tartan legs

When the weather was good in summer, the women would wander round the rows, sit with a neighbour on the front step and enjoy a good blether. When indoors at night it was nice to sit on the footstool at the fire and make toast, using a toasting fork. Sometimes it would break off and fall into the fire. Some of the elderly women had 'Granny's tartan legs'. This was mottled marks on the skin due to them sitting too long in the heat of the fire.

At New Year the Benwhat Band would play march tunes and parade round the rows using carbide lamps to light the way, bringing in the new year. Many of the band members would be a wee bit tipsy, but it

A cutting from the Ayrshire Post of March 13 1970 when the Benwhat Reunion was held allowing former villagers to reminisce and remember a village they were all proud of and recall special days of yesteryear.

was all good fun. All the men and women would come out of their houses and they usually had a bottle of something, often port or sherry. Every door was open.

Clothes

Maybe on Mother's Day or on birthdays the women would get something new to wear. It was usually a new pinny (apron) or slippers. These were greatly appreciated. A woman always wore a pinny. Sometimes especially the older women wore the wrapover style, known as the Dutch overall. But even when they were dressed, for instance at Christmas, they at least wore a 'daidle', a wee front apron. Clothes were handed down or passed on, so if it fitted you, well you simply wore it.

During war years, even clothes were rationed, so you just wore what you had. After having a baby, a woman's treat was either new slippers or a pinny. If you were lucky enough to have something nice to wear, that was just fine. But you had little chance of having matching things to set it off. I fondly remember my first swimsuit. It was a knitted green one bought at Girvan.

Working clothes for the men at the pit were just their own clothes, shirts and old suits. But they had moleskin trousers. Men, women and children had really very little and the women had to make do and mend and make sure things were washed and dried as they were needed.

Some things were frowned upon as villagers mostly had high moral standards. If a woman stayed with a man and was not married to him she was called a concubine and she was looked down on by others. Also in those days if a family had a handicapped child, he or she was generally kept indoors, almost hidden away. That's just the way things were then.

Random memories

Many people had dogs and cats but the dogs were just put out for a walk. You didn't take them, and naturally they went looking for easy pickings. One dog, owned by the Bunyan family, nabbed a salmon from the van of Iain Marr the fishmonger. This was really a financial disaster for the fish seller. Another fish seller was 'Scous' Dunlop who came up to Benwhat with a van selling herring. This was very tasty when coated with porridge oats and fried.

Bus service

The first bus service to Benwhat was a charabanc, owned by Mr Gibson, the grandfather of Sandy Gibson, well-known former garage owner in Dalmellington. But the first real bus service was provided by Percy Hill, with a service running to Lethanhill and Rankinston. That enabled local folk, none of whom had a car, to make contact with the outside world without first having to walk down the road to Craigmark and Dalmellington or walk down the incline to Waterside.

Ringlets

Wee girls with long hair wore it in ringlets, the style then. To get this look they got their cloots in at night. Long strips of material, usually ripped from an old sheet, were entwined with the hair and tied up at bedtime, so in the morning the hair was in ringlets, which was very stylish.

Children could play outside safely. They had the freedom and joy of running all over the moors. They had a carefree and safe place to enjoy themselves. They had no fear of perverts, in fact, villagers had never heard of that word. It was unknown. The children respected their elders and all married woman were given the title of Mrs.

The mares (moorburn)

Even today I love the smell of burning grass – mares or moorburn. The smell reminds me of Benwhat and brings happy memories of when I was young. It meant to me that another spring was on the horizon. I happily remember being a right wee rascal and quite daring for a laugh. With my pals I played at kick the door on our way down the rows, both as a child and adult. We were a wee bit boisterous even as adults!

Games

There was a pond in Benwhat known as the Mosie which froze over in winter and this was used for curling or sliding by the children of the village. Both boys and girls played at bools (marbles) with their glass jawries, the coloured ones and gongies, which were white. Mothers would take a jawrie bool and keep it inside the kettle to keep limescale from forming. All the children played hide and seek and kick the can. We really did have the time of our lives.

Girls played with skipping ropes and peevers (beds). If you really were lucky you might get a broken bit of marble from the butcher, or we used a polish tin filled with mud as our peever. Boys would search out birds' nests and have a collection of eggs. When they found eggs they wanted, they were carefully carried home and the yolk removed by putting two small holes in the eggshell and blowing the yolk out. The eggs were then kept in a box of straw and identified to a particular type of bird.

The boys would go guddling for fish in the burn. This is where you stand still and put your hand under rocks, tickle the fish's belly before grabbing it and pulling it out of the water.

Granny Currie

Old Meg Currie, also known simply as Granny Currie, used to get me and my pals, when we were just girls, roped in to help make rag rugs. This way old Meg had more and nicer ones than most other villagers because she had a lot of help from the village weans. The back or base of the rug was made of sugar sacks, or even flour sacks. The top patterned area was made from old woollen jumpers and cardigans.

Any old knitted garments in those days were unpicked, ripped out and the wool was used again to knit something else, but if the garments were really past it, they were recycled for rag rugs. Old Meg had some of the girls cutting the jumpers into strips and some of them had to use a hook or even a wooden clothes peg with a nick cut into it to pull the fabric through the sacking. They were usually worked into a nice pattern, matching the colours.

Sometimes we even designed something special such as a dog or cat, which was very clever indeed. We worked at this all year to get special rewards at Halloween with a party. Meg would make us dumplings and these were shared between us with some homemade toffee which she pulled and stretched into stalks. It was all worth it and great to see something you had made yourself.

Religion

Religion brought no problems in Benwhat, at least not that I was aware of. There were meetings held in an empty house by the Brethren for the children, who really enjoyed the meetings, singing 'My cup's full and running over' and 'The wise man built his house upon the rock' and doing all the actions. We were all given a cookie and a cup of tea and I remember at one time we were all given a Bible.

I remember Margaret McGuire, who was a Catholic girl, attending Benwhat School. She waited outside in the corridor until the morning prayer was over and then she came in. Each Sunday the minister from Dalmellington came up to Benwhat School to hold an evening service. George Connell and Robert Bryan were elders.

The store

The song 'I Owe My Soul to the Company Store' certainly rings true with old folk of Benwhat. The Dalmellington Iron Company and later Bairds and Dalmellington owned the pits where the men worked and the houses the mining families lived in. They also owned the store where we got all our supplies. So the Company gave the men their jobs, houses and wages, and then got the wages back off them as the people needed to buy supplies to live.

There was a railway line running along the front of the Laigh Row (Low Row) to Lethanhill, which was used to bring supplies up from Waterside to Benwhat store. Sanny Orr was the store manager and he was the grandfather of Sheena Orr (Armour). In later years there were vans that came up from Dalmellington to Benwhat, mainly the Co-op. This brought a wider selection of goods and the villagers had the choice of what they could buy.

The Co-op

The Co-op took over most things as they could offer services such as the butcher, baker, grocer, drapery and shoe shops and their vans came up the hill providing these services. Even although most things were rationed, it worked quite well. Joan Connell came round the houses to get the message list so your order could be made up and ready for you to collect. During the war years when food was rationed the allowance was 2 oz butter per head per week. Sugar, tea, everything, corned beef was rationed. You were allowed one egg each per week. There was even a van came up from Ayr to Benwhat, operated by Lipton the Grocer, who supplied goods and collected money on a Friday.

Words we used

Some guid auld Scots words are still used in oor ain twang, honestly spoken, because we are proud of our roots. We daunert doon hame or roon the raws at nicht. Someone might say: 'Come in bye, ye're aye welcome.' If it was really cold we were 'foonert richt tae the bane'. If more space was needed in the front room I'd say: 'Shift the claeshorse and sit doon roon the fire.' If the table was problematic someone might say: 'This auld caird table's a bit shoogly.'

Benwhat to Bellsbank

The friendship and community spirit continued from Benwhat to Bellsbank when people were rehoused there in the early 1950s. The allocation of houses was based on the date on marriage certificates, so most of the older people moved there first.

The hut from Benwhat was moved and reconstructed in Bellsbank at the top of Ness Glen Road close to where the present-day shops are. This hut was well utilised for a number of social events. Wee Mary Ferguson sold sweeties in the shop at the front of the hut. The remainder was used for various purposes for the weekdays. It was a reading room, a hairdresser's salon for ladies operated by Anna Clark, barber's for men operated by Cudder Murphy, and the locals played carpet bools and billiards, bingo was held on several nights, and the Sunday School was also held there.

Stages of Life

I left Benwhat when I was thirty-one, and had lived there from the age of five, going through all the stages of life until I was a married woman with three children. The housing conditions were by today's standards rather grim. It was a nice feeling leaving, knowing that we were going to a new-built house in Bellsbank. We threw all the stuff we didn't need into the midden and among them were old carbide lamps which today are collector's pieces. But of course when one door closes another opens and you have to remain positive.

Benwhat was slowly being depopulated and we were happy to leave, but our memories of our time in there grows ever brighter with each passing year. The memories will never fade, because it was our home: all we ever knew and we counted our blessings.

Benwhat today

All that remains now of Benwhat is the war memorial overlooking the former village from its hill command; the herd's house at Burnhead Farm which sadly is also now a ruin; some foundations of the school remain and those who search will identify the foundations of the rows where their former homes were situated. That can be very humbling and brings back so many happy and some sad memories of the past.

When returning for a nostalgic visit, former residents will search for the house where they lived and very often will select a brick from their former home to take back as a memorial – a wee keepsake. There are many of these DICo bricks used in gardens in Bellsbank and Dalmellington today and they are proudly pointed out to friends and relations. It keeps us in touch with our past.

Philosophy of life

Benwhat folk want to keep something visible to remind them of happy times in their special little village high above the valley of Doon. I think I was lucky to have been born there and experienced a special life with all its challenges. I often think these words by Anne Frank (1929–45) are important to remember: 'Think of all the beauty still left around you and be happy.' Now, to me that's not a bad philosophy to follow! How I really enjoy thinking back to good old Benwhat and its outstanding scenery and lovely folk. Those happy, special days can never return, but my auld hame will be forever in my heart.

Ae fond kiss, and then we sever;
Ae fareweel, alas, forever!
Deep in heart-wrung tears I'll pledge thee,
Warring sighs and groans I'll wage thee!

Aye Fond Kiss
Robert Burns

Chapter 16

After Benwhat – What?

Stuart Williamson

Stuart Williamson features in: After Benwhat, What?

Tho wandering now must be my doom,
Far from thy bonie banks and braes,
May there my latest hours consume,
Amang my friends of early days!

The Banks of Nith
Robert Burns

Stuart Williamson of Seattle, Washington, looks back to his mining roots in the Doon Valley at Benquhat now better known simply as Benwhat. This once again demonstrates that folk who worked as miners in the Doon Valley spread their wings far across the globe.

Pocket watch

After many years of pondering the origins of the only relic of my Scottish great-grandfather passed down to me by my father - a fine old pocket watch with the name Dalmellington on the dial, I finally did the smart thing and enlisted the aid of a skilled genealogist based in Scotland, John McGee.

He soon determined that my great-grandfather had been a foreman in the Dalmellington Iron Company (DICO) colliery at Benwhat until the early 1880s, when he suddenly showed up as a tobacconist in Ayr. What a strange transition for a poor coal miner in his 60s!

Wages of 1870s

Then we read that throughout the first years of the 1870s the miners' wages in the Doon Valley had soared by a multiple as high as eight. The mining families had gone on a splurge of spending on non-essentials like American organs and watches.

Evidently my canny great-grandfather rewarded himself with a good watch but also put a few pounds under the mattress and was able to buy the tiny shop at the end of the Auld Brig in Ayr, which had once been the port guardhouse.

A plaque on the wall of this building on the historical Auld Brig now marks the location, but makes no reference to its eventual use for the sale of tobacco, candy and penny-dreadfuls. Which is why my own father grew up in Ayr, rather than in the colliery housing in Benwhat.

Born in Canada

I was born in Canada and now live in Seattle, Washington, USA. My family history is strongly associated with the Doon Valley. My grandmother Agnes Williamson was born on 23 October 1861 in Dalmellington, Ayrshire to my great-father Robert Williamson, a coal miner and great-grandmother Agnes Stewart.

The birth was registered by Robert Williamson on 11 November 1861 at the Dalmellington Registry Office. Although Agnes was not born during the 1861 census her mother Agnes would have been pregnant and carrying baby Agnes at that time and the Williamson family were residing at 14 Old Church Street, Dalmellington.

1871 Census

In 1871 census my grandmother Agnes, 9, was a scholar and she resided at 2 Benquhat, Dalmellington, Ayrshire with father Robert, 41, a miner, mother Agnes, 42, and her other siblings. After leaving school Agnes was destined, like many young girls of the Victorian era, to a life of domestic service, possibly starting as a house maid in one of the many farms dotted around Dalmellington in Ayrshire.

Domestic service

By the time she was 19 years of age Agnes had managed to get one of the more sought after positions within domestic service. Agnes was appointed as a scullery maid at the fashionable Killochan Castle in nearby Dailly in Ayrshire, one of the many properties owned by the rich Gordons of Cluny dynasty. Although the job at Killochan would have been sought after by many young girls, Agnes would have found that she had to work long, hard hours below stairs in a life of servitude for very little pay.

1881 Census

In 1881 census Agnes, 19, was a scullery maid and residing at Killochan Castle, Dailly. The head of the household was English-born Michael W Kencage, 48, late Lieutenant Colonel in the Coldstream Guards with his wife and two children. On 30th January 1882 my grandmother Agnes Williamson, a domestic servant, was back with her parents when she gave birth to my father Robert at 1 Benquhat, Dalmellington.

Going back further in time my grandfather Robert Williamson was born on 20th February 1829 in Drumcrool in the parish of Durisdeer, Dumfriesshire, but by 1853 Robert Williamson had moved into the pit village of Dalmellington, working for the fast expanding Dalmellington Iron Company.

There he met his future wife Agnes Stewart who had been born in 1828 in Dalmellington. Robert Williamson married wife Agnes Stewart on 16th January 1853 in Dalmellington, Ayrshire. Robert and Agnes had eight known children in Dalmellington; Jean, Helen, David Stewart, James, Agnes, Isabella (likely to have died in infancy), Isabella and Menzies Blackwood.

1861 Census

In 1861 census Robert, 31, a coalminer, resided at 14 Old Church Street, Dalmellington with wife Agnes, 32, children Jane, 7, Helen, 5, David, 3, and baby James, 1. Agnes was almost certainly carrying my grandmother Agnes at the time as she was born in October 1861.

By 1870 the Dalmellington Iron Company was in a boom period and new miners' rows were constructed at the high moorland village of Benquhat. In 1871 census Robert, 41, a miner, resided at 2 Benquhat, Dalmellington with wife Agnes, 42, children David, 13, a labourer, James, 11, a scholar, Agnes, 9, a scholar, and Isabella, 5.

Big money

This was a period in time in the Ayrshire coalfields known as the time of the 'big money', but this was not to last. In 1881 census Robert Williamson, 50, was recorded as an iron miner oversman, still residing in Benquhat in the parish of Dalmellington, Ayrshire.

Auld Brig Shop

This meant that Robert had risen to the level of a foreman in charge of a shift of ironstone miners. However, just a couple of years later my great-grandfather was running his tobacconist shop on the Auld Brig of Ayr made famous by Robert Burns. My great-grandfather died in Ayr in 1907.

Back to Benwhat in memory

When I was able to return with some of my family to Ayrshire to search my roots and visited the barren site of Benwhat, we found almost no evidence of its existence other than the ruins of what was the 'new school.'

The shop and the terraced house on Gordon Terrace in Ayr where my father grew up were also lost to redevelopment. We did learn that the watch was first sold in 1874, and it still hangs in its bell jar in my living room.

Like so many other miners, my grandmother's brothers emigrated to the USA or Canada and became coal mine managers. My father chose to go into wholesale groceries.

Benwhat Bluebell circa 1905 was the successful local football team in Benwhat. Benwhat sat on the plateau above Dalmellington. This met the Dalmellington Iron Company policy of accommodating their workers as close to the mines as possible. Most of these men would have worked in the local ironstone and coal mines.
Back row (l to r): Neil Dempsey, Dan Parker, John "Baillie" Armour, McGee, Pat Murray, George Long, Thomas Hodgson*, John Hodgson*, J "Skip" Bryan, E Miller*.
Front row: Yates, 'Sand Dancer' Murray, Duff Hannah, J Murray, Kennedy, Charles Fisher.
*Thomas Hodgson, John Hodgson and E Miller were killed in action in the First World War.

A memorial to Benwhat (earlier known as Benquhat), keeping alive its spirit, was organised and paid for by these three men whose families lived at Benwhat.
(l to r): Willie Rowan, Willie McCluskie and Scott Filson
(Photo: Courtesy of Scott Filson)

I occasionally think back to my family roots and wonder how life would have turned out for me and my family, had those in whose footsteps I now walk, chosen to remain and work in Ayrshire.

But boundless oceans, roaring wild,
Between thy love and me,
Thy never, never can divide
My heart and soul for thee

Farewell to Eliza
Robert Burns

Chapter 17

Miner's Tale of a Lost Village

Neil Dempsey

Fond lovers' parting is sweet, painful pleasure,
Hope beaming mild on the soft parting hour;
But the dire feelings, O farewell for ever!
Anguish unmingled and agony pure.

Thou Gloomy December
Robert Burns

Neil Dempsey, 94, fondly known to all locally around Dalmellington simply as Neilly, is the oldest interviewee in this book project recording the memories of the last miners' of Ayrshire's Doon Valley. Interviewed in May 2015, Neilly is a fascinating character who spent his entire working life from aged fourteen years as a miner in the Doon Valley. He still has a longing for the folk and scenes of his early boyhood days on the high moors around dear lost Benwhat.

Benwhat

I was born on 27 May 1921 at 129 Laigh Row, Benwhat, Dalmellington, at what was known locally as the Laigh Row. This consisted of several long rows of cottage type houses and located on the high moors above Dalmellington. Benwhat sat immediately below Benwhat Hill and it had fantastic views out across the Loch Doon hills and towards Arran.

Remote Village

It was remote and exposed to the elements, especially in the winter months, and yet we all loved that wee village. Perhaps we were being emotional, but you ask any of the Benwhat folk and they will tell you that they just loved that wee village on the hill.

My father was Thomas McCall Dempsey, who was a miner and spent fifty-two years in the pits here in the Doon Valley. He was born in 1894 in Dalmellington at 25 Benwhat, for our family was very much dyed-in-the-wool Benwhatonians, although the roots of my mother and father's side came from the Emerald Isle.

Family Background

My father was a coal miner. He started in Benbrannigan mine which was located above Chalmerston mine and then he moved to work in Pennyvenie and remained there for close on fifty years. He died in 1961 having retired in 1959, so he didn't see much of a retirement.

My mother, Sarah Reid, was from Circubben, Newtonards, Northern Ireland. My father was over there playing football with an Ayrshire select team. They met at a social function. Needless to say he was a regular visitor across the water thereafter and they married on 4 June 1920 in Ards, County Antrim.

My Family

In my family, I was the oldest of six. There was John, Tommy, Willie, Mary and Elizabeth who died in infancy aged 9 months and the youngest, Mary, who still lives in Dalmellington.

I heard my father say that Elizabeth, who died in infancy, took an infection in her ear and she died. That was before there were antibiotics or other effective medicines and things would probably have been different nowadays. I'm overjoyed to have lived a long life and experienced my working life in coal mining. I never for a minute believed that I would still be going strong at such a grand old age – ninety-four years.

Football Focus

Father played with Benwhat Heatherbells Juniors. The Dempsey boys were all good footballers – and my father had six brothers, three of whom made their own mark on the world of football.

Uncle Neil played with Luton Town; my uncle Willie played with Smallheath, Birmingham; and my uncle Matthew played with Bradford City. Now that's not a bad football record for a wee mining village located high on the moors of the upper Doon Valley, don't you think?

They were all very proud to belong to Benwhat and football was the main sport played by young folk of their era. And of course the Benwhat folk were very proud of them, because it was a great honour to have villagers who excelled and made their mark in a sport such as football.

Mother's Irish connections

Because of my mother's family connections, I was across to Northern Ireland every year since I was born until I was aged sixteen. My parents always took the family back to Ireland at some point every year, because my mother was very keen to keep in touch with her ain folk back home.

All the relations in Ireland died many years ago and we don't have anyone there now that I'm aware of. Most of them were older when they got married and consequently didn't have any family, so when they died that was essentially the end of the line.

Grandfather visits Benwhat

My grandfather in Ireland, John Reid, was a professional gardener, working to a wealthy man who owned a large estate. I remember that he also worked in the court in Belfast as an Usher at one point. He used to travel to Benwhat every year until he wasn't fit. He'd stay for a few days to see his daughter, Sarah - my mother - and all the family.

Grandfather had been a working man all his life and he loved visiting Benwhat where he was always made so welcome by everyone. He enjoyed the village store where he would have a pint and a blether with the local men, most of whom were miners. He seemed to get on very well with them, because they were a down-to-earth lot, just like him.

Father's Father

My paternal grandfather was Irish, too, and was raised in a village near the Giants Causeway. His name was Neil Dempsey and I carry his name, albeit I never actually met him. According to my father, he came from Ireland to work at the Steelworks at Glengarnock in North Ayrshire.

He then moved to work in the Ironworks at Waterside and this would have been before the onset of the Great War. He was allocated a house at 25 Benwhat. His wife was Sarah (Martha) Wren and he met her in Kilbirnie where she was living at that time, although she was born in Stranraer on 11 June 1895. I have a photo of them both but have no personal memory of them.

Neil 'Neilly' above and with John Dempsey. Two brothers on the last day of work at Pennyvenie Colliery in July 1978.

Fitba' Daft at Benwhat

When I was a boy in Benwhat you either played football or you watched football being played; joined the harriers or played in Benwhat band. When I was at Benwhat school our boyhood hero was a local man, James Arthur Murray (born 8 June 1880 – 29 October 1933).

He was known locally as Jimmy 'Lodger' Murray, born in Benwhat, he began his football career playing for Benwhat Heatherbell, before joining Ayr in 1897. He then went on play professional football with Aston Villa. He also played for Birmingham Small Heath as a right-sided forward.

Murray scored in his only competitive outing for Small Heath, when they lost to Sunderland in the First Division. In an old newspaper cutting I have he was described as 'fairly fast, has capital command of the ball and can shoot excellently.'

He moved to Southern League club Watford in 1903 and remained in non-league football thereafter. He died in Glasgow in 1933 at the age of fifty-three. Playing for a top English team was quite something in those days and he was our local hero.

What I can say is that all these men who left Benwhat and made their own special mark on the world of football, were always talked about with great pride in Benwhat. There was also Joe McGhie from

Benwhat who went on to play with Everton.

It was quite amazing that all these men from a wee village on the high moors above Dalmellington produced these fine footballers who went on to play at professional level. Perhaps it was something to do with the good fresh air and the outdoor life at Benwhat.

Local Heroes

These great lads from Benwhat were playing great football in the 1920s and 30s when I was just a wee boy at school. We often talked about them in the same ways as a boy today would talk about their football heroes who play for Rangers or Celtic. When we played football we would choose to be one of the local heroes or some of the other established and popular players in Scotland. Football was part of the daily lives for the boys in Benwhat.

David Scobie & Tom Murray

The last really good footballers who played with Benwhat Heatherbell were David Scobie and Tom Murray. They were the best players that I saw and that would be in the late 1930s. These were the last good players for Benwhat Heatherbell, although they never became professional. Around that time the Heatherbell ceased to function and was replaced by Benwhat Rising Star.

My father played with Benwhat Rising Star. I still have several of the medals he won in the Ayrshire District League. It was around that time (1930s and 40s), although I can't be exactly sure.

What I do know is that several of the upper Doon Valley junior teams such as Dunaskin Lads, Benwhat Heatherbell and Burnfoothill Primrose all packed in, but they were fondly remembered by those who played or supported them. Due to my age – 94 - I am one of the very few who will remember those wonderful days when Lethanhill and Benwhat could boast such good football teams.

Craigmark Juvenile Team

I later went on to play with Craigmark Burntonians when they were a juvenile team, which was during the Second World War. I won four medals playing with them and I'm proud to say I still have them to this day.

The four medals were awarded for winning the Scottish Amateur Juvenile Football Association (SAJFA) league cup in season 1945-46; Amateur Juvenile Football Association (AJFA) Ross cup in season 1945-46; SAJFA Commander Leake Cup in 1945-46; SJFA Commander Leake Cup in 1946-47.

We had a great team at Craigmark in those days. The team I can recall of my time was a chap Gibson, John Murphy, Matt McLaughlan, myself, Tom Mathieson, David Torbet, Peter Johnstone, Willie Higgins; and Boyle, Corrigan and McGee, but I don't remember their first names.

We played at the old park at Burnton behind Sillyhole Farm at that time. There was an old wooden pavilion with a coal fire and that's where we changed. There were no showers in those days. I think it was around 1947 that Craigmark moved from Burnton to Dalmellington to their present home at Station Park, behind the community centre, where they still play today.

Changing Facilities

I fondly remember at Benwhat we played football on the Hearth fitba' park. Team members and supporters would carry buckets of water from the standpipe in front of the rows and empty them into two large tin baths – one for each team.

The teams had to wash in the cold water in the tin bath to get the worst of the muck off before they got changed. It was very basic, but in those days the lads just loved playing football. They didn't bother much about the conditions they had to wash and change in. Just playing the game was their personal goal.

There was no such thing as showers in the changing rooms in those days. All the players just loved the game and it was special to be in the village team, so you didn't even think of getting cleaned up and washed after playing as a big issue.

A typical scene of Craigmark which is now but a happy memory to the very oldest former residents. Most of the men from the village worked at Chalmerston and Pennyvenie as well as other pits in the area. Around 1924 the Dalmellington Iron Company began construction of modern rows of houses at Burnton and the residents of Craigmark over the next few years began to move to Burnton and Dalmellington. The road leading to Benwhat can be seen in the background.

At the pithead at Pennyvenie. The first chap is greasing a locomotive used to haul hutches underground. There is a large number of skills required to ensure safe operation in any colliery.

I remember that there was a club official who stood beside each bath to make sure that the players washed their faces before they put their feet into the water. That's how things were then – very basic, but great fun with lots of joking and a right good carry-on.

Nowadays we read in the newspaper about footballers and their managers complaining about poor playing surfaces in winter in the professional game. In our day we simply loved playing, irrespective of the weather and didn't care about the rough park. It was the game that was important to us and trying to win as a team.

Inspired Footballers

Benwhat had a lot of keen footballers and when you think of those who went on to play professionally, it really was a remarkable feat. We were all so proud of that special heritage of football developed 1,000 feet above sea level in a very rough park which was badly affected by the wind and rain. And yet it did produce inspired footballers who would have played all day long and never complained.

School Days

I started school at Benwhat aged five. I remember that the headmaster was Mr Ferguson and the teacher was Miss Kidd. Among my class was Eddie Dick, John Dempsey (my brother); James Relly, George Faulkner; Hugh Gourley, David Whiteman, David McEwan, Jeannie Mowatt; Alex Gardiner and May McHattie, who was a brilliant scholar.

There were also Elizabeth McPhail, Ethel Thomson, Margaret Dunsmore, Annie Hannah, Nelly Filson and Janet Robertson. These are the ones I can remember off the top of my head. School was enjoyable and we all seemed to get on really well.

I generally knocked about with Eddie Dick who stayed near me and we used to go about together, invariably kicking a ball. James 'Dykes' Relly was another I played with and I still fondly think about them from time to time.

I was also in the Benwhat school team when I was ten. I played with Rising Star at Rankinston when I was 16 and also in that team was Eddie Dick, big Alan's brother. (Alan Dick was well known in Benwhat and a good goalkeeper).

It was rough in those days, especially at away games, but I suppose teams visiting Benwhat would say the same about us. On one occasion I went to take a shy and an old lady on the sideline, who was shouting and swearing at the top of her voice, kicked me hard on the back of the legs.

High Pennyvenie with No 4 Pennyvenie, otherwise known as the Big Mine, seen in the background. This was where the railway system terminated, albeit a bogey line ran onwards to Beoch Mine.

Benwhat School class of 1939 gather for a photograph around the time of the beginning of World War 11. One can only imagine their hopes and aspirations mingled with fear growing up during a time of great uncertainty.
Back row (l to r): Tom Gardiner, Willie Filson, Andrew Armour, Sam Pyper, Richard Armour, Guy Deans and Andrew Galloway.
Second back row: Jeanie Thomson, Betty Bennett, Annie Stewart, Thora Bakkom, Moira Hill, Betty Gracie and Sadie McKinstry.
Second front row: Effie Douglas, Nellie Wilson, Ella Douglas, Anna McHattie (wearing a jersey which she had knitted herself. Anna is well known in Dalmellington and a tireless worker for the local Kirk) and Mary Coughtrie.
Front row: Andrew Wilson, Paul Relly, Adam McHattie, Sandy Robertson and Neil Hainey.
(Miss Anna McHattie collection)

Afterwards I went in for tea and the same old lady who kicked me was serving. She approached me and said: "I'm very sorry for kicking you on the legs. I got carried away, because I always want my team to win. But I've given you an extra scone on your plate to make up for it." That was how things were then. After the game everyone's sins were forgiven including the lady who kicked me.

Some Early Memories

As I mentioned I was born at 129 Laigh Row, Benwhat. It was only a room with a wash house at the back. There were two beds in the living room. We then moved to the Top Row or Heath Row in Benwhat. I think we were allocated number 75. It had a big living room and a smaller bedroom at the back which was attached to the wash-house.

The house was heated by a coal fire, but there was no central heating or anything like that, only a big coal fire to try to heat the entire house. My mother cooked on top of a range and there was a swee which came over the fire to heat the kettle or to make girdle scones. My mother was a good cook and baker and the smell of baking scones is a memory I hold dear.

Groups in Benwhat

Everybody was friendly in Benwhat. They all had their own special attachments to groups such as the football teams, the Benwhat brass band, Benwhat Dramatic Society or going to meetings of the Rechabites.

I well recall attending shows in the school hall produced by the dramatic society including 'The Dim Man of Manchester' and 'Auld Robin Gray.' I can say that I had a very happy childhood in Benwhat as did the other folk. I don't think I know anyone who was other than very proud to say they were brought up in Benwhat.

Into the Coal Mines

When I was aged fourteen I started working at Chalmerston Pit head. My role there was sending the empty tubs down the mine and receiving the filled ones as they came up from below. I would then push them along the line to be emptied.

My first wage when I worked at Chalmerston starting aged fourteen was 2/- a day working six days a week. The pit was owned by the Dalmellington Iron Company initially and then it went to Bairds and Dalmellington Ltd., before the NCB took over in 1947.

Domestic Arrangements

As a wee boy I would leave the house at 5.30am to walk to Chalmerston and then two miles back home for 2/- a day. Young folk wouldn't believe it now. There were no baths at the pit in those days, so you had to get washed in the wash-house at home when you trudged back.

I remember that I was very tired and hungry by the time I arrived home. The wash-house was also where my mother washed our pit clothes. If the weather wasn't good, she always had washed clothing piled high waiting to be hung out to dry. All my brothers worked in the pits locally, so it was a busy house and it must have been hard for my mother doing all that washing every single day.

My mother also had to make two dinners. The first dinner was at 3pm for me and my father when we came off shift. The second dinner was prepared at 10pm for my brothers coming in off backshift and they also had to get washed before dinner, so there was lots of hot water on the fire.

Working Underground

I left Chalmerston when I was aged fifteen to go down No 2 Pennyvenie pit. At first I worked at the pit bottom sending the filled tubs up in the cage and taking the empties off the cage to go to different districts within the pit.

When I was sixteen I went down the pit full-time and began working at the coal face working alongside my father. At that time it was common for family groups to work together as a team.

It was hard, hard work filling the tubs with coal or dirt and they were sent along to the pit bottom to be taken up in cages to be emptied and returned underground.

I was at the coal face most of my working life and it was hard, hard graft. However, there was a great bunch of men and there was always plenty of what we called 'pit humour' on the go or playing tricks on one another.

Salvage Work

Sadly, Pennyvennie closed in 1978 and that was the end of deep mining in the Doon Valley. However, it wasn't the end for me because with my brother, John, we carried on at the pit on salvaging duties for several months.

This involved recovering machinery and equipment from the pit and anything else such as rails, borers and other items which could be reused or were of some value elsewhere in the industry.

Last Men at Pennyvenie

There were, if I remember correctly, about six men working on salvage duties at Pennyvenie to start with including Alex Gillespie and Neilly Robertson but eventually they left as the work got less.

There was also an engineer, John Blane and an electrician, Tom Wilson, as they were needed to keep the pumps running to stop the mine flooding while we worked on salvaging equipment.

My brother John and I were the last two in the pit. There was a photograph taken of us when we finally finished all the work at Pennyvenie and went into retirement. It was certainly sad to see Pennyvenie close, but I had spent the majority of my working life there with some fine miners.

But the writing had been on the wall for years before that, so finishing at the age of fifty-seven after a lifetime in mining was a poignant moment. I often think back to working at the coal face and reflect on many of the characters I enjoyed working with at Pennyvenie.

Flitting from Benwhat

We flitted from Benwhat in 1938 to a house in Dalmellington living initially where the Army Cadet Hall is now. But we later got one of the first houses built in Dalton Avenue. It was a big change to get a half decent house and it made a huge difference, not only to mother who could cope much better, but also for everyone in the family.

It was definitely a wrench to leave Benwhat, but getting a decent house was the greatest thing, especially for my mother. And besides Benwhat was being gradually run down and folk were moving down into the Doon Valley. There were many empty houses in the Benwhat rows.

We were in our second house in Benwhat for about five years. But when we later got the very first council house that was allocated in Dalton Avenue, Dalmellington, it was just amazing having great amenities and the house being brand new as well as all the amenities in the village right on our doorstep.

There was a wheen o' Benwhat families moved into Dalmellington about the same time including Jimmy Armour, Jimmy Hill, Jimmy Lindsay and Robert Kirk. Others moved in over the next fourteen years when it was finally abandoned and demolished in 1952.

If we had had the same amenities in Benwhat as we had in Dalmellington, no one would have left Benwhat, that's a certainty. Everyone at Benwhat came from ordinary working families. They made their own amusements; everyone rallied round yin another. That's how it was in those days. It was clear even in 1938 when I was aged seventeen, that Benwhat would eventually be abandoned and demolished. So I suppose we were lucky getting out at that time.

Benwhat calls you back

I regularly returned to Benwhat to play for the Rising Star and to visit friends. On these visits it was always a wrench to see where my old home had been because it had been such a big part of my life. However this was compensated by being able to meet some weel-kent faces still living there and to enjoy many a blether. However, you have to accept that times change and you move on, but memories linger and the nostalgia for Benwhat was strong then and got even stronger with each passing year.

Nostalgia for Times Past

In fact I can honestly say that the longing and love for Benwhat is even stronger today some sixty-seven years after my family left Benwhat. Sometimes as I think back to happy boyhood days with my parents and family living on the high moor above Dalmellington, I do have a wee tear in the eye, because your first home is always special and inevitably, even as an old man now, I still think fondly of my mother who worked so hard in what were tough housing condititions.

Sarah Hainey's Wee Shop

Sarah Hainey, well known to older folk in Dalmellington, had her wee shop just next to our house and many a great fish supper I had there. It was a magnet for local weans because she had a great range of sweeties. Sarah and her sister, Nell, ran the place and were always lovely to everyone. Annie McCulloch, (John 'Jubie' McCulloch's sister), used to serve in the shop and it was a great place in those days.

The wee shop was right next to the railway line and there was a set of gates that were closed across Gateside Road when a train was due to arrive at or leave the station, so all the traffic would have to stop. Mind you, in those days there wasn't very much traffic because very few folk owned a motor car.

I was a member of the local Home Guard in Dalmellington during the war years, but that's another story perhaps for another time.

Marriage to Mary Hastie

I married Mary Hastie, known to all as Molly, in 1959 and we had a very happy marriage. Molly came from Sandhead, Stranraer, where we met. I was with Sam 'The Sheriff' Semple, a well known Dalmellington character, and others in Stranraer to play in a five a side tournament.

We went down on motorbikes, but a local farmer said he would put us up overnight in his barn, so we could enjoy the social life of the village. I met Molly and needless to say there were quite a few visits to Sandhead after that.

We got married in Sandhead Church by Rev James Campbell. We got our one and only house on 24 March 1961 at 19 Burnton, Dalmellington, and we've been very happy ever since. We have two girls, Primrose and Mary and one son, Neil and grandchildren, Faye, Arlene, Sarah, Bronwynn, Rory and Robbie and great grandchildren, Emily Rose, Ava, Elizabeth and Brooke. So, you could say that we've been very lucky to have such a large family and they visit regularly

Walking to Benwhat

I used to walk to Benwhat every week from my home in Burnton. It was usually on a Tuesday and I would invariably be accompanied by my pals Alex Gillespie, Willie Blane and my brother John.

We walked up to Chalmerston from the coal loading point at Minnivey and cut along the moorland to Benwhat. Alex Gillespie was a Burnfoothill man and Willie Blane was from Dalmellington.

Arriving at Benwhat all the houses of course had been demolished around 1953 and all that remained were the foundations of the rows which by that time were beginning to be covered in grass and bog myrtle, as nature reclaimed what was rightfully her own.

You could also see the remains of a small part of the new school

The young folk of Benwhat (circa 1939), like many other towns and villages, had a branch of the Independent Order of Rechabites. The sole aim of the rechabites was to preach the message of total abstinence.
Back row: (l to r) Drew McHattie, John Douglas, Sandy McHattie, Tommy Filson, Adam McHattie (Dalmellington), John Galloway, Margaret Campbell, A Mullen, Willie Lindsay and Andrew Filson.
Middle row: Marion Campbell, Betty McDicken, Mr James Hopes, Jessie Andrews, Mr Robert Bryan, Betty Templeton, visiting member of the Rechabites and May Stevenson
Front row: Adam McHattie (Patna), Jean Weir, Marion Lindsay, Ann McHattie, Beth Hill and Adam McHattie (Bellsbank)
Miss Anna McHattie collection

building. Above us on Benwhat Hill the war memorial proudly stood out, recording the names of the Benwhat men who fell in both wars.

Reminiscing

I'd stand and enjoy the scene and point out where the different rows of houses had been located and blether about who stayed where and some of the characters we knew and fondly remembered.

We'd talk about Benwhat harriers and some of the runners who made their mark, especially Robert Reid, who was a terrific runner and later joined the Birchfield Harriers. Robert died in 2007, but he will always be remembered in any discussion about Benwhat by local folk who were very proud of his athletic achievements.

We could also see the hearth football park where the Heatherbell and Rising Star played and there was a field behind where the younger boys played. These were always happy times on our wanderings, especially when someone would recall something special about our days at Benwhat. That would lead on to more discussion of days past.

In a way these discussions made the past come alive in special ways and perhaps even added to our love of our old village. I have to say that due to infirmity, I fair miss not being able nowadays to walk up to Benwhat, so I just have to rely on my memories of times past.

Granny Murray

For example, there was an old woman called Granny Murray. She used to make what we called Bosun cream, which was a drink. She also made terrific toffee apples which the weans loved. I was her runner to the store (pub) every Friday. She sent me there to get a big bottle filled with beer which cost 9d. She enjoyed sitting out the back door and drinking the beer.

She charged a halfpenny and a penny if it was a large glass of bosun cream. My pay on a Friday was a cup of bosun cream for carrying the beer to her.

Happy Days

My memory is not as good as it used to be, but I still try to get out for a wee walk every day to keep my legs active and to meet and blether to local folk. Having lived in my present house at Burnton since I was married, I'm really in with the bricks and couldn't be happier. I still potter about in the garden and grow my own tattics and onions and a few other things.

It was sad but inevitable that Benwhat was abandoned and demolished. Little now remains to show for just short of one hundred years of life on the exposed plateau which was dearly loved by so many of the villagers. Mind you, at the time, many did moan about the poor housing in Benwhat, but nostalgia does kick in strongly once you leave.

The war memorial erected on the face of Benwhat Hill in 1921 is still the most prominent feature marking what is now regarded as a lost or ghost village. This was restored around 2011. You can also see part of the 'new' school and the foundations of the rows - some close to the foundations of 17th century farms which were victims of earlier clearance policies!

Opencast Mining

The moors are now inhabited only by opencast coal working, also recently abandoned, but huge craters have been left on the plateau and have scarred the lonely moor. These gigantic man-made holes known as open pit mines are as spectacular as they are extreme.

Serious machinery is needed for the vast amount of earth moving that goes on in mines that operate around the clock, and for years I watched these operations on the plateau above Burnton, Dalmellington and around Benwhat towards the Craig.

I'm told that visiting Benwhat nowadays you will still see the scars of opencast mining, but there is still birdlife and perhaps, if you have a vivid imagination, you might also see the folk of Benwhat of yesteryear. I still remember many of them clearly and I smile when I think about them.

Ghosts of the Past

Most of my pals from Benwhat days of my youth have sadly passed on. But my memories of them will hopefully live on through these special recollections. Perhaps those who follow in my footsteps and visit Benwhat will wonder about how this village came to be and how the landscape has changed so dramatically with open cast mining.

The ghosts of the past will doubtless linger on at Benwhat and right across the high moors – destroyed and wilfully abandoned by opencast mining practices – in this once beautiful upper section of the Doon Valley.

Thinking of Yesteryear

For my part I like to think back to the sound of youngsters playing football, harriers running along precarious and overgrown paths which had formerly been the old Hill railway system and the sound of a fine brass brand, all familiar scenes that my departed pals knew, dearly loved and were part and parcel of their boyhood days at dear lost Benwhat

With future hope I oft would gaze
Fond, on thy little early ways:
Thy rudely caroll'd, chiming phrase,
In uncouth rhymes;
Fir'd at the simply, artless lays
Of other times.

The Vision
Robert Burns

Chapter 18

Beoch Birthday Blethers

James Chalmers

For a' that and a' that,
Our toils obscure and a' that,
The rank is but the guinea's stamp,
The man's the gowd for a' that.

A Man's A Man for a' That
Robert Burns

James Chalmers with daughter Anne Park.

The following are notes taken in 1996 by Mrs Anne Park of Dalmellington from her father's reminiscences as they sat and chatted about his early years.

James Paulin Chalmers was born in 1909 at North Beoch, a row of miners' houses located near to Beoch Mine, some 4 miles north of Dalmellington and about 1 mile north of the B741 road.

James was the fourth of eleven children - seven sons and four daughters - born to David and Annie Chalmers. The family lived at North Beoch row until James was aged twelve in 1921 when they moved to Dalmellington. He died on 12 February 1997.

Donald L Reid is grateful to the daughter of James Chalmers, Mrs Anne Park, for recording his precious memories including information taken on his birthday, thus allowing readers an insight into life at Beoch in the early 20th century.

The article is recorded in 'braid Scots' as spoken by most folk in Ayrshire's Doon Valley. Older readers, who may remember James Chalmers, will probably be able to picture him in their mind's eye, as they read this article. This reminiscence is rather special.

Choaclit Mint

Aye hen, ye aye hae mind o' ma birthday. Ah'm no ower fond o' thae chocalit mint things though, I'd rither hae a poke o' caramels oany day. It's a guid job you like them or they'd jist sit aboot an go mooldy.

Down Memory Lane

A wis born in 1909, my that wis a gey lang time ago. Ye ken, it's a peety yir Granny never leeved (lived) lang enough tae see ye, she'd hae spiled (spoiled) ye somethin' afwy.

A kindly, gentle soul she wis, mendin' pit semmits when she jist drappit back. Deid! Nae wunner, eleeven weans - seeven sons an fower lassies. A' in a twa roomed hoose at the Beoch. That's thirteen folk yaisin dry cloasits.(outside toilets) Mind ye, we boys usually jist yaised the fields! That was how things wur in thae days.

Beoch Boy

The Beoch wis ma hame an ah wis prood tae belong there where ah spent ma young years.

Oor hoose wis at yin end o' the row an there wis a readin' room in the middle o' the raw. Johnny Morgan wis in charge, cleanin' it and keepin' the fires in an the tramps oot!

Eva Eaglesham wis yin o' the teachers at Beoch schule. She leeved at the far end o' the raw. An when her boyfreen came tae visit her, we a' got a holiday! Noo an again we were geen (given) a penny, bit there wis naethin' tae spend it oan, so we'd wait for the butcher tae come tae the raw wi' his horse n' cairt an bocht a link (sausage) an ate it raw!

Spring Water & Winter

We had tae cairry watter fae a tap doon at the bottom o' the hooses, but in the summer it gey often dried up an' so we had tae go away doon tae the spring fur water. Ah hae mind the summer when the youngest o' the family wis born, (yir Auntie Jean) an her nappies hid tae be washed in the burn.

In the Winter it wis usually the case that the conveyances (delivery vehicles) couldnae come oany farther than the main Dalmellington - Cumnock road (B741). The track doon tae the row fae there wis gey steep an rough and often blocked by deep snaw.

So we took the big wicker claes baskets an' walked the mile or so tae the main road an filled them wi' the essentials. Oor big widden girnels (storage chests) in the scullery were stappit fu' wi' floor, salt an oats tae keep us gaun tae the snaw melted.

Christmas

The weans a' went tae the Beoch Sunday schule. An' at Christmas there wis a present for every wean in the place. Miss Walker fae Camlarg big hoose, jist ootside Dalmellington, wis a generous benefactor tae us young yins at Beoch.

At hame oan Christmas morning – it wisnae a holiday, ye ken – we were happy to see oor stoackins filled wi' ashes wi' an orange or apple sat oan the top.

I've mind o' a lassie yin time who got a pair o' shin, (shoes) an she wis the envy o' a' the weans in the place. Her brither's present wis the box they came in an' he tied string ontae it an' had a gran' time pu'in it up an doon the raw. Life wis simple and expectations few!

Move to Craigview

When ah wis twelve we flitted tae a bigger hoose at Craigview, Pennyvenie, nearer Dalmellington. These hooses wir newer than at the Beoch but made o' puir (poor) stuff an' had damp wee rooms. There wis an ootside watter cloasit at each o' the hooses an a cauld watter tap in the scullery, but in the summer when the watter dried up, it wis often back tae the fields again and that wis nae bother for the boys!

Doon the Pit

Ah wis 14 years auld when ah went doon the pit wi ma three brithers an ma faither. Aye, an' ah've mind being checked an' telt tae keep up wi the rest, an' at the end o' the shift bein sare in every bone an' muscle.

Oor wee scullery wis a busy place wi' seeven sons an faither a' waitin' their turn tae wash in the tin bath efter feenishin' their work. There wis wet semmits, drawers, moleskins, flannelette shirts knee-pads an' pit bunnets a' ower the place, tryin tae get dried aff before the next shift, so the wee hoose wis gey thrang (crowded).

Life at Beoch

The life wis hard, but we hid some grand times, tae, mind ye. Simple guid fun wi' ginlin'(to catch fish in the hand), in the burns, takin' a piece an' a bottle o' watter an gaun' awa' alang the glen oan a picnic.

We hid dances an' coancerts, an' at times entertainers wid visit an' put oan a show -grand fun- an' the schule room wis aye filled tae capacity. Folk jist loved the Beoch.

Lookin' back' there wis few really auld folk. Ye were thought auld at 60 an gey often folk jist 'took tae their bed' or donnert (strolled) aboot hingin' oan tae their stick.

There wis nae set retirin' age in thon days and men jist worked oan as long as they were able, sometimes only workin' two or three days in the week or takin' a lichter joab at the pit-heid. Aye, and the work in the pit wis hard for every yin of them.

Food at Beoch

Oor meat (food) wis simple. Parritch, guid thick vegetable broth made wi' a bone stock, hame-baked treacle scones an' pancakes. Auld Granny Clark wis a gran' oatcake baker as weel as deliverin' a guid few o' the bairns at Beoch! We caught rabbits an' hares an' had tatties an' mutton that had made the soup aforehaun' (before).

Jimmy Smith fae the Beoch Ferm wid come along for a lend o' the big axe when it wis time for him tae kill the pig. The weemem made 'potty-heid' that wis made fae the bone scrappins, then boiled up in it's ain jeely an' left tae set. Great for pit pieces!

Clootie dumplin' wis made oan special days, birthdays an' the like. The smell o' the spices were a' through the hoose. Silver threepennies were put intae the dumplin' if they were oany tae be got. Ye could hardly wait till it wis dried aff, sliced up an' sat there steamin' fernent ye. (opposite).

Pennyenie Colliery and a rake of dirt hopper empties await being filled with spoil and taken to the dump at Laight near Waterside.

Games we Played

Us weans played aboot wi' girds an' cleeks, peeries, bools an' balls. Then there wis buttony – a bit the same as tiddly winks an' there wis nae shortage o' buttons. Sledges were made in the winter an' gey often cairted the messages (provisions) fae the toon at Dalmellington through the snawdrifts. Aye we hid some hard, hard winters at Beoch, because it wis on the high moors and very remote.

Wash-Hoose Gossip & Mairrige

Then there wis the wash-hooses fernent the rows, an' as weel as the claes gettin' washed, this wis where a' the gossipin' went oan, an mony a row wis brewed ower wha's turn it wis tae wash in it, or the state it wis left in.

A wummin seemed tae be judged oan how sober, god-fearin' an' clean she wis. Ah believe she micht hae gotten away wi' murder if somebody could've gi'en evidence that she wis spoattlessly clean!

Folk maistly mairrit (married) a lad or a lassie fae the same place, an' it jist wisnae the din thing tae mairry a body fae oany where else. So when ah mairrit yir mother, who came fae Ayr, the faimily were gey huffed. An' ah wis asked whit wis wrang wi the lassies fae the Beoch.

Mind you, ah thought ah chose weel. An' yur mither and me, we hid a very happy mairrige! Nae Beoch lass could hae been better than yir mither!

Looking back, it certainly wis a hard life especially for Mither and Faither rearin' a' these weans in a wee hoose wi' few facilities, but we knew and expected nothin' else an' us young yins were contented.

Different Life

Ye ken, here ah am sittin' here bletherin' away, an' here's yersel' sittin' wi yer een shut chowin' choaclit. But ye ken, ah'll no aye be here, an' your weans'll hae a different kind o' life a' the gither, an' ah daresay they'll maybe ask aboot the auld days an' think aboot a' the changes that hiv ta'en place since their Grandpa wis a boy.

Listen tae ma Story

Maybe ye should pey mair heed tae ma ramblins hen, so ye can tell them a wee bit aboot their faimily history and how the world has changed. Aye, an changed no always fir the better!

Oanyway, it's high time ah wis awa' ben tae ma bed noo.

So, guid-nicht tae ye dochter an' God bless ye.

To make a happy fireside clime
To Weans and wife,
That's the true pathos and sublime
Of human life

Epistle to Dr. Blacklock
Robert Burns

Chapter 19

Childhood Memories of Lethanhill

Ann MacLean

Amidst thy desert walks the lapwing flies,
And tires their echoes with unvaried cries.
Sunk are thy bowers, in shapeless ruin all,
And the long grass o'ertops the mouldering wall.

The Deserted Village
Oliver Goldsmith

Ann Donohoe arrived in Lethanhill, aged seven, when the village was in terminal decline. When she finally left, aged fifteen, it was a deserted village, the whole population having been rehoused in the Doon Valley, mainly in Patna. Ann married Donald MacLean in Irvine in 1966. They have two sons, Niall and Colin. Niall and Lorraine live in Paisley and have two children, Cara and Ruth, while Colin and his wife Narin have settled in Germany with daughter Emma. Donald and Ann have lived very happily in Kilmaurs for many years. She worked as a secretary in Ayrshire Metal Products, Irvine, for some ten years and thereafter became a full-time housewife and mother.

She is involved in voluntary work and is an elder, choir member, and past convener of the Guild, in what is now New Laigh Kirk, Kilmarnock. She is thoroughly enjoying retired life with her husband Donald. Her second youngest brother, Brian Donohoe, was MP for Ayrshire Central from 2005 – 2015. His formative years were also spent at Lethanhill.

All the Donohoe family are very proud of their association with Lethanhill. They still enjoy taking a journey down memory lane to visit their former home, now a private dwelling and the only house remaining near Lethanhill. They also visit the lonely village war memorial as well as the remains of the ghost village on the high moors above the River Doon, lost amid a small forest of sitka spruce. Ann dips into memory recalling the way of life she experienced in this lost mining village.

Headmaster at Lethanhill

George and Catherine Donohoe moved to Lethanhill from Kilmaurs in October 1951 with their three children. I was the eldest, aged seven, and my brothers George and Brian were five and three respectively. Dad, who was the new headmaster of the Lethanhill Junior Secondary School, had travelled from Kilmaurs (a journey involving three different buses) for some considerable time before the schoolhouse at Lethanhill was ready for the family to live in.

Shortly before leaving Kilmaurs, Dad learned to drive and became the proud owner of a second-hand Hillman saloon. Although the houses at Lethanhill had electricity installed in 1926, our newly decorated schoolhouse was without electric power. Lighting was by Calor gas, and the kitchen was kept cosy by a Rayburn stove, from which Mum produced mouth-watering meals and superb baking.

Domestic bliss

Washing was done by hand with the help of an Acme wringer. To iron clothes, she used a heavy Calor gas iron, with gas jets round the inside of the base, always having to be especially careful when ironing garments with fringing or frills, in case the gas jets singed them. There was of course no television set, but we enjoyed listening to the battery-powered radio.

Our water supply came from a hillside storage tank to which lime was added from time to time to purify it. After such treatment the water looked like fizzy lemonade. On fortunately rare occasions, small frogs would emerge from the taps.

During the summer, if there had been a dry spell of weather, we could be completely without water. This normally happened during the school holidays, when thankfully we were able to use the school's storage supply, sometimes going into the cookery room to have a good wash in the large deep sinks.

Playground songs

On my first day at Lethanhill School the other pupils were very friendly and welcoming. The teacher for my class, which was a composite class of Primary 3 and 4, was Miss Parker. At playtime the girls formed a large circle, singing such songs as 'The big ship sails through the Illy Ally-O', 'Water water wallflower', 'I sent a letter to my love' and 'In and out the dusty bluebells'. When the weather was fine we would draw beds on the playground and play with peevers or use skipping ropes – one of the many songs we used to sing was 'Oh there she goes, Oh there she goes, Peery heels and pointed toes, look at her feet, she thinks she's neat, black stockings and dirty feet'.

At other times we would bring a couple of tennis or small rubber balls and bounce them off the wall, singing 'Plainy, clappy, rolly, backy' etc. The boys played with marbles, peashooters and conkers, but were always happiest kicking a ball about. We often played rounders, tig or hide and seek.

Moorland memories

The moor was an exciting extension of the playground. At weekends and holidays there was always plenty to do to fill our time. We played with metal fenders turned up at the front, using them like sledges to slide down the grassy slopes. Playing in the burn was great fun. We had races in the burn using empty tin cans, we looked for frog spawn, or tried to build a dam. In the spring we used to help the shepherd set the moors on fire, the lovely smell of burning grass filling the air. There was always a breeze blowing on the Hill, ideal for flying kites. Making a kite was a serious business, needing brown paper, canes and paste, with old newspaper and string for the tail. Some flew better than others, soaring to great heights before diving to the ground, startling any sheep that may have been grazing nearby.

Some distance behind the school was a disused quarry where there were still some tracks with bogies lying around. In the quarry, which was at least 1,000 feet above sea level, we found fossils of shells, showing us that the sea had at one time covered the area. We must have walked for miles, going by foot to visit friends down in Patna, or to the sweetie shop on Saturdays to spend some of our pocket money.

I can remember after a winter shopping trip to Ayr with my mum, getting off the bus at the foot of the hill at Downieston Farm. I was about ten at the time, it was very dark, and I must confess that I was just a little scared walking up the road to Lethanhill, and hearing strange sounds, my imagination running riot.

Coronation 1953

A date in history which I will always remember with great pride and affection was the Coronation of Queen Elizabeth. To commemorate the

Ann MacLean, better known in her Lethanhill day by her maiden name, Donohoe, recalls growing up on the hill.

LethanHill School class of circa 1943.
Back row: (l to r) Robert Ferris, Jim McVey, Bob Finlay, Bobby Kirkland, Edgar Ierland and Cecil McCormack.
Front row: Jean Brown, Nan Kirkland, Margaret Winning, Betty Wallace, Margaret Bowie, Ina Reid, Nettie Curry, Annie Conway, Jean McCulloch and Margaret Stevenson.
(William Stevenson collection)

Coronation on 3 June 1953 the pupils of my age were presented with a long flat metal box which had a picture of the Queen on the lid. The box was filled with Cadbury's chocolates and was to be used as a pencil case afterwards. Some of the younger children were presented with Coronation mugs, and the older girls were given brooches in the shape of a crown with red, white and blue stones. There was a special Coronation Gala day in Patna with Queen Lily Gilmour and attendants. The schoolchildren were asked to come in fancy dress. Mum was kept busy before the big day making our outfits.

The outside of the schoolhouse was decorated in red, white and blue, as was the car. We received a prize of £1, which was quite something at that time. One of my brothers still has the note, which is twice the size of today's notes. In August of that year (1953) my youngest brother, John, was born at Lethanhill. I can remember proudly pushing him in his pram past some derelict houses so that a friend who was still in the village could see him.

The process of re-housing all the people of Lethanhill and Burnfoothill took seven years. The first families were allocated houses in Patna at the end of 1947 and by summer 1954 the last person had moved, and the once busy rows were completely deserted and forlorn. It was really quite sad, especially for our family, who were the only family to remain on the Hill.

Old and new schools

When Dad had come to Lethanhill as headmaster, the younger primary pupils were taught in the 'Old School', which had been built in 1912 and had three classrooms. Older primary children along with secondary pupils were taught in the 'New School', which when opened around 1927 was one of the most modern and well-equipped schools in the county of Ayrshire at that time. However, within a year or two of him being appointed headmaster most families had moved to Patna. The influx of primary-age children was more than Patna School could cope with, so it was arranged that nine to eleven-year-old pupils would be taken by bus from Patna and taught in the 'Old School' at Lethanhill. They were regularly visited by Mr Baird, headmaster of Patna Primary, whose oft-repeated mantra to his pupils was 'Speed, Accuracy, Neatness!' This arrangement continued until a larger school was built at Patna. For this reason, around 120 secondary pupils were also being bussed back up the hill from Patna to the 'New School' building.

This could be termed 'the last footballers on the hill.' This team, with Mr George Donohoe and Mr James Paterson, would likely be the last official Lethanhill School team. The school closed later in 1959 with these footballers continuing their education at Patna. Who do you recognise and what memories does this photo evoke.
Back row: Geroge Donohoe (head teacher), Richard Law, Billy 'Bunts' Hunter, David Brown, Andy Paterson (goalkeeper), George 'Punt' Ferguson, Willie Young, John McDonald and Matt McLelland (teacher).
Front row: Tom Tusler, Boyd Plenderleith, Tommy Campbell, Tom 'Max' Murray, Billy 'Buck' Robertson, Alex 'Shy' Kirkwood, David Fossett and ?
(Photo: courtesy of Ann MacLean)

Norman Eric Kirk, a descendent of the Lethanhill Kirk family, made his indelible mark in New Zealand. John Kirk, his great grandfather came to Lethanhill in the earliest years of the Dalmellington Iron Company and worked in various ironstone mines. Then in 1868 he left his home at 58 White Brick Row, Lethanhill, and took his family to a new life in New Zealand, when his youngest son, George, was only 6 weeks old. 45 years later George Kirk's grandson, Norman was born on January 6 1923 and went on to become 29th Prime Minister of New Zealand until his untimely death on August 31 1974. Interestingly, Norman Kirk visited the Doon Valley in 1968 hoping to trace family connections. Tom White, Dalmellington District Clerk, was able to put him in touch with two members of the Kirk family, Mrs Mary Logan and her sister, Mrs Isabella Ballantyne.

A sombre scene at Lethanhill which was by then a village in the process of being demolished. However, if you look closely you will see children playing happily in the school playground. The Hill was abandoned in 1954 yet children were bussed up to the school, which remained open, until 1959 when most were transferred to the new school at Patna.
(Photo: Courtesy of Ann MacLean collection)

A memorial to Lethanhill, known simply as the Hill, by former villagers. This remains in place today, albeit opencast coal mining commenced in the area in 2011.
(Photo: Donald L Reid)

KIRK YEARS
Margaret Hayward

1851~1954
LONG LIVE
THE 'HILL

Deserted village

Although the miners' rows at Lethanhill lay in ruins, the sound of young people's voices and much laughter echoed round the deserted village during the school term, which was quite strange when you think of it now. At other times the bleating of sheep and the cry of peewits and skylarks in the summer skies were the only sounds to be heard.

Last residents

I have a photograph of the Donohoe family taken early in 1958 at Lethanhill which I treasure. This, as well as the one of the schoolhouse and the other of the two schools, was shown on Cliff Michelmore's television programme *Tonight*. Our parents had been asked to go to the BBC studios in Glasgow to be interviewed for the programme. This had come about because of an article in the national press. Dad had refused to sign the missive of let for the schoolhouse, as he wished to move to more satisfactory housing in Ayr.

However, the 'powers that be' decided that he must 'stay put' in Lethanhill, although we were the only residents living on the high moorland, with a deserted and ruined village as our nearby neighbour. The new secondary school at Patna wasn't going to be completed for another year or two, and until then the Education Committee were not prepared to relieve him of his obligation to live in the schoolhouse.

In the summer of 1959 we moved to Irvine. Dad had been appointed headmaster of Loudon Montgomery Primary School, a post he filled until his retirement. We lived in the Lethanhill schoolhouse for eight years. As a youngster that seemed like a lifetime. However, we have many happy memories of the Hill and of friends we made during our stay. We have all taken our families back to see where we grew up and, in brother John's case, where he was born. It is remarkably humbling to think back on happy days on the Hill.

Donohoe family at Lethanhill school house circa 1958. Mr George Donohoe, headmaster, was decidedly unhappy at his family remaining in deserted Lethanhill, the remainder of the village having been abandoned in 1954 whilst the school remained open until 1959, the children bussed to the Hill. Brian Donohoe was later to become MP for Central Ayrshire.

(l to r): Brian Donohoe, aged 9, Catherine Donohoe, John Donohoe, aged 4, George Donohoe, headmaster of Lethanhill School, Ann Donohoe, aged 14, and George Donohoe, aged 12. It was a strange experience for them living in the only inhabited house on the Hill. Strangely enough, this house still survives and is occupied today, still on its own.

(Photo: Ann MacLean collection)

But now the sounds of population fail,
No cheerful murmurs fluctuate in the gale,
No busy steps the grass-grown footway tread,
For all the bloomy flush of life is fled.

The Deserted Village
Oliver Goldsmith

Chapter 20

A Lethanhill Lad in the Mines

Hugh Hainey

Hugh Hainey, still smiling in 2012, recalled some happy and sad days living at Lethanhill.
(Photo: Donald L Reid)

Away from the roar and the rattle,
The dust and the din of the town,
Where to live is to brawl and to battle,
Till the strong treads the weak man down!
Away to the bonnie green hills
Where the sunshine sleeps on the brae,
And the heart of the greenwood thrills
To the hymn of the bird on the spray.

A Song of the Country
John Stuart Blackie

Hugh Hainey was interviewed at the age of ninety-four on 20 May 2015. This sprightly nonagenarian remembers Lethanhill with affection, but several tragic events also occurred during the years when his family lived there. Hugh now lives in Alloway and enjoys gardening. He is a member of Lodge St Thomas (Kilwinning) Dalmellington, and on 21 March 2012 received a special certificate marking seventy years of membership of the Lodge from Archibald Chalmers, Provincial Grand Master Mason of Ayrshire. Here Hugh looks back to his many years spent on the Hill. His dear wife, Sarah, died on 4 March 2015

Born at Lethanhill

I was born on 18 February 1921 at 136 Lethanhill, Dunaskin. This was the year of the general strike and times were very difficult for everyone in that era. My mother was Ann Kersal Scott, a housewife, and my father was Hugh Hainey. Father worked at the furnaces at Dunaskin. Like everyone else in Lethanhill, he would simply walk down the Drumgrange incline to go to work at Waterside each day. His family was of Irish descent and came to work at the Dalmellington Iron Company ironworks at Dunaskin, as did many other folk from different parts of Scotland and Ireland at that time. One of the by-products of the operations at Dunaskin was ammonia and he was a general labourer in the ammonia works.

Hainey family

I was the youngest of nine, having three brothers and five sisters. From the oldest to the youngest they were: Margaret; John, who was killed in a gas accident at Chalmerston Mine in July 1942; Mary, who never married; Scott; Anne, who always complained at our father putting an 'e' at the end of her name when her mother's name had none; Elizabeth, who married Peter Murray who worked with Willie Ireland, the joiner in Dalmellington; Williamina, known simply as Minnie; James (Jim); and myself, the youngest in the family.

When war broke out in 1939 Jim was called up to the army and served with the Royal Scots Fusiliers. He was with the British Expeditionary Force in France until he was taken off at Cherbourg after

Dunkirk fell into German hands. He was missing for some time as he made his way from the tragic scenes of Dunkirk to Cherbourg. He re-entered the conflict after D-Day and fought through to meeting the Russians at Magdeburg. He later had a painter's business in Stranraer, and died aged eighty-nine in 2007. He was a larger-than-life character and perhaps that's what helped him get through the war largely unscathed.

Double wedding on the Hill

During the time when Jim was missing in France, as he made his way from Dunkirk to Cherbourg, two of my sisters were married in a double ceremony at Lethanhill Church, which obviously Jim missed. Margaret married Alex Wilson, a butcher in Hawick, and Anne married Dan Wallace, a miner. Sadly, Dan Wallace was killed in Pennyvenie by a rockfall in the early 1960s. His widow, my sister Anne, actually lived until the age of ninety-eight in Dreghorn. Isn't it strange how life can be so cruel to some folk?

Family tragedy

My father died in March 1938 and my mother, who was born in Hawick, went to the Miners' Home in Troon for a well-deserved wee holiday. Because of this my sister Elizabeth and her husband, Peter Murray, came to stay with us at Lethanhill while mother was at the Troon Miners' Home.

Peter and Scott were travelling from Lethanhill to Dalmellington to their work each day on a motor bike. One day at the bend at Jelliston, Patna, they collided with a brick lorry coming from Dunaskin and both were killed. It was a great shock to the whole family, and not least to my mother, who was also finding it hard to cope.

She died in March 1943, never quite getting over the loss of her son and son-in-law, especially as it came so quickly after the passing of my father. It was my birthday and I will never forget what happened. I came home from work and my mother said she had a surprise for me. It was a banana. We never saw fruit during the war years. As she was giving me the banana, she said she had a terrible headache. Within a short time she collapsed and she died ten days later without regaining consciousness.

It was a sort of tragic period of life for the family and it did teach me a lesson. Our time on earth is made up of all types of experiences, good and bad, and I think you simply need to accept both with good grace. The reality is that no one goes through life without pain and suffering, but that was a very difficult period for the entire family to come to terms with.

Home and railway

Our house at Lethanhill had only two rooms: a living room and one bedroom. There were two built-in beds in the living room. The toilet we had was a brick-built dry closet located in the back garden. The Lethanhill that I remember of my youth was rows of houses and everyone knew everyone else. It was a close-knit community. The road was made of stone chips, like an old farm cart track.

The railway was still working right beside the village until I was ten years old, with the pugs being an everyday feature of village life. The railway ran from Lethanhill, across to Benwhat, and further on to the Benbranigan Mine. The railway came to a stop in the centre of the village, running alongside the Stone Row and stopping near to the Store Row. I can remember the engine, with Alex Beattie as driver and Jock Campbell as fireman and Jim Stevenson, all well-known and popular Lethanhill men. There were always three men with each of the pugs in those days and they worked very hard indeed.

The incline

I remember that these same men also operated the Drumgrange incline, which ran down to the north side of Waterside. Alex Beattie operated the drum with Jock Campbell attaching wagons at the top of the incline and Jim Stevenson at the bottom. I remember them taking the boiler from Benbranigan Pit and taking it down the incline. Rails and all the other items recovered from Benbranigan were also put down the incline and taken away by train for disposal.

As a wee boy I once went to Benwhat on the railway with Alex Beattie driving the pug. There was one carriage which was used to take the men to and from their work in the coal mines. A group of Lethanhill boys and adults went on the train to see a football game at Benwhat between the local rivals, Burnfoothill Primrose and Benwhat Heatherbell. That was the only time I went on the engine on the Hill. I do know that before my time there used to be two engines on the Hill. One was used to run to the Bowhill pits out towards Rankinston and the other worked between the Hill and Benwhat.

School

I attended Lethanhill School. It was what we termed the old school at that time. In 1926, the year of the famous miners' strike, I can

Polnessan Row, Burnfoothill was a long row of cottages housing miners and their families. Gradually depopulated after 1945, it was deserted in 1954.
(Photo: Courtesy of Scott J Rarity Collection)

remember going to the soup kitchen in the school where we got soup and bread, because with the miners not working, there was no money to buy food or anything else for that matter.

My father suffered from bronchitis and had asthma and I think it was a result of working with ammonia at Dunaskin. I was seventeen when he died. I started school aged five and my teachers over the years were Mrs Miller, Miss Thomson, Miss Campbell and after that the class was taken by Miss Agnes Hill. Her sister, Miss Mary Hill, taught at Benwhat School.

There were thirty-two pupils in our class and as I recall there were nine classes in the old school, and they took children from age five to fourteen, so it was a busy wee school. The headmaster in my time was D B McLean and before him it was David Vallance. In fact I think the schoolhouse, which is still there today, was built for D B McLean. He was followed by a Mr J McAuley.

In those days there were no school dinners and no milk at break times. Everyone went home at lunchtime, grabbed a snack and got back to school as quickly as possible, usually eating a piece on the way, so we could play football before the bell summoned everyone back to our desks. A new school was built around 1927 and the old school was left and used as the village hall. Lethanhill School provided a top-class education in those days and I was mainly at the new school. I enjoyed science and it stood me well for the rest of my life, working as an electrical engineer.

Friends of early years

My close pals were Willie Gillespie, who later became a mine manager, and Jack Miller, who became a Church of Scotland minister and spent some time preaching in Cumnock. Sadly, both are now dead. Other boys I played with are all dead now, because I'm ninety-one, so most have predeceased me. Among the girls was Margaret Sim. I remember her because she later went for a time to Sierra Leone, where she was a nurse. She's dead now, too. That's the problem when you get to my age, most of your contemporaries are gone, but my memories of them remain fresh.

Names of the raws (rows)

In my time there were 202 houses in Lethanhill. The names of different rows included the three Laigh (low) Rows; the Step Row, so named because it ran up towards the school and was going uphill and had stepped gables; the Whaup Row was at right angles to the Step Row, and on the level with it was the Diamond Row and the Old School Row. And coming back into line with the Step Row you came across the village store. In my day Johnnie Miller was the manager and the store was operated initially by the Dalmellington Iron Company and after 1931 by Bairds and Dalmellington. It was a general grocery store with a pub attached and was a focal point for villagers.

Social life of the Hill folk

You had the church and the brethren for services on a Sunday and these were well attended by the young folk. They organised the annual trip, so you had to attend regularly or you didn't get to the trip. The trips would go by bus to Ayr shore and we enjoyed games on the Low Green; Alloway, Dunure and Maidens were also popular. You got to what to us seemed faraway places, because you have to remember that we were really very isolated, sitting at over 900 feet above sea level at Lethanhill, looking down on the valley of the River Doon.

Our village was able to boast a pipe band, a flute band and a male voice choir. The Women's Guild was active and popular. The janitor of the school was a well-known Scots comedian, Jock Park, and he organised the cantatas. He could fill the hall for a week without any problem and he was a wonderful storyteller and joke teller. Then we had the West Highland Players, who visited and held plays in the old school, turned into a hall for such entertainments.

Football was the staple game for the boys or we simply wandered about the countryside. There was a quoiting green for the men to play and gamble on who was going to win by getting the horse-shoe around the metal pin.

I was a Boy Scout, and our local troop also met at the Hill. The Scout Master was Billy Small. I think he was a Waterside man originally, later living in Dalmellington, but a great Scout man all his days. Such folk like Billy Small gave really outstanding service to these small communities and we were so lucky to have men with their commitment and talent.

Lethanhill Church and school taken from what was known as the crossroads. The village was abandoned in 1954 except for the school and the headmaster's house. The school remained open until 1959 with children bussed there and back each day.
(Photo: Scott J Rarity collection)

Marriage

I married Sarah Peters in 1946 on Christmas day. Christmas was a normal working day at that time. Scotland didn't recognise Christmas as a holiday, but did have a holiday on New Year's day. Sarah had come to the Hill from Dalmellington and started school in the infant class and we met at school and I suppose our romance was sparked from those early meetings.

My wife later taught primary classes at Ochiltree and Ayr. We celebrated our 65th wedding anniversary on 25 December 2011. We are very proud of our son, Alastair, and daughter, Sheila, and grandchildren, Kirsten and Scott.

Snowed in

In 1947 I well remember there was the most horrendous snowfall which crippled the Doon Valley and brought everything to a standstill. I remember that a chap McMillan, whose brother was a doctor in Cumnock, was trapped in his car outside Patna. A search was organised and he was found dead there in the snowdrift.

It was a really severe period of heavy snow and nothing could move. We all had just to remain indoors until it gradually got better and men with shovels – snow ploughs weren't available in those days – were able to clear the roads, allowing supplies in.

Vans on the Hill

Tommy Paterson, the baker, used to come round the village with his van, selling his baking. Driving up the Step Row, which was quite steep, Tommy discovered that his brakes wouldn't hold him, so he used to ask me to go round with him, and when he stopped, I jumped out and put a brick in at the back wheel to stop the van running back. I was only about twelve at that time. Later on he would give me a shot at driving the van, which was really great for a young lad.

Jimmy Hare from Patna came round with a vegetable van and the Co-op would come round with the horse-drawn grocery van, and the Co-op bakery was also delivered by horse and cart. I recall they had two horses at the Patna Co-op when I was a boy. The drivers would take orders and later in the week they would come back with the orders and deliver them. It seems to me that in those days there was a far better service because everyone came to your door.

You didn't have to go to Tesco or Asda like we do today, ploughing round never-ending rows to get your messages. Very few folk had cars in those days, so the service from the Co-op and elsewhere was really first-class. When you think about it, the big companies of today couldn't provide such a personalised service where the delivery man was on first-name terms with every one of his customers and probably knew all the family, too.

Hill road opening

I remember my mother telling me about the Hill road opening in 1923.

The children were taken down and walked up the road. Before the era of horse and cart service and later motorised vans, everything came up to the Hill via the Drumgrange incline. This was a self-acting ropeway that ran from the edge of Lethanhill and down a steep rail line to the north end of Waterside below. It was used to bring everything to the village before 1923 and for some time thereafter, too.

Moorland royals

I fondly remember great Sport Days at the Hill. The organising committee had the crowning of the Queen ceremony. On one occasion Andrew McBride and Lottie Grant were 'the Moorland King and Queen'. There was a nice piece in the *Ayrshire Post* around 1938 about this event, encouraging folk to come to Patna and walk up to the Hill or get Percy Hill's bus which ran regular services to Lethanhill. Percy was a great character, known to everyone. He had an advert for the event which read: 'Percy Hill's Busy Buses, brings Burnfoothill Bumper Business'. All great alliteration, don't you think!

I was the bugle boy in the Lethanhill Scouts and was quite good at this instrument. At the crowning ceremony, when the pageboys put the paper bugles to their mouths, I was in the background and had to play the bugle call, which was just wonderful and gave everyone in the audience a great laugh.

Willie Gillespie had what must have been the first car on the hill. But it was a ramshackle. This was used for the procession round the village, showing the royal party to everyone. It really was a great occasion for everyone.

Lifting the police

I remember when I was sixteen and driving the baker's van up to Lethanhill, Constable Campbell Stevenson, the village policeman in Patna, flagged me down on the Hill Road. I thought I was in serious trouble for driving without a licence, but he simply asked if we were going up the hill and he said that's fine, you can give me a lift, and he came into the van and we dropped him off in the village. That was how things were then – relaxed and sensible.

Great gardens

There were some wonderful gardens and keen gardeners on the Hill, despite it sitting nearly 1,000 feet above sea level on the high moorland. I remember Robert Filson of Benwhat gave me some chrysanthemums that had won prizes at a flower show. The folk on the Hill were very proud and enjoyed life to the full, of that there is no doubt.

I used to run in the Benwhat Harriers with Robert Reid. He waddled like a duck, but could he run! You'd run round and round and he'd lap you in no time. He was a baker in Dalmellington Co-op, but left the area to run with the famous Birchfield Harriers and everyone was very proud of his achievements.

However, it is important to remember that nostalgia can get folk carried away. I was really quite happy to leave the Hill in 1945. With the passing of my brother Scott and my brother-in-law Peter, and my mum, and the death of my brother John in the pit, it held some very sad memories. The physical living conditions were also very poor compared to what most folk expect as standard today.

Leaving the Hill

I left the Hill in 1945, at just about the end of the war. My wife's family had left the Hill in 1943 and moved to Doonbank, Patna. A lot of families were beginning to leave the Hill around that time. It was after the war that Ayr County Council began a major programme of building houses to enable folk from the Hill, Benwhat, Corbie Craigs and other small mining communities to be rehoused with modern facilities, hitherto unknown to the families of these remote communities.

Although it was a nice, friendly community, when you look back from our modern facilities of today, the conditions in Lethanhill were quite basic. However, everybody knew each other and we were all really at the same sort of level, which was poor, because nobody had very much and most folk lived from week to week with no great savings for a rainy day.

Nowadays where we live in Alloway we don't know many folk and they don't know us. That situation is totally different from the Hill, where there was a real sense of community spirit and a willingness to be neighbourly and supportive. I certainly miss that sort of relationship the most. It was a real hallmark of the Hill people.

Coal mines and TB

From the ages of fourteen to sixteen years I worked at the surface at Bogton and Chalmerston and then I began my apprenticeship as an electrician. I was sixteen in the February and started at Pennyvenie Nos. 2 and 3 in the July. When my time was out I was aged twenty-one.

Lethanhill Pipe Band in 1935. They were very successful in competition in demand for a range of events. They later moved to Patna. (Courtesy of John Relly collection)

Lethanhill was a small Dalmellington Iron Company village on the Hill above Patna and it and near neighbour, Burnfoothill were more commonly simply known as the Hill. However, they were able to boast an excellent pipe band which competed regularly and took part in the social life of the Doon Valley. Anyone visiting the 'Hill today will be struck by the number of wreaths which have been laid as tributes to former residents. The Hill was very dear to the heart of many former residents.
Back row: P McMahon, J McMahon, N McGuckin, W Bell.
Middle Row: "Pipe Major" J Clark, L Bain, T Carruthers, J Hollaway, H McClymont, A McMurtrie, J Thompson, J Roller.
Front Row: A Currie, C McCormack, S Hutchinson, J Ballantyne, J McFadzean.

I took TB and spent nine months in Glenafton Sanatorium. It was almost a self-contained community. They had a bowling green, pitch and putt and community hall. I was also asked to maintain some of the equipment. When I got out and told folk I had been there, they would take three steps back. Folk thought they would catch TB or some other terrible disease. There was a skeleton staff of nurses, but I think there would be 200 folk living there. I think Glenafton was on the go until penicillin came into its own.

When the war ended they started sending folk abroad to get them cured of TB. The medical world thought that TB was hereditary because in the past whole families had been wiped out by it. Once they discovered it wasn't hereditary and simply an infectious disease, they started shutting down the sanatoriums.

When I came out of Glenafton I went back to Pennyvenie to see about my job. Alex Stewart was the manager and he said I could start again. I don't think the fellows working beside me were too happy because of the prejudices against the disease, but I settled in quickly. I had also been attending classes at Ayr Academy to further my skills.

A lot of the tradesmen were a wee bit selfish and kept information to themselves. However, I worked away and between my fourth and fifth year, the electrician at Chalmerston Mine took ill, and the manager invited me to take over as the head electrician at Chalmerston. I explained that I'd lost nine months due to illness. He went out of the office and came back a wee while later with a letter confirming that I had served my full apprenticeship, so that was me off to Chalmerston. Apart from the apprentices, I was actually the youngest miner there.

Mining accident

One day one of the enginemen took ill and I had to stand in for him to bring the men up from the mine bottom in the cage. When I brought them up I met my brother John, who was an oversman at Chalmerston. He told me there was gas in the mine and he said that he had to go back down to clear the gas. I told him to be careful. Anyway, away he went with another deputy, Willie Galloway, and by the time I got home to the Hill I got word that there had been an accident at Chalmerston. My brother John and Willie Galloway were brought out. Tragically John was dead, but Willie Galloway fortunately survived.

I also worked at the Big Mine (Pennyvenie No. 4). The agent, Alex Stewart, asked me to carry out an inventory of all the equipment in the mine in 1945 and it turns out this was in preparation for nationalisation that occurred in 1948.

Scottish Aviation

In 1945 I left the pits and went to work for Scottish Aviation Ltd (SAL) at Prestwick as an electrician working on aircraft wiring. Later on I worked for the British Thomson Houston Company (BTH). They were a manufacturing company who equipped power stations. All the equipment and sub-stations in Ayrshire were BTH equipment.

Afterwards I worked with the South of Scotland Electricity Board (SSEB) and I married Sarah and moved to one of the wee prefabs in Patna. I retired in 1984, having been executive engineer with SSEB. I've lived in Alloway since 1992.

In my spare time I took up ornithology and went on various trips with my wife, visiting good places for bird watching. We also had a couple of holidays in Australia and one in Canada. We also went to Russia, so we've had a great retirement, something none of the old-timers in Lethanhill could ever have dreamed of.

Happy and sad

Lethanhill for me is a place where I spent my happy boyhood days, but it was also a place where our family experienced very sad events that I remember vividly. However, it was my happy home for many years and no one goes through life with constant sunshine without dark clouds overshadowing happiness. Accepting happiness and sadness with good grace is, I believe, the secret, but I am proud to say that I was from the Hill.

Yet they wha fa' in Fortune's strife,
Their fate we shouldna censure;
For still, th' important end of life
They equally may answer.

Epistle to a Young Friend
Robert Burns

Chapter 21

Cairntable Miner – Poacher Turned Gamekeeper

Jimmy Dunn

I'm truly sorry man's dominion
Has broken nature's social union,
An' justifies that ill opinion,
Which makes thee startle
At me, thy poor, earth-born companion,
An' fellow mortal!

To a Mouse
Robert Burns

Jimmy Dunn is a down-to-earth character of the old school and very proud of his association with Cairntable. He was responsible for arranging the memorial stone erected at the site of Cairntable village which was abandoned in 1963.

Parents and family

I was born at 26 Cairntable on 29 June 1931. The village memorial stone at Cairntable is located outside what was my front door. My father was James McCready Dunn, who was born in Drumclair, County of Slamannan on 6 April 1890, and my mother was Jane Stewart Baillie, born on 3 November 1897. She was always known as Jeannie and she was raised at No. 6 Lethanhill. I have a sister, Ella, who travelled for Patna Co-op taking orders from villagers and they were delivered later by van. Afterwards she was head of laundry at Ballochmyle Hospital. She then joined the police in England and remained there for about fourteen years, before leaving and working in Marks & Spencer. She is still alive today, aged eighty-four, living in Maybole. My younger brother, John, lives in Maybole and spent most of his working life as a plumber.

Walking

My earliest memories of Cairntable was when I was about four years of age. My father was a great walker and he didn't believe in using the bus. On a Saturday we would walk from Cairntable to Lochside, Ayr to visit my Aunt Aggie (Agnes). We also walked back and I would be 100 yards behind him and would be greeting (crying) and he would say: 'Lift your feet and they'll fall themsel'!' Some Saturdays we would also go to Crosshill to visit my Aunt Susan and we walked there, too. Father walked everywhere and plodded regularly to Dalmellington to see my Uncle Johnnie. We also went bramble picking in the autumn and we would have a big 14 lb basket and it took hours and hours to get it filled.

Call of the open road

I did a lot of cycling in my younger days. I was a member of the Dalmellington Wheelers and we met regularly. I also cycled with the Ayr Argonauts and the Ayr Roads boys. Every Thursday I would cycle with the great David Bell – fondly remembered by many under his pen name, the Highwayman, from his wonderful descriptive articles in the *Ayrshire Post*. And a nicer man you could never meet. He was a great encourager of young cyclists. I took up road racing on my bike in 1953. During the first season I took part in twenty-one road races, winning eighteen, losing two and retiring in the other because of a puncture.

My first racing bike was a Dayton Roadmaster, which was a ton weight. However, my second bike was a Rotrax and I got this machine from Hughie Main of Ayr, who had paid £90 just for the frame. He could see that I was going to be a good cyclist and he gave me the frame and it was a great bike for me.

Cycling events

I remember going to the Ibrox Sports in Glasgow in 1954 and taking part in the half-mile and I won out the park. I won by a mile and when I went through the line there was no one near me. The next race was the mile and because I won the first race I was put in as the back-marker. The place was crowded, thousands attended this event, and I also won the mile that day. The prize was a Westminster chime electric clock for winning the half-mile and a table lamp for the mile. It was a great day for me and I was really chuffed. After the race a lot of cyclists were asking me to join the Glasgow Wheelers, but it was too far away from Cairntable.

Another place I raced was at Kirkconnell Professional Sports. That meant that I had to go under another name to protect my amateur status. There were about twenty bookies at this sports event and they had some of the finest athletes in the country taking part. I remember that Barney Yulle, who was a Yank (American), was a world sprinter. Tim McPate of Patna was a great sprinter in those days and a lot of folk were backing Tim to beat the Yank. However, although McPate was given 11 yards in the 100 yards, the American passed him like a flash, so fast he almost gave McPate the cold with his speed.

I took part in the famous Cumnock Rally organised by the Cyclists' Touring Club and beat Jim Love of the Doon Valley, who at that time was Scottish Champion. The other top men in that race were E V Mitchell and his brother Peter Mitchell, but I managed to show them all home that day, breaking the record in the process.

I continued competitive cycling until I was about twenty-three. I took part in the Marymass 25-mile race, which was an invitation event. It was a race where the last man in each round dropped off and there were twenty-five of the best cyclists in Britain taking part. I hadn't been on the bike for about six months, when Stuart Hay of Cairntable and Burnside came out and picked me up and took me to Irvine. I got through to the final and there were only two of us in contention. We were neck and neck and the other chap kept bumping me, but at the line I beat him by a tyre length. I got a beautiful cup and £10 for winning that race. I donated the cup to the best Norwich Canary at Ayr Cage Bird Society.

Day cycle tours

On a Sunday the Ayr Roads Club met at the Auld Brig and it was about 10 miles to cover just to get there. Then we'd cycle to Strathaven and there would be twenty on the run. I hadn't a piece (sandwich) on that first run and nobody offered me a bite. They were a bit of a clannish lot at that time. However, on the way back I got the speed up gradually until I dropped them all and headed back to Cairntable.

Mining

I started working at the Bowhill Pit near Cairntable when I was thirteen and a half years of age. I got a six-month exemption to leave school early because my father had silicosis and couldn't work and someone in the family had to work in the pit or you were put out of the house and another family were put in. These were tough times. This pit was located on the hill right above Tongue Row, a small double row of houses less than half a mile from Cairntable. The houses were stone-built.

Jimmy Dunn, of Ayr, lived at Cairntable and worked in local coal mines.
(Photo: Donald L Reid)

The Bowhill Mine produced anthracite coal only. There was a row of buildings consisting of the manager's office, the first aid room, and the machinery room. There were no baths and you went home with the clothes you worked in. The coal went in six hutches at a time from Bowhill to a washing facility, called the Monkey, at Rankinston. The coal was then loaded onto wagons and taken by rail to Ayr.

When Bowhill Mine closed around 1946 I then transferred to the Drake Mine at Littlemill Colliery, which opened in 1860 and closed in 1974. It was located midway between Bowhill and Cairntable. I worked down the pit and was also a wire rope splicer. There would be over 300 men at Littlemill in those days. It was a busy place.

Horse sense

There were some characters at Cairntable. One was Sam McFadzean, who was a great yodeller and he could often be heard, happy as Larry, yodelling away. Another character was Woods Smith. During the Derby he was talking about this horse called Peter Flower. I gave him £2 and he assured me it was guaranteed to win. Wee Cowder lifted the lines (betting slips) for Wull Hunter, the Dalmellington bookie.

As it turned out, the horse wasn't even in the first three and Woods had put three weeks' wages on the horse. As you can imagine, he was in a right pickle, not least with his wife. Sam McFadzean met him at the Cairntable Brig and he was lamenting to McFadzean about not having any money. McFadzean gave him £1. He apparently doubled up on all the races that day and ended up with £500. Woods gave me £10 from his winnings as he was a very kindly individual.

There was also Jimmy Pool, who had a dog, a lurcher called Patsie, which he used to catch rabbits and hares. Old Flo McPike had a grey whippet called Flossie. I used to go down to the burn and I would whistle and Mrs McPike would let her out, and she was absolutely excellent at catching rabbits and bringing them back, dropping them at my feet.

Boxing

There was also Bob Gibson of No. 1 Cairntable. He was a former show boxer and had a face like a pound of mince, with getting biffed on the face so often. Bob encouraged me to learn boxing and gave me a bit of tuition. He had a double-barrel 4/10 shotgun and I was keen to get that. At the end Bob sold it to me and that was the beginning of a great poaching career for me as I developed a great love of nature and the great outdoors, spending some time as a gamekeeper.

Thin ice and hare chasing

I had a great time and supplied Cairntable folk with rabbits, hares, pigeon and ducks from the nearby Kerse Loch. A story I was told, which happened before I was born, was that in the 1926 strike, some of the local men were working on extracting coal from the old pit bings at Cairntable. The local farmer from Kerspark Farm would come across the frozen Kerse Loch to buy the coal from the miners. On one occasion on the way back to the farm, the ice gave way and the horse and cart went through the ice. When I was boy and swimming on the loch, you could see part of the cart wheels and it's still there to this day at the bottom of the loch.

Whenever the snow was 2 feet in height in the fields around Cairntable you could catch hares. Because of the high drifts, we would chase after the hares and actually catch them with our hands. Hares can jump anything up to 8 feet in the air and end up yards away. My pals and I would find the hole in the snow where the hare landed and dive in and it would sometimes get away and we would chase it again and again until it tired out, lay down and started to cry and you can simply

pick them up. The best field for hares was the field where Broomhill Fishery is today. Everybody in Cairntable enjoyed hare soup and the tasty meat.

In the swim

I went swimming one day in the month of March at Kerse Loch. I swam out to the middle and went to come back in to what was called the Coo-Creep, which was the lassies' dooking hole. It got to the situation where my arms wouldn't work and I went under. I was down in the silt and came back up and got a gasp of air but I was so weak and thought I was done for. Auld Bert Smith came in front of me like a vision and said to me: 'Ah telt you to do the Dogs Paddle if ever in difficulty.' I kept going until my knees hit the bottom. I was lying frozen until I recovered, but I was nearly gone that day.

At the pictures

Auld Bert Smith, a local miner, used to show films, the silent movies, at Cairntable, and this was a real treat for the entire village. He would show about two hours of film and charged a few coppers to cover his costs. He had a big white sheet up against a coal house and everyone was out, including the adults, to watch them. That was the entertainment in the late 1930s. He went all over, showing them at Rankinston, Drongan, Patna and the Hill.

Chalmerston 4/5 Pit sat on the hill high above Craigmark. Sinking and production commenced in 1925 and in 1948 it had an output of 180 tons per day. There were 128 employees. There were pit baths and a canteen. Coal hutches ran down the incline to the coal loading point at Minnivey. It closed in 1959 and was abandoned the following year. This was the fan-house building. Chalmerston No 7 was sunk in 1934 and closed in 1952 and was a surface mine. Sitka spruce trees now cover the area where the pit head was located.

The coal loading point at Minnivey which had an intricate system for loading wagons. The bogies that ran up to Chalmerston can clearly be seen in the background with coal wagons waiting to be loaded. Chalmerston spoil heap can be seen on the hill.

Shops and tramps

There were two shops in the rows at Cairntable. One was operated by Bob Deans and he sold groceries, whilst the other shop, owned by Elspeth Knox, sold sweeties. Each of them lived in the rows where their shops were located. In those days a lot of tramps came up through Cairntable. My mother always gave them a scone and a plate of soup. They went from our house up to Deans' shop and he would give them a roll of tobacco and maybe a piece and cheese. Mrs Deans would cut the cheese and a rat about the size of your hand would drop down from the rafters onto the cheese and steal a piece. Some of the things that happened in those days, you wouldn't believe.

Although Bob and Helen Deans ran the shop, their other income was from selling eggs. They had about 500 hens out the back door and they were scattered all over the place where he had hen houses. Bob did work in the pit at one time, because he worked with my father at one of the Littlemill pits. My father dug the coal while Bob loaded it onto the hutches.

Breast is best

I remember going on the train to Ayr with my mother when I was a wee boy and all the women who were breast-feeding would be in the one carriage and as a young lad I would be told to keep looking out the window while the women were feeding their weans.

Snow

I remember one year of the big snow. I was at the school and there was a huge amount of snow and everything was at a standstill. The army was out helping to clear the snow from the roads. All the houses at Cairntable were covered and it was even coming through the holes in the doors and inside the houses, such was the ferocity of the wind. We were off the school for what seemed like weeks. My father walked to Patna through the drifts and brought supplies back, but it was a tough time for everyone at Cairntable.

Moving to Dalrymple

I moved from Cairntable to Dalrymple about 1954. As older folk died or moved out of the village, younger couples moved into Cairntable. However, the rows which were established in 1914 at the start of the Great War had been totally deserted by 1963 and it was demolished shortly thereafter.

I have fond memories of Cairntable. It was very special to me. I could be here for a month telling you about what went on. In my day the village families included 'Ploxy' Smith and I remember my mother used to make suits for the Smith family for going back to school; David 'Buff' Brown; the Callaghans; the Eastons; Adam Kerr, Lindsay and McTimpany.

Memorial

I used to go up to Cairntable about three times a week and sit and reminisce. I could pass two hours with no bother, just thinking about

The incline leading to Burnfoothill. It was also known as the Drumgrange incline and it was laid down about the 1860s. It was half a mile in length and inclined at 1 in 6. This incline remained in use until about 1930, so with the passage of time no one now will recall it being in place.

things we did in my early years. It's strange, but it holds a special fascination for me. There were so many folk who would stop when I was sitting by the roadside there and ask me where Cairntable was. Of course it was gone. Nothing left!

One day I simply decided that it would be nice to put up a memorial stone so that former villagers, their relations and simply anyone passing by would know that between 1917 and 1963 a small community existed at this spot. I knew about a granite stone I came across years before on the Skeldon Estate. I got permission and had the stone transported to Cairntable.

I located the stone outside what had been my front door and got it concreted in place. In 2007 I arranged with Kevin Roberts, the sculptor from Patna, to put the following inscription on the stone: 'Cairntable Village 1914–1963. Erected by J Dunn'. I noticed a black mark on the stone and I asked Kevin to incorporate a wee mouse on the stone because I'm keen on the works of Robert Burns, as were many of the men of Cairntable.

I arranged for everyone I knew who was born in Cairntable to come along to officially inaugurate the stone and there was a great turnout and it was quite emotional. We were all rather proud to belong to that special wee place and still remember it with great affection.

What tho', like commoners of air,
We wander out, we know not where,
But either house or hal'?
Yet Nature's charms, the hills and woods,
The sweeping vales, and foaming floods,
Are free alike to all.

Epistle to Davie, a Brother Poet
Robert Burns

Chaper 22

Lethanhill – A Deserted Mining Village

William Murphy

We twa hae run about the braes,
And pou'd the gowans fine
But we've wander'd monie a weary fit
Sin auld lang syne.

Auld Lang Syne
Robert Burns

William Murphy with Mr Robert Bryce at Lethanhill. Bryce was apparently the last man to move to Patna.

William Murphy was born at Lethanhill in 1895 and spent his formative years in the village. He said a fond farewell to the village in 1925, aged thirty, but those formative and adult years living there gave him a special insight into village life.

In 1965 and aged seventy, then living as a retired headmaster in Fort William, he spoke passionately to an audience said to number five hundred at the Hill Re-union. He recalled his memories of living in what he later described as 'a deserted village.'

And it was indeed a deserted village on one of his last visits in 1962 with only the war memorial remaining from the village of his day. The rows of cottages where folk have lived had been demolished and the rubble removed.

His personal reflections on life at Lethanhill over thirty years, span the latter part of the nineteenth and early twentieth century, thus providing an illuminating insight into aspects of life on the Hill.
In this article and indeed in this book the term 'the Hill' is a generic name for Lethanhill and Burnfoothill, two small communities located side by side above Patna, but each with its own identity, albeit Lethanhill was by far the larger of the two.

Lethanhill – My Birthplace

If you are travelling on the Ayr – Dalmellington Road (A713) near the old signal box at Patna Station you will see a sign post,'Lethanhill one mile.' Follow that road across the grassy face of the hillside and you will come upon the ruins of this village, now the haunt of the peewit, the whaup and the lark. It was here that I was born, in the Briggate Raw, in 1895, at which time something like 1,700 people lived in 300 houses. At one time Lethanhill was the largest community in terms of population in the Doon Valley.

Crimean War Settlers

The Hill as it was best known in the Doon Valley, grew up in rows on a grassy hillside about 600 feet above sea level. The first settlers occupied the Whaup Row and the Peewit Row about the time of the Crimean War (1853-1856).

The Hill developed as a miners' camp, a supply depot for the labour force required to work the ironstone. To be more realistic, it was also an isolation camp, almost literally cut off from any contact with the outside world.

Road Closed

Certainly there was an access road, but that road crossed the railway in the valley and was kept locked and barred by the companies orders (Dalmellington Iron Company). No outside trader dared trespass up the Hill. The road was closed except for flittings (moving house), funerals, and urgent medical cases.

The company's provisions store supplied the essentials for life, and there were instances where what the housewife did not pay against her 'tammy book,' the man spent in the beer store, so that by the next week his wage packet was returned almost intact to the company's coffers. In 1908 this physical barrier to free trade was removed by the fine work of Mr Beale, the liberal MP for South Ayshire and Patna Co-op came up the Hill.

Burnfoot Primrose Football Team in the 1920s. This was the local team based at Burnfoothill which was a Dalmellington Iron Company village on the hill above Patna. Everyone seems to have had nicknames in the mining industry.
Back row: George Bowie, 'Adie' Park, 'Tanny' Anderson, Hugh Givens, Dummy ?, 'Buller' Dalziel. 'Pimpy' Moffat, and J Graham
Front row: Sam Gillespie, D Logan, S Riddicks, 'Ruchie' Leslie, J McDowall, 'Elkie' Clark and Tommy Kirk. The young boy holding the shield is George Sturgeon, later a miner and a member of the Mine Rescue Brigade. His son, George, still lives in Dalmellington. The small villages in the Doon Valley such as Burnfoothill, Lethanhill, Waterside, Craigmark and Benwhat all had football teams.

A class at Lethanhill School 1947/48.
Back row (l to r): Andrew Meldrum, Andrew Beggs, Jean Meldrum, Margaret McFarlane, Lilly Gilmour, John McEwan and John Kennedy
Middle row: Billy Johnstone, Margaret Johnstone, Ella Knox, Marjory Fawcett, Elizabeth Dalziel, Helen Torbet and Bert Daly
Front row: John McDermont, Francey Bryce, Billy Brown, Harry Ferguson and Hugh Gilmour.

Ironstone Miners

The men generally walked or travelled on a an old railway coach along the myriad of railway tracks to the pits, their job to mine ironstone for the blast furnaces at Waterside, opened by the Dalmellington Iron Company in 1847. And then it was not an eight hour shift – usually much longer. In the winter months they saw the sun only at the weekend. Nor was there compensation for injury received at work. The Workmen's Compensation Act as applied to miners did not come into operation until 1897.

Cost of Living

Holidays for the miners were, of course, unknown. Indeed, when this concession was finally granted, it was without pay, so that, when he resumed work, the miner was faced with double rent and an extra week's grocery bill.

Occasionally for one reason or another, the miners would suffer from broken time. This automatically meant loss of earnings. But in no case was his rent allowed to lapse or his coal go unpaid. These charges were deducted at head office before he drew his pay.

The company simply could not lose. If life was grim for the men and of that there can be no doubt, it was also grim for the women because there were no pit head baths so the men had to wash at home and the women had to help as well as washing all the filthy pit clothes, but that that was the way of it and and the human cycle ran its course.

Poor Amenities

In the houses on the Hill there was no provision for birth or death or even sickness. There was an open fire in the kitchen. Water, carried from the 'Spoot' in pails, was heated in huge iron kettles. Washing day was an exercise in sheer physical endurance. Much of it was done by hand. Women just had to ring out their men's heavy pit moleskin trousers, after having scrubbed them white on a corrugated board. It could never have been easy for the women.

Large Families

As for overcrowding, the problem was acute but just ignored and large families were the rule, not the exception. Ten was quite usual. Inside there was just not room to sleep everybody. As soon as the lassies reached school leaving age – sometimes sooner – they had to go out to 'service,' which usually involved working for a family in one of the larger houses in the district.

Three men who spent their working lives in the pits of the Doon Valley. Their pursuit away from mining was playing in Dalmellington Band in the bass section. Willie Kennedy, John 'Jubie' McCulloch and Tom 'Tam' Wilson were talented musicians.

Cradle for babies

As palliative the 'Whurlie bed' was contrived and in use. During the day it ran on wheels under the big standing bed, and was pulled out at night. It could accommodate two adults. But by far the most pathetic article in every-day use was the home-made cradle, complete with wooden rockers. In some families these cradles served several generations of babies and when the babies took the air, they were carried in a big shawl or plaids by their mothers or older sisters. I never saw a pram on the Hill.

Uniform rows

Undeniably, the village was unattractive, forbidding, even ugly. The drab, barrack-like uniformity of the rows, planned with no eye to beauty, but seemingly to conform to the alignment to the railway tracks that intersected the rows, presented a picture of unrelieved depression and deadness. We entertained few visitors on the Hill. The sedate valley folk who lived in Patna, Waterside and Dalmellington, called us 'the Hill Arabs.'

Tough lads & Bonny lassies

From the houses the immediate prospect, back or front, was horrible, open middens and old pit bings. On its eminence and refreshed by 'winds, austere and pure' our village should have had a clean bill of health. Yet enteric fever was not unknown, engendered by foul water. None the less, the 'Hill reared hardy, tough youngsters, and bonny lassies as well.

Somehow, too, the women outlived the men. I have been privileged to see a photograph of four generations, where the grandmother, well over eighty years of age, still looks healthy, straight and comely. How they did it, I don't know.

Culture call

But the spirit of the Hill folk, rose superior to their harsh, frustrating, physical environment, and in time they evolved some attempt at self expression, cultural and even aesthetic, social recreation and fun and games. Two houses knocked into one, served as a public library and a reading room. About 1905 a wee corrugated iron church took shape.

Kinderspiels, (a childrens' entertainment, both choral and dramatic) became the rage in the wintertime, after one of which a character was nicknamed 'Cat′ Mackie for life. The ring of quoits was heard on the green. A pipe band turned out, a male voice choir was trained. Pigeon breeders flew their birds from faraway places on the continent.

Ballroom dancing classes were regularly held and at the finale the dancing master appeared in full evening dress, white gloves, silk handkerchief and imperial beard. Amateur pansy growers won prizes for their Hill blooms, even in Glasgow. Hardy fishers practiced their art, not only on the River Doon and Loch Doon, but also Loch Enoch at the foot of the Merrick.

Nor must we forget 'The Roses,' (Burnfoothill Primrose), the redoubtable Hill football team of such wonderful memory. Women liked flowers, and, if you knew where to look behind the lace curtains, you would get a glimpse at a fuchsia, a hydrangea or even what the housewife called, her French not being too good, - her 'Glory de John' rose.

Blizzards

On dear Lethanhill I spent my boyhood close to nature. And it was extremely exposed to the elements, for blizzards struck us in the winter time. We were isolated. The snow reached the level of the porches of the houses, so that the passage along the backs of the rows was like a front line fire trench, complete with bays and traverses. Outside at night it was as dark as the mouth of the pit itself. You had to have cat's eyes.

Delightful summer

By contrast the summers seemed endless. We had the freedom of the moors from Rankinston to Benquhat Hill. Barefoot in jersey and pants, you could guddle and dook (swim) in clear running burns, all day long. School we never took very seriously, nor did I remember doing any homework. It was a delightful animal existence.

Mixed Emotions

That is all gone. By 1960 most of the village had been demolished and the wilderness took over. The garden, a riot of colour in the summer time, was over-run by the nettles, the thistle, and the docken. The peewit and the whaup and the lark could now nest in peace. The oldest inhabitant and the last to leave (Mr Rab Bryce, then aged seventy-nine) had reluctantly been re-housed to Patna. I left the Hill in 1925. Do I comeback? Yes. Do I enjoy coming back, yes and no!

Steam Locomotive

For I see people and hear things that are not there anymore. I see the wee pug engine cruising cannily along the front of Polnesson Row. The cannier locomotive engineman, with an eident eye on his nearside, seemed keenly aware of the potential for a thoughtless boy running headlong after the stray ball. The steam engine, chuffed along spewing white and black smoke, working hard pulling a heavy train-load of char-filled wagons, on their way via 'the incline' to the furnace bank at Waterside. These were all common scenes of my boyhood.

Scenes of yesteryear

I could also hear the spark and clink of the champion's quoit, as he steals the shot from his opposite number, from the nearby Kerse. From the beer store, as an aftermath to the quoits, the mellow rendering, in a rich baritone voice, of *Bonnie Mary o' Argyll*. It mattered not then who won or lost, it was time to socialise.

The purposeful gait of the stout, unofficial, though none-the-less successful village maternity nurse dressed in black shawl, tweed skirt and leather boots answering an SOS call, signalled the imminent arrival of a new baby for Lethanhill.

I also remember the brave muster of the Orangemen gathering in the village for the 12th July parade. They were deep-chested men, stalwart and resplendent in their orange and blue. This was a sight to behold for young folk and caused a great stir in the village.

A Place of ghosts

At the front door of the school the leonine countenance of the headmaster, set off by moustache and chop-whiskers, commanding attention without opening his mouth. I gaze at the war memorial, upstanding, solitary, and now so lonely and so forlorn. Sixteen of our 'Hill boys did not come home from the Kaiser's war.

I say 'No more, no more,' repeatedly. This village, the Hill, is no more; it has died. For me it is a place of ghosts.

We Twa hae paidl'd in the burn
Frae morning sun till dine,
But seas between us braid hae roar'd
Sin auld lang syne

Auld Lang Syne
Robert Burns

Chapter 23

Donaghadee to New Zealand – via Doon Valley

David Boyce

David Boyce was born on 28 February 1947, in Blenheim, New Zealand. A teacher by profession, he has taught internationally for the last ten years with three years in Kazakhstan and seven years in Singapore. He has found the experience most enjoyable and inspirational, with the students from so many backgrounds eager to learn.

He has always been intrigued by his family roots, especially where they link to Ayrshire's Doon Valley. Here he writes of some family members, ironstone miners in the Doon Valley, in whose footsteps he now walks. In his research he discovered that spelling of names varied, both first and surnames.

This is a tale told through the deeds of the family of James Boyce and Mary Dickenson. Interestingly, David came into contact with Donald L Reid when he purchased, Donald's book, The Lost Mining Villages of Doon Valley, whilst he was working as a teacher in Kazakhstan. It really is strange how paths cross!

Reflecting on 1846 – 1909

While obviously this is a genealogy of sorts, the aim of this article is to give a perspective on the lives of an ironstone miner's family and their legacy, from 1846 – 1909 in various places in Ayrshire, including the villages of Doon Valley.

On reading accounts of the Boyce family, what comes through is the strength of individuals and of family ties, the inter-marriages between iron mining families, and the importance of religion, sport and music. These values would have been true for many other Doon Valley families and the communities in which they lived.

My great grandfather, George Boyce, was a skilled fiddle player and highland dancer (listed as a sport when he arrived in Blenheim, New Zealand). There were, however, some 'differences' over religion!

Married in Donaghadee

My great great grandparents, James Boyce and Mary Dickenson/Dickson, were married in 1844 in Donaghadee, County Down. I am not sure what impact the potato famine had on their lives, or indeed what other hardships they endured.

However, many men in County Down were agricultural labourers and their work was physically harder and less well paid than that of an ironstone miner.

The wages for iron miners in Ayrshire in 1851 ranged from two shillings and six pence (2/6d) to three shillings and six pence (3/6d) a day. (*Scottish Mining website)*

Moving to Dalry in Ayrshire

As young newly-weds, James, aged twenty-one and Mary, aged twenty, emigrated to Dalry in Ayrshire in 1846 with their eldest child, John. Was it to follow family (most likely in my opinion), or the expectation that the dire life as an ironstone miner was more promising than the life they were experiencing in County Down?

The actual trip by boat was probably not too daunting as there had been regular trips between County Down and Ayrshire for work, religion and trade over the previous couple of centuries. Donaghadee is on the east coast of County Down.

The 1851 census has James and Mary with sons John, Hugh (born Dalry) and James Jnr (born Coylton) at 29 New Street, Dalry. James was a pitheads man. It's interesting to note that in Dalry at that time the Ironworks had commenced in 1844, albeit they fell silent in 1871. There were also around thirty ironstone and coal pits working in the area. With a population of 11,000 it was a large thriving to town.

1861 Census

At the time of the 1861 census the family was at No 7 Vil of Linn (Village of Linn perhaps), Dalry. In addition to the above three sons, there were now Henry (born Dalry), George (my great grandfather born 1853, Dalry), Margaret and Elizabeth (born Peesweep Row, Dalry) and Mary and David (born Linn Row, Dalry). Peesweep Row and Linn Row were iron miners accommodations provided by William Baird and company.

In 1861 their eldest son John was resident at 8 North Row, Lethanhill, Dalmellinton.

James' brother, Hugh, and his family had emigrated from Donaghadee by this time and were also in Dalry. There was at least one other Boyce family in Dalry.

James and Mary's other children: Thomas, William and Joseph were born in Kilwinning. Sarah and Jane (twins) were born in Dalry. Robert, the youngest was born in Dalmellington 1870. (Robert, his wife Mary Strachan and family migrated to New Zealand in 1904, their passage assisted by George.)

In the 1871 census the extended Boyce family was in Lethanhill, with James and his sons working as iron miners.

Bound for New Zealand

George and his wife Ellen Roy (pregnant with daughter Mary), both aged 22, emigrated to New Zealand in 1875 with their son Henry—for a better life and possibly to follow 'uncles' from County Down who had already emigrated. The story of their voyage on the ship Carnatic is told in a personal reflection entitled: 'Plum Duff and Cake.'

George inspected several vessels before deciding on the Carnatic—one ship he 'didn't like the look of' burned at sea. The Carnatic passed the burning ship as they sailed to New Zealand.

George had various occupations in Blenheim including one as a contractor, which involved carting wool from the large sheep stations in the South Island. Among his team of Clydesdales were two outstanding horses, Brig o' Doon and Bonnie Doon.

George and Ellen were followed to New Zealand in 1879 by his older brothers: John and his wife Jane Murray, and Henry and his wife Annie McBride, with their respective families.

Boyce marriages

David married Elizabeth McFadzean, 1879 in Lethanhill/ Burnfoothill
Elizabeth married Thomas Mullins at 40 Tongue Row in 1884. Thomas was an ironstone pit drawer living at 8 Tongue Row at the time.
John, Hugh, James (Jnr) and George all married daughters of iron miners.

Mary married William Smith in 1875 in Dalmellington. Also (cousins?): Mary Boyce married Robert Willie 25/7/1872, Dalmellington. Sarah Boyce married Thomas Thompson 1876, Dalmellington.

Tongue Row

In 1881 James, Mary and family are listed at 39 Tongue Row, Dalmellington. Tongue Row was a "hill village", also known as Tongue Bridge Row, and existed from 1840 –1920. Miners' accommodation then shifted to Polnessan, near Patna.

The caption at the bottom of the picture reads: Burnfoot lamp station. According to D L Smith there were eleven Burnfoot pits above Patna. (l to r) 'Nashy' McCracken, 'Addy' McNab, Bob Jess, Harry Burgoyne, Jimmy Hose, John Flynn, J. Blackwood and Mr Cunningham.

Tongue Row consisted of approximately 20 mining cottages for workers at the iron pits on the slopes of Bowhill outside Patna. The rows and iron pits were owned by the Dalmellington Iron Company, as were other close-by hill villages such as Burnfoothill.

It is chilling to read of the conditions that mining families endured in the various 'Rows' in Ayrshire, including Peesweep Row, Lethanhill and Burnfoothill in the early 1900's. The *Scottish Mining website* describes life in these mining rows as: 'Physical hardship, overcrowding, disease.' Grim living conditions indeed! 'Sixteen tons and what do I get, another day older, I owe my soul to the company store,' comes to mind.

In 1891, the Boyce family was still at 39 Tongue Row, Dalmellington. James died in 1892, aged 67, from chronic pneumonia and was buried in Patna cemetery.

"James Boyce is my name
Scotland is my nation
Tongue Row is my dwelling place
Heaven is my expectation"

His son Hugh was killed in 1893 in a mining accident in Lanark when part of a roof fell on him.

Bearing Witness

Having travelled widely I often ponder on what life was like for those family members in whose footsteps I am now privileged to walk. It really is important to recording past life and working practices in the coal industry. These can be all too quickly forgotten, along with the stories of hardy miners who once inhabited the industrial Doon Valley.

I am delighted that Donald L Reid and his colleagues in Barrmill Jolly Beggars Burns Club, in spite of their own advancing years, have managed to capture, through personal interviews with so many lively old miners, the vibrancy of their daily work at the coal face of life. These voices from the past will be heard by generations to come, thanks to their need to bear witness.

Benwhat Heatherbell was an excellent football team in the early 1900s just before the Great War. Descendants of those in the photo still live in the Doon Valley.

Back row (l to r): Neil Dempsey, Dan Parker, John 'Baillie' Armour, McGee, Pat Murray, George Long, Thomas Hodgson (killed in First World War), John Hodgson, J 'Skip' Bryan and E Miller (killed in First World War).

Front row: T Yates, 'Sand Dancer' Murray, Duff Hannah, J Murray, J Kennedy and Charles Fisher.

(Courtesy of John Relly collection)

All these shops in High Main Street were occupied by various departments of Dalmellington Co-operative Society which was established in 1879. By 1951 the society employed 71 people and had a membership of 1,455 with an annual turnover of £144,000. This photograph is circa 1920 and the man holding the horse is Tom Bryden of Burnton Farm. From its earliest days until after the Second World War, the Co-op had several horses and carts for delivering groceries and butcher meat.

Chapter 24

The Human Cost of Coal Extraction

David Scobie

When the grim foe of life below
Comes in between to make us part,
The iron hand that breaks our band,
It breaks my bliss, it breaks my heart!

The Day Returns
Robert Burns

David Scobie, 81, was interviewed in June 2015 by Donald L Reid. He reflected on his years working in the pits of Doon Valley. His whole family from his grandfather, father to his son were involved in the coal mining industry.

Tragically, David's son, Iain, was killed in an accident at Hall of Auchencross opencast site, New Cumnock on 21 March 1997. This demonstrates that even after the closure of traditional deep mining in Ayrshire, fatal accidents were still occurring as men continued to extract black diamonds.

I was born at 17 Burnton, Dalmellington, on 29 October 1933. My father was David Scobie, miner. He worked 52 years in the pits of the Doon Valley. He worked at Beoch and later at Minnivey. He retired in 1953 and died in 1984.

Family Mining Connections

My mother was May Limond of Dalmellington, born and bred. They married in 1933. I was the oldest of a family of three. My younger brothers were John and Tom. Both were in the mining industry.

Tom was an engineer at Minnivey Colliery where he began his coal mining career as an apprentice and then went on to work at Killoch Colliery.

David Scobie of Patna has a watch presented to his grandfather by the Dalmellington Iron Company on his retiral. David's memories are recorded in a chapter entitled: The Human Cost of Coal Extraction. (Photo: Donald L Reid)

Iain Limond Scobie, son of David Scobie, who was accidentally killed on 21 March 1997 aged 33 years at Hall of Auchencross Opencast site near New Cumnock.

John was a joiner with the NCB working initially at Waterside then going on to Lugar workshops and finished up at Killoch Colliery. It was really impressive when you realised the number of different trades, skills and abilities required to keep a coal mine running safely and efficiently.

So you could say that all my family were in the mining industry in Doon Valley in some capacity over many long years.

Tour with Abe Moffat

My grandfather, David Scobie, was also a miner. I remember that one May day holiday, about 1947, when the industry was nationalised, he was taken round Edinburgh in a car with the miner's leader, Abe Moffat.

This was at a miners rally to celebrate the nationalisation of the coal industry and he used to talk about how he toured Edinburgh with Moffat celebrating nationalisation of the coal industry from which he had just retired. He was very proud to be a miner, but also realised that the conditions had to be improved to ensure that safety was paramount.

60 Years Service

I still have a gold inscribed watch given to my grandfather when he retired from Bairds & Dalmellington and the inscription reads: *"On completion of 60 years service, December 1946, presented to David Scobie by Bairds & Dalmellington Ltd."*

Heirloom

I treasure the watch very much because I was called after my grandfather, my father, and my grandson is also David Scobie. I will pass this watch onto my grandson and hopefully he will take the same pride in it as I do and it will remind him of the long mining tradition in the family.

School Days to Beoch

I was educated at Dalmellington Higher Grade School which I started in 1939 and Mr Thomson was the headmaster. I finished in the 3rd year when I was aged 15 years and I immediately started work at the Beoch Mine located on the Dalmellington – New Cumnock (B741) about 5 miles from Dalmellington and a further 1 mile off this road. We had some tough times getting to and from Beoch over the years because it was often snowbound, lying on the exposed high moors.

I started in the pithead at Beoch and then I got into the work-shops to serve my apprenticeship as a colliery engineer. I went to night school in Dalmellington and day classes at Ayr College of Technology which was out the Maybole Road in those days. I finally retired aged 51 from Killoch Colliery in 1984.

Engineers Shop

When I went into the engineers shop at Beoch as a youngster, my gaffer was John Niven, who was the chief engineer at Beoch Colliery. The manager in my early years was Jackie Bunyan. He was good to the boys and the auld men. In winter he put out an enamel pail which was full of hot Bovril and you helped yourself to a nice hot drink. I served my time at the Beoch and worked there for quite a few years, eventually leaving in 1960 to work at Pennyvenie.

At Beoch Jim 'Gentle' Boyle was a workmate and John Blane and Jock Hamilton, were amongst the several who travelled from Lanarkshire to work. David Shankland was from New Cumnock and in fact there was a lot of New Cumnock men worked there. David Bowie was an electrician.

They all worked with me in the engineers shop together with electricians and blacksmiths.

The main role of an engineer was to build and repair machinery. We were basically fitters. An engineer would be in charge of a section whilst on the backshift and nightshift.

I did inspections and carried out repairs. There were coal cutters and conveyer belts and these were the vital pieces of machinery that had to be maintained otherwise coal could not be produced. If the conveyor or coal cutters broke down, then the pressure was on to get them repaired and back working because producing coal was the top priority for everyone.

Fatalities at Beoch

I was on the backshift the night that Richard Armour of Dalmellington was killed down the pit, apparently electrocuted. That was in early November 1955. I was working at a machine and I was told about the accident. Jock Kennedy was the manager and he came in with Doctor Campbell, the local GP in Dalmellington.

Tom Henderson and I were told by the manager to get hot water bottles and some blankets and take them down the pit to the scene of the accident. Kennedy and the doctor immediately set off for the scene. Meanwhile I got hot water bottles and blankets from the baths attendant.

I remember running down the main road into the mine and at the bottom Tam (Henderson) and I got into a hutch and were taken along the road to near the scene of the accident. When I got there Richard (Armour) was lying there and I could see that Dr Campbell was exhausted from the exertion of getting to the scene and attending to Richard.

Tam (Limond) and his neighbour had given Richard (Armour) artificial respiration for about an hour before the doctor got to the scene. That was without doubt one of the saddest days of my life. Richard was a really nice quiet fellow and it was so tragic for his wife and very young family.

It could never have been easy for someone like Dr. Campbell going down the mine after rushing up from Dalmellington, because it would be a scary place for anyone not used to the conditions. I know that Dr.

Richard Armour, pit electrician, who was accidentally killed in a mine accident at Beoch Colliery on 2 November 1955. (Photo: Armour family)

Campbell and Dr Lee attended many accidents in the local pits over the years, so they were very dedicated men and greatly respected by the miners.

Jimmy 'Pimpy' Moffat was acting as manager on another occasion I recall at Beoch. Tam Jess from New Cumnock had died down the pit as a result of a heart attack rather than a specific mine accident. He was a big man and when he was brought to the surface and certified dead by the doctor, the undertaker later arrived. I was asked to help move the body into a coffin and get it out to the hearse, a job I did with great sadness because there would be another family grieving at their personal loss. That was another sad day for everyone at Beoch.

I also remember Willie Carlyle from Dalmellington being killed at Beoch in late 1954. His father, also worked at Beoch on the turbine pumps, so it must have been extremely upsetting for him being a fellow miner.

Willie was killed by a rock fall at No. 7 section of Beoch 3 and 4. I remember that Willie was killed on the backshift. All the men were sent home, because that was what happened when a fatality occurred. The miners were more or less local and knew each other well, so any death impacted on everyone. I think it also made us even more conscious of the potential dangers that were ever-present down the mine.

Beoch Highest Mine

At the time I worked at Beoch it was reputedly the highest mine in Britain and it was a cold place to work. In my day you walked down the Beoch and walked back up and it was a long walk before you even started work.

After I left in 1960 to go and work at Minnivey they put in a mini-rider and this took the men up and down the mine rather than them having to walk long distances. It was a small enclosed carriage, which took them safely underground.

However, by that time Beoch was really on its last legs and didn't last a great time after that. In fact it closed in 1968. Most of the men who worked at Beoch came from Dalmellington or New Cumnock area.

My Son – Fatal Accident

The cost of mining – on this occasion – opencast mining, was brought home to me in the most tragic way. My own son, Iain Limond Scobie, aged 33 was killed on 21 March 1997 at Hall of Auchencross opencast site near New Cumnock.

He had only started working at this site some eight weeks before the accident. In fact he had been commended the day before the accident for the way he carried out his duties in fuelling the huge earth-moving vehicles involved in the opencast operations. These giant vehicles would come in to the fuel loading point and Iain would begin filling the tanks from a bowser.

He would signal to the drivers when the operation had been completed so the driver knew it was safe to move off. On that particular day the earth moving truck seems to have moved away before the refuelling process had fully finished. The fuel line seems to have sprung back and struck my son, killing him.

The accident happened on a Friday and the way things are with communications, I think everyone in Patna knew about the death of Iain before our family were told. My wife Jean passed on in 2004, but to be honest she was never quite the same after this tragic event.

I think for about two years we just mainly stayed in the house and never ventured out very much. It really had a devastating effect on our lives. We received great support from our son, Hugh, better known to everyone by his middle name, Ferguson; my daughter, Fiona and son, David.

My family and Iain's widow, Lynn, were so supportive and we, of course, tried to be supportive of her. But despite this it was very difficult coming to terms with the loss of a dear son, in such dreadful circumstances. Of course you never expect that any of your children will die before you.

The really tragic part was that Iain had just set out on married life with Lynn (Madden) from Patna in August 1996, only a few months before he was killed, so it was a very difficult time for Lynn. In fact she stayed with my wife, Jean, and I for a couple of years after Iain's death. They had been very happy together and had a house in Patna. Fortunately, she married again several years later and moved to Ayr.

I spent all my working life in the pits mainly in the Doon Valley. The coal mines could be very challenging. I think that working with so many good people was what made a difficult job mainly enjoyable.

For me mining was and remains a place of precious memories – happy times intermingled with heart-rending tragedy that still makes me cry and ask why? My personal experience is that life is definitely not all roses. You have to take the good with the bad and face life head-on because there is no other choice.

Fare-thee-weel, thou first and fairest!
Fare-thee-well, thou best and dearest!
Thine be ilka joy and treasure,
Peace, Enjoyment, Love and Pleasure!

Ae Fond Kiss
Robert Burns

A dramatic scene showing a train accident at Waterside near to Cutler sidings. The pug with a rake of coals left the line. The spilled coal would have disappeared later that night! On the left the compulsory 'three men and a dog' watch over proceedings! They were (l to r): James Kerr, John Kerr who was himself a former engine driver and Thomas Rowan, formerly the traffic foreman.

Chapter 25

Colliery Tradesman

John Collins

Thou'll break my heart, thou warbling bird,
That wantons thro the flowering thorn!
Thou minds me o departed joys,
Departed never to return.

The Banks of Doon
Robert Burns

John Collins

John Collins recalls his days working in the coal mining industry in Ayrshire, starting off as an apprentice engineer. He was born and raised in Dalmellington where he still lives today.

He is married to Jean Bell, daughter of Neilly Bell, who ran a popular bakery business in Main Street, Dalmellington for many years. John and Jean are very proud of their family. They have three children - Elaine, Dorothy, and Andrew, and three grandchildren - Lyndsay, Rhiain, and Adam.

Now enjoying retirement after leaving the coal industry in 1970, he worked for another 24 years at Grants Distillery, Girvan and 15 years at GE Caledonian, Prestwick, retiring in 2011. John's hobbies are golf, watching sport, and his grand-children.

John, who was interviewed by Donald L Reid, in June 2015, is very proud of and values his years involved in the coal mining industry working with some clever engineers and fascinating characters.

Family Background

I was born at No 43 Broomknowe, Dalmellington on 25 May 1946. My mother was Jean Limond who was born and raised in Dalmellington from a mining family. My father was Joseph Collins who worked all his days in the local mines. He started off at Clawfin before moving to Chalmerston and after that he worked at Minnivey, retiring from there in 1973.

He never missed a shift and took his work seriously. He was very proud to be a coal miner. In fact he wanted to retire earlier than he did, but John Kennedy, the manager, kept putting him off because he knew my father was reliable.

Mr Kennedy needed someone he could count on to brush (mine drive) the big road at Minnivey and he knew my father would work hard to achieve success.

School Days

I was educated at St Xaviers Primary School, Waterside and then at St Margaret's Ayr. I left school aged 15. This was the year that 'O' Levels started and that would be 1960-61. I got the chance to stay on and take some technical subjects at 'O' level.

However, my father had other ideas and was quite polite in telling me that I was going to work for a living as he wasn't going to chase me out to school for one more day of his life.

He was a no-nonsense type of man and always tried to explain the importance of earning a living honestly and doing your very best at work. I think my father did pass on these same values to me, because I have always tried to do my work to a good standard.

Apprenticeship in Mining

I applied for an apprenticeship in the pits. The day I sat the exams there was 60 boys sitting in the same room hoping to get an apprenticeship as an electrical or mechanical engineer. I was accepted as one of the 20 boys taken on for mechanical engineering and there were also 20 for the electricians training.

I started on 21st August 1961 at Sherwood Road, Prestwick, which was a NCB training centre located next to Atlantic House at Prestwick Airport. Glenburn Mine was right next door. I did 9 months in the apprentice school where you learned to turn, do basic welding and soldering as well as practical training at the pit.

You had to undergo tests for all the practical aspects of the job. You would spend perhaps a week on a lathe getting used to working with precision tools. You also had to do one day a week at Ayr Technical College which at that time was based at St Leonards Road, Ayr, later relocating to Dam Park.

I did quite enjoy the whole experience and you learned a range of skills that were put to good use in the coal mines. The instructors were Bob McClatchie, Jimmy Mackie and Willie Dick on the mechanical side.

Working at Minnivey

After one year in the training role, I was transferred to Minnivey Colliery at Burnton, Dalmellingon. As an apprentice going to work in the pits, you were given a list of tools you needed. These were supplied by the Coal Board and you paid them up the cost coming off your wages at 10/- a week.

I've still got some of my original tools to this day. The old miners often said: "Look after your tools and they'll look after you, son" and that's something I took on board and it proved to be very good advice.

Workers

The chief engineer was Jack Seawright with Jimmy Dempsey and Willie Kennedy as his assistants. The other engineers I remember were Dick Wallace, Ian 'Purdie' Allan, Hugh McClymont, Jimmy Dick, Jimmy Murray, Roy Wright, Hugh O'Neil, Dick Law, Tom Buchanan and Billy McCormick.

Alex Johnstone was foreman blacksmith with Tommy McColl, Steve Poole, Jim Boyd, Abe Shannon and Bobby Kirk, and the apprentice was Tommy Paton. Jim Tanner was chief electrician and Jock Easton was his assistant. Jim Kennedy, Tom O'Neil, Tom 'Tam' Wilson, Jack Learmouth were the electrical crew.

In our workshop there was also Hammy Wallace who was the greaser; Pat Dooley, 'Pan' Bryce, Timpsey Thompson, Willie Tyson and they were belt men and dowty men – dealing with belts on the machinery and pit props. I got into trouble for not calling men by the surname – Mr McColl, Mr Boyd, but that was soon changed and we were on first name terms.

Temporary Change of Trade

On one occasion I caused quite a stir when I drove the forklift truck straight through the work shop doors. In his report on the incident, Jack Seawright said that the brakes on the forklift were not working properly.

I was called in to see the manager, John McArthur, who was the top man. He asked me what happened and I told him the truth. He then said: "What is it you do here at the mine, Collins?" I told him that I

The Running Dog was the name given to the pub in Craigmark in 1960s and frequented mainly by local miners. In 2015 it was still operating at the Craigmark Inn. Miners dressed up as cowboys and Indians and attended charity events. Sam Semple, a popular Dalmellington character and former miner, is holding the gun. Next to Sam is Billy 'Rocky' Campbell and Alexander 'Sanny' Aitken.

The car park at Minnivey Colliery in the 1960s. Minnivey was sunk in 1955 and its short life ended by faulting and subsequent closure in 1975.

was an apprentice engineer. He looked at me sternly saying: "Well son, until that door is fixed you are now a joiner, so get to it, son." So I spent about a month working with Hugh Relly in the joiners shop and the door was eventually fixed to the satisfaction of the boss and I could return to being an apprentice engineer.

Practical Mine Training

At Minnivey you then did underground training. I was sent to Muircockhall Colliery, Dunfermline, which was an NCB training establishment. It was a pit which was kept open for the purposes of training apprentices and others coming into the industry.

The training establishment at Dungavel near Muirkirk was also on the go, but the coal board apprentices at that time went for 4 weeks to Muircockhall.

Muircockhall

I stayed in private digs in Dunfermline and the apprentices were usually billeted with old miners and their families who were paid to look after the apprentices. I was in digs with Tom Buchanan, also of Dalmellington. We were able to walk the short distance from the home of Mr & Mrs Whitfield to Muircockhall.

There were nine of us from Dalmellington who went to the training centre at the same time. There was George Dunn, Tom Buchanan, Billy Thomson, Jim Plenderleith, Ian and Adam Gillespie, Billy Blain and Clifford Wilson.

We went from Dalmellington in a mini-bus driven by Bill McMinn. Bill picked us up on a Friday evening to bring us home from Dunfermline and took us back up on Sunday night, so we could start work on Monday morning. Bill was well known in Dalmellington as he delivered coal and briquettes around the village.

There were four boys to one instructor learning to cope with working underground. You learned to do the basic skills required underground such as putting up props, packing to support the roof and basic underground safety such as testing for gas and learning how to use a Glennie lamp.

Swearing was Endemic

There was a saying in the pit that I always remember and we learned this as young apprentices from the old hands. If you did the job and got hurt you were a silly bastard, but if you refused to do the job, perhaps because you thought it unsafe, you were then a lazy bastard, but either way you were a bastard!

Swearing was endemic in the pits and it was simply the way men communicated. But that was the sort of logic that prevailed, but most of it was highly humorous and I enjoyed many a good laugh among miners, because there were some real characters.

Underground at Minnivey

On returning to Minnivey I was then allowed underground, but with a qualified tradesmen under close personal supervision. Safety was all important and that was constantly hammered home to us as we trained.

Addie Johnstone was the safety officer at Minnivey. His role was to check that everyone underground and above ground were adhering to good practice. He would be on your top if he saw anything that was potentially dangerous.

Rail Accident at Cutler sidings which is located on the south side of Waterside on the branch line to Dalmellington. This accident occurred in 1929 when the engine toppled down the banking and two men were killed.

At the Coal Face

Face training followed next and that involved working with a responsible miner at the face for three weeks. You followed his shift pattern for that entire period. He assessed your fitness to be allowed at the coal face. I worked with Adam McHattie. He lived in Merrick Drive, Bellsbank near to the shops. On the first day he asked me if I'd like a bit of an apple. He took an apple out and with his bare hands he halved it and gave me one piece.

Adam was a great dog lover and he was what was called a dog physiotherapist. He had built up a great reputation for that line of work. Folk brought their dogs from all over the west of Scotland to have Adam work with them to help injured dogs, especially greyhounds.

He could work with dogs in the most wonderful way and folk really respected him. He died many years ago, but he was a miner all his days and never married. He stayed with his two sisters, who were much older than him. I learned a lot from Adam during my face training.

Dark Ages Beoch

At that time you weren't allowed to serve your apprenticeship at only one mine, you had to get experience elsewhere so I went from Minnivey to Beoch mine and I can tell you it was like stepping back 100 years.

Minnivey, being the last of the mines sunk in the Doon Valley, was modern and well planned. On the other hand Beoch was a scatter of Nissen huts. It was 200 yards from the baths to the workshops and two hundred yards in the other direction from the baths to mine mouth and the lamp station. There was no flow about the layout.

Beoch was reputedly the highest above sea level working mine in Scotland at that time. I went there in 1964. John Kennedy was manager, Nat Airlie was assistant manager, Henry Forsyth was under manager and John Niven was the chief engineer.

Driving a Road to the Big Mine

There was a move to drive an underground road from Beoch to the Big Mine (Pennyvenie No. 4). The aim was to do away with the double endless rope haulage that ran across the moors between the two mines and do everything underground. These rope haulages were Carron of Falkirk engineered.

So, the three Clegg brothers from New Cumnock were in charge of driving the mine from Beoch to the Big Mine. This was almost finished but was never actually used because the Beoch was on its last legs by that time and it would have been uneconomic to fit it out with an underground rail system. In hindsight, part of the problem with the coal mines was poor planning which must have cost the NCB a fortune, but that was the way things were in those days.

Tradesmen at Beoch

I was based at the workshop at Beoch which was busy. The manager was John Kennedy and under manager, Henry Forsyth. The blacksmiths were Sandy Gourley and John Limond, both of Dalmellington. Jimmy Hart was another blacksmith hailing from New Cumnock. The engineers were John Niven (Chief Engineer), Nat Airley (assistant engineer), James 'Gentle' Boyle, David 'Sticks' Shankland, John Donnelly (Dalmellington), Joe Collins, Norman Kellock of Bellsbank, Eric Hughes, George Allan and Billy McDowall. And Drew Galloway was another great character at Beoch. He was a member of the Magic Circle and enjoyed showing us many of his card and other magic tricks.

The electricians were David Bowie, Dick Anderson, John Riggins,

Ian Gillespie, Andy Cochrane, Eddie 'Ned' Kerr was assistant chief electrician and keen member of Dalmellington Band. There were also others that I can't immediately recall, but it was always a hive of industry with lots going on.

Off to Barony

I remained at the Beoch for three years when a job came up at the Barony because they were going to reopen sections after the Barony disaster in 1962 when four miners were killed and their bodies never recovered when the pit shaft had collapsed. The powers that be were going to sink a new shaft to reopen the pit and they needed tradesmen, so I went. I thought it would be good experience working in a big pit. I remained there for two years.

NCB Workshops Waterside

I have to say that I didn't like a big pit. Coming from wee pits you were put into a position where you knew very few others which wasn't great. I was there for nearly two years when Leslie Pryce, Chief Engineer at Waterside, a big Welshman, was at the Washer at the Barony one day and we started talking. He knew me from my days at Beoch. He asked me what I was doing and asked if I'd like to work at Waterside because they needed an engineer.

The workshop there covered the steam locomotives, otherwise known as pugs; the washer and the brickwork which was still part of the NCB as they owned 51% of the brickwork. This meant I got a lot of experience as an engineer. In fact I'd say I got more experience at Waterside than I did anywhere else in the pits.

There was an excellent team of tradesmen there. The foreman engineer, Jim Larmer, was nephew of David L Smith, our Dalmellington born railways historian; Tom McGill played in Waterside Band; Sandy Taylor, David Gemmell, John Halbert, Jackie Burgess, George Hainey, Davy McCulloch from Patna was the waste welder and Hugh Yair and Allister Glass were the electricians.

Roll on Death

John Halbert, was a fascinating character at Waterside. His favourite saying was: 'Roll on death.' The wind was always blowing in John's face. He was never happy.

He told me that during the war he worked at Runcorn in the big steelworks there. He used to boast about the number of pies he ate at that time. One wag told him that he reckoned he'd eaten about two tons of pies during the war, because that seemed to be the staple diet.

But there can be no doubting that he was a good tradesman, but he was always moaning, even about the work of other folk. He wore his specs on the edge of his nose and his bonnet was always at the side of his head - Benny Hill style. He had this humorous air about him.

Steam Locomotives

I really enjoyed working there. At one time there were seven locomotives to look after. In fact Waterside was one of the last places where steam was still used. The locomotives were worked on every day, so the brass bearings had to be moved in, so you were always busy.

Locomotives are so technical. A real work of art when you get into the workings with steam valves, injectors, connecting rods, steam boilers and forward and reverse gear. It was an education to work on them.

At Barclays in Kilmarnock, the railway engineers, the tolerance on the bearing was 25,000 of an inch whereas at Waterside the tolerance we aimed at was 9,000 of an inch, so it was a very high standard. All the men at Waterside were good tradesmen and proud of their work.

The locomotive drivers/firemen in my time were Tam Bruce who drove No.24 and also drove the steam crane when it was required; Mick Rooney who drove No. 17; 'Sparra' Black on No. 19; Hugh Hainey, No. 12; Jackie Heggie, No. 9 and Norman Sutherland, No. 1.

The whole team at Waterside was really first class and genuinely nice people. It was such a busy vibrant place but to see it today, almost ghost-like, is sad. I really did enjoy my time there and definitely increased my skills and abilities working with so many talented tradesmen.

Who made the heart, 'tis he alone
Decidedly can try us;
He knows each chord, its various tone
Each spring its various bias;
Then at the balance let's be mute,
We never can adjust it;
What's done we partly may compute,
But know not what's resisted

Address to the Unco Guid
Robert Burns

Chapter 26

Benwhat – The Music Plays On

Tom Filson

Content am I, if heaven shall give
But happiness to thee,
And, as wi' thee I'd wish to live,
For thee I'd bear to dee.

It Is Na, Jean, Thy Bonnie Face
Robert Burns

Tom Filson reflects on mining and Benwhat

This interview with Tom Filson took place in January 2012. He reveals some of his happy memories of Benwhat, especially playing with the village brass band, a lifelong interest for him, which he always said greatly influenced his life. His brother Andrew was also a lifelong member of the band. The two brothers used to meet weekly at Tom's house in Bellsbank, where they enjoyed a happy blether, when Benwhat and its famous band were regular topics of conversation. Sadly, Tom passed on in February 2012, but some of his precious memories live on through this book. His brother Andrew died later that same year.

Twins

Benwhat was a smashing wee place. My father was Thomas Filson and my mother Sarah Armour. The others in my family were Sadie, Jack, Jean and Willie. I was born at Benwhat in 1933, a twin of Andrew. Our family lived first in No. 14 Benwhat, the row beside the school. We later moved to No. 52, which was slightly bigger and had an inside toilet, which our first house didn't have. However, we more or less always went up to what was called 'the privy', which was a stone dry closet toilet located in the back garden. There was running water in both houses and there was a back boiler, which enabled us to get hot water once the fire was lit.

Like two peas

The birth of Andrew and I seems to have been straightforward enough, despite it being twins. We were delivered at home by Nurse Brecknie of Dalmellington. Andrew was older than me by two minutes, according to my mother. My brother and I were so alike that for years Mother had bother distinguishing between us. As you can imagine, that caused a bit of bother when one of us had been up to no good and the other got the blame!

Benwhat School

Andrew and I began at Benwhat School aged five. The head teacher initially was a Mr Frank Ferguson and his replacement was Mr Jim Jeffrey. Mr Jeffrey was a great footballer and was well respected. He came to the school about 1943 and remained until it closed about 1951.

The teachers also had trouble sorting out who was who between Andrew and I, and that often led to the wrong twin being blamed when things went wrong. Although we still argue about it today, Andrew was most often up to no good, but he would like as not tell you different. We love each other dearly, but we still argue, but always leave on the very best of terms to argue again the next week and we've been doing this for years.

A local harrier, Robert 'Bobby' Reid with No 40 vest is beaten by Peter Atwell of Beith Harriers as they race along the front of the rows at Benwhat. Reid went on to be successful with Birchfield Harriers.

Doon Harriers were the local athletic club based at Benwhat where this photo was taken in 1948. Back row (l to r): William Currie, Walter McEwan, George Hannah, George McConnell, Neil Robertson and Addie Hannah. Middle row: Jimmy Galloway, Jim Bigham, Robert Mullen, Richard Armour, George Mowat, Andrew Filson and Bruce Hainey. Front row: Tommy Filson, Tom Wilson, John Wilson, Andrew Galloway and Eddie Uriarte.

Tom Filson (left) and Andy Filson both born and raised in Benwhat, emerging from the mine entrance at Minnivey around 1973. Both men spent their working lives in the coal industry and also played in Benwhat Band which was formed in 1871. (Photo: Scott Filson collection)

The other teachers at Benwhat during my time were Miss Rollo and Miss McLean, but I forget the names of the others. Schooldays were happy. I looked forward to going there. I wasn't clever, but did my best. Strangely enough, my favourite subject was algebra. I just loved it. I remember that there were five classes and with the lads from Corbie Craigs also attending I think there would be about twenty to twenty-five in each class.

There would be about twenty in my class at Benwhat and it was a composite class. There were five classrooms in the building and when you finished class 5, around the age of twelve, you went down the hill to Dalmellington Higher Grade school. McGuire's bus took us from Benwhat each morning and brought us back in the evening.

Pals

My boyhood pals were the McHatties and Lindsays and all of them have passed on now. Thinking back, we were all football daft and I was the goalie. We played on an area of grass known as the hearth, probably going back to the times when ironstone would be laid out and dried on these areas. It was a really good football park for a wee village. As long as there was a ball, I was there, because I loved the company and the fun of taking part.

There wasn't much trouble in Benwhat as I recall. There would be the occasional scrap, but nothing like the trouble you get in communities nowadays. It was friendly and because everyone knew one another and lived together, it probably had a controlling influence on behaviour.

The Coal Mines

I left Dalmellington School aged fifteen in 1948 and went to work in Chalmerston Pit and later Minnivey, where I was a coal stripper working at the coal face. Although it was gruelling work, I can honestly say that I enjoyed working in the pit. There was great camaraderie among the men, although the work was very demanding. I worked in the pits for thirty-seven years, retiring from Killoch Colliery after the closure of Chalmerston. I worked with some lovely characters in the pits and got on well with most of them.

Marriage

I married Jessie Bone of Broomknowe, Dalmellington, in 1954 in the Kirk o' the Covenant, Dalmellington, with the Reverend John Morton officiating. Afterwards, we had a social in the church hall. My brother

Bottom left, clockwise:
Benwhat School team 1931/32 with John Relly, captain, showing off the team mascot.
Back row: (l to r) Hugh Gourlay, Tom Tinman, Eddie Dick, David McEwan.
Middle row: Tom Hodgson, Bill Gage and Sandy McFadzean.
Front row: James Relly, Tom Fraser, John Relly (captain with team mascot), David Wightman and Neil Dempsey.
(Courtesy of John Relly collection)

Benwhat School Woodwork class in 1930/31. Each boy holding a woodworking tool.
Back row: (l to r) James Adams, Alex Robertson, Hunter Torbet, Mr Hugh Ferguson MA, headmaster and John McKnight.
Front row: Vincent White, John Relly, John Wilson, Ritchie Campbell and Sandy McFadzean.
(Courtesy of John Relly collection)

Benwhat School Cookery Class in 1930/31. Each girl neatly dressed.
(l to r): Mr Hugh M Ferguson MA, headmaster, Mary McKnight, Margaret Murphy, Jean Hay, Georgina Dick and Mary Ferguson.
Front row: Peggy Murray, Agnes Tinman, Chrissie Relly, Mary Hodgson and teacher unknown.
(Courtesy of John Relly collection)

Andrew was the best man and we've always been very close, although some would have you believe we fight like cat and dog. It's always in good fun and I'm always right, anyway!

Family

My wife and I have a son, Scott, a daughter, Norma, grandchildren Laura and Mark, and great-grandchild Leah. When first married we lived in digs, it was just a single room, with Rab McKinstry in Ness Glen Road, Bellsbank, before getting a council house in Riecawr Avenue and after twelve years there we moved to Ness Glen Road where we currently live.

I had two older brothers, Jack and Willie. Both worked at Minnivey and Chalmerston pits. Jack moved to England when he was quite young and didn't keep good health. Willie was raised in Benwhat and later Dalmellington and spent his life in the pits.

My father was a miner and worked at Chalmerston Pit. There was a gas explosion in the pit when I was about twelve years old and it badly affected his eyes and he never worked after that and passed away in 1977.

We left Benwhat to come down to Dalmellington to attend the Higher Grade School when I was about twelve (1945). We moved to Newbiggin Terrace, Dalmellington, later moving to a smaller house in Hopes Avenue.

Benwhat Band

My uncle, Jimmy Armour, was the conductor of Benwhat Band, formed in 1871. This band was born and grew in the village. The band members met and practised in the drill hall in the village school. The band was an important part of village life. There was a great but friendly rivalry between them and Dalmellington Band, in the valley below.

When I was about ten years of age, I was brought into the band by my Uncle Jimmy and I was given a bass trombone and that was my instrument throughout my banding career right until the late 1970s, when the band ceased to function. My brother Andrew joined at the same time and he was also put on the trombone and for many years was solo trombone of the band. Brother Willie played tenor horn and Jack was on cornet.

My Aunt Nellie Armour and Uncle Jimmy always had band members in their home practising, so as well as practising at home, my brothers and I were regulars at the home of the conductor, so we got

Benwhat school in 1942. Several in this photograph are still among the older residents in Dalmellington today and perhaps this will bring back many happy memories of the school days.
Back row (l to r): Sandy Robertson, Andrew Wilson, Tommy Dempsey, Richard Armour, William Filson, ?, Adam McHattie, ?
Front row: Jeannie Thomson, Sadie McKinstray, ?, Mora Hill, Anna McHattie, Thora Bakkom, Nellie Wilson and Betty Bennett
Front row: Neil Hainey, Betty Gracie, Ina Filson, ? Effie Douglas,?, ?

more than our fair share of tuition. However, we all came to love playing brass instruments and taking part in the many and varied engagements with the band.

Benwhat was really a village of music for many of us because it dominated our lives. The band was made up mainly of men from Benwhat and the band met on a Monday, Wednesday and Friday for formal practices. We took part in Scottish brass band competitions as well as leading Sunday School trips, fetes, concerts and other events happening not only in Benwhat, but widely in Ayrshire. I had a wonderful life in the band and when I think back I am very grateful that Uncle Jimmy encouraged me to learn the trombone.

Some time after, the band moved down to Dalmellington as the village was being run down and folk were moving out. The band moved into a lovely wooden band hall situated on the edge of Dalmellington near the Path and on the far side of the Muck Burn. That remained the band's base until it eventually folded around 1978 due to a lack of players and money.

Personal reflection

Benwhat was a very happy place and it was one of those places where you never locked a door. Everybody knew everybody else and with the hills, valleys and streams right on your doorstep, it was a great place for boys to play. Mind you, the winters could be very severe and often the place was snowbound. I remember once when the snow was about 15 feet high in places with drifts, but as you can imagine, we boys really did enjoy that.

I regularly journey down memory lane to reflect and remember my boyhood days in Benwhat and those who influenced my life. They were great times, despite the poor living conditions, but I'm now one of the older folk and the last of a dwindling group who were raised at Benwhat. I'm very proud to say that I was a Benwhatonian and although my dear brother and I enjoy our weekly blethers on a huge range of subjects, we always agree on one thing – Benwhat was a great wee place.

Chapter 27

Happy Years at Pennyvenie Colliery

George Brown

George Brown features in Happy Years at Pennyvenie Colliery

There's aye a place, ye'll keep in mind as hame:
Ye'll hae a thocht for't sometimes faur awa',
That hillside whaur the brume's a yellow flame,
An caller breezes blaw.

To An Exile
W D Cocker

With his roots firmly set in the upper reaches of the Doon Valley in Dalmellington where he was born and raised, George Brown, 76, says it was natural that he would end up working in the local pit at Pennyvenie. He was interviewed by Donald L Reid on 19 May 2015 focussing on his eleven years working underground at Pennyvenie from 1954 - 65.

He left coal mining to work at Chemstrand, Dundonald. Later on he spent a few years in Africa (1968 – 78) living near Johannesburg where for a time his mining experience was put to good use when he worked in the 'City Deep Gold Mine.'

He then returned to Ayrshire and Drybridge. However, he still has a special place in his heart for old Dalmellington and the folk he worked with underground at Pennyvenie. Today, George enjoys nothing better than working in his very large vegetable garden and pottering in his shed.

Raised in Dalmellington

I was born at Bellsbank Crescent, Dalmellington on 23 April 1939, son of Jackie Brown and Barbara McKenzie of Dalmellingon. My maternal grandfather, Albert McKenzie, was well known in Dalmellington and worked as a porter at the village railway station. He actually came from a farming background in the New Galloway area.

Halfway to Hell

After my education at Dalmellington Higher Grade School, I left aged fifteen. On leaving school I went to Poulton's Office which was located in the middle of Main Street across from the railway station. I suppose it was the equivalent of the Job Centre today.

I had an interview and started at Pennyvenie Colliery quite soon afterwards. In those days it was easy to pick up work, but most men in Dalmellington tended to go into the coal mines or get work in Ayr at places like the Stamp Work.

I often tell folk jokingly it was like half-way to hell working in the pits, but in reality it wasn't so bad once you got used to it, like most other things in life. But working down a pit deep under the earth was always potentially dangerous, so you always had to be on your guard and you did have to rely on the mineworkers where you were operating.

When I started in coal mining at Pennyvenie in 1955 the manager was Mr Willie Drysborough and he lived in a cottage at the foot of Low Main Street in in Dalmellington.

Mine Training at Dungavel

I went to the pithead first and worked at what was known as the 'picking tables.' This was where the dirt was picked out by hand from the coal by a line of mine workers – usually the younger chaps and older miners – leaving the clean coal to be loaded at the end of the line. Everybody started here before going on training. I did my training at Dungavel, a large mansion with extensive grounds located just outside Muirkirk. It had been converted for training miners.

Training was very interesting and quite exciting for all the young men. The training programme was that one day the trainees went down the pit and the next day it was classroom work. At night we did ambulance training and shot firing training. It was a 12 week course and you got home every second or third weekend. I was there during the winter and the snow was bad, so you didn't always get home because the roads were blocked with drifting snow.

Staff I remember included Mr Gemza, he was Polish and the sports instructor, a Mr Hope who was an instructor and Willie Bone was the bricklaying tutor. They were all former managers or senior folk in collieries who were specially trained and qualified to train the young miners.

It was an enjoyable course. I came from a big family of eleven in Dalmellington, so for me to go to Dungavel was a bit of a holiday, because our house was always jam-packed and chaotic. The local lads who were with me included Willie Ferguson; a lad McEwan; Jim 'Sparky' Auld and several others, but I don't recall their names at the minute, it was so long ago. I've worked in too many places since I left the coal industry in 1965.

I do remember that there were several lads from Patna and Drongan on my course. So, after twelve weeks of quite intensive training we went back to our own pits to begin work at the pithead. It was exciting times! Back at Pennyvenie I did my brush training with two weel kent characters, Neilly Dempsey and Sam Black and that was an enjoyable time because they were always cracking jokes and telling tales, most of them very tall!

Underground at Pennyvenie

I went down Pennyvenie full-time when I was eighteen years old. The initial jobs down the mine included loading up the lie for the cages. The lie was the area where the hutches arrived to await being raised to the surface.

There were two lies for the hutches coming into the pit bottom and one of my jobs was to uncouple the hutches and push them onto the cage to be raised to the surface. You had to be careful doing this because they moved very quickly and many of the fatal accidents in Scottish pits resulted from doing this particular job. This was the job for the full shift.

There were two locomotives working underground to move the coal hutches at that time in the west mine and the north mine and there was a set of traffic lights. You switched the lights from red to green depending on which locomotive you wanted to enter the area to deliver the hutches to be unpinned from the train and subsequently loaded onto the cage to go to the surface.

You also dealt with empty hutches coming down from the surface. It was a busy job and you constantly had to be on your guard, because moving hutches in the dark was always potentially dangerous.

In some respects it was really like a mini railway traffic system, only underground. Later on they changed the cage layout to provide capacity for four hutches to be raised at the same time rather than the two, so it got even more hectic at the loading point.

Once you learned what they called your 'pit feet' which meant that you were familiar with the underground working - basically you knew your way around underground including escape routes as well as the safe procedures and processes and you were confident in what you were doing - you then moved on.

Ben Kennedy, was under-manager, a real gentleman of a man, and he would decide in consultation with the Fireman, where the new lads were most suited to work. Ben was a great guy with a lovely manner and I don't think you will ever hear anyone say a bad word about him.

Clipping and Brushing

I then went to what was known down the pit as the Burnton dook. This was a road which dipped steeply before rising back up. I worked there with Alex Torbet, John Reid and Johnny Fyvie, who was the locomotive driver.

We worked at what we called 'benching' or 'clipping' which involved looking after the overhead haulages where we clipped and unclipped the hutches. There were dozens of hutches moving in pairs along the line, so you had to unclip them ready for them to be loaded onto the cages to be taken to the surface.

Next I went to work on what was called 'the brushing.' This involved making airways for sections off the main underground road

This was the end of an era in Doon Valley deep mining. The last NCB operated coal mine in Ayrshire's Doon Valley at Pennyvenie closed on July 6 1978. Here some of the last stalwarts are seen with pit manager, Mr John Kennedy (hands clasped).

Back row (16) (l to r): Davie Galloway, Matt Reid, Jim McCracken, Neil McKnight, Nikolay Melnitschuk, Jim Auld, Tom Robertson (under manager), Tom Meechan, Drew Napier, John Kennedy (manager), Tom Archibald, Willie Calder, John Dempsey, Willie Calderwood, Neil Dempsey and Jimmy Stewart.

Kneeling left to right: Jim Gemmell, Jack Thomson and Billy McClelland.

into the west mine where the roadways divided. This was hard physical work with pick and shovel. The belt shifters would then go in and move the belts to the new track and the coal would be loaded onto the belts and taken to the coal loading point on hutches to the pit bottom.

There was myself, Rab McCutcheon, Joe Spence and Harry Ritchie all working in this section. Four of us brushed that road. The machines would undercut the coal on the nightshift some three hundred feet long and the strippers on dayshift at the coal face, perhaps thirty of them, would take the coal away.

Coal Cutters & Belt Shifters

Among the coal cutters at the face in my time whom I knew well were Tommy Meechan, Gavin Boyd, who went Australia; Hugh Phillips, Mark Hamilton and John Stead. The colliers went in on the dayshift and removed the coal from the face and set props to make sure that the coal face was safe and secure for further work.

The belt shifters started a couple of hours earlier in what was known as the ham and egg shift, to move the belts closer to the face which was progressing all the time as coal was removed, so that the brushers could create more roads around the area to allow air to be circulated.

They also put in circular girders to support the seam. It was a continuous moving process to recover the coal, support the seams, create side roads for safety and always made sure that it was as safe as possible for everyone.

Blind leading Blind

There were many characters in the pit. Harry Ritchie was one. He was an old hand and a good brusher, but he only had one good eye, so he always had to have someone walking in front of him in the mine, because it was always dark, albeit there was lighting along the roads. You did get used to working in these conditions, but you always had to be careful.

Harry was a big man, over six feet, and he enjoyed a laugh. If I was walking in front of Harry you would sometimes pretend there was an obstacle on the ground and say: "Watch out Harry. Take a big step," and you would lift your leg high as if to step over an object on the ground and Harry would do the same.

He would then realise that he was being tricked and would give you a right tongue-wagging with a few expletives thrown in and if he could reach you, he would thump you on the back. But it was all just good fun which he took in good part.

Working the Seams

There was always a run – a potential new coal face – which had been partially developed and was on standby for working and if there was gas, water, sinking or other problems with the main working coalface. They would then begin work on the spare run, often this would be an area with what we called splint coal. This was a very hard greyish coloured coal which was in great big lumps. It was generally used for coking coal and in factory boilers for steam generation.

On the other hand Camlarg coal was very soft, but gave off a very high heat and was used in the domestic setting and was in big demand. The high coal, was also known as Pennyvenie jewel, and it became famous for use in ships and factory boilers because it had a low ash content. Other coal from Pennyvenie was used in factories or schools or for powering steam locomotives.

Fatality

In my time at Pennyvenie, between 1954 and 1965, now that's about sixty years ago since I started down the mine and fifty years since I left, there was only one fatal accident I can recall, but there may have been others after I left that I'm not aware of. The man who sadly was killed was a chap by the name of Alex Baird from Dalmellington. He died in November 1956 when he was struck by a falling stone. That was always a very real danger in any part of the underground workings because the ground was constantly moving despite the supports, so you had to be very careful.

Shot Firing Debris

There were occasional accidents, especially when shots were being fired to blast out the coal and the debris could travel some distance along the roads causing injury, but usually it was nothing too serious. One chap regularly got caught and was injured by shot firing debris and such incidents had to be reported to the manager and this was reported as a miner being shot. Someone went up to tell the manager about a miner being shot by blast debris and the frustrated manager said: "That bugger has been shot more times than the wild west's most famous cowboy, John Wayne."

Tragedy at Barony

The man who was the engine driver for Burnton Dook West where Camlarg coal was brought out was a well respected mineworker called Johnny Fyvie, who lived in Dalmellington. He had strong Christian beliefs as indeed did his two sons, John and Tom. You often saw them with a group, which included another Pennyvenie miner, Charlie McDonald, all adherents at the local Bethany Hall in Dalmellington. They would be singing hymns in the Square regularly on a Saturday and Sunday and sometimes mid-week, depending on the weather.

However, the whole community was stunned when John Fyvie's son, Tom, also a miner, was tragically killed in the 1962 Barony

George Sturgeon was a respected and popular figure in Dalmellington. He was born and raised in the lost mining village of Lethanhill and was involved in many of the Hill reunions. He worked at Pennyvenie and is seen here marking its closure in 1978.

accident. The bodies of all four men were never recovered. This accident happened on 8 November 1962. Tom Fyvie was a mine borer who lived in Ayr. Also killed were John McNeil, a pit deputy from Drongan; Henry Green, colliery oversman from Cumnock; and George Wade, a borer, from Carluke. All four men were killed when there was an inrush of heavy sludge into the underground seam, so it was doubly sad because none of the bodies were ever recovered because there would be thousands of tons of sludge which would be impossible to move.

I don't think Mr Fyvie ever quite got over losing his son in such tragic circumstances and there was great sympathy for him and all the family as well as those folk connected to the other victims. It must have made going down Pennyvenie quite a traumatic occurrence for Johnny Fyvie after that catastrophe. Once again it highlighted the heavy price paid in winning coal.

Great Characters

Looking back sometimes we laugh and sometimes we greet (cry) when we think of some great mining folk we had the privilege of working with. Many sadly are no longer with us. Many were really very clever and talented folk. Quite a few miners played in Dalmellington Brass Band, in fact most of the band was made up of miners who worked in the Doon Valley pits, all talented musicians. Jimmy Graham, who was a pal of mine, left Pennyvenie to join the army. He's still playing euphonium all these years later at Whitburn Band.

Some of the older miners played mouth organs as they waited underground for the cages to return them to the surface. Others enjoyed a wee song or simply told stories. Looking back it was a really fantastic atmosphere. There was what we called "calling you ben" which meant that the man in front of you was about to go onto the cage and that meant you were next up to the pithead, so you had to be ready to move.

Stoppages

Pennyvenie was famous for strikes and disputes. Down the pit you'd be working away then you'd here 'Chap 3' which was a triple bell on the cage and everyone underground would eventually come up to the surface because of a dispute of some kind and we would all be sent home.

Some of the miners were annoyed about yet another stoppage and would say: "What's the strike for this time," and some wag would jocularly respond: "I heard someone's got jam on their piece, so it's all out until it's sorted, no matter how long it takes to get her to put cheese in the piece!" You see, you only got paid for the time you were down the mine. Such instances of stoppages happened regularly at Pennyvenie. Some would say they'd call a halt for absolutely anything because in my time our pit was famous for strikes for just about any reason!

Miners of My Time

Miners who worked during my period there (1954 – 1965) included Jimmy McLarty, Bobby Calderwood; Matt McCrae; Andy Buchanan and David Ritchie who were all colliers; Jimmy Pettigrew (surface foreman), the screening plant mechanic was Willie Barber; Willie Young and Stewart Jackson laboured in the wood yard; John Calderwood was in the oil store; the clerk was Willie Filson; Sam Coughtrie was blacksmith foreman and Charlie Baird was the apprentice.

In the electrical shop was Willie Brechney and Louis Uriarte; Symon Reid was No. 2 banksman with Hugh Ballantyne at the back as the dogger. Eric Taylor was No 7 banksman who chapped the cages up and down on dayshift and Joe Roney did the same on backshift and Duncan Murphy on nightshift. 'Dixie' Jackson was on the drawing off alongside Sam Piper who had a stutter. 'Spud' Murphy was on the retarders to stop the hutches because they could fly along at some rate of knots and could easily jump the rails and cause an accident.

Jimmy Graham was on the points and I took over from him when he left Pennyvenie and joined the army. Willie Pettigrew and Jock Sadler were on the weigh box. John Stead was on the pins. Jock Bell was on the brake stick. 'Tanny' Anderson and Kenny Murdoch were on the tumblers where the hutches were turned onto the screes and the dirt was removed.

Danny Young was the security man. John Allan and Davie McLeod were in the baths where the men showered at the end of shift. Rab Clyde was in the lamp cabin. Lenny Watkins handed out the tokens and lamps in the time office. Adam McClure was the wagon shifter on the screens.

Matt Park operated the haulage for the No 7 bing, which stands sentinel over Dalmellington. This was where the hutches full of dirt ran up a rail line right to the top of the bing, emptied automatically and the debris cascaded down the length of the bing. The hutches then returned to the bottom empty.

John Kennedy of Dalmellington was manager of Beoch Mine and Pennyvenie. His father, also John Kennedy, was under manager at No 2 Pennyvenie for 34 years. His brother, Ben, was also under-manager from 1954-1968. The family were steeped in mining.

William Allan cleaned the wagons. Andy Hare, Stewart Ray, John Fairbairn and three or four others were mine drivers and their job was to drive new coal seams. Jim Auld, known as 'Sparky,' was the grease monkey on the conveyor belts, pans and scrapers. The conveyer system was quite complicated and had to be carefully maintained.

During my time Willie Dryborough was the manager and Ben Kennedy, under-manager. George Sturgeon, Frank Small and David Torbet were fireman; Tom Bingham was an oversman; two brothers Andy and George Brown were dayshift and nightshift oversmen as was Sam Kennedy.

Jimmy Sutherland was a conveyor belt technician and he could turn his hand to absolutely anything and he was a well respected engineer. David Blair was the rope splicer in Pennyvennie and checked everything was safe and carried out plenty of air and gas checks. He also made sure all the pumps were running. He was responsible for safety in each section of the mine. There were dozens of other men, but it's now fifty years since I left and my memory is not that great, but I can still picture many of them in my mind's eye!

It was a very close-knit community in the pit. Once you had been there for a few years, you generally got to know most of the men in the pit. Not only that, you also knew their families and their background because they all tended to live in the Doon Valley, especially Dalmellington and Patna.

A Wee Story

I already mentioned a great wee character, Sam Piper, who had a very bad stammer. They say that on one occasion he was standing in Dalmellington Square when a man driving a fancy car stopped beside him and asked directions to Ayr. Stammering throughout, Sam very slowly replied: "You're driving a big fancy car like that and you're lost looking for Ayr … well sir, you're still lost," and he walked away leaving the bemused driver scratching his head!

No Regrets

My wife was never happy with me working down the pit. Her family were all miners in the Barony and she could see how mining had affected them with poor health. So she was always keen for me to get out, so when I got the chance, I took it. I left Pennyvenie in 1965 to go and work at Chemstrand, Dundonald as several others at Pennyvenie did too. I was on around £5 a shift in the pit, whereas at Chemstrand in 1965 I was on 13/- a shift, so I didn't leave the pit for the money.

I don't regret leaving, but was sorry to see the jobs in the Doon Valley coalfield disappearing within a few short years of me leaving. Mind you, I think folk who left mining would have seen their health improve.

There were some challenging seams at Pennyvenie which were extremely difficult to work. In the north mine the seam was just two foot three inches and you had to drive a road through it. It was difficult to remove the debris and coal, really hard graft. Miners in these areas had to work the face with pick and shovel. In what we called the splint road the seam could be up to four feet which was much better, but still not easy.

What do I think about my time down the pit? I can honestly say, and perhaps this is memory playing tricks, I really enjoyed my time among some great characters. But my wife was always fearful for my safety. They say you shouldn't forget where you've come from and I hold that to be true. Being from Dalmellington and raised among miners, I was proud to have been a Pennyvenie miner. I enjoy nothing better than meeting old colleagues and remembering days down the pit with some wonderful men.

There was a great camaraderie and some great laughs, especially at piece time, with my fellow mineworkers. No, I don't regret my time working coal at Pennyvenie - not for a minute. I often think back to those days and I always smile and have a wee chuckle. I believe I was so lucky to share some great times with the proud miners of Dalmellington.

Thus ev'ry kind their pleasure find,
The savage and the tender;
Some social join, and leagues combine,
Some solitary wander.

Song Composed in August 1783
Robert Burns

Bobby Jackson, blacksmith at Pennyvenie working away. The blacksmith produced a variety of metal accessories for us in the coal mines and they were very skilled in their trade.

Chapter 28

Mining to Music

Hugh Johnstone MBE

These were the folk before us,
Be proud of them, be proud
These Scottish folk who bred us
We sing their praises loud.
With all of our endeavours
The future will abide,
May the sons of our sons remember,
Dalmellington with pride

Arthur W Wilson - January 1963
Set to music by Stuart M Robertson.
(Both were respected teachers at Dalmellington High School)

Another Craigmark man, who spent many years in coal mining and subsequently made his special mark on the world of brass banding was Hugh Johnstone MBE. He is one of those wonderful, knowledgeable characters, who possessed boundless energy, talent, skill and professionalism. He was born at 61 Craigmark and moved to Burnton when he was about six years of age.

As a young lad he joined the ranks of the band and that became a commitment for life. Hugh conducted Dalmellington Band when they became Scottish Champions in 1969 and again in 1976. He worked in the coal mines for many years, later taking up an appointment as a teacher of brass instrument playing to young people at Auchinleck Academy.

A greatly respected man in the Doon Valley, Hugh tutored many brass players who made their mark in major brass bands and orchestras in the UK. His commitment to brass banding in Scotland, is unlikely ever to be equalled, let alone surpassed.

His commitment to the Dalmellington Band is admired by all who know him. He is still (2015) at the age of ninety years, a tireless worker for the Scottish Brass Band Association and his outstanding services to brass banding in Scotland resulted in him being awarded an MBE in 1982.

In this chapter Hugh reminisces about his life and times in the coal mines and happily flits between various subjects, his memories always lively and interesting ranging from mining to music.

Early Years

I was born on 1 April 1925 at 61 Craigmark, Dalmellington. My father was William Johnstone and my mother was Mary Murphy. They were both Dalmellington folk.

Family members

There were seven sons and three girls in our family. My sister Kate, who went to Canada and ran into bad times, had to return to Scotland. She died in 1930 at Beoch in childbirth. Mary, who lived at 63 Burnton worked at Craigengillan, Dalmellington in the 1930s right up to the war and she was aware of the many high profile visitors who came to visit there.

My brother William worked at No. 3 Pennyvenie. Because he was the oldest son in a big family he was allowed to leave school at age twelve and began work in the pits. He later joined Manchester City Police in 1932, spending thirty-five years policing that city.

Adam (Adie), was a miner at No 7 Chalmerston all of his life and finished up as Training Officer at Chalmerston. He lived at Wren's Nest, Pennyvenie and married an Irish girl from Bushmills, Margaret McFeeley, and after four years there, they moved to 43 Burnton.

Brother John worked at No 2/3 Pennyvenie all his working life and finished as deputy at Pennyvenie No 7 for the last ten years before retiring.

Alex was the pit blacksmith at Chalmerston all his life and later became a Councillor for Dalmellington for some six years after he retired from the pits.

Quintin worked in No 7 Chalmerston. He went to Canada in 1948 flying from Prestwick to the Toronto area. He worked for a short time for a firm called Massey Harris and they subsequently had a large factory in Kilmarnock producing combine harvesters under the banner of Massey Ferguson. Quintin later ran a gas (petrol) station and had taxis in Toronto. He visited Dalmellington the year before he died.

Sister Janet was three years older than me. She worked in Dalmellington Co-op and latterly at the Patna Factory where they made cloth for womens' dresses. She was age ninety-two when she died. She was a great supporter of Dalmellington Band.

I was the next of the family born and the only one still surviving aged ninety. I married Jenny Baird of Galston in June 1948 in the big kirk in Galston. She was a great supporter of Dalmellington Band all her life. She passed away on St Valentine's Day 2003.

The youngest in the family was Drew, who was born the day that coal was brought up from the Bogton mine. That was on 19 May 1931. He was the only member of our family not born at Craigmark. He was born at Burnton. He worked at Minnivey until it closed.

My Father

My father, William Johnstone, began working underground at No 6 Chalmerston mine after leaving school at age fourteen. A few years later he was involved in an accident when an electrical cable broke and he partially lost the sight in one eye, so that put paid to his underground working.

He was then given a job on the surface maintaining the mineral line that ran from Dunaskin to the loading point at Minnivey. The pit owners were good at looking after miners who were injured and usually managed to keep them in work.

My father's job was to be one of a team that kept the line in repair. It was a very busy line with trains running night and day from the pits to the washer at Dunaskin.

My father's mother, Jenny Good, had a wee shop up the Black Bull Close in Dalmellington. She sold sweeties and also took in blankets which she mangled. Drying large blankets couldn't have been done with a house wringer and she had a big mangler which squeezed the water out to make it easier to dry.

Grandmother remarries

My grandmother Jenny's first husband was killed in the Great War. He had been a regular soldier. My grandmother remarried in later life to Robert Howatson who farmed at Auldcraigoch which was located in the wilds beyond Dalcairney Farm to the west of Dalmellington.

Auldcraigoch was totally isolated in those days (1930s). The only way in was via Glenhead, located high above the Straiton road, with a two mile hike over the hill. Nowadays there is a rough road to Auldcraigoch via Dalcairney.

Hugh Johnstone, MBE, whose extensive knowledge of the Doon Valley is a great benefit to those carrying out local research. His contribution to Dalmellington Band (aged fourteen to ninety at time of writing) is immense. Many fine musicians, including famous Scottish composer, Sir James McMillan, have benefited from Hugh's guiding musical skills.
(Photo: Donald L Reid)

Sadly, Hugh Johnstone MBE, passed away quietly on 17 August 2015 in hospital following a road accident a few weeks previous. He will be fondly remembered by generations of brass band musicians who were fortunate to have been tutored and encouraged by this giant original man of Dalmellington. His contribution to the Doon Valley was immense through his involvement in Dalmellington Band, Doon Valley Golf Club as well as his personal knowledge and love for Ayrshire's Doon Valley.

His contribution to brass banding in Scotland saw him awarded the first ever Lifetime Achievement Award by the Scottish Brass Band Association.

The trumpet sounds!

In Memoriam

Life at Auldcraigoch

At Auldcraigoch in the 1930s they kept a thousand sheep as well as cows, pigs and four hens and that kept them going. In October they came to Dalmellington to the shop of Scott and Simpson, grocers in the Square, and bought a large casket of tea in 1lb boxes and a twelve stone bag of flour and a full sack of oatmeal and that did them through the winter together with what they killed on the farm.

My grandmother did all her own baking. She went out to the burn with an enamel pail and got their water for the farm because there was no piped water in those days. They had an outside toilet at the rear, so things were tough and I think she must have been very lonely at times.

New Year at Easter

In 1937 at Easter I had been talking about my grandmother at Auldcraigoch and wondering how she was getting on. I picked up a piece of coal and my mother said "On you go, son." And believe it or not I was their first foot at the farm. You can imagine that my grandparents were delighted to see me after months when never a soul was to be seen passing their remote farm. She just talked and talked and wanted all the news about our family.

Post by pony

The Howatsons had a letter box at Wee Berbeth near to Dalcairnie Falls. At that time Jimmy Ireland was the postman who covered that area. Jimmy lost his arm during the Great War. He also served on Dalmellington Band committee for years. Robert Howatson would ride his pony, Donald, twice a week to pick up the mail left for him at Wee Berbeth.

My grandfather was only six weeks out of Auldcraigoch and had moved into Wee Berbeth to be nearer Dalmellington when he died. He was buried in the auld cemetery in Dalmellington on 3 January 1940. My grandmother, Jenny, left to go and stay with her daughter, Kate, in Muirkirk, as she was in failing health.

My uncle John Howatson, grandfather's son, had been the shepherd at Clawfin, above Pennyvenie. So he came to stay with our family at 59 Burnton when he retired from shepherding at Clawfin in the late 1940s. He died around 1948.

School to Mines

I was educated at Dalmellington Higher Grade School leaving school on 1 April 1939 and on the following morning I was working at Chalmerston No 7 and straight away was down the mine with my brother Adie. I worked underground for ten years.

The pit I was working in was in decline and I then moved to the new mine at Pennyvenie which was just in the process of sinking. I worked there underground for the following 20 years on nightshift from 10pm until 7am.

Nightshift

The main duty on the nightshift was preparing the coal face by doing an undercut of around three and a half feet with advancement of around a metre. The dayshift would then blast the coal face and blow it down and burst it up so the coal and dirt could be removed.

The coal was then put on the conveyor belt and taken along to the tubs which were filled and it then ran on rails to the pit bottom. The tubs were then taken up to the surface in the cages for the dayshift to remove and process at the screes.

There would be roughly forty men working on the nightshift at Chalmerston No. 7. There were different faces to be tackled and there were various other jobs such as maintenance work by electricians and engineers whereas during the day the main aim was always to be getting the coal out from the face to the surface.

Workmates

Over the years I neighboured a German chap, William Kinnel. He was formerly a seaman and when war broke out his ship was in Wick and the crew was interred. He eventually came to Dalmellington and worked at Pennyvenie Pit on the nightshift. He initially stayed in Dalcairnie Road, Bellsbank, and when he retired he moved to Waterside Street. He had a son, Jim and a daughter. She became a school teacher in England.

There was Hugh Phillips who was the senior machineman or coal cutter operator; Jimmy Baird who held a similar position; Matt Hamilton, Graham Lees and two stars, Auld Gavin Boyd and 'Auld Okie Doak' (nickname) who lived in the Glebe Hostel across from Broomknowe. These were all the machine pairs on constant nightshift whom I worked with.

We worked six days a week and got Saturday night off. There was no work on a Saturday night and only a minimal work on Sunday with cover for the pumps to prevent flooding. The deputies would be there to ensure safety in terms of gas accumulation.

The roads in the pit bottom were quite big.The fans would draw air

Dalmellington Band bass section, with bandmaster William Oughton, taken in the band hall around 1953. This group had just won the Ayrshire contest. This qualified them to go to the Scottish Championships where they played Eric Ball's Quartet for Tubas and took fourth prize.
Back row (l to r): Hugh Johnstone, later conductor of the band and lifelong servant who was awarded the MBE for his services to brass banding; Robert Oughton (conductor) and Willie Kennedy, another valuable and unsung servant to the band.
Front row: John Paulin and Jim Hose. John Paulin died as a result of injuries sustained in mining accident at Pennyvenie No. 4. All four players were miners.
(Photo: Dalmellington Band)

out and bring fresh air into the pits. At one time the Doon Valley was almost totally based on coal mining with few other major employers. All the coal was on the north side of the River Doon right from Houldsworth to Beoch, a distance of eight miles.

Dayshift

On dayshift I went down at 6am and came up at 2.30pm. At piece time in those days the single men were not allowed to sit with married men. I had to sit down 320 yards away at piece time. That went on until 1947.

You only got fifteen minutes for your piece and then it was straight back to work. It was hard work at the face and you were constantly moving large amounts of coal and waste. The boss made sure that everyone was doing their fair share of work and he wanted to know what was up if there was any let up in coal production.

All Systems go

We would generally eat something before going to the face. This was because our jackets with the piece could be half a mile away. Folk like Tam Wilson, Willie Kennedy and Jim Stevenson were the men who would carry out the repairs if breakdowns occurred to any machinery in the pit.

They would also do preparatory work when the pit wasn't in full production, so that all systems were ready to run without delay the following week. The objective was always to produce coal and there was constant pressure on you to make sure that the coal was coming out.

The Bosses

The manager in my time was initially William Dryborough and when he retired a man called Robert Blair took over. They were incomers to the Doon Valley and would have come probably from Lanarkshire. The under-managers were generally local men, John Kennedy (dayshift – and later manager), William Wallace (nightshift oversman) and Jimmy Baird (backshift oversman).

These were men of vast experience. When a face run came against a fault and was finished, all the machinery had to be prepared so that it was ready for the men starting again on Monday at a new face. Whenever possible it was vital that time was never lost and production kept going. At its peak time (1952 – 1969) Pennyvenie No 7, a deep pit, was working four different seams at the same time and produced about 1,000 tons per day, 6 days per week.

Splint Seam

What was known as the splint seam where I was working was four-and-a-half feet thick. The other seams were three feet and two-and-a-half feet producing good quality coal. Some of the splint coal went for railway work to feed the steam locomotives whilst other coal was used in factories and for house coal. No 3 Pennyvenie produced a house coal which burned away to two percent ash in what was called the Sloanston section

This was an area located below the Sloanston Burn and it became famous for producing domestic house coal sold in Prestwick, Ayr and Newton Mearns. It was very popular and was known as Pennyvenie Jewel.

Chalmerston No. 7 was rich in domestic coal and it was known as Craigmark Coal. It was a very high quality house coal. When some of the pits were on idle time, it was always in production because there was such a demand for it.

Strike of 1941/42

The one big strike in my time was in 1941/42 when there was a three days strike over poor wages and management not being prepared or allowed to negotiate. It affected all shifts, but after three days it was resolved. There was a slight increase in wages awarded and that satisfied the miners to get the strike over. There was never the violence or confrontation that was evident in later strikes such as in 1984/85. I think both sides simply wanted to get things sorted and the men back producing coal.

Home Guard

During the war years many folk aged sixteen to forty-five volunteered for or were conscripted for the Home Guard which was initially known as the Local Defence Volunteers. The dayshift miners paraded on a Tuesday and Thursday. The backshift paraded for duty from 10.30am – 12am on Tuesday and Thursday and on Sunday everyone paraded together in Dalmellington School playground. Parties were taken in groups to the rifle ranges to learn about using arms.

Reserved Occupation

There was a shooting range located behind Benwhat Hill and another over towards Maybole. Mining was what was known as a reserved occupation because the miners were needed for industrial purposes and coal production was essential for just about every industry. For that reason and because the Doon Valley was all mines, the local miners were the mainstay of the Home Guard. Most other men, not in the mining industry, were already conscripted for military service.

A lovely clear photo of 'Dear Auld Craigmark' so described by Billy Greig in his poem of this now lost mining village. The reader will be able to make out the outline of the road leading upwards to Benwhat on the plateau above. The first row was known as the Laigh (low) row.

On Parade

At these parades everyone who was present had to give their number and if for any reason a miner missed a parade, he was called up in front of the mine manager and had to give an explanation for absence from parade. If the explanation was unsatisfactory he would be punished, for example, by not getting his next load of concessionary coal.

The mine manager had a lot of power in those days and his decision was final. This pertained to all adults up to age forty-five and you were trained and made to keep fit. There was a regular army sergeant and he supervised the training. Major Tom Auld, a First World War soldier, was the local commander in Dalmellington. However, the Home Guard was disbanded on 31 December 1945, but it did prove an interesting and enjoyable time for the mining members.

Weil's Disease Rat Attack

There were young men killed through no fault of their own. Danger was never far away in the pit. In my time there were several such accidents. In 1941 we worked in an 18" high section in Chalmerston No. 7. This section only lasted for about 18 months. The purpose was to allow expansion deeper down to reach Craigmark Ell Coal seam, which was a quality house coal.

Chalmerston No 7 was riddled with rats. They were all over the place. Three of our fellow workers died of Weil's disease. They were Stewart Blane, (21) Patna; John McFarlane, (21), Burnfoothill and Tommy Winning, (28), Patna. There were eighteen of us in the section and three died. How the rest of us escaped I'll never know. They are all buried near each other in Patna cemetery.

On another occasion the problems with rats at No 7 Chalmerston was highlighted very well indeed. Jim Allan was a miner, who lived in Bellsbank Crescent, Dalmellington. He was a keen cyclist and because of this, unlike the other miners, he refused to wear a string around his moleskins. He said it restricted the blood flow and wasn't good for his legs as a cyclist.

Well, this came home to haunt him on one memorable occasion. We were sitting underground having our piece when a rat ran up the inside of Jim's trousers. What a commotion that caused. John 'Joe' Paulin and the others grappled with the rat inside Jim's trousers and eventually they managed to kill it, but it was a frightening experience for all of us and most of all for Jim Allan. The rat was screeching like a banshee and that was pretty powerful and frightening. However, it was eventually killed and removed from Jim's trouser leg, but what a mess his leg was in. It was covered in scratches with the rat trying to get out and it was blazing red.

Jim was taken up the pit and was attended to by Dr Campbell. I remember it was on a Thursday nightshift, but he was back at work on the Monday. From then on, having experienced what a rat could do, he always chose to have a string around his moleskin trousers having learned his lesson the hard way.

Accident – John 'Joe' Paulin

One of our band members, John 'Joe' Paulin, died on 26 September 1959 following an accident in the Big Mine (No 4 Pennyvenie) a few weeks before. He was only thirty-five years of age and left a wife, daughter and two sons. He was a very committed member of Dalmellington Band. He was injured underground when a big wall of stone buried him. He was taken to Ayr County Hospital, but died of his injuries a few weeks later.

There were lots of accidents in the pits, most not too serious, but you had to be very careful because danger was always present. All you had was a wee tiny light to see with so it was little wonder that accidents did happen from time to time.

On 1 January 1947 the Government nationalised 1,400 pits in the UK. Locally here in Dalmellington they moved all the offices to Glenburn in Prestwick. The wages had always been paid to a bank in Dalmellington and they moved it to a bank in Ayr. This caused absolute chaos, because men were unable to access their pay and eventually when a strike was threatened, the authorities transferred the wages back to Dalmellington bank.

Snowbound Beoch

In February 1947 there was a full month when Dalmellington was snowbound. Folk down in Ayr don't appreciate that whilst they can have absolutely no snow, at the upper reaches of the Doon Valley the roads can be impassable.

During this period of heavy snow, the backshift men were working away at the Beoch, the highest pit above sea level in Scotland. The manager, seeing the weather forecast and noting the levels of snow locally, phoned the pit telling the men to get home as soon as possible to avoid being snowed in.

Walking Through Snowdrifts

As transport was unable to get through to the Beoch, the men had no choice but to brave the elements and walk through drifting snow to get home. It must have been a long difficult walk for them. However, two sixty year old men were down the pit, and for some reason they didn't get the message. They were Frank 'Peasy' Harris and William 'Mulley' Hill. They were stuck at Beoch mine for some 14 days.

Mind you the reality is that these two men actually saved the pit, because they made sure that all the pumps were running and this stopped the mine from flooding. If it had flooded Beoch mine would almost certainly have had to close. One of the men went down Beoch No 4 and the other tackled No 5 and their efforts saved the pit. Put simply, these two men were real heroes.

The pit authorities arranged to drop food by aeroplane to Beoch out of Prestwick Airport. The manager, Jack Bunyan, stayed in Castle Road, Dalmellington, so he knew how difficult it must have been at Beoch when Dalmellington was also cut off by drifting snow.

He roped in all the men he could get in Dalmellington, around twenty-five of them, into clearing the main road up to Beoch. You have to remember that in those days there were no snow ploughs so everything had to be done by manual labour. It took them almost two weeks working flat out to shovel snow the five miles and eventually allow access back to Beoch and get the miners back to work.

Bread rationed

Bread was even rationed during that time. The Co-op had twelve bakers and two apprentices in Dalmellington and they were working flat out to provide bread for the local population. The apprentices were 'Mid' Park and Robert Reid. Robert was a noted runner and in fact beat an Olympic champion at Hamilton Racecourse on one occasion. He and his family were later recruited to Birchfield Harriers, Birmingham and he spent the rest of his life as a runner and coach down there. He only died a few years ago.

Strange Names

I spent a large part of my life in mining and I have fond memories of those years working with some great characters, always up for a joke and a carry on. I remember at Pennyvenie, one man was the clerk in the powder house and handed out gelignite recording the names and amount of gelignite each received in his log book.

The first man went up and the clerk, who was quite new to the job, and said: "Name please" and the man replied: "Jimmy Baird," and received his gelignite. The second was Willie Barber and he too received his gelignite. The next two were Andy Hair and Willie Whiskers, all genuine names and they received their gelignite. The next man, Danny Onions, went up and asked for 6lb of gelignite.

The clerk was scratching his head as he looked at the list of names and thought that the miners were perhaps having a joke at his expense with surnames such as Baird, Hair, Barber and Whiskers. He came out the office clasping a brush and chased poor Danny Onions all the way to the mine entrance. Danny didn't have a clue what was going on because his surname was indeed Onions and he did need 6lb of gelignite. He must have thought the clerk had gone mad.

Cycling Holiday

I remember that in 1943 I received a holiday bonus of seventeen shillings. Hunter Smith, an older miner, had said that he was going on holiday that year and he encouraged others to come with him. Eight of us ended up going on holiday together on bikes. There were two tandems and four single bikes. We all came up the pit after our shift and went home, got our gear and began our cycle holiday

The cycle tourists on that occasion were me, Hunter Smith, Johnny Killen, Bobby Banks, John Pinder, Hugh Clark, John Paulin and Tom Brown. We cycled all the way to Blackpool and back. We also had several other biking holidays to Blackpool over the years and that was quite a common thing in those days. Folk didn't have much spare cash and holidays abroad were largely unknown for miners. Of course, there wasn't a huge amount of traffic on the roads then, so it was reasonably safe.

Opencast Mining

The last NCB mine to close in the Doon Valley was Pennyvenie and that was in July 1978. It was around five years later when the Opencast mining started - around 1983 - at the Hare Craig to the left of Benwhat Brae Then they moved to Chalmerston, removed the coal and back filled the ground, which was nicely covered over and has now returned to nature.

Later on a huge amount of work was carried out at Pennyvenie taking in the Beoch coalfield. Unfortunately, the further extension of the opencast mining at Lethanhill area met with financial issues with the operating company going into liquidation, leaving a veritable disaster scene on the ground in the Lethanhill moor. This was so disastrous that it is unlikely ever to be rectified with deep mines and huge mountains of waste scarring the hillside and moors over a large area.

Dalmellington Band

Dalmellington band, throughout the war years and right up until the pits closed in 1978, was fully maintained at a playing level by mainly mineworkers. Thereafter the sons of miners made up the most of the band personnel which had traditionally been all male.

However, in recent years the band has become popular with a good cross-section of the wider community in Ayrshire. This was particularly so after a meeting of the band committee in 1983 to look at ways of getting new players on board. After deciding to work towards getting women into the band, Tam Wilson, a retired miner and committed band member and bass player ruefully said: "The Dalmellington Band will never be the same again."

Women and banding

Tam Wilson was absolutely correct, but not in the way he thought. The band was indeed never quite the same. In fact it simply got better with the influence of women in all playing positions as well as women working hard on the committee. That was the start and it proved very good and has been built on over the years with women making up half of the band playing personnel.

As bandmaster at that time the committee were afraid to tell me of plans to bring women in as they thought I might be against the idea. However, I was already teaching at Auchinleck Academy and five key positions there were filled with women in principal roles. So I was all in favour of women knowing that they could produce excellent music to a high standard and with great personal commitment.

First Three Women

In 1983 the first three women to join the band were Elaine Clelland who married David Roxburgh; Shona Thomson who married Archie Hutchison and Jan Weir who married Les Henderson. This happy trio of husbands and wives are still playing and involved with the band in 2015 which does show that Tam Wilson's prediction was well off the mark.

I left the pits in 1970 and took up a brass teaching post with Ayrshire County Council and eventually retired in August 1990. I was six weeks retired when I was asked to return to Queen Margaret Academy and within a month I had organised a school brass band. I stayed there for a further five years before retiring in 1995.

Music my life

Brass band music has been my life and it was also a key part of the lives of many miners who played or served on the committee of Dalmellington Band. A large part of my personal memories of being involved with the band for over 70 years was recorded in the band book entitled: *150 years of Dalmellington Band – A Sesquicentennial Celebration*, published in 2014.

Since I retired from teaching brass instruments at Queen Margaret Academy, I have concentrated on tutoring young players at Dalmellington Band. This has given me great pleasure over many years and even at the grand old age of ninety, I still tutor some wonderfully talented young players most days.

Miners and Music

Coal mining and brass band music have been a huge part of my life. I've had the privilege of working with many talented and well educated men who were hard working miners. I've also had the satisfaction of encouraging so many young folk in music, many of them going on to make their own special mark on brass bands, top orchestras and in music composition – one of whom is now Sir James McMillan. That gives me great satisfaction.

And, who knows, there may be another young boy or girl among my current crop of up and coming musicians just waiting to be inspired by the fun and fellowship and the mystery and magic of playing a musical instrument and go on to great things in their musical career. I hope so anyway.

I count each day a little life,
With birth and death complete;
I cloister it from care and strife
And keep it sane and sweet.

Each Day a Life
Robert W Service

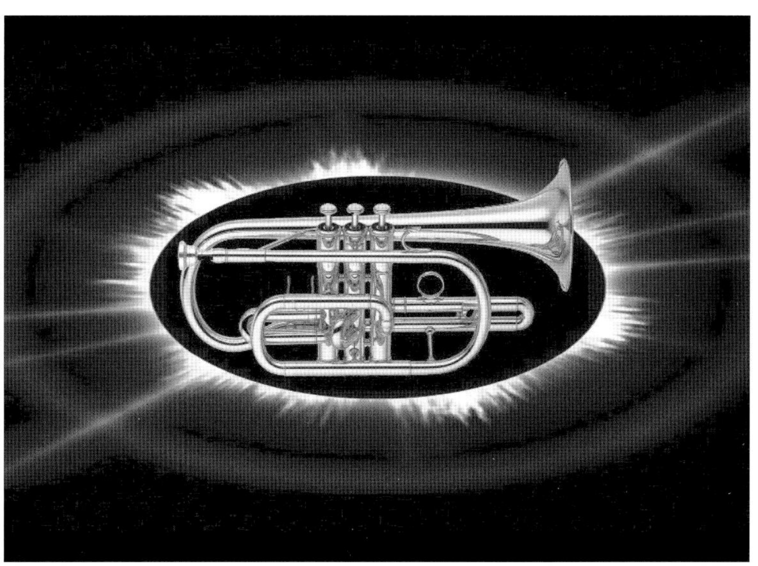

Chapter 29

Alexander Sloan MP His Family of the First World War

Esther Clark

My mirth and guid humour are coin in my pouch,
And my Freedom's my lairdship nae monarch daur touch.

Content Wi Little
And Cantie Wi Mair
Robert Burns

In 2014 Esther Clark of Ayr, originally from Rankinston, was asked to write down what she could remember of family stories, particularly about her grandfather, Alexander 'Sanny' Sloan, who died in 1945 when she was three years old. He was M.P. for South Ayrshire and his funeral was the first time double decker buses ever came to the village and there were a few of them.

Her aim widened to researching family history and a family tree, providing information for those who follow in her footsteps about family life experiences. She would wish to encourage other ordinary folks to look at their family histories.

Esther started on a fascinating and heartrending journey and here reveals some of what she has discovered, particularly about Sanny Sloan and his outstanding commitment to fighting not only for the rights of mineworkers, but everyone in his community and much wider.

She hopes readers will enjoy learning about the Sloan family and particularly about Sanny Sloan and his battles on behalf of ordinary working class people in South Ayrshire during tough times. He lost four younger brothers in the First World War and there are many like them commemorated in Coylton cemetery. About 25 % of Scottish miners volunteered to fight. Times were hard in war and peace.

Interestingly, Agnes Graham/Davies, Sanny's granddaughter, was a Labour district councillor for Kyle & Carrick and then South Ayrshire for twenty years until her death in 2003. Sanny's great granddaughter, Katy Clark, was to follow in his footsteps serving as a radical socialist Member of Parliament for North Ayrshire & Arran from 2005 – 2015. She has independence of mind like him. Radical roots run deep and there are weavers further back in time in the family.

This is a very poignant story of family struggles, loss in war time and reveals part of the price paid by ordinary people in the countries need to win coal at a crucial time in the twentieth century when ordinary workers were struggling against the power of coal owners.

Sanny Sloan – The Miners' MP

Sanny Sloan, a man of principle and vision, was well ahead of his time. He was known in Ayrshire as The Miners' MP. Someone suggested that I write out what I could remember of family stories about my great grandfather Alexander Sloan, fondly known as Sanny.

After a lifetime of service to ordinary folk, he died on 16 November 1945 when I was three. My aim is to try and interest ordinary people in their own family history. The centenary of the First World War seemed a good place to start.

I always knew that my great-grandfather Sanny Sloan was a firebrand socialist MP representing South Ayrshire from 1939 to 1945. He had been involved all his life in trade unions and local government. I always knew that he had experienced great poverty and injustice and the dreadful effects of war.

He fought against these evils on behalf of ordinary people, for individual rights for workers, for better employment conditions like safety at work, better housing, better education and training, freedom for the colonies, proportional representation, a republic and for lots of things now accepted as reasonable but then seen as radical. I also knew that old men would weep at the mention of his name and recount what he had done for them.

Sanny was teetotal until he was about 60 years of age when he took up having a glass of wine when he went out with his grown up grandchildren. He also had an ironic sense of humour and was good fun to be with.

I also knew that four of his youngest brothers died in the First World War in France. It transpired that two of them, had emigrated to

Canada and came over to the UK with the Canadian Expeditionary Force.

Family Migration

Four brothers had emigrated to Canada but were able to come home to visit family after a couple of years. It was a place of great opportunity for them and many others from the West of Scotland at the time.

Two of the brothers, Robert and William, joined up in Canada when war broke out. The third of these young men, Thomas, was at home in Scotland and joined the Scots Guards. Another brother, Donald, who had not emigrated to Canada, also joined the army, specifically the Black Watch.

The fourth Canadian, Charles, seems to have come back home at some point to Scotland to marry but spent the rest of his life in Canada. I started to look not just at what these young men had done in the Great War but how they and their parents and families had lived. The family had such a lot of drive and intelligence. The story unfolds…

A Mining Family

Alexander Sloan was born on 2 November 1879. His parents were John Sloan and Esther McCloy who had married in Dalry, Ayrshire, on 27 December 1872. There were twelve children born to the couple, two daughters and ten sons. The first three were born in Dalry, a mining town in North Ayrshire. The rest were to see the light of day in the south of Ayrshire in a mining village called Rankinston.

The ironstone miners and their families transferred to Rankinston when one ironstone mine operated by the Glengarnock Iron & Steel Company shut and another opened. Whole families all had to walk some thirty miles from Dalry to Rankinston and as the two sites were built to the same plan, they moved into the same street address. Any belongings they had were sent on the mineral train running between Dalry and Rankinston. This was how things were done then.

Early Death

Three of the twelve children of John Sloan and Esther McCloy died of natural causes before their time. The second child and elder daughter, Margaret, died aged ten years of tubercular meningitis. James died aged thirty of tubular nephritis and the second last birth was of twins and one died. His name was Robert Thomson Sloan and he died at age three weeks of bilious vomiting. They named their next and last child after him. The family grave featured a 'wee Robert' the twin who died as well as the Robert who died, aged nineteen years, in France.

Hill Reunion guests gather before the event in Patna Community Centre in 1978. These reunions began in 1965 and ran for 31 years. The last speaker was Brian Donohoe MP in 1996.
Back row (l to r): John Gilmour, James 'Cherry' Bryce, Bobby Knox, William Stewart, Bertie Smith, Hugh Ferguson, Tommy Hose and George Sturgeon.
Front row: Peter Conway, Annie McFadzean, James McFadzean, Mrs Bella McCormick and Jim Carruthers.
(Courtesy of John Relly collection)

Life in an Ayrshire Mining Village

In the nineteenth and early twentieth century, mining families lived in the appalling housing supplied with expensive rents by the mining company. Miners' rows were part of the social fabric of that period. The homes were tiny, one or two rooms often with earth floors under the set-in beds, where often coal had to be stored if there were no coalhouses.

In Rankinston the miners' houses had coalhouses but no washhouses which was a great problem, with all the filthy coal dust being brought home. Water was carried home in buckets from standpipes in the village coming from the spring up the hill.

In these villages the few outside earth toilets were shared with many others and strangely they were often built without doors. There were effectively stinking open middens which caused disease and ill health to miners and their families.

In Rankinston the earth toilets were shared among only five families and had doors. This still meant sharing with a lot of people. These toilets were much better built than in Dalry. They were easier to keep clean and were safer for everyone to use. The housing was newer in Rankinston so tuberculosis was not such a scourge then.

The Truck

The illegal 'Truck System' operated widely in coal mining areas throughout Scotland and thrived in Ayrshire. It was a barter and exchange system. Earlier it had meant labour in exchange for the necessities such as food and clothing. The housing provided by the company was expensive compared to the wages miners received.

There were villages which were closed by a gate at night. The mining company owned the village shop, the pub, the school and even provided a doctor to look after the health of the mining community and villagers paid a penny a week for this.

Everyone was obliged to pay through the nose for whatever was needed and were forced to use the company facilities. In some places they had a 'mark-up' of up to 30% in the company store. No one was allowed to open a shop or bring in a horse-driven mobile shop, such was the level of control exercised by the mining company.

Some employers in Scotland paid wages tokens, but not in Ayrshire. The miners lived in abject poverty in what was a controlled environment. They would also be mindful that protesting could often result in them losing their jobs, which meant that the family also lost their home which was tied to the job. The fact that the 'Truck System' was illegal was ignored by the coal owners.

Family Life

Despite having seven children at the time, the Census of 1891 shows that the Sloan family had an elderly lodger to help make ends meet and this was common with miners and their families. He was an ironstone miner from Inverness, aged sixty years. Many families had relatives living with them as well as lodgers.

With poor living conditions, it was surprising that so many of the Sloan children survived childhood. All the sons of the family left school at twelve years and went to work in the ironstone or coal mines.

Hours were long and working conditions dangerous with little concern shown for safe cages to take miners to the coal face. Even much later, for example in 1900 a thousand coal miners a year died in UK pits and many more were injured.

Their only surviving sister, Esther, became a farm servant at the age of twelve, just about the only job open to young women there. She later married a miner. The hard life was alleviated to some small degree by the closeness of families.

Next door to the family lived Esther McCloy's younger brother with their widowed mother, Esther Wilson, as housekeeper. He had three small children, the youngest being two years old, his wife having died in childbirth. They all supported one another but it was a constant struggle.

Family at War

Four of the sons at the younger end of the Sloan family died in the First World War. Robert the youngest son was the first to make the ultimate sacrifice and died at Ypres in 1915 aged nineteen. He emigrated to Canada in 1913, going with his brother William, who had gone across there in 1910 with another brother, Thomas. Robert joined the Canadian Infantry's Alberta Regiment and seems to have been killed when chlorine gas was first used by the Germans. He was lost without trace on 22 April 1915, aged 19.

William died next, the surviving twin, who had gone to Canada in 1910 and stayed two years, had come home briefly and then returned with Robert in 1913. He seems to have settled in Burnis, Alberta, serving as a Sapper in the 2nd Tunnelling Company of the Canadian Engineers. He died aged twenty-three on 28 June 1916 and has a grave. His death was not confirmed at first, only that he was missing.

Thomas was the next brother to die. He had gone in 1910 to Canada for two years but had returned home to Scotland. He went back to Canada with his brother, Charles, in 1912 returning once again to Scotland and joined the Scots Guards by the start of the war. He fought in France and Flanders. He was killed aged 28 on 15 September 1916. Like so many other soldiers who fought in the Great War, he was lost without trace.

Telegram News

The telegrams telling their mother that both William and Thomas were dead came on the same day. She was distraught at this tragic news. Sanny immediately wrote to the War Office requesting that another

A group of workers at Dalmellington Iron Company Waterside with the date on the board 1896. No names are known, but doubtless many of their descendants will still be living in Ayrshire's Doon Valley. Clearly no one asked them to 'smile for the birdie.'

brother, Donald, who was fighting at the Front be moved to a slightly safer posting. The response came back refusing the request, saying 'it was an honour to die for your country.'

Donald died on 1 January 1917. He was the oldest of the brothers who died. He was in Royal Highlanders' Black Watch. He fought in France and Flanders and died at the age of thirty-three. He was married with an eleven year old son, Donald, and a younger daughter, Esther. He is buried at Arras. His wife came from Belfast and she went back there.

Unveiling Rankinston War Memorial

The Sloan boys' grieving mother, Esther, was later given the unwelcome honour of unveiling the Rankinston War memorial on Sunday, 19 December 1921, because she had lost the most sons. Donald Sloan, Robert Sloan, Thomas Sloan and William Sloan all have their names recorded on this memorial.

In addition one of the Canadian immigrants was said to have been married to a French Canadian woman, who came to Scotland after the war with her young son, hoping to settle near her dead husband's family but she returned home. She was a French Catholic and although members of the family were supportive, she did not settle and they paid her fare home.

There are no photographs of any of the Sloan family apart from a couple unearthed of Sanny Sloan. However the two Sloan boys who were in the Canadian Expeditionary Force and died in the First Word War (Robert and William) have photos in their war records kept in the Canadian Archives.

Robert died aged nineteen, had fair hair and fair complexion, blue eyes, was 5 ft. 11" and stares at you from a black and white photocopy. This may be of interest to others. It certainly personalises his death.

After the Great War

There were five Sloan siblings left at the end of the war. One was Esther who was bringing up a family. She began her married life living with her parents, as was common, and some of her children were born in Rankinston. Brothers, Henry and John, the eldest were coal miners and lived and died in Rankinston.

Both were involved in the coal mining union. Indeed Henry actually served a prison sentence during the 1921 Hunger Strike with Sanny which was really a lockout by the mine owners when there were large coal stocks.

Charles had been to Canada in 1912 to Burnis, Alberta and went again in 1926 to Nova Scotia and later Oshawa, Ontario. He had married a young Rankinston war widow with four daughters in 1923 and they had a son, Thomas.

They all joined him in Canada in 1929. Thomas was their only child together. He died with another Canadian Expeditionary Force in World War 11 aged twenty years. It is not known if Charles returned to Scotland before or after the war or whether he fought in either the Canadian or British forces.

Defiance against Injustice

Sanny Sloan, the miners' MP, was the fourth child and second son of John Sloan and Esther McCloy. Soon after he started working at the coal mine at the age of twelve there was a pit accident and he was among the injured.

He lost the sight of an eye. He then got a lighter job in the mine. He became very involved in the struggle for the rights of ordinary people through fighting the injustice which he had first experienced himself working as a miner in what must have been atrocious conditions for a young lad.

Underground at Pennyvenie No. 2. How many folk today would like to spend their entire working life in such conditions? The author's grandfathers, father and many of his uncles worked in the mining industry locally.

Sanny Sloan - County Councillor

He had a strong social conscience and was just as concerned about injustice to others as well as miners. He wanted equal opportunity for all. He was passionate about education and joined his local School Board from 1900, was elected and served on the County Council from 1920 for twenty-five years. He was on the Education Committee for the whole of that period and held several convenerships, including Housing.

He had married Agnes Sloan (no blood relation) who also came from Dalry, Ayrshire. She had left school at ten years of age to work in a mill. She was short in height and had to stand on a box to reach the machine.

Agnes Sloan – Village Shop

Agnes was a bright go-getting woman and once she had settled in Rankinston, she purchased a piece of land from a farmer. It was just below the village and unlike everything else, did not belong to the mining company.

She built a grocer/general store/drapery there and began to set up what became a profitable business. This act of defiance was initially ignored by the powers that be for some unknown reason.

The coal owners knew the 'Truck System' was against the law but that did not usually affect them. A new doctor came to the district to look after the farming community. The miners already had a doctor chosen by the company and paid a penny a week for this service. However, Agnes felt that the new medical practitioner, Dr Macrae, was much better than the existing one, so consulted him instead.

Sanny Sacked & Family Evicted

When no sanction was imposed on Agnes by the mining company, others followed suit. This was rank disobedience and went against the system so Sanny and his pregnant wife and two small children were evicted and he was sacked.

He was blacklisted and barred from working in any pit in Ayrshire. His family was also blacklisted, so they would have had extreme difficulty in getting work in Ayrshire.

Meanwhile Agnes and Sanny lived in a barn lent by a farmer while they built a house beside their shop. The new doctor guaranteed their mortgage or they would not have got a loan at all. The income from the shop kept them going.

They already had two children, Robert and Esther, and whilst they were living in the barn their last child, John, was born. He became a mining engineer and then a teacher so his unfortunate start in life did him no harm.

Eviction and Water Cut Off

The building of their new home, Kerse Cottage, was problematic for them. They wanted to put running water into the house, which was not a village feature at the time, water being obtained from standpipes located around the village streets.

The coal company owned the spring and the pipes to serve the communal stand pipes and when asked they refused permission for water to be sourced to Kerse Cottage. However, Sanny found that the pipes ran through their piece of land and so water was installed without the permission of the authorities.

Village without water

Someone happened to say to a pit manager that Mrs Sloan was awfully lucky having hot and cold running water in the house. The company response was to cut off the water for the whole village. Sanny did his homework and discovered there was a byelaw which said that all schools must have running water.

The school was next door and without water as were the seven hundred people of the village. Sanny went to court and his determination and well argued case meant that the water had to be restored to the people of Rankinston, who had been without it for three days.

Agnes Sloan's Death

Agnes Sloan's shop thrived but had to close in the 1926 General Strike as all the food and other goods had been exchanged for union promissory notes. The union printed notes which could be used to buy food, promising to pay later. Of course this was not possible as the union was bankrupt.

The soup kitchen for preparing food for the village had been based in the Sloan family washhouse. They had no regrets about losing all the stock and also a great deal of money. The failure of their fight was a blow.

A bigger loss that year was Agnes Sloan's death at forty-seven years of age of phlebitis. Her family background in Dalry, Ayrshire, was more typical of the time than Sanny's, with four siblings dying of TB, three in their twenties and another aged thirty-two. The average lifespan in their family was thirty-nine, about the same as Sanny's, but war was not to blame in this family.

The horrific housing conditions, poor sanitation and unhygienic water supply coupled with poverty and lack of medical care, were the real problems. Only two of the seven family members of Agnes Sloan's siblings reached old age.

Agnes was a remarkable woman in her own right. Apparently she used to go to auction sales and buy items of porcelain to sell in her shop. While she was at it she would buy furniture to give away to people who had none. She was always a giver, typical of her community and many of the folk of that era, who whilst having very little themselves, were mindful of the needs of those around them.

The Hunger Strike

During all these years, Sanny had real problems finding work because of his reputation as a union activist and another factor was his poor

This was the first dam created at Loch Doon before the current dam was built in the mid 1930s. On the other side of the dam is the famous Ness Glen which became a huge tourist attraction in the late 1800s.

eyesight. He sold Singer sewing machines and he was an insurance salesman. He had also been a union check-weighman in the coal mines.

After many attempts in Parliament eventually unions were allowed to pay for and employ a man to make sure that the mining company did not cheat the workers who were paid for the weight of coal they produced.

Sanny did this job and later became a miners' agent. In 1921 he became involved in an industrial dispute when in the middle of a coal strike. This was in fact more of a 'lock out' by the mine owners against the coal miners. It followed the Sankey Commission set up to examine the mining industry which required changes after the Great War.

The Royal Commission report was to recommend nationalisation. However, Lloyd George did not implement this, causing great disappointment and resulting in pay cuts of 60% to miners when the mines were returned to the owners' control.

The owners had large stocks of coal so wanted the miners to stop work but wanted the pits to be in working order and free from flooding for when the market improved. Sanny had been asked by a group of miners to go with them to Houldsworth Colliery, Polnessan near Patna which he did.

Arrest of Striking Miners

The miners had come to Sanny's house at about one o'clock in the morning on their way to stop volunteers from maintaining the colliery in good order by pumping out water. On arrival at the colliery at approximately 2.30am, five of the seventeen men went into the office and confronted a dozen or so volunteers who were due to carry out maintenance work .

The leader of the five, Sanny Sloan, advised the volunteers that there was a large crowd outside and that they should put the fires out and close the pit. The volunteers co-operated and went home.

The five men, Sanny included, were subsequently charged with mobbing and rioting and were taken to Barlinnie Prison. If the men were to be found guilty on this charge, it potentially meant life imprisonment, at a time when a life sentence was until death.

The case went to the High Court of Justiciary and in a stated case in 1921/22, it was found that the five men could not be considered a sufficient number to constitute a mob. The five, who included Sanny, his brother Henry and elder son Robert, were imprisoned on lesser charges.

Sanny was sentenced to three months imprisonment whilst the other four received sentences of six weeks imprisonment.

Unfortunately, the family did not keep Sanny's papers, letters and books when he died and it was only in the 1980's, when a member of the family studied law that the full importance of the case became clear. At a lecture entitled 'The Use of the Criminal Law against the Working Classes' the case was discussed and sounded familiar. It is one of many occasions when strikers were victimised and falsely accused.

Voice of the Poor

Sanny Sloan went on to become a powerful voice for the poor and the underdog. He often appeared in compensation cases in court and got good results for union members who had been injured in the coal mines of Ayrshire.

There had been a long history of compensation being denied by the courts, even when safety measures were the clear responsibility of mine owners, like providing safe cages for men to use to get down the pit.

Some thirty years after Sanny's death, a relative contacted the National Union of Mineworkers in Edinburgh, asking about records concerning Alexander 'Sanny' Sloan. The receptionist said that they had no records, but asked if it was an enquiry about a compensation case, as she had heard of him. It transpired that he had argued many a case in court successfully, with no legal qualification. He was still remembered.

Sanny Sloan in Parliament

Apart from his twenty-five years on Ayrshire County Council, where he championed housing and education, he was also Secretary of the Scottish Miners Federation for nine years and a Labour MP for six years. Popularly known as 'The Miners' MP,' among other things he got miners extra rations of cheese in wartime.

Work in Parliament

A man of wide interest, he was involved in the fight for Colonial Independence, being particularly involved in the India League. Once elected to Parliament, he raised these issues, as well as concerns about poor treatment of serving British soldiers, arms profiteering and children getting time off school to harvest potatoes.

In his six years in Parliament he made 640 interjections. A pacifist all his adult life, he opposed the First World War, and subsequent wars, he was a republican and wanted abolition of the House of Lords.

He favoured Home Rule of a federal variety for UK and the Commonwealth and he spoke out for proportional representation just as he had spoken out on equality for women. He seems to have been into everything.

Well Read

Perhaps his greatest passion was education. He had educated himself throughout his life. He was apparently a passionate speaker on the political stage and a great Burns man, popular at Burns Suppers and well read. Whilst he fought for better public provision, which he wanted, it was also about personal commitment and self-help.

Sanny's Helping Hand

Agnes Graham/Davies, Sanny's granddaughter, met a fellow teacher on the local bus one time. They joined in conversation and the lady asked Agnes where she came from and she said Rankinston. Then the stranger asked if she knew any Sloans and Agnes said that she was a Sloan on her mother's side.

It transpired that Sanny Sloan had been asked when he worked for the union, for advice by a miner with several children. The miner could not afford to send his daughter, who was at school in sixth year, to University.

The fees could be obtained as a loan from the Carnegie Trust but the father could not afford to pay her living expenses any longer. It was before the days of educational grants. Sanny said that he would send the money quarterly to the miner to pay for her living costs.

He added that if the daughter subsequently became rich she could pay him back, but if not it was fine to forget all about it. None of Sanny's family knew of the story, which only came out thirty years later when two strangers met and talked on the Patna bus. Sanny had a habit in a discreet way of helping people out.

Family who Cared

So what do you make of such a family of ordinary working class heroes? These were heroes who proudly struggled and fought in war for their country, struggled and fought for a better life for everyone and for a dream of an egalitarian society with international co-operation.

There were many like them in the mining and other working communities where the injustice was so great. Many of their aspirations were achieved after the Second World War under Clement Attlee and some more in the Wilson Government in the 1960s but now we are slipping backwards.

Better World

Are the people who fought through the centuries for progress, human rights and dignity really the 'enemy within,' as some might say The Sloan family story shows the resilience and the aspirations of one ordinary working family, including soldiers fighting a cause or pacifists fighting for peace or socialists attempting to right wrongs and end poverty or just struggling to make the world a better place.

Like brethren in a common cause,
We'd on each other smile, man,
And equal rights and equal laws
Wad gladden every isle, man.

The Tree of Liberty
Robert Burns

Chapter 30

Houldsworth, Glenburn and Littlemill

Alex Green

This memory brightens o'er the past,
As when the sun, concealed
Behind some cloud that near us hangs
Shines on a distant field.

Did Walk With Me That Day
Henry Wadsworth Longfellow

Alex Green, 75, is married to Sheena and has one daughter, Julie, and two sons, Steven and Scott. They also have grandchildren and great grandchildren. He recalls his career in mining which seems to have featured too many stoppages at Houldsworth. He later took up a job as a BT engineer, but was still proud of having experienced life at the sharp end in the pits.

Early years

I was born on 6 January 1940 in Seafield Hospital, Ayr. My father was Patrick Green who worked in Ayr Stamp works. My mother, Annie McGhie, was originally from Barrhill.

As a family we lived in Limonds Wynd, Ayr. I attended St Margaret's School, Whitletts Road, from aged five until I left at fifteen. On leaving school, I applied to become a miner but I had to wait for medicals and interviews, so in the meantime my father got me a job at Alexander Sawmills in Ayr where I was a general labourer. I was only there for a few weeks when I got word to start at Houldsworth Colliery on the hill above Polnessan, Patna. I was just sixteen when I started.

Houldsworth Pit

Like other new starts I began work at the pithead and I was given a job in the wood yard. I always remember that it was cold because the Houldsworth sat high on the hill and was open to the elements, so it tended to be very cold. The job was to take wood and steel girders from the storage yard to the pithead where it was then taken down in the cage to the pit bottom.

Where I worked

The Houldsworth pit was a steam winding operation. This was a system where the cage was lowered up and down using steam power. There was a large chimney and a variety of different buildings including pit baths. The most prominent feature was the pit winding gear which brought the cage up and down the shaft.

The cage was huge and held sixteen men. It was also used to bring the hutches and other equipment and supplies up and down the pit. Houldsworth was a very deep pit and it was a jerky ride up and down. It occasionally stopped without warning and that was always a bit scary for everyone.

Steam free meant strike

There was only one shaft in the Houldsworth. This was a weakness because this was the only way in and out. In fact, I remember going on the bus from Ayr to Polnessan and as we approached the pit, the older miners could tell about three miles away that the pit was on strike. This was because they could see in the distance that there was no steam rising at the pithead. This was a good indication that the cage to the mine was not operating.

On the job training

After working in the wood yard I then progressed on to the screes. It was nicknamed the craw-picking which meant that you stood at a chain belt which ran past full of coal and dirt and you picked out the stones and dirt. I worked on this for a couple of months.

The first job I got after my period of training was underground, but not at the pit face. I was working with an experienced miner to load the hutches onto the cage and take off the empty hutches coming back down. This was a standard job for the young mineworkers to give them experience and probably to test if you would be comfortable working down the pit.

Dungavel Centre

Part of the off-site training was to go to Dungavel Training Centre,

Muirkirk, on a residential basis. Dungavel was a large mansion house which had huge grounds. There was a stable block and an outdoor swimming pool with no water in it during my time there. There were also playing fields and extensive grounds to walk in with wooded areas.

Horses at Kames

When I did my training at Dungavel there were still horses working in the Kames. It was absolutely fascinating. I saw a couple of horses there and they had protective helmets on their heads which was basically a leather shield. That was intended to protect them if any loose material fell from the roof as they walked the roads underground.

Activities

There were two classes operating when I was at the centre. There would be around fifty trainees on the course which lasted around a month. I actually enjoyed my time there and there were some good lads on the course and we got on well.

The training involved one day on classroom work learning about the theory of mining and safety issues. The next day we were taken on a bus to Kames Colliery where we did underground training. That was the general format of training for the four weeks.

In the morning the gym teacher, Mr Gemza, who was a Pole, had us out running round the block and doing physical training. There was a large hall where they showed films and there were two full sized snooker tables. There was also a small shop which was open at night where you could buy sweets and other items.

I was pals with Jim Cairney who also worked at Houldsworth. He came from Dalmilling, Ayr, so it was good to have company with someone you knew. We got home at weekends, but had to be back on a Sunday night to begin first thing on Monday. The classroom training consisted mainly of first aid, woodwork and pit safety procedures.

Down the pit

After this formal training period I went back to Houldsworth. You were considered to be trained and it was then time to work down the pit. You did a stint down at the loading and unloading of the hutches, you then progressed further into the mine. This was to the point where the hutches were loaded as the coal came off the conveyor belt from the face and the hutches were loaded to be taken to the pit bottom to be brought to the surface. You had to clock in and out before going down the mine. You were given a token at the same time as you picked up your lamp. The token had to be handed back in when you returned to the surface to allow a count kept of who was underground.

Alex Green.

Canaries

When I was at Houldsworth there were canaries kept at the pithead. They were used to help check for gas. The canaries would die if there was gas present, but this gave an early warning of gas which hopefully helped to identify the problem and prevent any danger to the miners. When the men went down the pit the canaries were taken down with them. This was especially so if the mine drivers were going to open a new seam. It was at these times that it was most likely that gases could be released or be present, so the canaries served a very important role in pit safety.

All the miners took their piece down the mine and had a right good blether. If you were working on extra time, then a piece was sent down to you from the pithead, so you simply worked away at your job. It was a long tiring day working down the pit even without doing overtime.

At the cage bottom at Houldsworth there was a small train with bogies which the men sat in and they were pulled along the roadway which took you quite a long distance towards the coal face. However, once the train stopped there would be another ten minute walk to get you into the coal face. This was the same at Glenburn where I later worked. The roads there ran right out under the sea for some distance.

Strikes Prevalent

Houldsworth tended to be on strike on a fairly regular basis. In my opinion some of the miners were daft because they seemed to want to stop work at the drop of a hat for reasons that didn't honestly justify going on strike. I got fed up with the stoppages because it affected the amount of money you earned. You got a bonus if you worked fifty-three days, but if there was a stoppage for any reason, the bonus was gone. It was unusual to get a bonus there. I decided that Houldsworth wasn't a good long-term prospect because of the strikes.

Glenburn

I had always wanted to work at Glenburn pit because it had a good reputation and it was much handier for me living in Ayr. However, I couldn't get a transfer, so I eventually left Houldsworth and went into Dickie's Stamp Work for a short time. I then applied to get into Glenburn pit.

I got started right away in 1958 probably because I was a trained miner. I began working there at the pithead at what was known as the tumblers. That's where the hutches came off the cage at the pithead and headed for the tumblers which emptied the coal from the hutch by turning it upside down into a large coal wagon located below the tumblers.

There were two tumblers at Glenburn and I told the foreman that they were similar to the ones operated at Houldsworth. He asked me what I did at Houldsworth. I said I worked down the pit, so he arranged for me to work down the pit at Glenburn. I was soon put on coal face training there.

Coal face training

I was only eighteen or perhaps nineteen years old at the time, doing my coal face training. This involved working on what was called long wall stripping. The coal seam at Glenburn wouldn't be more than three feet high so the miners had to kneel while they stripped the seam of coal. It was all hard graft doing the shovelling work, the coal having been previously blasted down by the shot-firer on nightshift. The great thing about Glenburn that really pleased me was the fact that there were no strikes. That meant we didn't lose money.

A Houldsworth miner is homeward bound after a shift. Houldsworth was one of the deepest mines in Scotland.

Wet money

I can recall that there could be a hundred miners standing outside the baths at Houldsworth on strike over something that now seems ridiculous like a few shillings for dirty money or wet money. If you got wet in the pit you could ask to get away early and there could be extra money for working in water, so these things sometimes caused strikes, which now seems absolutely ridiculous.

Pit fatality

There was no one killed in Houldsworth during my time. However, when I moved to Glenburn I would only be there weeks when the manager's son, a chap Dyer, was killed while working a loading machine. I can't remember the date exactly but it would be around 1957/58

Wall stripping

At Glenburn I worked with John Gillan of Annbank on what was known as wall stripping. This involved pushing the hutch in towards the coal face and filling it by hand. We called it the bullring which was a slang name for it, but I don't know why it was so called. I was 'John's boy' and he kept me right on safety and procedures and I did learn a lot working with him.

Holdsworth Pit in the 1930s with its distinctive winding gear.

Littlemill

I left Glenburn in 1960 to go and work at Littlemill Colliery. We'd been told that because it was a more modern pit there was a better chance of getting to work at the coal face where the money was much better. However, that turned out to be a load of nonsense. When I went there I didn't like it. I started off on supplies where I brought materials from the yards to the pithead for transfer down the pit.

In the underground they had mine cars which were large steel bogies, much bigger than hutches that I was used to. They were used to bring the coal and debris from the coal face into the pit bottom for transfer to the surface. I was only there for a few months because I was disenchanted that I wasn't working on the coal face which was what I really wanted to do.

Leaving the pits

I applied for a job with British Telecom which I got and I remained there for 35 years, retiring in early in 2000. I got soaked on a much more regular basis working outside for BT than I ever did at Houldsworth or Glenburn and we were never on strike.

In 1984/85 strike I was very sorry for the miners, having been a miner myself. I remember that the miners in Ayr would come round the doors looking for donations of food. I asked two of them into my home whilst the wife got some donations for their collection. We had a right good chinwag about our days in the pits.

Fish for Killoch

A wee while later my son, who was a fisherman, phoned to ask if I could use two boxes of fish. I got them and straight away drove up to Killoch Colliery where there were several miners standing round a lit oil drum which was blazing away. They were delighted to accept the two boxes of fish. I went back to the office and the Telecom Inspector was waiting for me. He said: "We've had a phone call. I just want to know where my fish is?" Someone had told him about what I had done. He was joking and quite happy that I had been helping to support the striking miners because he knew I had been one in my time.

Fond of Miners

In retrospect, had it not been for the strikes, I might well have spent all my working life in the coal mines. However, knowing what I know now, I think moving to BT at that time was the right decision. I will always have a special place in my heart for coal miners who did the most dangerous job I know, but with great humour.

Maybe when you're snug and warm in bed,
And sleep had come to you all -
The miner, 'ere the night has fled,
May have paid the price of coal.

(anon)

Chapter 31

Days Doon the Pit

Sammy Ballantyne

The honest heart that's free frae a'
Intended fraud or guile,
However Fortune kick the ba',
Has ay some cause to smile:
And mind still, you'll find still,
A comfort this nae sma';
Nae mair then, we'll care then,
Nae farther we can fa'.

Epistle to Davie, a Brither poet
Robert Burns

Sammy Ballantyne, was born on 30 April 1908 in the Hill village of Burnfoothill, located on the high moors above Patna. He later moved to Hopes Avenue, Dalmellington, and then to Bellsbank. He was very happily married to Margaret 'Peggy' Clark who passed on in 1994. They had eight of a family – Annie, John, Hugh, Sam, Phillip, Christine, William and Margaret.

In his younger days, Sammy played the pipes in Burnfoothill Pipe Band. He remained at the Hill until he married Peggy on Hogmanay 1934. He spent his working life in the coal mines of Doon Valley, with forty years working underground at Pennyvenie, Chalmerston and Minnivey. His final thirteen years were spent working as pit baths-man at Minnivey. He retired in 1973.

He recalled some of his mining memories in a taped interview recorded on 1994 when he was aged eighty-six. He died in February 1997 a few weeks short of his eighty-ninth birthday. This is an edited extract from that tape kindly provided by his daughter, Christine MacLellan.

Early Memories

I was born and raised at Burnfoothill (the Hill), on the moors above Waterside. I started work in the coal mining industry of the Doon Valley in 1922 aged fourteen years. I worked for a short time at the furnaces at Waterside which were then in their last days.

When I was a wee boy in Burnfoothill you could look down from the Hill and see the flames from the furnaces glowing bright and smoke spewing out the large lums (chimneys). It was a very busy place Waterside in those days. As my wee pals and I played bools (marbles) in the street I was fascinated at the brightness of the glowing flames and we used to say that it helped us see better in the dark.

Pennyvenie

A lot of Spaniards came to work in the ironworks at Waterside in those days for the Dalmellington Iron Company. After two years at Waterside I started at the pithead aged sixteen years at Pennyvenie No. 4. I got my pit bag with my flask and pieces ready and got the old carriages, hauled by a steam locomotive, on the short journey up to Pennyvenie.

Getting to work

Most of the miners who came from Patna and Waterside and from the Hill villages, travelled in the steam train in old carriages to Pennyvenie. At the end of the shift the men got back on the carriages and returned along the railway lines to Waterside and Patna. Miners simply didn't have cars in my youth. In fact it's probably hard for folk today to understand this, but it was very rare to even see a car, you would just stand and stare in awe when you saw one. Nowadays in my opinion folk take so much for granted.

I was occasionally sent by train from Pennyvenie No. 4 down to Waterside to pick up supplies for the engineers shop and then back by the next train with the packages. The trains were going up and down there all the time empty to pick coal and return full, so you could always get a lift. I sometimes used to go up in the tender of the engine and blether to the driver and fireman.

A short while later, when a new start came to the pit, I went from doing odd jobs at the pithead to the screes. We called it craw-picking – where you took the stones and dirt out of the coal. Then you progressed and went down the pit.

Working the Coalface

I remember getting four and a tanner a day (4/6d) in wages. The way things worked then was that perhaps you had a father or an older brother who was a collier. You would draw off him – remove the coal and the dirt - at the face and put it on the conveyor belts to go to the hutches. You would work away and later you would get a place of your own to work the face and someone would draw off you, perhaps a family member or a friend.

You got the big money working at the face if you were producing the coal, so most men wanted a job at the coal face. Others were happy to work elsewhere underground as they perhaps felt it was too dangerous at the face. The reality is that it was dangerous anywhere underground.

Pit ponies

When I started underground, there wasn't much machinery to work the face. It was done by borers and blasting, so it was hard heavy work to remove coal and dirt. When I started there were also pit ponies which pulled the hutches on the underground railway.

In fact when I started in Pennyvenie No 4 there were lovely stables half roads down the mine and the ponies were stabled there when not working. The stables were cut back into the rock. They were well kept and the miners were fond of the ponies and they often brought them down a carrot or sugar as a wee treat.

When I went to Chalmerston they also had ponies. One of the on-cost workers looked after them. Three ponies ran the underground bogies. One would work each shift. The ponies would pull the hutches and they had a lamp on the front of their chest, just like a light on the front of a train. I remember the workers who did this job escorting the ponies. It was Tommy Medine, Tommy Higgins, and 'Tarry' Gault. It was in my time at Pennyvenie and Chalmerston that the ponies were done away with, as mechanisation came in more and more. The ponies were replaced underground by diesel engines.

Mechanisation & tools

I remember when the first coal cutting machines were introduced. The machine men were always on the ten shift (nightshift) cutting the coal. The dayshift men stripped the coal and you put girds in to hold the coal and support the area being worked.

It was all hand boring in my early days. There were different sizes of borers otherwise called ricketies. Later on it was electric borers that were used. You carted your tools into the coal face. And you treated them with respect because you had to pay for all your own tools in my early years. If they broke, you had to personally replace them.

Sammy Ballantyne in his Lethanhill Pipe Band uniform taken at the Hill on 30 April 1930.

Later on the NCB supplied everything. They got free graith (tools) and some miners played on it. One day a miner would get a new shovel from the big store at the pit where all the graith was kept. After a day's work he'd fling the shovel onto the waste and get a new one from the store the next day, rather than carry it back to the pithead.

In my day you had to lock up your tools – pick, mash, saw and borer. You had to keep a box and padlock it. You had to look after your graith, but once it was supplied free, some workers didn't appreciate it, perhaps getting things far too easy. We even had to buy our own gelignite – 1/6d a pound at that time from the pit store.

I remember we had to send our saws to the workshops at Waterside to get sharpened and it cost 6d. If your pick handle broke, it went down to Waterside and a new handle was fitted. Later on these jobs were done at Chalmerston. It was the same with your pit boots and they could be repaired by the pit cobbler.

Head protection

When I started in the pit things were very basic. All we had for a light was a wee oil lamp and you just wore an ordinary bonnet. These were less than useless if there was a fall of stones from the roof. Most of the miners of my early days would cut a bit of leather off an old boot, sew it on to the pit bonnet and make a hole for the lamp to be fixed to your bonnet.

Some miners would fix a tie so that the bonnet was secured to your head under your chin. Later on it was all those pit helmets made out of bakelite, then they came to the very hard safety helmets. They were white in colour. They had webbing in the inside to protect your head and to cushion it on impact.

Lamp Lights

Carbide lamps came in after the oil lamps. I had one in the house for years. During the war, I mind that some of them that didn't want to sign on for the armed forces were put into the pits and several were sent to work at Pennyvenie. They were called Bevan Boys throughout the country.

I recall one from Glasgow who was staying in Dalmellington and he was away home every weekend and back in time for his shift on Monday. He took his carbide lamp with him. I sat on the bus to Ayr with him one day. He took the bottom off the lamp, spat on it, put the bottom back on and sparked it to light his cigarette. There were some right roasters in the mines during the war.

Moved to Chamerston

I shifted up the hill to Chalmerston Nos 4/5 mine in 1929 and I remained there until it closed in 1960. Chalmerston had a small pit forty-five fathoms deep and three mines. It fact you could shout up to the decker (engineman) at the top of the pit, if you wanted a piece sent down or a drink and he would arrange for that to be done.

In 1956 I took ill and was off work for three months. I was physically exhausted working at the stripping. That was the only time I was ever off. After that I gave up the stripping and got a lighter job down the pit. There were different grades of pay. Grade 1 was a collier or a brusher and I was put down to grade 3 which was a lesser pay, but the work was not so demanding.

As I got older the job down the pit became more difficult because it was still hard physical work, but not as tough as at the coalface where coal production was always a top priority. You knew at the end of the shift that you had been working.

When Chalmerston closed I moved to Minnivey. I applied for a pithead job, but after interview it went to the older man. The manager was good at looking after older miners who were finding it hard going down the pit. So I said to myself, the next few jobs that come up, I'll apply and I'm bound to get one of them.

Ropeway from Bogton pit to the washer at Minnivey where it crossed over the houses at 40 Broomknowe. This ropeway was removed and re-erected at Butlins Holiday Camp, Ayr around 1957 where it was used to transport holidaymakers from the site entrance down to the camp.

Bath Attendant

So, after about a year another job came up for bath attendant. There were two applicants in for it. We were lucky as we both got jobs. One was cleaning the Glennies (Glennie lamps) and looking after the batteries to get them recharged. The other chap got that job and I got the baths job. I was thirteen years baths attendant at Minnivey. Baths attendant was a busy job. You had to keep them clean with Ajax powder and keep the drains clean to avoid them getting clogged up. I enjoyed this much better than down the pit.

Mind you, I wasn't making the same money, but I got my pay every Friday. Whereas down the pit, depending on how much coal they brought out, they could get a good pay week or one not so good. That's how it went. I enjoyed my thirteen years in the pit baths and I never lost a single shift.

Bevan Boy

There was another Bevan Boy who came from Galloway. He went home every weekend. He walked up Loch Doon and over the hills and came back on Sunday evening to start on Monday. He was hardy and I

NUM branch meeting with local manager at Minnivey Colliery, Dalmellington circa 1964.
L to r: J Thomson, deputy manager; Sam Graham, NUM; J Miller, under manager; J McArthur, manager; David Connell, clerk; John Easton, electrician; H Murphy, NUM and Adam Johnstone, safety and training officer.

became friends with him as he was a really decent lad. After the war he used to send a postcard to Chalmerston every year asking after everyone. I just forget his name, but he was a great spud. It was a good experience for him and he loved the banter with the miners.

Smoking down the mine

At the finish up in the 1960s it was all safety lamps in the Doon Valley pits. You had a belt and battery for the lamp which was held in the belt and a line came up round your back to the lamp to provide the power. By that time there was strictly no smoking allowed in the pits. Every second morning there would be a fireman down the pit before you, and he'd be standing along the road a wee bit away waiting to search everyone coming off the cage.

There would be water running at the channels at the side of the underground roads and if we spied the fireman, you would see cigarettes and matches flying everywhere into the water, so no one would be caught. You could be sacked on the spot if you were caught with cigarettes or matches, so you didn't want that to happen or you would have been out of a job.

I smoked the pipe, but I never took it underground. We laid them past until we came back up and then you had a smoke after you went into the baths and got washed. The baths were a great thing. As baths attendant I had to keep the water warm. I had also to clean the boiler out twice a shift. I would be burning a ton of coal a day. There were more than two hundred men getting baths each day, so it took a lot of hot water.

Rag trade

I also had to clean the entire baths every three months. The men had to take their working clothes home when the big clean was on, otherwise they were stored initially to be burned later. The men in the rag trade got to know about this, and they called every few months and took them away. They gave me 7/6d for a bag of clothes, so it must have been worthwhile for them.

Rats at Chalmerston

There were loads of rats when I worked at Chalmerston. There were no mice. It was said that the rats went down in the bags of grain used to feed the horses. It was all rats. It's funny. The rats were bloody sensible. They kent fine if there was going to be a flood or fall of stones. They had the sense to move out. The rats never bothered you, but they would go for your piece if you left it sitting. If you threw a crust away, they would nab it right away. Eventually we were warned, under threat of the sack, not to throw food or feed them.

Underground work

The brushers did all the stone work. They put in what was called 'a pack' to support the walls at the face and the rest of the waste from the face was removed. Afterwards the miners came in with the blast borer and pulled the face down. The waste was removed and taken out. There were big belts four feet wide that would take the waste away to be taken up the pit. So much of the waste would be retained to provide support at the face.

The 'doughty men' advanced the props. They counted and inspected them every night. The doughties were handy. You didn't need to hammer them in with a mash as you did during most of my time with the wooden straps. You put the doughtie in and it was raised by pressing a button and getting it hydraulically to the right height.

Benwhat Heatherbell circa 1894 with the Dalmellington Challenge Trophy snapped outside Benwhat Store. The door on the left led to a room used as a surgery by the doctor on his rounds to the village. Back row: (l to r) Willie Dick, James Allan, David 'Wheatie' McBride, Alex Orr, John Conner, Willie Orr and David McGarvie. Front row: James 'Punch' Hainey, John Rae, David 'Dad' Torbet, James 'Lairdie' Armour, Andrew Hainey, Neil Dempsey, Adam McHattie and Alex McCall.

In my day it was all wooden props you worked with. You put them in three foot apart and there would perhaps be twelve to be set in place during a shift. If the conveyor stopped you put up more wood as you could then get easier access.

Wet Money

We regularly worked in water at Chalmerston. You got a shilling a day extra for doing this. I mind once this mate of mine worked in the dry side and I was in the wet area. On pay day he said: "Whits the five shillings extra in your poke. I've not got that." I said: "Naw, you won't get that extra money because you were working dry." Mind you, he wanted in the water the next week. I said: "On you go, son. I'm happy to forego the water money, to stay dry."

Well, to be honest, even not working directly in water, you still got wet working underground. In each big road and the side roads underground, the water run into the pit bottom, known as a sump. From there it was pumped out of the pit. If water built up to a high level, the pit could have flooded and that would have been very dangerous, perhaps even resulting in closure.

When the coal mines were nationalised there were men running about with pads and pencils asking you what you were doing. There were jobs galore on the go for pen pushers. Then there were the women in the canteen. One covered each shift and provided a great service to the miners.

Every so often the x-ray motor would come to the mine and check each man for silicosis, which was a lung disease. Mind you quite a few men wouldn't go. I've been x-rayed a wheen o' times.

What I can say with certainty is that when the NCB came in to run the pits in 1947, they were much more conscious of safety than under private ownership. On the other hand there was an awful lot of money wasted on jobs.

Social life

We had great pit socials and lots of friends in Dalmellington. The miners were always up for dances and enjoyed singing a song at the breaks during the socials. Every pit had its own pit social. They were always held in winter time. Each was held on different dates, usually a Saturday, so you could go to more than one if you wanted.

Special men

I've been fortunate to see mining develop from the early years of the 20th century when thing were very rudimentary until the introduction of modern methods of coal extraction. It is with mixed emotions that there are no coal mines in Scotland today, because they did provide lots of work and gave men a sense of belonging to something special.

But I passionately believe that it's important to remember how the coal mines operated over the years in the Doon Valley and those who walk in our shoes might also give some thought to that special band of men who were proud to call themselves miners.

Nae treasures, nor pleasures
Could make us happy lang;
The heart ay's the part ay,
That makes us right or wrang.

Epistle to Davie, a Brither Poet
Robert Burns

Some of the members of Barrmill Jolly Beggars Burns Club, Beith, Ayrshire. (Photo: Donald L Reid)

Author, Donald L Reid, with some of the members of Dalmellington (33rd Ayrshire) Scouts at the launch of his book, *The Lost Mining Villages of Doon Valley*, in 2011 (Photo: Kathleen Reid)

The spoil heap or pit bing at Pennyvenie bears testimony to the millions of tons of waste which culminated in this now overgrown man-made hill. Pennynenie Pit closed in 1978, but this bing will always be remembered by the many miners who risked life and limb to win coal. To the rear can be seen Benbeoch Craig and in the foreground is a local nursing home.

Looking from above the KGV playing field towards St. Barbara's RC church with Benbeoch Craig in the background and the KGV playing field on the left.

Benbeoch Craig from the Pennyvenie Opencast site 2005. (Photo: Donald L Reid)

The ruins of the ten houses at Corbie Craigs, known locally as The Corbies. Behind can be seen Burnhead Farm, sadly now a ruin. (Photo: Donald L Reid)

Two sets of twins that we know of, The Galloway girls and the Filson lads, were born in Benwhat. It was timely to photograph them at the rededication ceremony of the war memorial on June 12 2011. Sadly Tommy Filson died in February 2012, but his story had been recorded earlier.
Back: The Galloway twins – Effie (left) and Jean
Front: Tommy Filson and Andy Filson.
(Photo: Donald L Reid)

Craigengillan Dalmellington Curling Club is the oldest surviving social and recreational club in Dalmellington having been established on 3 December 1841 at a meeting in the Black Bull Hotel.
Back row (l to r): Michael Shaw, Gavin Clyde, Jim Morrison, Gus Cochrane, Ed Baines, Gordon Neil, Craig Coulter, James Dee, Tony Bell and Kerr Alexander
Middle row: Andrew Linn, Fiona Deans, Jinty Haddow, David Stewart, Ian Alexander, John McLeod, Anne Hay, Susanne Howie, Ruth Clyde, Edith Kerr and Jim Nisbet.
Front row: Robert White, Alex Paterson, Ian Hay, Margaret White and Kenny Ferguson (secretary).
(Photo: Courtesy of Craigengillan Curling Club (Kennedy Ferguson)

Loch Doon which is a popular tourist attraction for its beauty and history and also for the ospreys, their nest just seen on the high point of this photo.

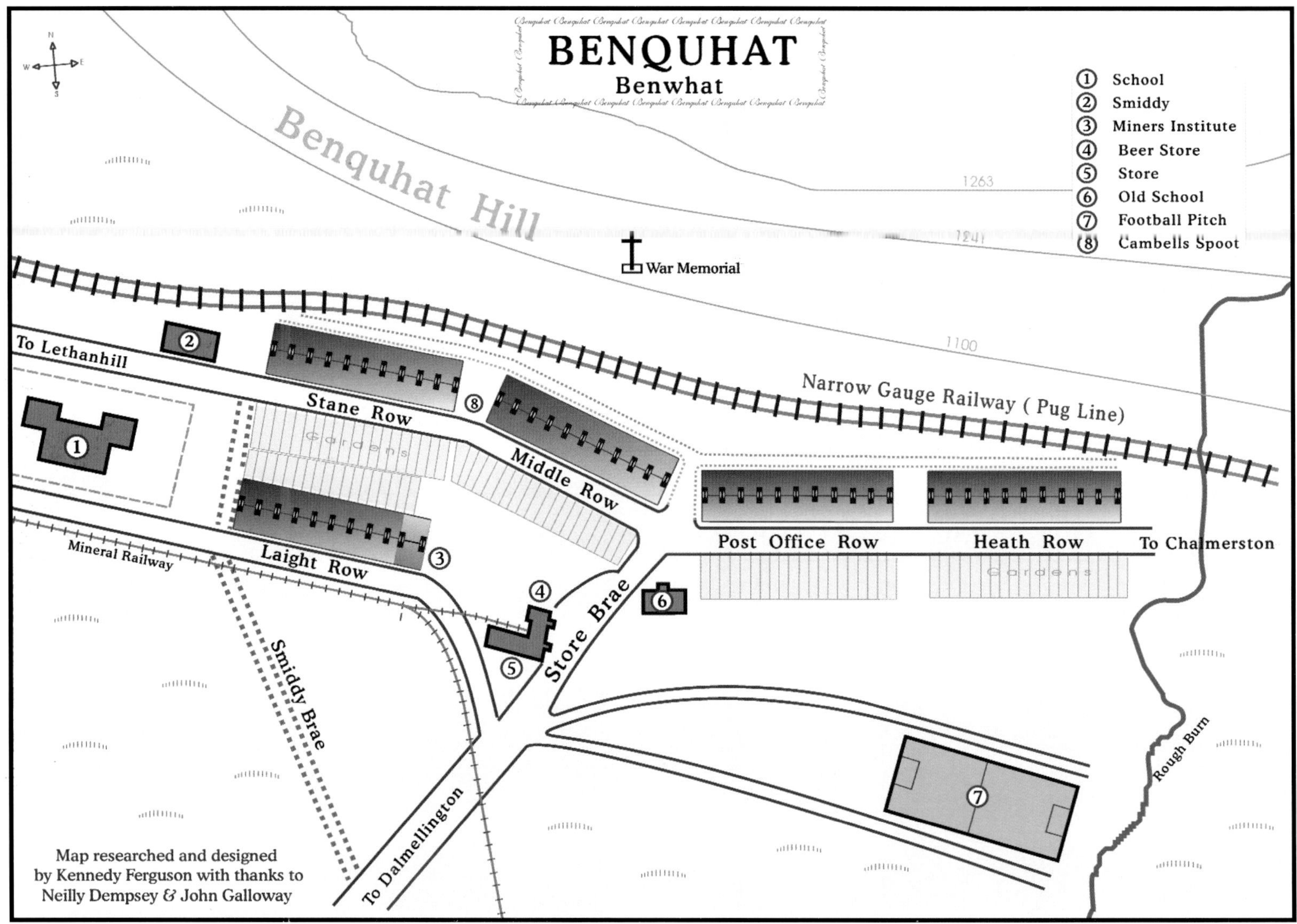

A detailed map of Benwhat, sometimes spelled Benquhat, from the pen of Kennedy Ferguson, which will prove invaluable to anyone wishing to learn more about the village.
(Courtesy of Kennedy Ferguson)

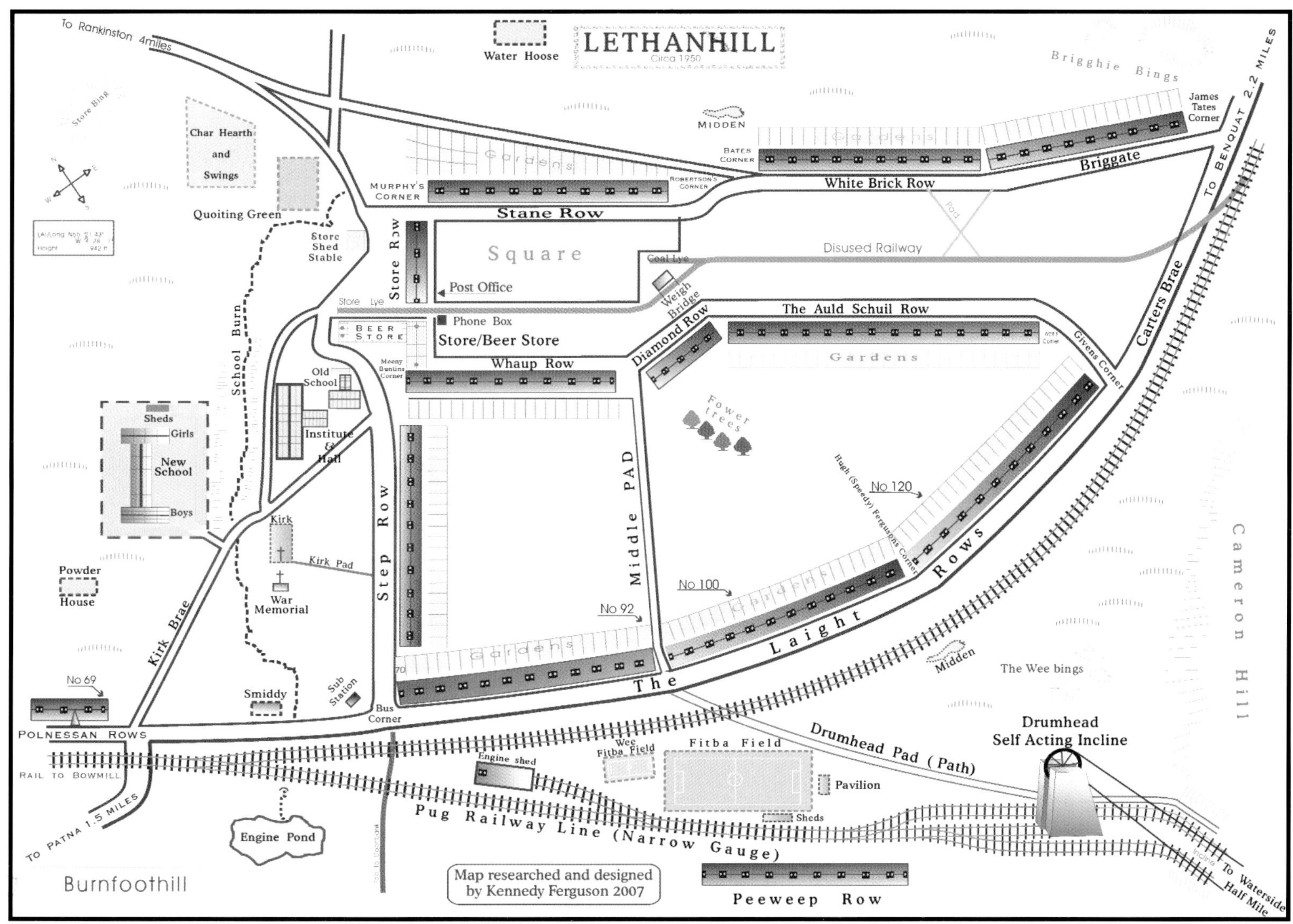

A plan of Lethanhill as recalled by former resident Kennedy Ferguson, now of Dalmellington.
(Plan of Lethanhill: Courtesy of Kennedy Ferguson)

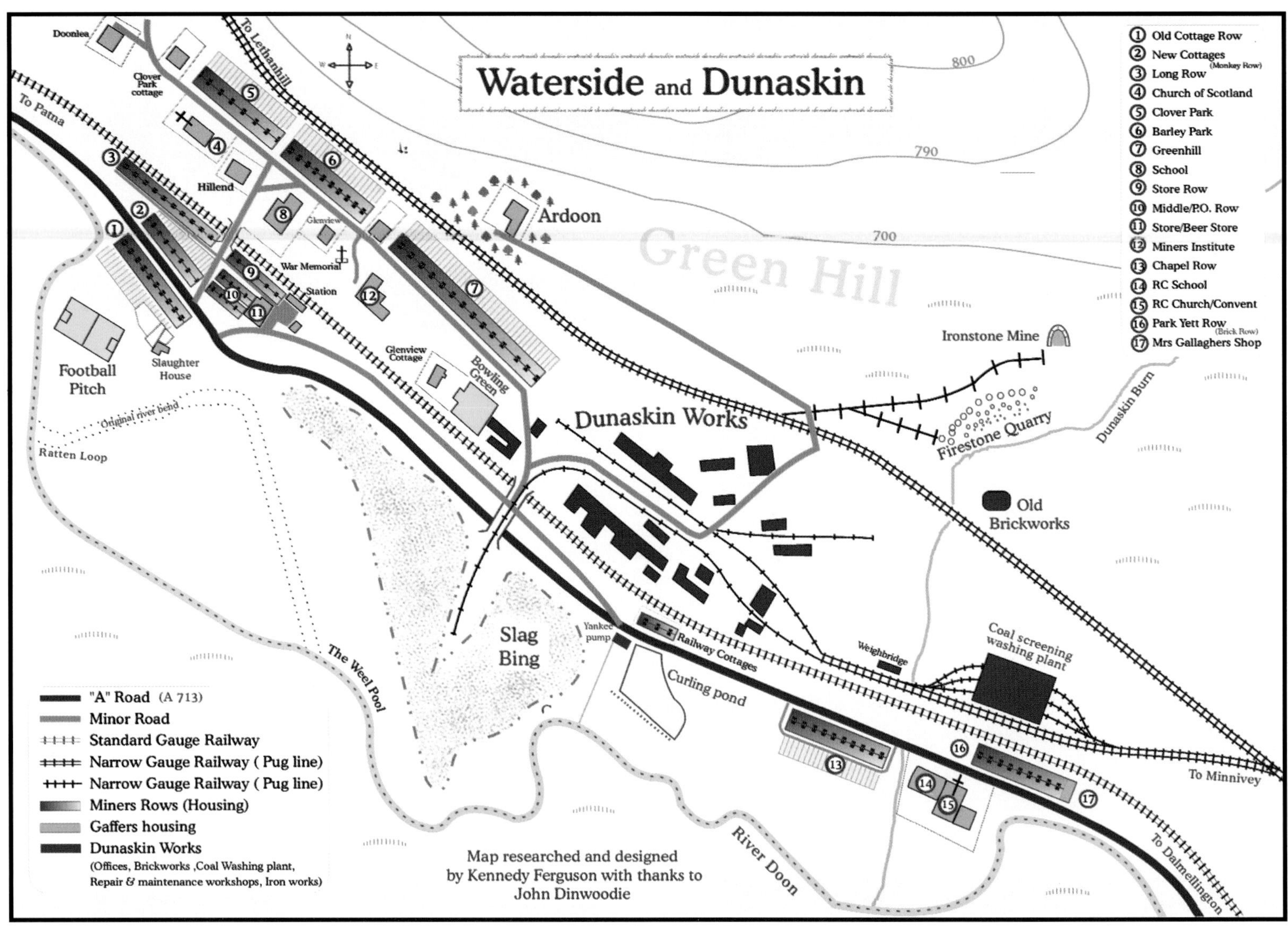

An excellent map of Waterside, carefully prepared by Kennedy Ferguson of Dalmellington.
(Map by Kennedy Ferguson)

Pennyvenie just around the time of its closing in 1978. The winding gear still in place and the bing to the right. In 2015 you would never have believed that this was the pithead. It is covered in trees and bushes. Nature has claimed it back.

Pennyvenie bing in July 2015 which burned for many years after the pit closed in 1978. Nature has now reclaimed it.
(Photo: Donald L Reid)

The children of P6/7 at Patna Primary School enjoyed hearing about the industrial and social history of the Doon Valley from Donald L Reid.
(Photo: Donald L Reid)

Robert Douglas, born at Benwhat where he spent his formative years, visits the refurbished war memorial, which sits sentinel on the front of Benwhat Hill, affording wonderful views across the Doon Valley, prior to the re-dedication service on 12 June 2011. As a boy Robert recalls that several of the rows were already being demolished as they used to play in them when the workers went home. The opencast site at nearby Lethanhill can be seen and the Clyde coast and Arran are in the background on the right, highlighting the wonderful views from Benwhat Hill.
(Photo: Donald L Reid)

Chapter 32

Random Memories of the Pits

Arthur McCrail

But Och, mankind are unco weak,
An' little to be trusted;
If Self the wavering balance shake,
It's rarely right adjusted!

Epistle to a Young Friend, May 1786
Robert Burns

Arthur McCrail

Arthur McCrail, 83, is a retired Doon Valley mineworker. He has lived in Kilmarnock for several years. Here he reflects on part of his time spent as a tradesman at Pennyvenie Colliery from 1960 until it closed in 1978 and thereafter moved to Seafield Colliery in Kirkcaldy. He thought working at Pennyvenie was the best time of his working life.

Early life

I was born on 7 November 1931 in Dennistoun, Glasgow. My father was John McCrail, a marine engineer working at sea. My mother was Jean Donald. Both my parents were Glaswegians.

I was educated at Knightswood Senior Secondary School. I began work in Glasgow and served my time as a marine engineer in a company called Drysdales in Yoker. They made marine pumps. I married in 1957 and at the time was living in Vale of Leven.

Pennyvenie calls

Housing was hard to get in those days in Glasgow and the house in Vale of Leven was pretty poor. I saw an advert in the newspaper for a diesel mechanic in a colliery in Auchinleck. I got an interview at Prestwick. I was offered a job as a diesel mechanic working at Pennyvenie Pit, Dalmellington, in 1960.

There were four underground locos there and my job was to make sure they were maintained in good working order. Mechanisation was beginning to take off and the National Coal Board (NCB) was employing more skilled men to look after machinery. They also had a first class training programme for apprentices. At that time I think there would be around eight apprentices working on the mechanical side and the same number on the electrical side at Pennyvenie.

As a key worker coming into the Doon Valley I was allocated a Scottish Special Housing Association house in Dalcairnie Road, Bellsbank. It was a four-in-a-block house. It was a four apartment house and in good condition. I lived there with my then wife, Margaret, and daughter Lynn, who was aged three years.

While we were in Bellsbank my daughter, Wendy, came into the family. After around four years I bought an old house in Dalmellington at what was known as the foot o' the Mains, at the bottom of Main Street opposite Bellsbank Crescent. My son, Keith, was born there.

Pit Training

On taking up my position at the pit, I did training at Dunfermline to learn the underground work. This took place at a disused pit called Muirkirkhall. I got home at the weekend, but stayed in digs in Dunfermline during the working week. The training focussed quite a bit on working haulages underground. One day it was practical underground work and the following day it was classroom work on mining theory and practice.

The practical work underground involved coal face work removing the coal and dirt. It was very much about safety issues and safely working underground haulages. There was a self-acting incline operating with the loaded hutches running out that pit. One lot of hutches pulled the others without power and it was a very ingenious system.

I worked at Pennyvenie for two weeks before going for my training, so I was actually working underground right away getting used to the pit, but under supervision. I was working on servicing Hunslet locomotives. One of the engineers from the Hunslet company had come up and I worked along with him to fit a water tank and water system for cooling the exhaust on the loco. He was there for a week and I worked with him learning exactly how the engine worked and after that I was able to work on the locomotives and maintain them to a high standard.

Good place to work

I can honestly say that Pennyvenie Colliery was the best place I have ever worked. It was a small pit and you could go and see the manager at any time. He had an open door policy and it wasn't a problem if you wanted to discuss any issues.

Everyone knew each other and we were on first name terms with the oversmen and the manager. This was completely new to me coming from working on Clydeside where, if you saw the manager or the senior foreman, you were probably in trouble. Pennyvenie was a much more relaxed and friendly place.

If all was going well and the mine was working away, quite often we were quiet just doing maintenance work. Most of this work was done on the backshift and nightshift when the main work on the face was stopped because getting coal out without interruption was essential.

Good managers

I worked at Pennyvenie for almost 19 years right up until it closed in 1978. The first manager I worked under was Bob Blair and Ben Kennedy was the under-manager. Both were gentlemen. Bob Blair was a really nice man and came from Ayr. He was a very fair man and I think he was quite a shy man. I don't think he liked confrontation very much. I became union delegate, so I had regular meetings with him, but he was good to work for and always fair.

Ben Kennedy, David McHugh (pit engineer) and Paddy McCutcheon, (lamp-man), all lived at Craigview, Pennyvenie, near to the mine, but Ben Kennedy died while he was living there. He always seemed to be a big healthy man, but died not that long after he retired. He was replaced by Danny Crockett as under manager. Danny proved to be a different personality and could be very dogmatic. He wasn't very popular with the tradesmen at the pit.

Wet money

On one occasion when I had just been appointed as the tradesman's delegate a situation arose down the pit over what was known as 'wet money.' This was where a tradesman, Mick Inglis and the oversman, Jock Johnstone, were in dispute. Mick had been working in a wet area and was looking to get a 'wet line' which would have entitled him to an additional 4/- provided the oversman gave him a line authorising the payment.

Johnstone was too busy and said that Inglis wasn't that wet anyway. However, things escalated after that and I called a meeting of the tradesmen to discuss this dispute over the wet money. It was suggested that if it wasn't resolved by the Monday, that a strike be called.

However, common sense ruled and a compromise payment of 3/- was made to Inglis, thus averting a costly strike. In essence none of the tradesmen wanted to go on strike for such a trivial occurrence. However, this did put me in a good position to work with the management on behalf of the tradesmen. I usually managed to resolve all working issues amicably at Pennyvenie.

Types of accident

Folk often assume that accidents were always caused by roof falls. In my time there was less and less of those types of accidents. The majority were actually caused by men using machinery such as the haulages, moving belts and not surprisingly, the main problems were caused by miners tripping and falling on the underground roads.

I worked the ham and egg shift where you started at 10am and finished at 5pm. I also worked the backshift as well, being the diesel mechanic. I came into the lamp cabin and the belt shifters were there. They moved the belts forward nearer to the coal face as coal was

No 1 Pennyvenie in the late 1890s. In those days the winding engine was operated by steam, hence the large chimney. This photo seems to have been staged to demonstrate the various trades involved in the mining process.

removed and the face progressed. If they were finished they came up the shaft early, but every now and again the manager had to remind them not to abuse the privilege.

Down a hole

I remember a chap Whalen, his son Jim was an engineer in the pit. He wasn't a very fit man and was given a job at the pit head. He was working on scrap and it was the last day before the holidays. There was a big metal plate about five feet square lying on the ground. Jim went forward and put his hand under the plate and lifted it up and suddenly fell forward and disappeared down a hole ten feet deep. The sheet was covering the large deep hole.

John Skinner, an engineer, heard the frantic screaming voice. When he moved the plate back they discovered that Whalen had broken his leg. They had to go and get a ladder to get him out. This happened just past the electrician's shop where no one went very often. He was lucky that John Skinner happened to be passing or goodness knows how long he would have been stuck down that hole.

1972 National Strike

In 1972 a national strike was called when Ted Heath was Prime Minister. Several of the local miners went to Braehead Power Station, now a shopping centre on Clydeside near Govan. We had an arrangement with the railway union where, if a member was on official duty, they would not cross the picket line.

Three of us, Jack Buchanan, Davie Murphy and I, went at night to picket Braehead and a police car turned up with a sergeant and constable. The five of us just stood chatting. There was a yard nearby and the rats were running about all over the place and they came close to us. The young constable got his baton out to throw it at the rats and the sergeant said: "Put that away. If the press see you, they'll accuse us of police brutality." We all had a good laugh at that.

The only folk working at Pennyvenie, during the 1972 strike, were a few of the deputies. Their role was to maintain the pumps to keep the pit from flooding. Keeping the pumps going was essential and the pump-man at that time was Tommy McGuigan.

Old Tramp

There was an elderly tramp living beside the screening plant at Pennyvenie. There was a small brick building with some benches where the pithead men would have their piece on the dayshift. This old tramp stayed there.

He was supposed to have been twenty-one years in the army. He used to shave himself every night with an old fashioned cut-throat razor. He kept out the road, but would put the cans on with boiling water for the men coming to the bothy for their piece.

Bob Blair, the manager at the time, let the old man stay as he wasn't doing any harm. However, he had to have an address which was Hillview, Pennyvenie Pit. The manager had to sign papers confirming he was living there. A couple of times a week the man in charge of the pit baths would let him in for a bath.

I don't remember when he went away or what eventually happened to him. He kept himself clean and tidy and he was a right old soldier. Sometimes I would speak to him on the nightshift and he was always well mannered and articulate. This was just another example of how Bob Blair, the manager, could be sensible, caring and compassionate for someone like the old tramp.

Nicknames

Dalmellington was an awful place for miners having nicknames. They seemed to run in families. 'Ringy' Maxwell was a miner and 'young Ringy' was an electrician. There was 'Tarry Gault' and 'old Tarry,' the father was a bricklayer. I remember on one occasion, Jock Kennedy, the manager at that time, spoke to 'old Tarry' about a wall he built underground.

Jock asked 'old Tarry' if he thought the wall was plumb. He replied: "I can tell you it's not only plumb, it's a little more than plumb."

The chief electrician was always called Tommy 'Cauder'which I only later discovered was actually Calderwood. The lamp-man was Rab Clyde and his proper surname was Clydesdale. There was also 'Disher' Graham, who was a miner, and he cleaned the locomotives. The ones who were getting on in years were given jobs that weren't so hard. 'Pale' Scally was another, but most nicknames carried on to sons.

No Time

One night I phoned across to ask the lamp-man, Rab Clydesdale, the time as I'd forgotten my watch. I knew there was a big clock on the lamp-man's wall. He apparently was busy filling the Glennie lamps for the nightshift and he simply said: "I canny tell you," and put the phone down.

When I met him later I said: "I've heard of folk wouldn't give you a break, but you're the first man I know who wouldn't give me the time." He seemed to take the huff at this remark because a couple of days later I met Bob Blair, the manager. He asked if I had problem with Robert Clydesdale. I told him what happened and the manager burst out laughing. It transpired that Rab had complained about me, saying: "A geelygaw fae Glesga comes here and thinks he's running the bloody place." And that was all because I asked him the time.

Rab didn't speak to me for a long time until one night we both finished backshift when it was snowing heavily. He was waiting on a bus. I offered him a lift and he kind of hesitated but took the lift, so we got on fine after that.

Crossed wires

One Saturday morning I was working to service the locomotives down the pit so they were ready for Monday morning. I came up the pit to the engineers shop and I was having my piece. Someone phoned across from the lamp cabin and time office, which were in the same building, and I was told I was wanted on the national phone.

Pennyvenie Pit around the time of closure in 1978 with the colliery headgear and winding tower still in place. This was the last deep mine in Ayrshire's Doon Valley. Here you can see the small hutches used for loading coal and spoil underground.

I went across and saw that Tommy Calderwood was there with Lewis Uriarte and the lamp-man. Wee Lenny Watkins, who was in the Time Office, said very seriously: "Arthur, it's Mick McGahey, the Scottish Miners President looking for you." I took the phone and said hello Mick. It was in fact a man called Mick McGaffney, a miner at the pit and not the national union boss.

When I put the phone down Lewis said: "Was that really Mick McGahey, the top union man looking for you. What did he want?" Jokingly I told him he was asking my view on the possibility of a national strike.

This caused a real stir among those present who then assumed a strike was in the offing. Lenny Watkins was asking others how come I knew Mick McGahey, the firebrand miners leader. Someone said: "Aye, they're all bloody communists anyway." That was another time in the pits when I had a good laugh.

When Pennyevnie closed in 1978 I moved to Lugar workshop where I worked for a year and then I moved to Seafield Colliery in Kirkcaldy, Fife, but it was also on the way out and closed in 1988.

Poaching

In my spare time I was keen on fishing on the River Doon with a pal called David Murphy, an engineer at Pennyvenie. I recall Tommy 'Tarry' Gault was making a gaff in the engineers shop. When it was ready I suggested we try it out. We went to the burn adjacent to Pennyvenie pit and it was in spate. 'Tarry' took his overalls off from the shoulders and leant into the pool. He flung out a 7lb salmon. I said: "Listen 'Tarry' not only are we in danger of losing our jobs for being away from the pit, but the polis might jail us for poaching."

Funeral fun

Jimmy Stevenson, was a Lethanhill (the Hill) man and he was my gaffer. I remember him telling me about his happy days at Lethanhill. He was passionate about it and he said how much he missed his old village which had been abandoned and demolished about 1954. He said that a funeral on the Hill was more fun than a wedding in Dalmellington.

Lost at the Picket

I remember being on strike and going through with Arthur Scargill and the infamous flying pickets to Longannet Power Station in 1972, with several men from Pennyvenie. There was more polis about than miners.

The only confrontation was picketing at the power station in Kilmarnock One day the pickets stopped a lorry about to enter the power station. I asked the driver if he appreciated that he was crossing an official picket line. He replied: "Thank hell I've found you, pal. Can you give me directions to Templeton's carpet factory? I thought this was it." He was lost! We happily joined in the laugh and pointed him in the right direction. We always tried to keep things light hearted.

At the age of 57 I went to university in Wales and got a BA degree in literature and drama. I've been working on a novel and I've got most of it finished. It's based around Dalmellington some twenty years after the 1984 miners' strike.

I can honestly say that I thoroughly enjoyed my years at Pennyvenie. It was a good job, a happy place to work and everyone got on famously. What more could you ask for?

Ay free, aff han', your story tell,
When wi' a bosom crony;
But still keep something to yoursel
Ye scarcely tell to ony.

Epistle to a Young Friend, May 1786
Robert Burns

Chapter 33

Working Pennyvenie Coal Face

Harry Kennedy

The sun that overhangs yon moors,
Out-spreading far and wide,
Where hundreds labour to support
A haughty lordling's pride:
I've seen yon weary winter-sun
Twice forty times return;
And ev'ry time has added proofs,
That man was made to mourn.

Man Was Made to Mourn
A Dirge
Robert Burns

Harry Kennedy spent most of his working life in the coal industry mainly at Pennyvenie working at the coal face for thirteen years. This pit closed in 1978 bringing to an end NCB deep mining in the Doon Valley. In this chapter he reflects on his personal experiences working at the coal face at Pennyvenie. Married to Mary they have two daughters, Ena and Anne and grandchildren, Colin, Steven, Stephanie and several great grandchildren.

School to pit

I left Dalmellington School when I was fourteen years old and started work at the NCB Dunaskin Workshops. After two years there I went to Pennyvenie No. 2/3/5 pithead. After various jobs I was sent to No. 2 pit shaft. When the cage from the pit bottom landed on the surface with a full hutch of coal, my job was to shove the full hutch clear of the cage and then make sure that the empty hutch was put back on the cage to go underground.

Cage and Hutches

There was a wire rope above my head with a ring attached to it. At the other side of the cage, the banksman, Joe Roney, had to stand on a pedal which was known as 'the monkey' to release the safety bar so that the hutch could only move when everything was secure. This was to avoid accidents because a loaded hutch was a real danger if you got in its way.

I reached up, pulled the ring twice that indicated to the winding engine operator that the surface was all clear. The pit bottom bell would ring once to let the operator know that it was clear to send the cage up to the surface and it was two bells to send a cage safely down to the pit bottom. This was a non-stop operation because without hutches going back and forth no coal or dirt could be brought to the surface. You had to be thinking and watching all the time during this operation because it was a constant process.

Winding Engine Operator

There were some incidents I recall. There was a window in the winding engine house so the operator could see the hutches coming on and off. On a few occasions he saw my hand going up and must have assumed I was going to pull the ring to indicate that it was safe to move the cage. However, he didn't wait for the bell to sound and jumped the gun. He anticipated that all was fine and sent the cage on its way.

However the hutch was not correctly positioned on the cage. The result was that the cage moved and the hutch jammed at the pithead. This happened a few times. The end result was that the window of the winding engine house was blocked up so that the operator would have to depend on the bell, rather than anticipating what was happening by simply looking. Accidents could happen so easily and in a pit environment they could be costly.

The engineman had to follow the strict procedures to avoid accidents happening. It was probably boredom or perhaps wishing to speed up things that made him act without hearing the bell.

No. 7 Pennyvenie

My turn came to work underground at No. 2 Pennyvenie where I had carried out my coal face training. Later on No. 2 closed and the men were transferred the short distance to work at No. 7, the only one left. No. 7 was twice the depth of Nos. 2/3 and the cages were much larger. They held something like twenty-eight men and they had a double-deck cage which could take four hutches.

Coal Face Stripper

One morning at the pit bottom I was asked to wait as the under manager wanted to speak to me. There was a bad flu epidemic on the go and due to this there was a shortage of strippers. Strippers were the men who produced the coal at the face. He asked me if I would be able to strip a cut of coal. I said that I was up for the challenge telling him that I would try my best. I left the pit bottom with a shovel, coal pick, saw, and a 2lb mash all bundled together. I had to walk one-and-a-half miles to reach the coal face. I felt that I had actually worked a shift by the time I got there.

Feeling Inadequate

I was shown my cut at the face and by that time the rest of the strippers had been working for an hour. There was simply no way I could catch up with them. I had visions of me, a young man aged nineteen, with no real face experience, working on hands and knees in a seam of coal less than three feet high in unbelievable darkness and simply being unable to do the job.

Help at Hand

It didn't look too good for me when other miners arrived and they could see that I was well behind the others, but they wouldn't appreciate that I started an hour after them. Two other miners, working near me, had completed their work and they then got stuck in with me working on my cut of coal. I think they appreciated that I was new to the job and would be feeling a little ill at ease.

Those two men were Tom Roberts and Jim 'Can' Buchanan. Every day thereafter until that section finished the three of us made our way to the pithead together. They were my best friends from then until the end of their lives. That was one of the great things about the pits, you made great pals because you shared the same hard work and faced the same dangers. We were all genuinely in it together and looked out for each other.

Pit Baths

In the pithead baths you had to get someone to wash your back. All coalface workers bodies were caked with sweat and thick coal dust. Someone would shout: "Can you oblige and wash my back, Harry." When you went out your cubicle to help, it was not uncommon for cold water from a hose to hit you square on the chest. That was the type of carry on that we enjoyed in the baths.

Harry Kennedy.

Injured at the coal face

When the section finished Tam (Tom Roberts) and Cam (Jim Buchanan) were sent to another job. I was also sent to another section in the pit as a stripper. Most coal face workers at some time were likely to get an injury of some kind or lucky escapes.

One day I was lifting a six foot wooden strap up to put it in place to support the roof. I was shoving a wooden prop under it when the backend of the strap got caught on a moving pan. The pans were used to bring the coal out to main belt for onward transport to the loading point.

The strap flew out striking me on the mouth, bursting my lips and knocking six front teeth clean out by the roots. Two inches higher up or down and I could have been killed. You can bet that I wasn't smiling for many weeks after that particular incident! It was a good lesson for me to be vigilant at all times.

Buried at the face

Another lucky escape was when I was shovelling coal onto the conveyor belt when the roof above me caved in. I had all my roof supports in place to protect myself. I was completely buried and I hadn't a clue what happened because it was so quick. One minute I was working away and the next I was buried under wet rubble and frantically trying to push dirt and stones off the top of me. I have to say that I got the fright of my life and I was shaking and sweating. My heart was beating ten to the dozen.

Willie Murphy, the stripper next to me, later told me that he heard the crash and when he looked all he could see was a pile of stones. He thought I had been killed. He managed to get me out. When incidents like that happened it was common for it to be simply one huge block of rock, often three or four hundred weights and it was usually fatal. I was lucky because it was water that caused the fall in my accident. I had bumps and bruises and small abrasions, but nothing serious, so I carried on, thankful that I had escaped serious injury.

I walked down the railway line after work with Willie (Murphy) to Burnton where we lived. We both got a real fright that day and it did hammer home to me once again just how dangerous it was working down the pit and how it was the luck of the draw whether you sustained a minor or major injury or be killed. Reaching the end of every shift was a big relief and most miners, if they are honest, would agree with that opinion.

More modern pit

No 7 Pennyvenie was a more modern pit, but one thing that could not be changed was the coal face. The roof still had to be supported by wooden pit props in the first few years of operation. It was only later on that hydraulic props came to the coal face along with steel bars to support the walls and roof. This made a real difference to the safety of the strippers.

Fault in Coal Face

In the west mine in one of the sections a step appeared in the coal face. A step was basically a geographical fault where we were working. You would have a straight seam of coal then you would hit solid rock just like glass. The coal would disappear and it would be found again four feet higher or lower and this caused havoc in that area as it was always best to get a straight road to advance on.

I remember at No. 7 one incident when I was renewing broken props. The pressure was snapping the wooden supports like match wood. I was wriggling through the step to get to the other side and the space was only sixteen inches high and six foot long. I just reached the other side when a stone fell and hit the floor at the side of my hand. I had only a scratch when I got through, but again it could have been very serious indeed.

Props snapping

David Torbet, the fireman in charge of my section, wanted me to come up to the loader so that he could bandage my hand. I told him I was fine, but he insisted and attended to my hand. I was actually glad to get out of that section. The props simply couldn't stand the extreme pressure and when you see them snapping it can be frightening and an indication of an imminent collapse. Later that whole section closed from one end to the other and all the equipment at the face was lost. This was known as total closure. That again brought home to me the constant danger of working at the coal face.

The same thing happened later on in the north mine in the high coal section. It had hydraulic props and steel straps for support at that time which was very much better than the wooden props. When the coal was taken out in the dayshift, the backshift packers would put in packs of stone where the coal had been removed to provide support. This was done to take the pressure off the coal face and to maintain a safe working area.

Packers removed

We were informed that the management at Pennyvenie had been told from the powers that be from NCB HQ, Edinburgh, to withdraw the packers. They were of the opinion that packers were no longer needed because of the hydraulic props allowing the weight of the roof and sides to reduce slowly and in a controlled way. The bottom line is that by withdrawing the packers they could be relocated elsewhere and that would save money.

This system of hydraulic props would, in theory, stop any roof falls before there was danger to the face workers. After the hydraulic props were positioned, there was a withdrawal from that section for two weeks to allow any movement to take place and for the face to settle. The stripper would then return to the face after two weeks and assess it for safety. If all was well, it would be back to producing coal.

Total Closure

On one occasion when the packers had been removed from the section and the two week period had passed to allow the natural movement of the face, I returned to find that the props had reduced in size right to the danger line on the hydraulic props. I could hardly crawl in that area and I could hear the sound of rocks cracking, going off with a real bang, so that there was clearly movement going on. The strippers decided that enough was enough and it was dangerous.

Pennyvenie Colliery showing the road skirting round the spoil bing with the small wagon-way running to the top to allow spoil to be tipped. Pennyvenie Nos 2/3/7 was operated by the Dalmellington Iron Company and from 1931 by Bairds and Dalmellington Ltd., until nationalisation in 1948. It had an average workforce of 581 and the output was 124,000 tons per year. Pennyvenie No 4 was sunk in 1911 was closed in 1961 whilst Pennyvenie No 5 was also sunk in 1911 and closed in 1953.
(Photo: Courtesy of EAC Doon Valley Museum)

Harry Kennedy at Pennyvenie in his mining gear.

Doon Valley miners often took part in sporting events. This was an NCB five-a-side game with No. 7 Pennyvenie Colliery against Chalmerston Mine. Pennyvenie won by one goal to nil.
Back row (l to r) G Phillips, R Mullen
Front row: F Gormanley, O Murray and Harry Kennedy.
(Photo: Courtesy of Harry Kennedy)

I recall that the sweat was rolling down my face with real fear. We all managed to crawl back to the main road when the pressure burst the props and it was total closure right to the coal face where we, as strippers, would have been working. We all agreed that there should be no more brain waves from Edinburgh. From their safe offices in Edinburgh they clearly had little knowledge of the practical issues around working at the coal face.

Shift Working

The working day started at No. 7 Pennyvenie Colliery at 6.20am when you entered the pithead baths. You went to your clean locker, hung your clothes up, put a towel round your waist and went to your other locker and put on your working clothes for the pit. You then went to the lamp cabin to get your lamp and a self-rescuer. They both had your token number stamped on them. You attached them to your belt adding an extra 5lb in weight.

Token system

You then went to the token office to receive two tokens. One was round and the other square in shape and they had your lamp number stamped on them. You then went to the pit head to the cage to be lowered underground straight down the main shaft. You gave the banksman your square token that was to let the management know that you were underground.

Down on the cage

At the end of your shift, you handed the round token in at the token office which was to indicate that you were not left underground. When it was your turn to go underground and you entered the cage, everything turned silent. When the cage started to move you thought 'here goes' because working at the coalface you never knew what to expect when you got there.

The shaft was a sheer drop about a quarter of a mile or more. The cage ran down the shaft face on wheels and steel rails like a great big lift. You could not hear a thing because it was so noisy and you were moving about 20mph. Sometimes the cage was travelling too fast and would automatically cut out and stop dead. Your knees felt as though they were going to hit your chin. You didn't know what had happened for a minute. It would start again and everyone gave a sigh of relief when they set foot safely on the pit bottom.

Walk to coal face

You had to make your way on foot to the coal face which was around one-and-a-half miles from the pit bottom. The coal face was three foot high or less. Sometimes the bottom corner would be flooded and you had to wait until the water was pumped out. That could take an hour to achieve. It was common in some sections that the face belt stopped at 10am until 10.20am, that was your break when you took your piece.

Stripping coal

The strippers would sometimes ask the management to keep the belts running at piece time as it was so wet. It was a case of being soaked to the skin and then to stop for twenty minutes when you were actually sweating, which meant you got frozen. So, we often just worked on eating as we went. All you wanted was to complete your stint and get back to the surface for a warm shower.

Each stripper had stint of thirty feet and they had to shovel twenty-eight tons of coal onto the face belt. If the belt stopped you had less time to complete your work as you couldn't get your coal out. Shovelling the coal could be the easy part, as you had a lot of hard work to do before you reached that situation, for example always making sure that the roof was safe. You ignored safety issues at your peril.

End of shift

The only men, in my opinion, who knew and faced the real daily dangers, hard work and unbelievable conditions that had to be worked in, were the men on their knees all day long at the coal face. At the end of a hard shift, when you reached the pit bottom, and you were on your way to the surface, there was a feeling of elation when you saw the daylight. And when your feet touched the pithead you could almost hear every man say under his breath: Thank heavens. We've made it again!

Proud miner

I worked in the mining industry for thirty-nine years. In later years I saw so many of my friends with coal dust related illnesses and hard work that killed them too early and before they could enjoy their retirement. As long as I live I will never forget their 'never say die' spirit and I am proud to have worked side by side with so many fine family men.

'Yet let not this too much, my son,
Disturb thy youthful breast:
This partial view of human-kind
Is surely not the last!
The poor, oppressed, honest man,
Had never, sure, been born,
Had there not been some recompense
To comfort those that mourn!

Man Was Made to Mourn
A Dirge
Robert Burns

Chapter 34

Memories of Waterside

Alexander Mackenzie

What happy visions to delight,
And save us from despair.
What balms to smooth an endless night,
What joys and beauty there.
The perfume of those bygone days.
Drifts on the air tonight.

Memories of a Lost Mining Village
Maureen Henderson

Alexander Harvey Mackenzie was born 16 November 1896 at 30 Drumgrange Row, Waterside, Ayrshire, to John and Sarah Mackenzie (Harvey). He emigrated to Fergus, Ontario in 1927, with his wife Bessie and family of Jim and Jack and daughter Jean. The last in the family, Elizabeth (Pearce), was the only family member born in Canada.

These memories of Waterside by Alexander Mackenzie were written in October 1960. Due to a heart condition he had to retire aged sixty-three. He passed away in Fergus on 6 August 1963 and is buried in Belsyde Cemetery. He was very proud of his Scottish background and there is a large Scottish thistle etched on his head stone.

This reminiscence and poetic reflection are important because they reveal a personal dimension of life in an industrial village, Waterside, which rescues part of the lived experience of working class men of the early twentieth century.

Alex's daughter, Elizabeth, tells that her dad was a self-educated man. He was only fourteen when he had to leave school to work in the coal mine to help support his brothers and sisters. His mother died when he was only twelve leaving a family of eight. His Dad couldn't except her death and drifted away from the family.

When Alexander Mackenzie had a family of his own, he didn't want the boys going into the coal mines, so decided to emigrate to Canada. When he arrived at the railroad station in Fergus he had $35.00 in his pocket. They did have a place to stay as he had family already living in Fergus for about a year.

Having arrived on a Friday, by Monday he secured his first job building a stone wall around the home of the owner of Beatty Bros. Within two weeks he had a job in the Beatty Bros. factory. They made farm equipment and washing machines. A self taught man, he worked himself up from a lowly factory worker to Assistant Personnel Manager. In this position he was in charge of hiring and firing.

He was also known in Fergus for his poetry which was occasionally published in the local paper, Fergus News Record. Some people called him Fergus's own Rabbie Burns.

His older brother, John Mackenzie, was also a miner, but never left Scotland. He lived in Patna where he was well known in that area as a great entertainer. A popular ventriloquist and musician, he made his own 'dummies' and one of them even played the mouth organ. He also had the ability to carve images in coal. He had one that he called the Lady with the Violin. It was carved from one block of coal and at one time was on display in Ayr Town Hall. The voice of the interviewee speaks out in our own Doon Valley Ayrshire dialect as he recounts memories of Waterside from his home in Fergus, Ontario.

Schule days

O' weel I mind those happy days, I spent aroon Truffhill, when wi' barefeet in the summertime, we dandled tae the schule, where oor teacher, auld Miss Burgess, taught us oor a.b.c's., and when teachin' us oor numbers, made us hum like bumble bees. And then, Miss Lizzie Anderson, in standard one and two, put us through oor tables as oor wee brains slowly grew. Then there was Alex Scott, in standard three. We made his hair turn grey, as he tried to teach us grammar, long division an' history.

Next on I went to standards four an' five; Mr. Sinclair was there then, it was in his class that we first learned to write wi' ink an' pen. I never saw anither man who could throw a strap (the belt) sae true when he saw a pupil talkin' or misbehavin'; straight through the air it flew and it landed at the feet o' the culprit, who quivering in fear, had to take it back to him, an' believe me when he used that strap, he fairly laid it on.

Mr. Williamson wis heid maister, taught standards six an' seven an' I tell ye very truly, it was onything but heaven. Poor Mr. Williamson,

Hammy Gray with his horse and cart and his son (wearing hat) at Parkyett, Waterside in the 1940s. This was the common means of making all sorts of deliveries and uplifts in Waterside for many years until motorised transport became more common.

Workers at DICo store, Waterside in the early 1900s. This store supplied just about every need anyone in the community could wish for.
L to r: Willie Smith, Hugh Borland, Nancy Kerr, Peter McGeachan, Margaret McMillan, Bob Dunn, John Thomson, Tom Campbell, Billy Thomson (boy).

often he was appalled at oor spellin' an' oor grammar - nae wunner he was bald. Oh my, how mad he used tae get at Pete Rowan an' the like, Bullock Hervie, (Harvey), Geordie Richmond, Tommy Bryden an' James McKnight. We caused him as much trouble as we possibly could. Archie Winning, he was just as bad; an ill mannered little brute. Well that's what the 'headie' said aboot him.

Band o' Hope

An weel I mind on Friday nichts wi' us he had tae cope when he assisted Mr. May tae rin the Band o' Hope. He must hae thocht we were a band o' hopeless wee bad boys, as we sat up in the gallery; just kickin' up a noise as he tried to tell us aboot the bible and the evils o' drink.

Then there were the cantatas all of which he supervised. I remember once I got a part which made me quite surprised. The part was Granny Brander in *Springtime Holiday*. How proud I was that I got such an important part to play. And then there was the Sunday Schule. It started at eleven, and it was there we boys learned mair o' hell than we ever did o' Heaven.

Mr. Dalghetty was the minister; he lived abin' the village store at Waterside. My how I used to marvel, at the fluent way he swore. He talked about damnation, hell's fire an' sic like things. When by masel I often tried tae copy him; but jings, I couldna dae it half sae weel nae matter hoo I tried; although I kent a lot o' words I could only use outside!

Soiree

Another happy memory was the Band o' Hope soiree, when we a' got a bag o' buns an a cup o' milk or tea, and every time it came aroon; of one thing we were sure. The minister, Mr. George S Hendrie frae Dalmellington, would be there. He'd stan' up on the platform an' thunder oot the grace; then tuck a napkin 'neath his chin, an' start tae feed his face. He used tae scare me half tae death, wi' his voice sae gruff an' lood, an' I've never seen anither man who could swallow sae much food. Jam rolls, buns an' cookies he ate the whole darned lot; you could see his adam's apple jerk as he crammed them doon his throat.

Happy times

My thoughts won't let me skip, the times we went to Ayr Low Green for the Sunday Schule Annual Trip. Frae the schule doon tae the station, we mairched behin' the Dunaskin Band; wi' oor tinnies hingin' roon oor neck an' a wee flag in oor hand. An' weel I mind at the same time, I had a sweet wee lass; when the ither weans were racin' we sat thegither (together) on the grass. Oh we were really deep in love. We'd baith be nine or ten - an I was Mary Burgess lad an' she was my lass then.

Up to nae guid

Oh, memories keep crowdin' in, as my thochts I backward turn tae dookin' in the shallow land; catchin' minnows in Kiers Burn; stealin' tatties oot the gairdens aboot Waterside was really graun' and we took them tae the furnaces, tae roast them in the san'. They tasted jist wonderful. Oft-times it was up tae the stables, along past the bowlin' green and we'd slip ow'er tae the biler an' steal the horse beans. We'd be fillin' up oor pooches, when Jimmy Carr or Hammy Gray wa'd drive in wi' the horse and cairt for a load o' coal, an chase us a' away.

At Nancy Stewart's Sweety Shop near the Kirk we'd spend oor pennies on sugarally chewin' gum or a lucky bag, where we were keen to open them tae discover the prizes in each one; a wee balloon, a whistle, a brooch or a wee plastic gun.

Memories flood back

Oh I could ramble on an' on aboot my memories an' some o' them would bring a laugh, an' some would bring a tear as I think o' my pals of these days, all passed on. Pals like Wull Fulton who played fitba wi' the Dunaskin Lads fitba' team, along wi' brither Sam, 'Happy' Young, 'Spitty' Campbell and wee 'Pinkie' Grant an' my Uncle Tam Harvey wis the team manager.

A happy trio of Hugh Hainey, Tom 'Big Tam' Bruce and Drew Barclay standing beside NCB Pug No. 24 at Waterside in the 1960s. Waterside was one of the last places in the United Kingdom where steam engines could be seen working after the demise of steam on British Railways after 1967.

Matthew Anderson, born in Waterside, was known as the policeman-poet of the Ayrshire Constabulary where he served for 36 years working at places such as Dalmellington, Symington, Ardeer, Barrmill and Kilmarnock. He died on 14 November 1948. (Photo: Donald L Reid collection)

Hugh the butcher wi' his one horse cart was never known tae fail when weighin' oot a pun' o' steak, tae pit his thum' upon the scale tae gie him extra profit. 'Midge' Keatly and 'Roons-a-Hoop', 'Greaser' Grant an' 'Creacher' Blain, Sammy Tear an' Joe the Pole. We'll ne'er see their like again.

Och memories keep pourin' in o' those lang happy days, when Paddy Rooney had a drink; he'd hide frae Father Hayes, the Waterside priest, yet he'd stan' up tae 'Barney' Woods, a real tough fightin' man. I tell ye that was somethin' I could never understan'.

Auld Liza Quinn, pearl fishin' in the 'Din'(River Doon) was quite a sicht. A' she wore wis a waistcoat an' it really was too ticht: She never had it buttoned, but Liza didna' care it wadna fash (annoy) her one wee bit if the King an' Queen were there. Auld Liza's only worry was tae fish up some good pearls; so she didna care who saw her; be it princes, dukes or earls.

Ither folk like auld Molly wi' her barrow; sellin' herrin' roon the raws; Tam the milkman; Patna Dummy, (William Alexander born 1849 – 1921), they'll a' hae passed awa' years ago, but I min' them fine. Johnny Campbell who worked in the joiner's shop, I remember he was lame; and he enjoyed the draft board, playing monie a hard fought game against ma faither. Pete McCreachan sellin' drapery; Bob Hood sellin' beer; Mr Kerr the station maister, his wee Nancy was a dear. Getherin' firtops in the plantin' or collecting conkers in Kiers' Glen and climbin' the trees. Och many times I ponder o'er these happy memories and hae a wee tear in ma eye.

And then there was the Institute a real boon at ony price where we played billiards, carpet bools an' summer ice. The tournaments we played in the winter. The walks we took on Sundays; stealin' turnips oot the fields an' then we'd shake like potty heid, meetin' Constable Greenshields in case he knew whit we'd been up tae.

Gettin' pennies for jeely jars frae Jim Rankin in the store; buyin' sweeties frae Geordie Park, who always gave us extra. We never went to auld McDougall, we aye felt kind o' scared o' his big shaggy eyebroos, an' dark, thick, heavy beard.

Sneakin' into Swallows' picture show where we'd see Charlie Chaplin, Pearl White or Clara Bow. These were happy times that bring a smile tae me every time I think aboot them. Waterside wis a great wee place in ma boyhood days.

Tho' many years hae come an' gane;
an far ower the sea I bide, I ne'er forget
those boyhood days, I spent in Waterside.

Dunaskin

Alexander (Alex) Harvey Mackenzie

This is just a wee verse, frae a lad frae Dunaskin,
'Where's that?' is a question, a few will be askin'
Weel, it's richt on the Banks o' ye old Bonnie Doon,
Twelve mile an' a half frae Ayr, the Auld Toon.

'Noo if ony o' you come frae onywhere near
Just cast yoursel's back for a few years,
We'll start at Truffhill, where I first saw the light
Now just have a look, noo ain't that some sight.

'Now ! now! dear folks, don't shed the tears,
Just take a look -why, there's the Kiers
An' there's Davie Burgess, oot on the hill.
Wi' his gun an' his ferrets all set for the kill.

Noo we'll go for a stroll before it gets late,
Doon Murray's Brae and past the gate,
Noo pass the gas burn, and what do we see?
Well ! well ! the umbrella tree!

And look ! why, there's the glaury sheugh,
An, Neilly McLarty, treating them rough,
Well I don't want to take any more of your space,
But I tell you, dear Editor, right to your face,
I don't want a prize, for this wee simple letter,
To hear from someone who's been there, would be better.

Chapter 35

Doon Valley Mining – Press Reports

Extracts from Various Newspapers

"If you were born with the ability to change someone's perspective or emotions, never waste that gift. It is one of the most powerful gifts God can give—the ability to influence."

Shannon L. Alder

The following are extracts found in a number of newspapers which relate to mining in Ayrshire's Doon Valley. They are self-explanatory and make interesting reading.

27 October 1848 – Glasgow Herald
Dalmellington Iron Works
Those works, belonging to Messrs. Houldsworth, Glasgow, were blown in for the first time on Monday week, and the first casting took place on Wednesday. The machinery was found to work smoothly and everything went off well. Ayrshire is now nearly girded round with ironworks.

15 April 1857 – Ayr Advertiser
Housing at Waterside
It is reported that the proprietors (Houldsworth) of these works (Dalmellington Iron Works) intend erecting houses for their workmen adjacent to the mines. We hope that the cases of disease at public works, reported in the newspapers, will cause the proprietors to see that the site chosen is properly drained, and the houses are of sufficient size, and well ventilated."
Note: Waterside, named after the nearby farm, was completed in 1851 and consisted of 89 houses next to the ironworks with a further ten at Corbie Craigs near the ironstone pits and Corbie Craigs incline. The other Hill villages of Benwhat and Burnfootbill/Lethanhill were completed after 1857.

26 July 1860 - Ayr Advertiser
Fatal Accident near Patna
On Tuesday morning some men were engaged putting pipes in a coal pit that the Dalmellington Iron Company are sinking on the farm of Dalharco, Patna. Two of their number were in the shank, on a platform suspended from a windlass or crab, which went out of gearing, when they were precipitated to a depth of eight or ten fathoms.

One of them was fortunate enough to catch hold of a projecting piece of wood in the shank, and in this manner was saved; while the other fell the whole depth, and was so much hurt that he died in the course of three hours after the accident.

No blame is attached to the person who was in charge of raising and lowering them by the windlass. Peter Bennett left a widow and seven children to mourn his sudden and awful death.

15 September 1860 – Ayr Observer
Fatal Accident at Patna
We are sorry that we have to record a most distressing event in this locality. On Monday night, about 10 o'clock, two men were changing shift at Pit No 2 Dalharco, Patna, and being raised higher than the level of the pithead, the engine keeper, on being instructed to lower them a little, made a mistake and lifted them to the top of the frame, from whence they fell to the bottom of the pit - forty or fifty fathoms - and were dashed to pieces.

The names of the two men were Kennedy and McGribbon, the latter of whom was recently married. We understand that the authorities are making strict investigations as to the carelessness of the engine keeper who, although experienced, was only on as a substitute for the shift. It is just six weeks since Peter Bennett, the overseer, was killed at the same pit.

21 January 1863 – Ayrshire Express
Fatal Coal-Pit Accident Patna
About half-past six on Tuesday evening, a fireman named Adam Reid, about twenty years of age, and unmarried, met with his death at the Dalmellington Iron Company's pit No. 4, Downieston, Patna.

He and the engineman being the only persons about the pit-head were engaged in hoisting a hutch of coal from the low shuts to the scaffold, about ten feet above, for the use of the fire-lamp. The engineman lifted the cage from the bottom, and stopped it about half-way between the low shuts and the scaffold, intending to lower it as soon as he received the signal from Reid that the shuts were closed for the cage to rest on.

After waiting a considerable time, he came round to ascertain what could be detaining him; and not finding either him or the hutch, he suspected something wrong, and at once gave the alarm. On descending the pit, which is sixty-five fathoms deep, Reid's mangled and lifeless body was picked up; whilst the hutch was found sticking at the high doors, about eighteen feet from the bottom.

The supposition is that he must have been under the impression that the cage was ready for him; and having pushed forward the hutch in the dark, both fell to the bottom. He was a quiet and steady young man, and will be much missed by the younger members of the family, whom he helped to maintain - his father having been killed on the works some years ago.

NB Sad to report that Adam Reid (senior) died of burns following a fire damp explosion on 23 November 1856.

27 February 1875 – Scotsman

Colliery Accident at Patna, Ayrshire - Three Men Killed

A melancholy pit accident occurred on Thursday afternoon at Dalharco Pit, Patna, about nine miles from Ayr, belonging to the Dalmellington Iron Company, by which three men lost their lives and a fourth is so severely injured that fears are entertained regarding his recovery.

In connection with Dalharco pit there is an old working which has not been wrought for about eleven years past, and ever since that time appearances of fire have now and again exhibited in the working. About two months ago the proprietors, seeing that the fire was gaining ground, sent a number of their workmen to explore the old working and, if possible, to extinguish the fire, and in this work rapid progress was being made.

On Thursday four men were engaged on the first shift at this work viz., James M'Culloch and Daniel Stevenson, oversmen; William Bell and Francis Cunningham, miners. Shortly after one o'clock in the forenoon, from some unexplained cause, a fall took place from the roof of the working.

This completely demolished the bratticing, putting off the above named four men from their connection with the current of air and locking them up in a space of only a few feet. Nothing was known of this occurrence till about an hour afterwards, when another three men arrived in the pit for the purpose of working on the second shift.

After they had descended the shaft and gone some six hundred yards from the face of it, they heard cries for help, and immediately ran to assist. The cries had proceeded from the overs-man, McCulloch, who was now the only survivor of the catastrophe. When taken up he was totally exhausted. On clearing away the rubbish the dead bodies of the other three men were found.

The oversman, David Stevenson, and Francis Cunningham were lying locked in each other's arms, and the body of William Bell was lying close beside them. All the bodies were badly scorched. No time was lost in getting the survivor, McCulloch, conveyed home, where he was able to relate what he knew of the occurrence.

He states that after the bratticing fell, cutting off their communication with the air, he made two attempts to get relief, and at last discovered a hole through which he could, with difficulty, get his head. He likewise states that he saw Bell and Cunningham make two ineffectual attempts to escape also. The three dead bodies were removed to their homes.

David Stevenson, who resided near Dalharco pit, was about thirty-three years of age, and leaves a widow and five young children; William Bell resided at Kerse Row, was about thirty-seven years of age, and leaves a widow and three children; and Francis Cunningham resided at Waterside, was about twenty years of age, and unmarried.

30 May 1884 – Edinburgh Courant

Fatal Colliery Accident

An accident whereby a miner named Isaac McLachlan lost his life occurred at Pennyvenie Pit, near Dalmellington, on Wednesday night. It seems that McLachlan had been working at the roof of the pit, and had accidentally stumbled off the scaffolding; but as no person was near him at the time, it is not known exactly how the accident occurred. He belonged to Dalmellington.

12 June 1891 – Ayrshire Post

A Model Ayrshire Mining Village Thirty Years ago.

A Scottish Canadian Minister contributed to a Toronto Journal the other day an account of the miners in the Motherwell District among whom he laboured recently as a missionary. His paper presented a frightful picture of ignorance and moral degradation.

Another Scottish Presbyterian pastor, who has been longer in the Dominion, writes expressing his astonishment. He did not think any such experience was to be had in any part of Scotland, and he endeavours to relive the picture by giving an account of his experience as a missionary nearly thirty years ago (1861) in a mining village of Ayrshire, Waterside, on the banks of the River Doon.

The dwelling houses of the miners were self-contained consisting of a but and a ben or a large kitchen with two enclosed beds. There was also an entry or hall with a pantry and a large room with two enclosed beds. Between the rows there was a large open green and behind were the gardens. The houses in general were very comfortably furnished, many of them had stuff-bottom mahogany chairs in their rooms.

The people were an intelligent, sober, industrious class as a whole. The children in my Sabbath and bible classes were well dressed, well bred and well taught class. I was often amazed at the questions put by some of the collier's wives. Questions asked to me included those on religion, philosophy and poetry. I happened to stay overnight at the house of Mrs W, and a more enjoyable and unexpected evenings pleasure in my wanderings I have seldom met.

Mr W was a quiet thoughtful man. Mrs W had much to say on many subjects and she could say it well. Most astonishing of all, she had studied astronomy from observation and books. She had also tried her hand at poetry. Some of her lines are in my desk. She showed me a treatise she had written on the stars; the language was chaste glowing and reverent. One thing I often marked to the credit of the people was their cleanliness.

My visiting was three days in the week and I do not remember finding a slovenly kept house. In my prayer meetings I lectured on the attributes of God on the doctrines of the atonement, Election, Justification, the Perseverance of the Saints and the Use of Confessions of Faith.

I found during the week that the people had an intelligent grasp of all the subjects. These colliers were members of the Rev E Hayman's church, Dalmellington (Free) and the Rev Mr McFadyen's (Patna Established Church) and mostly Scotch.

Some of them had been lead miners at Carsphairn and who because of their attachment to the Free Church had to leave. I have, however, for many years had experience of life as a miner as it is in Dalry and Kilbirnie and only in exceptional cases and among Irish Roman Catholics could one find a state of things such as Motherwell represents.

In the school at Kilbirnie Ironworks, it was said that Mr Wilson, regularly had one hundred percent of passes by his pupils. The houses were good, squares and rows clean, and the gardens well kept. Prizes were given for the best kept houses and gardens and this doubtless accounted for their cleanliness to some extent.

When I left Waterside, I left a mining village the inhabitants of which were tidy, intelligent, liberal, warm-hearted people and the memory of my sojourn among them is one of the pleasant things of the past.

Saturday 24 March 1900 Ardrossan & Saltcoats Herald
Benwhat Heatherbell V Burnfoothill Primrose

Considering the big attraction at Ayr (Kilmarnock were playing Ayr in the final of the Ayrshire Challenge Shield Cup) the same afternoon, the attendance of spectators was very gratifying, over £15 being realised out of the proceeding. The contesting teams were Benwhat Heatherbell and Burnfoothill Primrose.

It was generally expected that the game would have a close issue and in that respect at least few were disappointed. During the first half Benwhat played with the assistance of a strong wind and had the monopoly of the play during that stage. Burnfoothill, however, offered a good defence and when a halt was called, Benwhat had only secured a lead of two goals against nil for their opponents.

The change of ends now saw Burnfoothill pretty much in evidence, in fact play was conducted on somewhat similar lines to the first half, only Bunfoothill were the main aggressors. They, however, scored on only one occasion and Benwhat were thus hailed champions of the shire by the narrow margin of two goals to one.

The game was to the rough side and for this the referee was to blame, having allowed the players too much scope. At the close of the game, which was good value for a draw, several of the players quarrelled and a pugilistic display closed the day's proceedings

Benwhat Heatherbell: Tait, Torbet, Hunter, Hannah McHattie, Watt, McCreadie, Parker, Fisher, Murray and McCall.

Burnfoothill Primrose: Kirk, Young, Hutchison, Kelly, Lunnie, English, Highet, McDowall, Watt, Dougal and Ballantine.

Saturday, 25 October 1902
Ardrossan & Saltcoats Herald
Scottish Junior Cup Second Round – Benwhat 4 V 2 Kilbirnie Ladeside.

Arriving on the scene of combat weary and footsore after an arduous march of something like 3 miles from the nearest Railway Station (Dalmellington) o'er hill and dale, our fellows (Kilbirnie Ladeside) were rendered totally unfit for anything in the nature of a fast game, and it was their circumstances which merely found them wanting in the last fifteen minutes of the game when the (Benwhat) Heatherbell began to apply the pressure and succeeded in bringing about the downfall of the Kilbirnie goal, twice in succession, thereby qualifying themselves for the third round.

7 January 1905 – The Scotsman
Fatal Result of an Accident
John McDonald (81), surfaceman, in the employment of the Dalmellington Iron Company, at No. 1 Bowhill pit, Dalmellington, has died in Ayr County Hospital from injuries received by being knocked down and run over by a wagon. Deceased, who was a native of Portree, Skye, had been in the employment of the Dalmellington Iron Company for fifty years.

5th July 1905 – Glasgow Herald
Pit Fatality at Dalmellington
James Bell, (13), son of William Bell, pit fireman, was run over by a loaded hutch at No. 2 Pennyvenie, yesterday morning and was so severely injured that he died within half an hour. He had only started work the day previous and this was his first trip to the pit bottom.

They brought him up the pit shaft,
And took him out of the cage.
His face was covered with coal dust,
They could not tell his age.

In fact, he was a young lad,
On his first day down the pit,
He did not hear the noises
Just before the pit prop split.

Down came the roof and crushed him,
Against the stone hard floor,
Squeezing out a young life,
That would run and laugh no more.

Who would tell his mother?
Who would tell his dad?
That the coal had claimed another
And this one just a lad.

The Lad
Ian Winstanley

The last shift to finish up at Minnivey Colliery in December 1975 and another colliery closes in Ayrshire's Doon Valley. The present mine began production in 1958 and of the 280 miners, 148 were transferred to nearby Pennyvenie, whilst 64 were being retrained for salvage purposes and a further 64 accepted early retirement. The newspaper commented: "As coalmines in South Ayrshire gradually become a dying industry, so the area becomes more depressed."
(l to r): William Filson (union rep), James Auld, William McMahon, David McGill and John McPhail.
(Courtesy of Ayr Advertiser - December 4 1975)

5 November 1919 - Evening Times
Pit Fatality at Dunaskin
Hector Jones, (17), residing with his parents at 139 Lethanhill, Dunaskin, was killed by a fall at the working face in the Dalmellington Iron Company's No 3 Pit, Pennyvenie, yesterday. He was working as a drawer with his father and brother, and was in the act of filling the first hutch when the accident occurred.

18 August 1921 – Ayr Advertiser
Death of Notable Character – William Alexander (Patna Dummy)
The death of William Alexander, known to few by that name but to

thousands as "Patna Dummy," a notable character, has passed away. Deceased who was about seventy-two years of age, was a native of Dailly Parish, and came as a child with his father to Patna, almost seventy years ago. For his schooling he was indebted to the late Mr John Hunter, manager of Dalmellington Iron Works, and, despite his dual infirmities of being deaf and dumb, became quite intelligent.

He was apprenticed to the late Mr Alexander Steel, shoemaker, Patna, but that trade did not suit his temperament and he became stabler and odd worker at Patna Inn, under Mr McCulloch, the then manager of that hostelry, which was more to his liking. Later he was employed for a short period at some of the Dalmellington Iron Company collieries, before doing every needful odd job about the village, which he continued to do until about a year ago, when he was admitted to Kyle Home, Ayr, where he succumbed on Friday.

By the kind attention of the local councillors his remains were brought from that institution on Monday afternoon and interred in Patna Cemetery. Even one individual from far away Canada, presently home on holidays, assisted in the obsequies, which were largely attended.

Alexander was greatly respected and well-known in the district. He was a great mimic and could let one understand in his own way quite easily any information he wished to impart. Whenever he wandered beyond the confines of the village, he was followed by a crowd of children who were in their glory when he made after them.

17 April 1927 – Sunday Post
Dunaskin Miner Killed

Dunaskin, Saturday - In No. 3 Pit, Pennyvenie, Dalmellington, yesterday. Thomas McCutcheon, brusher, was killed as a result of a fall from the roof. Deceased, who was forty-three years of age, leaves a widow and two children. He resided at 66 Waterside, Dunaskin, and was very popular, being green keeper of the local bowling green and solo euphoniumist of Dunaskin Brass Band.

26 April 1929 – The Scotsman
Engine Overturns - Two Ayrshire Men Killed

Two workmen in the employment of the Dalmellington Iron Company were killed under somewhat extraordinary circumstances near the Company's works at Waterside, South Ayrshire, yesterday afternoon.

The Company own two branches of railway lines which converge upon their premises and bring coal from Pennyvenie and Craigmark mines. It is not definitely established how the accident occurred, but it is believed that at a place known as the Cutler siding someone got down from the engine of a train, with the object of altering the points, and it is supposed that the man was not in time to do so.

The train was conveying the last consignment of coal for the day from Pennyvenie, the load being over two hundred tons. From whatever cause, the engine toppled over, and John Ferguson, the driver, and a man named David McGill, who was on the engine at the time, were crushed and killed.

Both men were married, and the former resided at Long row, Waterside, while the latter lived on the Company's premises. McGill was a pitheadman employed at Beoch mine, and he was returning home after his day's work.

26 April 1929 – The Scotsman
Fatal Burning Accident in Ayrshire Mine

Three miners, one of whom, Edward Cathcart (29), 122 Lethanhill, South Ayrshire, has died in Ayr County Hospital, were involved in an accident which occurred in Pennyvenie Mine, Dalmellington, in the early hours of yesterday morning. There was, it is stated, an ignition of gas. Peter Fagan, brusher, and Robert Gillespie, miner, lie in Ayr County Hospital suffering from extensive burning injuries.

29 April 1929 – The Scotsman
The Ayrshire Pit Explosion - Another Death

The death has occurred in Ayr County Hospital of Robert Gillespie (26), miner, 22 Burnfoothill, Waterside, who was involved in the explosion at No. 4 Pennyvenie Mine, Dalmellington. He is the second victim of the accident.

It is curious that the two men who were thought to be least injured at the time have succumbed, while the other man, Peter Fagan, rescued from his working place after the explosion, and who ran a big risk of being suffocated, is still alive and under treatment in Ayr County Hospital.

27 January 1935 – The Sunday Post
Died In Ambulance

Douglas Kerr (18), son of Hugh Kerr, Burnton, Dalmellington, died in the ambulance from injuries sustained in No. 2 Pit, Pennyvenie Colliery, while being conveyed to Ayr County Hospital.

Camlarg Cottages with Pennyvenie to the rear. All have now been demolished.

22 August 1936 – The Times
Miner Killed at Pennyvenie

A miner, James Blane, was killed, and his son, Willie, and another man, Jimmy Johnstone, were seriously injured by a stone fall from the roof in Pennyvenie Pit, Dalmellington, Ayrshire, yesterday.

Note: Hugh Johnstone, MBE, (2015) recalls the funeral of James Blane which took place from Burnton to Dalmellington Cemetery. It was a Masonic funeral with two horses drawing the carriage bearing the coffin. It was said to have been extremely well attended.

26 August 1938 – The Scotsman
Pit Fatality Littlemill Colliery

William Wallace, (41), who resided c/o Henry Walters, 33 Cairntable, Patna, was killed by a roof fall in Littlemill Colliery, Rankinston, early yesterday morning.

2 July 1954 - Ayrshire Post
Beoch Pithead Baths

New pithead baths were opened at Beoch Colliery, Dalmellington, on Saturday by Mr Henry Black, BEM, veteran miner of the West Ayr Area. Mr A B Dyet, manager of the colliery, introduced the area general manager, Mr A M Ritchie, who spoke of the changes in working conditions and in particular of the great boon in having pithead baths.

If there had been baths in his day, housewives' life would have been much easier. He took the opportunity to congratulate the workmen and management on their fine relationship and on the fact that no stoppages were recorded against the pit this year (1953/4).

The baths were handed over to the welfare committee and the key was presented to Mr Henry Black who opened the baths. The company had tea in the Beoch canteen when the presentation of a flycase with flies (for fishing) was made to Mr Black.

Mr Daniel Sim, who made the presentation, spoke of Mr Black as being a good hard, honest workman. He started work at eleven years of age and was still working at aged eighty-four. For his long service in the mining industry he previously received the BEM, and a gold watch from Bairds and Dalmellington Ltd.

A Vote of thanks was proposed by Mr James Douglas to the officials, contractors, area catering officer, Mr Andrew McHattie, who provided floral decorations, and all who helped to make the baths available.

The baths have locker accommodation for 454 men, together with open and cubicle type sprays. Lockers are heated to dry clothes and there is a special drying locker for extra wet working gear. The medical centre at Beoch is well equipped for the prompt treatment of injuries.

The canteen supplies tea, cigarettes, confections, meals and packed snacks are available for men who have to work late. The water supply which is pumped approximately half a mile, is treated for drinking and bathing. The baths were open to the public on Sunday when large numbers inspected them and sampled the wares at the canteen. Monday morning saw the baths in use for the start of the dayshift.

25 October 1962 – Ayr Advertiser
Facets of Doon Valley Life – Fishing for Pearls

This article appeared nineteen years before it was illegal (after 1981) to fish for fresh water pearls. It is stressed that anyone interfering with pearl-beds in the River Doon or any other Scottish river, commits a serious breach of the law which could result in imprisonment or a fine. However, in the time referred to in this article, pearl-fishing on the River Doon was only carried out by a few skilled individuals.

Of the countless numbers of people who have, at one time or another, given voice to the Immortal Bard's heart-warming lines about the Banks and Braes o' Bonnie Doon, how many, apart from those in the immediate vicinity, are aware of the unparalleled beauty that lies hidden in the depths of the river itself?

Yet, if one but knows the proper place to search, one may have for the picking up gems which for purest beauty and quality are unsurpassed anywhere in the world.

Mr John Peters of Patna is one of the leading exponents of the art of pearl fishing in Doon Valley. It is an education to listen to what he has to say on the subject. In fact he is a sprightly sixty-nine years and can still be found at odd times, between May and October, on his eternal quest for the elusive mussel in the river which he has fished from Doonfoot, Ayr, to Moss Bridge, Dalmellington.

The chief snag is that if the ordinary angler requires unlimited patience, it is nothing compared to what is demanded of the pearl-fisher On more than one occasion, when the waters of the Doon have subsided following excessive flooding of the river, Mr Peters has gone straight to the points where long experience told him the river would have thrown up some of its treasure. He has at these times been successful in discovering some wonderful pearls.

Normally he avoids the deep treacherous channels, because the river can be unforgiving – these have to be fished by boat or by diving – and prefers to operate by wading where the river bed is sandy or gravelly. In such haunts he knows just where to look, and has long since lost count of the number of pearls he has found and disposed of.

In his day, he has maintained contact with most of Ayr's jewellers, and has even been commissioned to find a pearl to match one already in a certain jeweller's possession. Knowing the uncertain nature of the art, this must be one of the most optimistic assignments ever undertaken, but 'Optimism' is the cheerful Mr Peters middle name, and he proudly states that he did not let the jeweller down.

It is unlikely that pearls will ever be found in large volumes in the Doon. But, there is always the hope that one day, in one of these beds, an aged, ugly, crooked mussel will be thrown up and opened to reveal a pearl beyond price. Such is the fabric of dreams.

8 June 1967 – Ayr Advertiser

Well Known Landmark to go – Waterside Slag Hill Sold

Despite denials in certain official quarters, it would appear that the well-known slag hill, for so long a feature of Waterside's scene, is likely to be removed, and, while few tears will be shed, the occasion will bring back memories to many of the local folk and exiles from the village.

Of itself, it is an eyesore, a blot on the landscape, a man made mountain with neither beauty nor grandeur, yet it holds a strange place in the hearts of the villagers.

Pennyvenie Mine showing part of the extensive rail network and the pit wheel. Many men from the Doon Valley worked here over the years. All that remains today is the huge bing which dominates Dalmellington on the approach from the north along the Moss Road.

Memorial to Better Days

It stands on its mute majesty, solid and defiant – a memorial to the 'better days' remembered with nostalgia by everyone who had any connection with Waterside in the days of its prosperity. Yet, like the boom period it symbolises, it is not for ever.

The hill is, of course, composed of the lava-like waste matter which came from the blast-furnances, and it took three quarters of a century of round the clock working to build it.

The slag hill records, after its own fashion, the progress made in iron smelting from the time the Dalmellington Iron Company opened their furnaces in 1847 until the depression forced their closure in 1921.

History in Waste

Improving techniques and changing processes were all reflected in the characteristics of the waste products but, to the layman, the most obvious change came when a new system of disposal allowed the slag to be tipped over the edge of the hill in its molten state.

For many years – indeed until the heap was roughly half its present height – the slag was run into specially lined bogies and allowed to set, after which it was taken to the hill and dumped in solid rectangular blocks.

This procedure entailed a considerable waste of time, and it was a big step forward when the heavy iron 'ladies' were procured and the slag taken directly from the furnace to the hill and tipped over.

Miniature Volcano

Like a miniature volcano, the molten mass cascades down from its lofty peak, lighting up the sky for miles around. It was a comforting glow for those young people who chanced to be out and about on a dark and somewhat spooky road.

And now, apparently, the slag hill's days are numbered. Its removal will be a monumental task, but in these days of miracle-working machinery it is far from an impossible one.

Forgotten Things

One thing we do know. Whether you loved the slag hill or hated it, admired it or merely tolerated it, if you are of Doon Valley you will definitely miss it. For there is no person living who can remember when it wasn't there – arrogant, ugly, but bound up inextricably with the history of the community which was – but is no more. If there was ever an appropriate time for it to go it is now. Let it follow the furnaces, the workshops, the dwellings, the people themselves into the limbo of forgotten things.

My Memories of Craigmark

This article, in the form of a letter to the editor, appeared in the Ayr Advertiser in 1967. It was simply signed: Ipso facto. This is a philosophical term. It is Latin for "by that very fact." The letter does reveal part of that spirit of love for Craigmark by a former resident and tells of happy memories of times past revealing some fond memories from boyhood days. It was inspired by an earlier letter to the Advertiser from 'Rosemary,' who reflected on life in Dalmellington.

Sir, 'Rosemary,' has set us going folding back the years. Ever heard of Craigmark? It is right next door to 'Rosemary's' Dalmellington – or was. Now it is no more than a green patch. Even the tall trees of the auld hoose stackyard have gone. But my memories remain.

No one that remembers Craigmark can forget the life and the people. Mention of names like Rev. George S Hendrie, and Rev. Father Murphy make me even today gulp with respect – and often a little fear. Old John Wilson, and son Mattha (Matthew) Wilson, too, commanded great respect as did the Misses Smith and Anderson at the school house. Should I confess here today I still possess a slate pencil – a real Craigmark school slate pencil!

Sammy Orr at the Craigmark Store, both 'ends' comes to mind readily and I'm happy to say at the same store we still have our very good friend, Sanny Rankin. I don't know how many years I've known Sanny, but I hope it will be a lot more!

No radio and television then but we did have Craigmark Thistle – as good as any when the boss was there. The boss was Johnny Grier – and we boys would do anything to get into the pavilion when the 'big yins' were there.

For recreation there was always helping Bessie Eccles at Sillyhole (farm near Burnton) to catch her horse or going round on dark nights with the Co-op bread van holding the lamp for Jimmy or Jackie Currie – two gentlemen who had the respect of every house.

But we all had our regular parcel-delivery houses from whence came the cash to buy 'The Boy's Realm,' 'Boy's Friend,' 'Boy's Cinema,' or the new one just started, 'Adventure.' They were all great reads! Why, who didn't know the then world's greatest goalkeeper, Jimmy Power, introduced by 'Adventure?'

I never gained the distinction of being jump-the-burns champion – this was the every-Sunday afternoon competition in Craigmark, though I was never the worst jumper. The supreme jumper was Pat Bigham, now happily married and living in Seattle, USA.

Mrs Maggie Allan and husband, Willie, whose house was the back row of 'Dublin' side, I remember with reverence. Once weekly we would assemble (all religions) and sing hymns. A worthy couple indeed. I'm sure we boys must have been a trial – but none was ever refused admission.

Our playground was the first, second and the third hedge we jumped over, and that was great fun for us boys. The four glens, were all within shouting distance of the Dublin Green, where the Dalmellington band played twice a year. The blue billies, the bings, the auld line where nothing was dangerous except a runaway gir (ghir?) – I never could spell that word, though I doubt if I could run it. As Shakespeare puts it, 'Desire by far outlives performance.' Ah, yes, I see the cosy ingles as the mist comes o'er the brae!

13 July 1978 – Ayrshire Post

Pennyvenie – 'The Family Colliery' – Works its Last Shift

Pennyvenie Mine at the time of closure with under manager, Dan Crockett shaking hands with a miner signifying the end of an era for deep mining in Dalmellington. This was one of the last shifts before the mine closed in 1978 prior to salvage operations beginning. Background (l to r): Unknown, David Galloway, George McCutcheon, Joe Fairbairn and John Kennedy.

Thursday, 6 July 1978 was an historic and in many ways, a sad day, for Dalmellington and the Doon Valley. It marked the end of an era with the closure of the last pit in the area – Pennyvenie Colliery.

With the setting up of the Dalmellington Company in the early 1840s, coal has been produced commercially throughout the valley for upwards of one hundred and thirty years, indeed, in Sinclair's Statistical Account of Scotland, good quality Camlarg coal was being mined as early as 1790. The closure of Pennyvenie means a 450 job loss in an area already severely hit economically and socially, by other recent pit closures.

In 1960, 2,500 men were employed in the industry throughout the Doon Valley and now there are none. Three hundred of the Pennyvenie workmen have been transferred to Killoch or Barony. One hundred and twenty-five (including eighty over the age of fifty-five) have accepted redundancy payments which, at the maximum, will be around £2,500 and twelve men with their families are moving to England to continue working in the industry.

The fact that so little had been achieved over the years of declining employment in the industry, towards the introduction of alternative work to an area that had so much to offer to industrialists, is to be regretted.

Pennyvenie was a colliery which employed whole families over many years. The Dempsey brothers are one example of this. Neil Dempsey has been on face work for forty-three years and brother, John, for forty-two years. Two more brothers, Tom and Willie, have also been employed at Pennyvenie since leaving school and they have now been transferred to Barony Colliery. All followed in the footsteps of their father, the late Tommy Dempsey, who had no less than fifty-two years service underground at the colliery.

Other family names with equally long service are the Calderwoods, Wallaces, Patersons, Semples and Kennedys. John Kennedy who was the current manager, states that his father, John Kennedy, was under-manager at No 2 Pennyvenie for thirty-four years and his brother, Ben, was also an under-manager from 1954 - 68.

Apart from the job loss to the area, family life too, will in many cases, lose its old routine. At Pennyvenie, men were regularly employed on a particular shift. This does not apply at Killoch or Barony where alternative shift working is the rule.

Snippets of the Hill

Peter Conway wrote a brief snippet about his memories of Lethanhill (the Hill) shortly before his passing. Born on 8 September 1928 he died peacefully at Ayr Hospital on 19 July 2009, aged eighty years after a period of ill-health. Having lived in Dalmellington for many years, he was a popular local man, much involved in the life of the parish church and wider community. He was the much loved husband of Mary and a dear dad of David and Deborah and Pappy of Jamie.

I was born at Burnfoothill on 8 September 1928 and went to the Hill School. I started primary school when I was aged four. That was the old school and went to the new school at Lethanhill where I remained until the age of eleven when I then went to the higher grade school at Dalmellington till I was age fourteen.

The teachers I remember at the Hill school were Miss Aird at the primary and at the new school I remember Miss Devlin, Miss Park and Mr Taylor who was the headmaster. There was also a Mr McAuley and Mr Geddes there during my schooling.

Aged eleven I travelled by bus from the Hill down to Patna and got the train at Patna station which took me to Dalmellington. I was usually accompanied by James Baillie, Isa Gillespie and Robert Ferguson.

At the Hill the reading room was popular for billiards and dominoes and of course there was also a library where you could read books and magazines. We also had the Hill Store which was owned by Johnny and Betty Miller. Their son, Jack Miller, became a church minister. There was also the church and Sunday school at the Hill and the teachers at that time were Thomas Hose and Tommy Knox. We used to get a sixpence for reading extracts from the bible if we did it really well.

I stayed at the Hill until I was age twenty-one. I was very fond of the Hill and for around thirty years I was on the Hill re-union committee and served as president for a number of years. These were great events and there was a special pride by those who were able to boast that they came from the Hill. The entertainment at these events in the early years was by weel kent locals including Jock Park, Paddy Stratton, Freddie Galloway, Willie Clark and Bessie Stafford.

I was grateful for my upbringing on the Hill among some wonderful folk I fondly think of now and again.

1969 Benwhat Reunion

The 6th Benwhat Reunion was held in Dalmellington Community Centre in 1969 when Mr John P Kennedy, manager of Pennyvenie Colliery, proposed the toast to Benwhat. He was still manager in 1978 when Pennyvenie closed its doors, bringing to an end NCB deep coal mining in the Doon Valley.

Mr Kennedy, in an eloquent speech, began by saying that the audience, with links to Benwhat, do not come to reunions year after year to celebrate the hardships and privations, poor housing and hard, hard work for miners and the tragedies connected with coal extraction.

Mystique of mining

He explained that it is something more than that because mining communities, like Benwhat, developed what you might call a mystique of their own which only those who lived there and experienced it at the sharp end could fully comprehend.

You cannot examine it under a microscope, but what I can say with certainty is that same spirit of pride – that sense of belonging to somewhere special with so many social activities for ordinary people which they greatly enjoyed and worked hard to maintain – is present in this hall today. It is something one can feel.

Mr Kennedy then talked about the industrial history which led to communities like Benwhat, Lethanhill and Burnfoothill, and the other many mining villages, none of them now in existence, being developed by the Dalmellington Iron Company.

Local mills

He explained that the development of steam engines and railways had led to a demand for iron with the more traditional crafts of weaving and working on the land giving way. He said: that most mills at that time were water driven and there were two in the village of Dalmellington, which had a population of some eight hundred; and one in Patna with a population of some two hundred and fifty. At that time there was also some coal being produced at Camlarg on the outskirts of Dalmellington.

The cottage industries of spinning and weaving were facing severe competition from steam-driven complexes near to developing coalfields in Ayshire. At the same time the production and importing of cotton goods resulted in locally-based weaving industry going into decline. And with good deposits of ironstone in the Doon Valley and the opening up of the major ironworks at Waterside by the Houldsworth family around 1848 saw many local men moving to work in that emerging industry.

Benwhat

The exploitation of ironstone and coal on the plateau above the Doon Valley was ongoing and it was there that the birth of Benwhat took place. The first twenty houses were built around 1847 and another 110 between that year and 1874. The population drift to these remote moorland villages was very high during the 19th century.

Flocking to Doon Valley

The Highland Clearances, started after Culloden in 1746, were still continuing one hundred years afterwards. Conditions in the north of Scotland and Ireland were deplorable after the potato famine of 1846 and in our own part of the country crofters and weavers were embarking on a new means of livelihood. Mines were being exhausted in other parts of the country, and so over the years many people came from elsewhere to villages like Benwhat and Lethanhill to work for the Dalmellington Iron Company at Waterside.

Origination of incomers

They came from the mines of Cornwall, leadmines of Wanlockhead and Cumberland. More still flowed in from the quarries, the bothies, the cottage looms and linen mills of Wigtownshire, Argyllshire, Banffshire, Renfrewshire, Mull, County Down and many more points of the compass. The names Yates, Orr and Hodgson are still familiar names in these parts of the country as are the McCurdies, Hannahs, Nevilles, Curries, Dempseys, Fishers, Robertsons, McHatties, Filsons, Kirks, Wilson, Parkers, Armours and many other fondly remembered Benwhat names who came to work in and around the mines and formed a good part of the Benwhat population.

Ironstone

From 1850 – 1919 the Dalmellington blackband ironstone was mined in the Benwhat area. All the pits, eight in number, were inter-connected and the working depth varied from 250 to 720 feet. Of course all the pits were not worked simultaneously. Seams were thin and the working life of some of the pits were quite short, but each pit had its full equipment and at each was situated a great flat open hearth upon which the ironstone, spread in thin layers, interspersed with layers of coal, was slowly burned to rid it of its impurities

Blast furnaces

The resultant purified product was known as char, this was exposed to the air for a period of six months before going to the blast furnaces in the valley below at Waterside. The char was at the beginning, transported down the Corbie Craigs incline and over the viaduct at the bottom of the glen then by horse haulage to the furnace bank. The wagons carried approximately three tons. But the tonnage grew so quickly that a new incline to Burnfoothill (Drumgrange incline) was constructed to deal with the outputs from Benwhat and Burnfoothill mines.

Monuments

All that now remains (writing in 1969) as monuments to men's achievements, are the coal and ironstone bings, foundations of old winding houses and the char hearths. One must look below the moss to see what they really achieved. As a mining man I can appreciate that labour of two generations – over six hundred acres of extraction of the black band ironstone, approximately twenty inches thick, yielding a total of nearly four million tons. Not a great tonnage perhaps when one thinks of pits now producing a million tons of coal each year, but one must remember all this tonnage was hand-gotten, the laborious job of under-holing and blasting with powder.

Accidents

Ironstone is two and a half times heavier than coal and it takes no stretch of the imagination, especially to anybody connected with the mining of coal, to visualise just how hard and arduous the work must have been. The accident rate was very high. My own father and grandfather were badly burned in No. 6 Corbie Craig pit due to an ignition of inflammable gas. My father was only fourteen years of age at that time. My uncle, Jim Gourlay's father, was fatally injured whilst working at a beam engine in No. 4 engine house.

It is interesting to note that one of the first on the scene of the accident to my father and grandfather was that fine old lady, Mrs David Scobie of Burnton, now (in 1969) ninety-four years of age. She, her mother and father, had been walking past the pit at the time to visit an uncle in Burnfoothill when the alarm had been raised and they offered to help. Jim Gourlay was seven years old at the time and his mother was left with a family of six youngsters to bring up. Sadly this type of incident happened too often in mining in the Doon Valley, leaving personal tragedy for so many families.

Declining ironstone

By the early 1900s the demand for native ironstone was declining. It was not suitable for steel making and the ore was much cheaper to import from Spain. The miners gradually drifted into the coal mines of the district and finally the mining of ironstone came to an end in 1919.

Future mining

It is interesting to note that during the Second World War in 1940, at a time when this country had its back to the wall, the Ministry of Supply in London carried out a survey of the area around Benwhat and consideration was given to the re-opening of the shafts at No. 8 Corbie Craigs to mine the twenty-nine million tons of ironstone reserves known to exist in that area.

Mr Kennedy received rapturous applause from the audience, delighted with his speech and the memories it evoked for many Benwhatonians.

The Loch Doon School of Aerial Gunnery

The reader might wonder why Loch Doon is included in this book which reflects mainly on 'Lost Mining Villages of Doon Valley.' The reason is quite simple. The incredible story of the School of Aerial

Gunnery is a fascinating one in the history of Ayrshire's Doon Valley. It has been publicised many times in various books. However, it is rare to have a witness account of some aspects of what was happening at Loch Doon, hence the reason for including this piece in what is mainly a book about mining reminiscences. Loch Doon was close to the heart of many local miners and their families and was a place visited often during the summer months for fishing and relaxation.

Loch Doon can also be regarded in some as a 'lost community' because the plans towards the end of the First World War were huge with the loch being invaded by hundreds of soldiers, Royal Flying Corp members, labourers engaged on the construction of a sea-plane base and German prisoners of war who worked on the Loch Doon road.

There was even a 500 seat cinema constructed near to Beoch Farm to entertain the workers and the troops. That alone highlights the sheer scale of the proposed School of Aerial Gunnery project.

These reminiscences of that period are from someone who actually worked at Loch Doon during the frenetic period in 1917. Mr H G Johnston, who later lived in Swindon, recorded some of his memories of that period at Loch Doon in two letters written and dated 4 & 31 December 1990 to a Mrs Allen and they are recorded in full.

Letter of 4 December 1990 – Relating to Loch Doon

In reply to your letter of 28 November (1990), I am approaching the ninety-third anniversary of my arrival on planet earth and my memory is getting a bit dim! However, I will begin by answering questions arising in paragraph 2 of your letter as follows. In November 1916 I volunteered for service as an air mechanic (second class) in the Royal Flying Corp and in April 1919 was demobilised from Cologne as Sergeant Mechanic, Royal Air Force!

I was posted to the Loch Doon School of Aerial Gunnery in early January 1917, where my duties included road-making (using absurdly small hand tools), postman (Royal Mail work, not pay), cookhouse fatigues and other duties. I was also promoted to the rank of corporal (two stripes) in charge of six lower ranks and ordered to Nanterre, a small village on the banks of the River Seine, not far from Paris.

Why? To become familiar with the design and maintenance of six "Hydro Glisseurs" (HGs) which was lightly built flat-bottomed 'punts,' each one propelled by a seven-cylinder radial aero engine, thereby, avoiding interference from vegetation, floating objects and the like encountered by submerged water propellers as used in motor boats.

AN OLD SERVANT RETIRES.

This cutting from the Ayr Advertiser of 9 January 1931 is headed: 'An Old Servant Retires.' It refers to the horse, Tommy, which worked underground for 20 years at Houldsworth Colliery near Patna. It is believed there were no horses working in the Doon Valley pits after 1945.

Before we could get the six 'HGs' in action at Loch Doon the School of Aerial Gunnery was closed down. The 'HGs' were consigned to the Admiralty, Isle of Dogs, London, and I was sent to join a party from 149 Squadron at Ford Junction, Sussex.

Because I made no records of events at Loch Doon and because I had no camera, the extent of my contribution to your article is very small. However, thank you for writing to me and if you think I could help by trying to answer any questions, please do so. In conclusion, I may say that most of my working life was spent in workshops or technical offices of the Great Western Railway Company in Swindon, from where I retired in 1962.

The quite well known, almost famous workshops were closed down in 1986 and the site will provide accommodation for almost another small, but very modernised Swindon. Please excuse my handwriting, especially at the beginning of this letter. How I wish I could type.

Letter of 31 December 1990 - Working at Loch Doon

Thank you for your letter dated 6 December 1990, also for the enclosures it contained. The photo-stat was of special interest as also were the photographs.

I am sorry for this delayed reply due to several reasons, but my replies are as follows. In addition to picks and shovels we used hand-hammers with heads weighing about 10-12lbs for breaking up pieces of nearby granite rock which we then threw into the track where the road was supposed to go and watch them gradually disappear below the boggy surface.

Weather was changeable, always cold, sometimes wet and occasionally snowing. Strange to say, but while we worked away in these difficult conditions, the Germans in a nearby POW camp used to remain in their warm huts.

Living conditions in the wooden huts was no worse than my introduction to service life at Aldershot. Our bedding consisted of two wooden blocks supporting three boards, two mattresses and two blankets.

When we were on flying duty we marched about two miles along Loch Doon to a Bessonair type hangar which sometimes sheltered our one seaplane, which never became airborne while I was there. Hence the beginning of what became known as ‘the Loch Doon Scandal’ because of the huge waste of money trying to pursue a project which was, from the outset, clearly doomed to fail.

In mid January 1917 I was selected to act as area postman. I stayed in a private billet in Dalmellington. This was a single storey home occupied by a coal miner, his wife and son (also a miner), his daughter aged around twenty-three and their surname was McGarvie. The kitchen was heated by a coal fire which never went out and had a small table where I ate breakfast alongside two holes in the wall, giving sleeping space for the family, all somewhat primitive.

As an important member of the HM Forces, however, I was given a real bed in the parlour. The sergeant major also gave me the lock and key to a room in a small house in the High Street near to Dalmellington Railway Station where I went every morning about 9.20am to collect mail off the incoming train from Ayr.

I took it to my ‘office’ for sorting into three areas – Dalmellington, Craigengillan officers and Loch Doon. At about 10.30am a small RFC Crossley service van arrived to take me to those areas to distribute the mail. At 3.30pm it called for me to collect the outward mail which I handed to the guard of the train on route for Ayr. End of my working day.

In the evenings I visited the local reading rooms, had a short walk or read books, wrote private family letters, had my cup of hot cocoa and biscuit in my own room and so to bed. This ends my doings in Damellington.

Chapter 36

Shared Mining Memories

The following articles are shorter shared mining memories.

Mining Jottings
Robert Wallace

To sum up all; be merry, I advise;
And as we're merry, may we still be wise!

Address Spoken by Miss Fontenelle
Robert Burns

Robert Wallace, (78), was born on 7 October 1937 at 15 Broomknowe, Dalmellington, which was his grandmother's house. He was the son of George Wallace, BEM, and Margaret McLelland, both of whom were Dalmellington folk. Bobby, as he is affectionately known to locals, is a keen supporter and committee member of Dalmellington Band. Here he briefly recalls some of his mining memories.

Early years
The first home I remember living in was a brand new house in Hopes Avenue, Dalmellington. We were the first tenants at number thirty-one. My father was a miner, a Deputy Manager, at Pennyvenie. He was in charge of the sinking of No. 7 shaft which reached the bottom in December 1946.

My father retired from Pennyvenie around 1969 and died in 1979, the year before it closed, bringing to an end deep mining around Dalmellington. As a pit deputy he was in charge of the men driving the underground roadways in the pit.

Start on Monday
I attended the school at Dalmellington from age five at the primary and

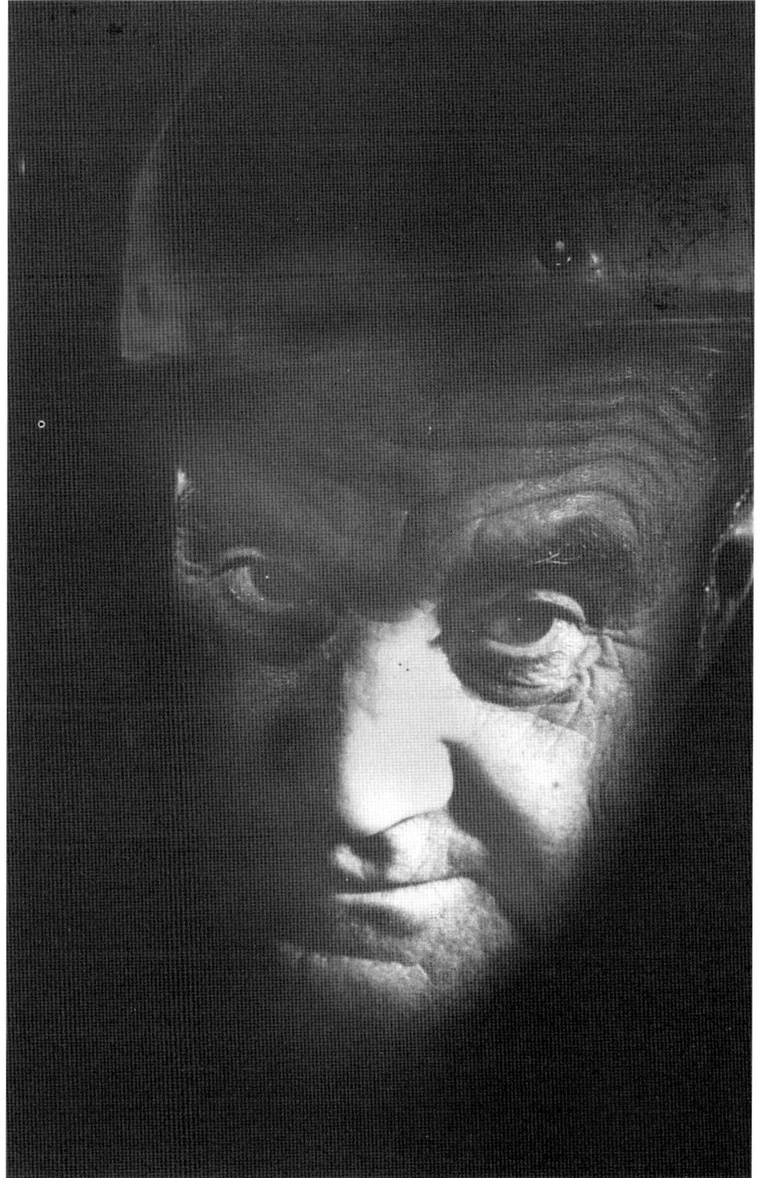

Matt Reid of Dalmellington wearing his mining safety helmet on his last shift at Pennyvenie. The closure of the pit was a poignant time for many of the Dalmellington miners.

Robert Wallace.

then the Secondary School until aged fifteen when I left in 1952. I remember walking out to Pennyvenie Colliery and chapping the manager's door – Mr William Dryborough – and he asked me in. "What do you want, son?" I said that I wanted a job in the pit. He asked me my father's name and when I told him he smiled as he knew him well. He simply said: "You start on Monday and don't be late."

Wood yard and screening plant

That was the extent of the interview which led to me spending the largest part of my working life at Pennyvenie from 1952 until 1978 when it closed. I then went to Killoch Colliery for a further eight years until its closure in 1986. I initially worked for a year on the surface at Pennyvenie in the wood yard and screening plant. I remember that many of the older miners at the pithead were still smoking clay pipes then.

Initial training

There was a period of initial training which took place at a pit in Mossblown, I recall it was Auchincruive No. 3 and week about we went from the pit to the old Ayr College of Technology in St Leonards Road. I think it was an eight week course.

There were four other boys on this course with me – Robin Anderson, Jim Orr, Danny Scobie and Ian Campbell. They were all from Pennyvenie Colliery. I think there was only myself and Robin Anderson who continued until Pennyvenie closed in 1978. Robin stayed in Patna, but died a few years ago. The rest didn't stay in mining as I recall.

At the age of sixteen and having the experience at the pithead and the theoretical work together with practical training at Auchincruive Pit, it was then time to begin my career in underground mining. I remember being a wee bit apprehensive on my first few days going down the shaft at Pennyvenie. To be absolutely honest, it was never a wholly comfortable experience for anyone.

Pennyvenie

At Pennyvenie I was often neighboured with Alex McGuinness whom I enjoyed working with because he was a lively character. We put the supplies of wood and girders onto hutches which were then sent down the pit on the same cages that took the men underground. The men, for safety reasons, went down separately from the supplies. There were two cages operating. One went down whilst the other came up. The mine was 96 fathoms, but the descent and ascent would take only around two minutes. The descent was in the dark, but the pit bottom had lights.

Supplies delivered

The supplies were already in hutches forming a small train which was pulled by an underground diesel shunter taking the supplies towards the coal face. This was the type of pit bottom work I did until aged eighteen, when I started supervised coal face training which lasted for some two months. This involved working at the coal face with experienced miners, moving the coal and dirt already cut by the nightshift machines, loading onto belts which ran it along from the face to where the hutches were positioned. The hutches were filled to be taken to the surface.

Coal face

I worked ten years on backshift at face work. The smallest seam I worked in was three feet and the highest would be around five feet. However, being small and wiry, I was able to get stuck in and the smaller men could get in closer to the face to remove the coal and the dirt. It was more difficult for taller men. They often had back problems due to working in such cramped conditions. It was hard, tiring work, but you got used to it.

Fond Memories

I spent 26 years down the pit in Pennyvenie until it closed in 1978, when I transferred to Killoch Colliery which subsequently closed in July 1986. The pit closure was a sad day for all the miners, but probably more so for their sons who would perhaps have also worked in the mines.

I've yet to hear any Doon Valley miners say they enjoyed working at Killoch. It was too big and impersonal. I can say that I mainly enjoyed my time in the pits, working with the likes of the Scobie brothers – Archie, Jimmy and Dan. The Dempseys – Tommy (senior), Neil, Tommy, John and Willie. Nowadays I have major breathing problems which no doubt was caused by my years down the pit. Despite that I still have very fond memories of my days as a Doon Valley miner.

This truth fand honest Tam o Shanter,
Ashe frae Ayr ae nighnt did canter

Tam o Shanter
Robert Burns

Memories of a Mining Father

Margaret Dale

Tho cruel fate should bid us part
Far as the pole and line,
Her dear idea round my heart
Should tenderly entwine

Tho Cruel Fate
Robert Burns

Margaret Dale was born and raised in Dalmellington, the daughter of Patrick 'Paddy' Leitch. She was invited to dip into memory to recall her father's working days at Chalmerston Mine, Dalmellington. Nowadays, Margaret lives in Mauchline, but has happy memories of growing up in Dalmellington.

Margaret Dale writes about her father, Patrick Leitch, a miner at Chalmerston and Minnivey.

My father, Patrick Leitch, known better to everyone simply as Wee Paddy, was well known to everyone in Dalmellington and district. He left school aged fourteen and went straight into the pits. It was sad circumstances that saw him begin work at Chalmerston when he was just really a wee lad.

A Boy Down the Mine

He was born in 1912 and raised at Craigmark which was located just beyond Burnton, Dalmellington and beside what became Minnivey mine. Craigmark was abandoned and demolished around 1938, but dad always said that he was proud to have been raised there in a large family.

Sadly his father (my grandfather) died when Patrick was only fourteen years of age in 1926 – the year of the big miner's strike - so he had to go down the mine to support his mother and his sisters – Mary, Sarah, Rosina, Winnie and Cathy. It must have been quite hard on him as a boy having to do a man's work and having responsibility for his family suddenly placed squarely on his shoulders.

Chalmerston Mine

He went on to spend all his days working at Chalmerston mine. And when it closed he moved down the steep Chalmerston brae and began work at Minnivey, located right beside his old village, Craigmark. But I can tell you that Chalmerston was a place he just loved. He spent the largest part of his working life there. He was an oversman and the miners were fond of him and called him Wee Paddy. He worked with and was a good pal of the Johnstone family, especially fellow miners, Addie and Hugh, and other such as Hugh Gourlay, who was a shotfirer and played in a local dance band as well as many more whom I didn't know.

Problem Solving

His manager at Chalmerston during part of his time there was Willie Ross, but I don't know the names of the others who were there before Mr Ross. My father just lived for work. In fact if there was a breakdown of any kind at Chalmerston, he would often be sent for and he would immediately go back out to deal with the problem. I also remember that he would go down the mines himself on a Saturday. I think it was to do with the pumps to stop flooding.

Chalmerston Brae

My mother and I would take his piece to him. We lived in Gateside Street, Dalmellington and would regularly walk out to Burnton and then up the steep brae to Chalmerston to give dad his piece. We would often stop for a picnic and enjoyed the lovely views across to the Loch Doon hills. How my father walked up and down that steep brae all his working life, I don't know. No wonder he was in his grave aged sixty-seven. He had no time for lazy miners.

He was always on the dayshift and would be away at 5am and was never back in the house until 4pm. My sister and I would be waiting at the Kirk o' the Covenant to get his pay. One week I took it to my mother and the next week it was my sister's turn.

Porrige and Bed

Father had no hobbies to speak of. He did enjoy his garden though. He would come home from the mine to Gateside Street and have a plate of porridge and then go straight to his bed. He got up at 7pm for his tea. That pattern went on all his working life. He lived for his work in the mines, his family and his church.

Fond Memories

After he retired through ill health, he enjoyed drives in the countryside and going to our caravan in Stranraer. He would often speak about his days at Chalmerston and I think he missed the company of other miners.

I have no doubt that working underground with all the dirt and poor air, did have an adverse affect on his health, because he did die at a relatively young age. I have fond memories of my father.

Till a' the seas gang dry my dear,
And the rocks melt wi the sun!
And I will luve thee still, my dear,
While the sands o life shall run

My luve is like a Red Red Rose
Robert Burns

Bus to Pit

Vance Harvey

Fate still has blest me with a friend,
In ev'ry care and ill;
And oft a more endearing band—
A tie more tender still.

Epistle to Davie, A Brother Poet
Robert Burns

Vance Harvey of Tarbolton recalls his time driving the mine workers to and from different pits around Dalmellington in an old double decker bus. He wrote a small poem about mining. An extract from it is included at the end of this short reflection.

For many years I was a bus driver for Western SMT. On my regular route I drove an old double decker taking the Doon Valley men to and from different pits such as Beoch, Pennyvenie and Minnivey.

I always enjoyed going into the pit canteen at Pennyvenie and Minnivey, listening to the different stories as the miners blethered. The funny thing was they all sat and laughed and then made for the cage which was to take them into the bowels of the earth for a hard shift in difficult conditions underground.

They never seemed to have any fear or at least they never showed it. At the end of the backshift some of the miners were sound asleep before the bus left the pit to return them home. I used to think to myself: "My God, how do they do it."

My better half had five members of her family working in the pits. Alas they are all gone now. But I do think back to the days when I was delighted to be driving the miners from around Dalmellington back and forward to their work in the mines.

Now on Monday at six it was back to the mine,
The cage left at five past, so you must be on time.
Then back to the coal face one mile underground,
There's no light, just darkness, not even a sound.
It's now they get started to dig out the coal,
Having a pick and a shovel I'm told.
Each man he will bring out his quota each day,
They have to work hard to make any pay.

When they emerged from the cage at the old pithead,
You could see they were tired and drawn.
They were the ones that were digging the coal,
That we put on our fires to keep warm.
Some would then make for the canteen,
For they had a terrible thirst.
After working all day far underground,
In nothing but dampness and dust.

The kids met their dads at the front door,
He'd cuddle each one in their turn.
An anxious young wife from the kitchen,
Shouts: "Hurry up or your dinner will burn."
Well this was the life of a miner,
From fourteen to sixty-five years.
Some certainly could tell you some stories,
Of which some of them ended in tears.

The coal mines have now closed in Scotland,
Much to the miners' delight
They don't have to go to that dungeon
In a place full of dust and no light.
Well here's to the men of the coal mines
They were the men I admired.
Yes, they were the men who did keep us warm
By digging the coal for our fire.

Memories from a Mining Family

Dennis McQuillan

Ye banks and braes o' bonnie Doon,
How can ye bloom sae fresh and fair?

The Banks o' Doon
Robert Burns

Dennis McQuillan, 66, was born in Patna in 1949 and raised in a mining family. In 1973 he moved south for work as a Podiatrist. He is now happily retired, but his fondest memories still relate to happy family days in the Doon Valley. He journeys into memory recalling some of the stories passed down in his family.

Family down the Mines

While I never worked in the pits I come from a family where the previous three generations were all coal miners in the Doon Valley. The extended family from Patna, Craigmark, Dalmellington and Polnessan had uncles and cousins who were miners too.

My father, John McQuillan, worked in three of the Doon Valley pits. He first worked at Chalmerston mine as a young man, Houldsworth pit when he married my Mother Liza, and then Pennyvenie pit when Houldsworth closed. My grandfather Dennis worked in Chalmerston mine. Uncle John in Beoch and Houldsworth, and uncle Leslie in Houldsworth and Polquhairn Colliery, Rankinston. Another uncle John worked in Beoch mine, Grandad's cousin 'Geordie' McQuillan, father of Tommy McQuillan who notably chronicled life in 'The Hill, it's People and it's Pits,' never worked again following a serious injury accident.

Family Life

When I grew up in the 1950s, families seemed to be bigger, better connected, more integrated and interdependent than today. Very few people had television or telephones at that time, they were considered unaffordable luxuries. National news was broadcast on the radio or read in the newspaper, and local communication was through the spoken word.

Families tended to associate very freely and regularly within their communities. Where they met, adult conversations about miners and mining issues were always likely. Children like myself were not expected to converse with their elders apart from appropriate responses when spoken to, so we listened and took note. The following anecdotes are all noted from such conversations at the meal table or the fireside at family gatherings.

Don't go Doon the Pit

Stick in at school and whatever you do 'Don't go doon the pit.' This was constantly said to young boys by adults in the Doon Valley. It reflected the dirty, dangerous and unhealthy underground conditions and the often awkward and strenuous physical work faced by miners. Post war there was better educational opportunities to enable young men to find other forms of employment, and in the fifties and sixties jobs were more readily available than nowadays.

Dirty Work

It was dirty! Coal is a naturally dirty substance and cannot be handled without becoming blackened. After a shift extracting and transporting the coal, the miners and their clothing would inevitably be filthy. My Father John and most other miners, left these clothes in a pit locker and changed into 'shifting clothes' to travel back home.

The miners had showers and lockers installed after nationalisation, and used the 'sprays' to wash after a shift. Periodically the 'pit baths' were cleaned and the underground clothing, including heavy 'moleskin' trousers was brought home to be washed. This prompted a strategy to locate and eradicate the fleas which would inevitably come into the home in these clothes.

In the times before nationalisation there were no facilities to wash at the place of work. The coal owners were not willing to spend money on anything which would reduce profits. The men came home dirty and washed in the sink or a tin bath beside the open fire. It is not generally known that at that time the men would not wash their backs. It was thought that too much washing would soften their backs and render them unable to work.

Calls of Nature

The men would regularly have to work in water which gathers naturally in the pits. While this could be pumped out, the owners were reluctant to install pumps due to the capital and running costs. This meant that the men had to walk sometimes many miles home in wet clothes, and we can imagine how unpleasant and unhealthy this would have been in a blizzard in the depths of winter. There were no facilities down the pit, calls of nature had to be answered with whatever discretion was available.

There were no opportunities for hand-washing. The men ate their 'piece' at break time with unwashed hands down the pit. Clean drinking water had to be taken underground, because dehydration had to be avoided at all costs. My Dad took a tin flask of tea which was wrapped in newspaper and consumed tepid.

As well as regular personal infestation with insect vermin, rats and mice lived in the pits too. These rodents are well known to carry disease, and were known to have caused outbreaks of Weil's disease. For some reason rats and mice were seldom found together at the same time. They were particularly manifest in pre war times when the pit ponies and their feedstuff were kept underground.

Dangerous Work

It is said that no other occupation in history had such a wide variety of ways to be injured maimed or killed. Accordingly the men and boys enjoyed elevated status in the home and were indulged by their mothers, sisters and daughters. The family depended on their health and fitness for an income, and the women were always very much aware that each time the men left home, it might be the last time they saw them alive or in one piece. When food was in short supply the women would often go short to make sure the men were well enough fed in order to keep them fit and healthy.

Firedamp or methane gas accumulates naturally in underground workings. It is highly explosive. While coal dust is explosive on its own, when mixed with methane it is even more dangerous. Underground fires and explosions have accounted for a great number of deaths and injuries in UK mining. Methane is difficult to detect, and naked flame or sparks will ignite it.

The men were not allowed to smoke or take smoking materials (contraband) underground. Anyone caught doing so would be dismissed. I was told by my father that one of our neighbours in Patna, a miner called Isaac Gillespie, had the misfortune to be met with a wall of flame following an ignition, and in surprise took a sharp intake of breath.

He survived the fire but his vocal chords were so damaged he could no longer speak properly.

Carbon monoxide, or Whitedamp, is also found naturally in pits, it occurs when coal is exposed to the atmosphere and spontaneous combustion results producing the gas. This gas is of course odourless, colourless and lethal. This is the gas that canaries were used to detect. Blackdamp is a mixture of Carbon Monoxide and Nitrogen. Where it is found in quantity, there is no oxygen and consequently can cause asphyxia.

Dennis McQuillan.

Roof Falls and Hazards

Most of the miners we would encounter in our daily lives would have visible blue scars on hands and faces. Working with coal and stone with bare hands to extract the one and discard the other would inevitably lead to injury. The broken skin would be quickly contaminated by coal dust and the blue scars never faded and were accepted as an occupational hazard.

Regular injuries were commonplace for most underground workers and most would recover. Some were less fortunate, the risk of a roof fall was a constant threat and many miners were killed or seriously injured by 'Stanes fa'in in' on them.

Where roadways were excavated to reach the coal and where the coal had been extracted, the roof had to be supported to prevent it falling in on the workings. These supports sometimes failed. Pit props made out of tree trunks were used as roof supports. Those from abroad were favoured as they gave an audible creak as a sign they may give way.

After the war, metal hydraulic props called 'Doughtys' were used. Where there were roof falls there could be fatalities, entrapment or often serious injury causing disability and therefore incapacity to work. Tommy McQuillan's father, George, suffered such life threatening injuries with multiple fractures. He never worked again and always walked with a stick. Such injury was financially calamitous for households until employers were made to compensate workers for work related injuries.

Mining and its everyday dangers was simply accepted as part and parcel of life by my father, the wider family male members who worked in the bowels of the earth and indeed all the local miners. They were proud to be miners, but were always acutely aware of the daily dangers they faced. It is my hope that their memory will never wither but flourishes forever in that lovely landscape of Ayrshire's Doon Valley which they knew, loved and called their home.

Thou minds me o' departed joys,
Departed never to return.

The Banks o' Doon
Robert Burns

The Knockshinnoch Disaster

Andrew Galloway

Farewell hours that late did measure
Sunshine days of joy and pleasure!
Hail, thou gloomy night of sorrow –
Cheerless night that knows no morrow.

Raving Winds Around Her Blowing
Robert Burns

Andrew Galloway, known as Drew, recalls his father's involvement as one of the rescuers at what became known as the Knockshinnoch Disaster, New Cumnock, on 7 September 1950. His father, also Andrew, occasionally spoke about the disaster and the role played by members of the local mine rescue brigade in assisting the rescue of one hundred and sixteen miners. Tragically thirteen lost their lives.

Andrew Galloway (sen) was born in Benwhat in 1908 and died in 1966. He spent most of his working life in Chalmerston Mine. He left the pits in 1953. Andrew (jun) was born in Benwhat in 1940. He started work at Chalmerston in 1955, followed by a year at Dunaskin starting his trade as an engineer, then worked at Pennyvenie No 4 (the big mine), Pennyvenie No 2/7 and finished in the mines in 1964 at the Beoch.

The thirteen miners who died at Knocksinnoch were 1. John Dalziel, 50 loader attendant; 2. James D. Houston, 46 coal miner; 3. Thomas Houston, 40 coal miner; 4. William Howat, 61 switch attendant; 5. William Lee, 48 coal miner; 6. James Love, 48 coal miner; 7. William McFarlane, 36 coal miner; 8. John McLatchie, 48 shotfirer; 9. John Taylor, 33 coal miner; 10. Samuel Rowan, 25 coal miner; 11. John Smith, 55 coal miner; 12. Daniel Strachan, 38 fireman and 13. John White, 26 coal miner

Disaster Announced

It was dinner time at remote Benwhat Primary School located on the hills to the north east of and just above Dalmellington. I remember that it was the morning of 8 September 1950 when the headmaster Mr Jeffrey gave us the news about an accident at Knockshinnoch Colliery some ten miles away where miners were trapped underground.

My father, Andrew Galloway, was at the time the captain of the local mine rescue brigade and Mr Jeffrey mentioned to me that he was already at Knockshinnoch with his team. I think everyone in the class was shocked, because all of them came from mining families. I remember a shiver running down my spine when I realised that my father would be going down the mine to help rescue trapped miners.

Rivers of Mud

After several days of heavy rain a field at Knockshinnoch had caved in causing rivers of mud to rush into mine workings, sealing off any escape from the pit and trapping one hundred and twenty nine men.

For the next few days my mother and I had to rely on the wireless, newspapers and men from the village who went over to

Knockshinnoch to help in any way they could, for information on the rescue operations. It was a time of great anxiety for our family and of course for the families of the trapped miners. One hundred and sixteen of the men had managed to get to a heading (high point) in the west mine as yet untouched by the mud, but tragically the other thirteen were lost.

Working Underground

By a stroke of luck the heading had a working telephone and they were able to tell officials on the surface their location. There was no chance of clearing the sludge from the Knockshinnoch tunnels in time to save the miners, but the neighbouring Bank mine had disused workings which had a road near the trapped men.

There was less than thirty feet of coal between them. My father remembered the hard slog through almost two miles of old abandoned tunnels to get there, but found that the road was filled with deadly firedamp, poisonous and highly inflammable.

His men were ordered to install a fan to try and clear the gas and as captain it was his job to throw the switch on the control panel. He was warned that if there was a spark it would not only get rid of the gas, but him as well. However, soon after the fan started up, he felt a gust of air hitting him and knew it was bouncing off the dense gas.

Digging to Rescue

He knew they would have to dig through to the west mine, some thirty feet, wearing their breathing apparatus and still with the constant threat of the ingress of more mud. The breathing apparatus used was the Proto system which consisted of a mouthpiece and a nose clip which took weeks of training to get used to and to work a shift wearing it would be tough going.

After some hours of challenging work by brigade men and teams of miners in the west mine digging towards each other, a hole was made large enough for much needed food and water to be passed through. During the dig the nose clip of one of my father`s team came off, but before it was replaced, he inhaled some of the gas and had to be rushed to a fresh air base for treatment. Thankfully, he made a full recovery.

Rescue seemed close at hand, but then a major setback happened. The extra fans which had been brought in to help to dispel the gas were ineffective and it was now seeping into the heading and the miners. Time was running out and drastic action was needed to get the men out. It was decided to fit each one with breathing apparatus. This ruled out the use of Proto as it would be dangerous for untrained men.

Help from Home and Abroad

The Salvus system was suggested which was used by the fire and submarine services even though it had never been tested underground. Naval stores and fire stations from all over Britain sent every Salvus set they could spare and even the USA offered to fly some over to Prestwick Airport.

Almost one hundred rescue workers were required as they would be stationed in pairs a few yards apart in the gas filled road leading to the barrier at the west mine where the hole was enlarged to take three men.

The procedure was that two brigade men went into the heading, fitted a Salvus to a miner, then as my father recalled, we were told to take an arm each and march him through the barrier, then pass him on to the first men in the chain and not to stop for anything.

If a man began to panic we were to drag him through if necessary. However, this was not a problem and it took almost seven hours to get all the miners out passing them along the chain, including two on stretchers who were too ill to walk, after two days being trapped.

Greatest Rescue

At the time of Knockshinnoch my father had completed fifteen years with the rescue brigade and had recently received a medallion for his service. Much has been written about this Ayrshire mining disaster and the heroic efforts of so many folk. I feel very proud that my own father, Andrew Galloway, was part of that operation which saved the lives of so many miners. It was his last rescue operation and as it turned out, the greatest in Scottish mining history.

Life is but a day at most,
Sprung from night in darkness lost;
Hope not sunshine every hour,
Fear not clouds will always lour.

Verses in Friars Carse Hermitage
Robert Burns

Doon Valley Miners at War

Gallipoli Press Report August 1915

I left the lines and tented field,
Where lang I'd been a lodger,
My humble knapsack a' my wealth,
A poor but honest sodger

The Soldier's Return
Robert Burns

The disaster of Gallipoli, the First World War campaign in which 42,000 allied troops lost their lives, was caused in large part by the poor quality of the maps used by the officers as well as poor planning and leadership.

It also had major ramifications for Ayrshire's Garnock Valley soldiers on one disastrous day of war – 12th July 1915 - when thirty local men from Beith, Dalry and Kilbirnie were killed in battle.

The following short press report is recorded from the Glasgow Herald dated 2 August 1915. It demonstrates that whilst mining was a reserved occupation, many miners from the Doon Valley area did serve in the Dardanelles and many other campaigns during the Great War and were wounded and in some case far too many made the ultimate sacrifice. The newspaper piece is simply headed: 'Ayrshire.'

The following casualties are announced in the 1st-5th RSF (TF). Private William Ferguson, 13 New Cottages, Dunaskin, is in Alexandria Hospital. He was a locomotive guard at Dalmellington Iron Works. Private John Fagan, 44 Waterside, Dunaskin, has been wounded. Private James Malcolmson and William Ferguson, Cathcartston, Dalmellington, are amongst the wounded. Both were brushers in the Dalmellington Iron Company's Pennyvenie pits. Private David Simpson, 91 Lethanill, Dunaskin, has been slightly wounded. Privates William Bryan and Edward Millar, both of 38 Benwhat, Dalmellington, are reported killed. Both were 33 years of age and were miners and were employed in the Dalmellington Iron Company's Clawfin and No. 3 Pennyvenie mines and respectively. Millar leaves a widow and five of a family. Private Ivy Lafferty killed; Private Hugh Hynds killed; Private John Ferguson, wounded and Private Hugh McCutcheon, wounded (the latter being in Old Mill Hospital, Aberdeen), all resided at Burnfoothill, Dunaskin prior to enlistment.

It's not the roar o sea or shore,
Wad make me langer wish to tarry;
Nor shouts o war that's heard afar –
It's leaving thee, my bony Mary!

The Silver Tassie
Robert Burns

Epilogue

Ill fares the land, to hastening ills a prey,
Where wealth accumulates, and men decay;
Princes and lords may flourish, or may fade;
A breath can make them, as a breath has made.
But a bold peasantry, their country's pride,
When once destroyed, can never be supplied.

The Deserted Village
Oliver Goldsmith

Time does pass quicker than we think and this book is timely in that it captures the precious memories of Doon Valley coal miners, many of them men in the autumn of life and some who are no longer with us, but it is fitting that through this book their precious mining memories will live on to benefit those who follow in our footsteps. These mining stories reveal a way of life that deserves to be recognised as a crucial part of the industrial and social history of Ayrshire and Scotland. These small mining communities of Ayrshire's Doon Valley were populated by real, caring people who lived life at the sharp end, facing adversity head-on. Sadly, too many families lost loved ones to coal mining.

The mining villages created by the Dalmellington Iron Company in the mid 1850s are deserted and demolished, but a loving bond still exists between yesteryear and today that will not be easily broken as long as family members of miners proudly tell their family about their mining heritage.

Thus in memory let it steep,
And in tradition let it keep,
That those that follow get a peep,
At days gone by;
And what we do enjoy today,
Whose beauty never fades away,
If folks still try.

John S McChesney
(For many years a popular teacher at Dalmellington High School and a Dalrymple resident)

Ghaists

A fitting way of concluding this revealing and humbling insight into personal memories of mining folk who experienced life in Ayrshire's Doon Valley, especially in the lost mining villages, is with yet another piece of poetry. Matthew Arnold's assertion that 'poetry is simply the most beautiful, impressive and widely effective mode of saying things' is widely accepted, and certainly touches a chord with the author. I chose to sum up this book featuring the voices of The Last Miners of Ayrshire's Doon Valley with poetry, in braid Scots, from the pen of one of my own favourite rhymers, Rab Wilson of New Cumnock. Interestingly, Rab also worked in the pits for several years before training as a nurse.

In my view his poem nicely encapsulates the ebb and flow of mining life in Benwhat and elsewhere in the Doon Valley's lost mining villages. Let's hope that, in remembering, our children's children may also from time to time reflect on these thriving small communities where now only the ghaists of the past walk.

Here, oan this blastit hillside, stuid Benwhat,
Whaur haurdy men aince mined the Ironstane,
Till it ran oot – an then they mined fir coal.
Seen frae the heichts it's lyk some Machu-Picchu;
Weird plateaus an mounds define the grunnd,
Strange promontory's grassed ower nou wi green,
As natuir slowly hains back whit's her ain.
Ower-sheddaed by the mammoth Opencasts,
The spoil-heaps o Benwhat are shilpit things;
Worm-casts, neist thae muckle mowdie-hillocks.
That lane brick wa they say wis aince the schuil,
Ah stoop tae lift a waithert block o cley,
'Dalmellington Iron Company', it reads;
The faded legend o some lang loast empire.
There's naethin left o douce, trig miners' raws,
Whaes cobbles rang wi soun o cleek n' girr,
Or scrape o tackets, thud o leather club,
The flap an whirr o racin pigeons' wings,
White-peenied weemin clashin ower the dyke;
Whaur yae road taen ye in, an taen ye oot.
Thon aiblins wis 'The Sacred Way' fir some,
Wha laucht an daffed alang it as they left –
When Ne'erday cam, their friens turnt doun a gless.
There's naethin here nou, naethin here but ghaists,
Heich oan the hill the stairk memorial stauns,
A souch o back-end wuin blaws snell an keen,
Throu brucken iron railins, whaur it steirs
The tattert remnants o a poppy wreath.

Bibliography

The books listed below are recommended to the reader wishing to learn more about Ayrshire's Doon Valley. Those interested in finding out more are advised to contact the excellent local reference libraries in Ayrshire.

Rob Close, *Ayrshire and Arran* (1992)

Robert Farrell, *Benwhat and Corbie Craigs: A Brief History* (1983)

Alex Johnstone, *Craigmark: 1800 to 1937* (1995)

Hugh Johnstone, MBE and Donald L Reid*, 150 Years of Dalmellington Band – A sesquicentennial Celebration (2014)*

Dane Love, *Ayrshire: Discovering a County* (2004)

Dane Love, *Lost Ayrshire: Ayrshire's Lost Architectural Heritage* (2005)

T Courtney McQuillan, *The Hill: Its People and Its Pits* (1988)

John Moore (ed.), *Gently Flows the Doon* (1972)

John Moore (ed.), *Among Thy Green Braes* (1977)

Piggot's Directory Ayrshire (1837) GC Book Publishers Ltd, Wigton

Donald L Reid, *Old Dalmellington, Patna and Waterside* (2001)

Donald L Reid, *Doon Valley Memories: A Pictorial Reflection* (2002)

Donald L Reid, *Doon Valley Bygones* (2004)

Donald L Reid, *Yesterday's Patna and the Lost Mining Villages of Doon Valley* (2005)

Donald L Reid, *Robert Burns' Valley of Doon: An Ayrshire Journey Down Memory Lane* (2005)

Donald L Reid, *Discovering Matthew Anderson, Policeman-Poet of Ayrshire* (2009)

Donald L Reid, *The Lost Mining Villages of Doon Valley – Voices and Images of Ayrshire* (2013)

James Edward Shaw, *Ayrshire 1745–1950: A Social and Industrial History of the County* (1953)

David L Smith, *The Dalmellington Iron Company: Its Engines and Men* (1967)

Gavin Wark, *The Rise and Fall of Mining Communities in Central Ayrshire in the 19th and 20th Centuries* (Ayrshire Archaeological and Natural History Society Monograph No. 22) (1999)

Books by Donald L Reid

The following other books have been compiled by Donald L Reid.

* *Reflections of Beith and District: On The Wings of Time* (1994)
* *Yesterday's Beith: A Pictorial Guide* (1998)
The Beith Supplement: The Story of Beith's Newspaper (2000)
\+ *Old Beith* (Stenlake Publications, 2000)
In The Valley of Garnock: Beith, Dalry and Kilbirnie (2001)
\+ *Old Dalmellington, Patna and Waterside* (Stenlake Publications, 2001)
* *Doon Valley Memories: A Pictorial Reflection* (2002)
Beith Bygones: A Pictorial Journey Down Memory Lane (2003)
* *Doon Valley Bygones: A Pictorial Journey Down Memory Lane* (2004)
* *Barrmill and Burns* (2004)
* *Yesterday's Patna and the Lost Mining Villages of Doon Valley* (2005)
Robert Burns' Valley of Doon: An Ayrshire Journey Down Memory Lane (2005)
More Old Beith (2006)
* *Discovering Matthew Anderson: Policeman-Poet of Ayrshire* (2009)
Voices and Images of Yesterday and Today. Beith, Barrmill and Gateside: Precious Memories (2011)
* *The Lost Mining Villages of Doon Valley – Voices and Images of Ayrshire (2013)*
150 Years of Dalmellington Band – A sesquicentennial Celebration (2014) – with Hugh Johnstone MBE
* *Not in print and no reprint planned*
\+ *Only available from Stenlake Publishers, 54-58 Mill Square, Catrine KA5 6RD*

Author profile
Donald L Reid is a retired police superintendent, having served in the Ayrshire Constabulary and Strathclyde Police from 1967 until 1999. He was superintendent serving mainly in Glasgow City Centre area for the last seven years of his service.

Raised in Dalmellington, he is very proud of his Doon Valley roots where his father grew up at Beoch and his mother at Craigmark, two of the lost mining villages of Doon Valley. He has lived in Beith for the past thirty years with his wife Kathleen. His son, Fraser, and his wife, Heather, and their sons, Taylor and Owen, live nearby. Donald's daughter, Elaine and husband, Mark, also live in Beith.

Donald has now produced eighteen local history books since 1994 mainly about the Doon Valley and Garnock Valley areas of Ayrshire. He is the Garnock Valley correspondent for the *Ardrossan & Saltcoats Herald*, keeping locals abreast of happenings in Beith and district. He has been correspondent for Beith since 2002.

A past president of Garnock Valley Round Table, he was three times president of Barrmill Jolly Beggars Burns Club; he is also secretary and was honoured when in recognition for his services to the club he was appointed honorary president in 2008. Donald is a sought-after speaker on subjects ranging from Robert Burns and Dr Henry Faulds to the Doon Valley and Garnock Valley. With his good friend Iain D Shaw, he gives an illustrated presentation on the life and works of Robert W Service, a truly international poet with close links to Kilwinning. This is entitled 'Robert W Service – Poet of the People'.

Donald is the founder member and secretary of the Dr Henry Faulds Society, which achieved a fitting memorial in Beith in 2004 to the Beith-born medical missionary, writer and one of the early and minor pioneers of fingerprint science. Donald is a member of or assists several groups and organisations in Beith and district. He was Beith Citizen of the Year in 1994. In 2015 he was appointed as Regional Ambassador for Ayrshire for the charity, Age Scotland.

He can be contacted on: Tel 01505-503801 or E: donaldleesreid@hotmail.com. You can also visit these websites:
www.jollybeggars.org
www.facebookon/donald.reid.1401

All the world is beautiful,
and it matters little where we go.
The spot where we chance to be
Always seems the best.

John Muir, 1890

End Gallery

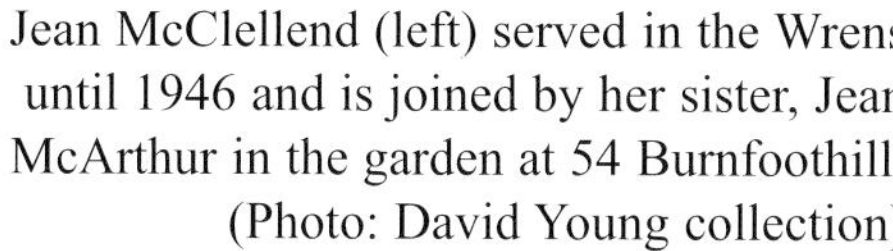

Jean McClellend (left) served in the Wrens until 1946 and is joined by her sister, Jean McArthur in the garden at 54 Burnfoothill. (Photo: David Young collection)

William and Maggie McClellend in their well-stocked garden at 54 Burnfoothill around 1944. (Photo: David Young collection)

A happy duo. Jack Young who was the last manager of Lethanhill Store with Jack Hunter, who was the immediate past manager. This would be taken about 1948. (Courtesy of David Young collection)

Fanny McClelland with three young children sitting enjoying the sun in front of 54 Burnfoothill in the early 1940s. (Photo: David Young collection)

Benwhat Heatherbell in the 1940s.
Back row (l to r): Jim 'Pim' Douglas, John Thomson, David Connell, William Barbour, Arthur O'Neil, unknown.
Front row: Jim Murray, Alan McCreath, Jim McCulloch with son John, 'Toy' Bennett.
(Courtesy of Flora Scobie nee McCulloch)

Lethanhill Group of men on a bus trip. In the centre a man is offering another a cigarette from his case. Those in kilts are likely to have been members of the Lethanhill Pipe Band.

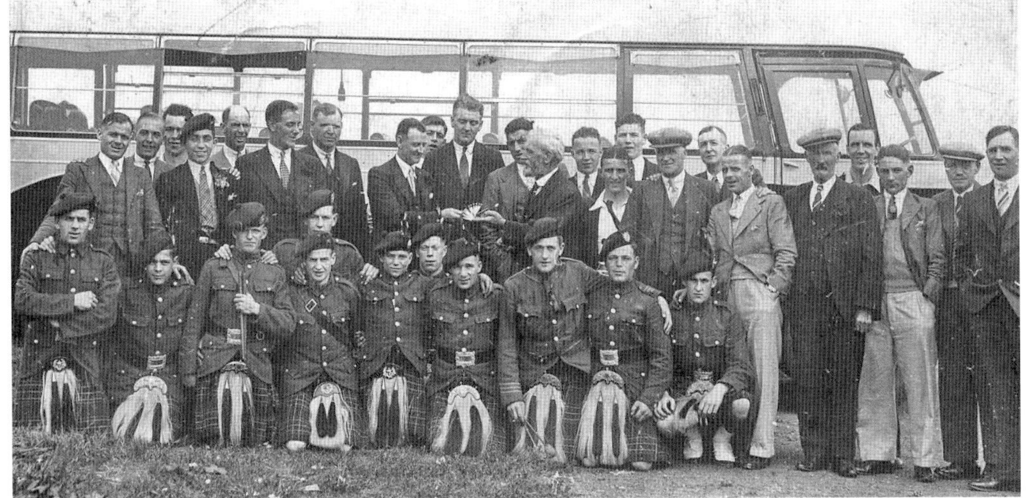

Lethanhill School staff circa 1951
Back row: Matt McLellan and Jimmy Paterson.
Front: William Faucett (Janitor), Sadie McIndo formerly of Smithston Farm who was the domestic science teacher; George Donohoe, headmaster. In addition to those in the photo, there was a Miss Faulder (infant mistress) and several other teachers.
(Photo: Courtesy of Ann MacLean collection)

A front view of Waterside Stores which remains largely unchanged today, although the building is no longer in use. Taken in the 1920s, this shows the extensive use made of horse and cart in transporting people and goods in the upper section of the Doon Valley. On the right of the building was the Palace Bar, a popular haunt for the hardworking men of the Dalmellington Iron Company who owned the premises. Women were not welcome in such establishments. The carriage on the left is sitting on what is known locally as Parliament corner, so called because local men gathered there and discussed the issues of the day. The carts are about to set off for neighbouring villages to replenish supplies and deliver orders. The sign on the centre wagon reads: 'Dalmellington Iron Co. Ltd., Stores, Waterside.'

Dr Lee with his wife, Mae Ireland. Dr Lee was a very popular General Practitioner in Dalmellington. Born in Singapore in 1906, he came to the village in 1933 and after 40 years of diligent service to the community retired in 1973. He will be fondly remembered by miners as he regularly had to go underground to deal with numerous accidents and fatalities.

Burnton village was erected near the farm of Burnton, less than 1 mile north east of Dalmellington. Built circa 1924 by the Dalmellington Iron Company, the village comprised of eighty-four houses. This was the Craigmark/Burnton Sunday School Cantata 'Ali Baba.' Back row (l to r): Mr Matthew Wilson (Sunday School Superintendent and a highly respected man in the district), Andy Smith, Sadie Calderwood, Annie Carruthers, Mary McCulloch, Mary Beck, David Henderson, William Campbell, Duncan Murphy, John Jackson and Mr J Torbet.
Middle row: William Blain, Jim McLellan (long white pinny and hat), Jean Kennedy, Sarah Connell, Mary Murphy, Jean Welsh, Barbara Boyle, Nancy Beck, David Torbet (later to become a very accomplished Flugal Horn player with Dalmellington Band), Sarah Murphy and Mary Carter. Front row: Rose Torbet (Jeanie), Betty McCracken, Nettie Calderwood, Margaret Hose, Mrs M Murphy, Nan McKie, Jean McCulloch, Jenny Kennedy and Nan Torbet.

Waterside was a very busy place for screening coal and there were regular steam workings until 1978 when Pennyvenie Colliery closed. No. 24 is working at Pennyvenie and the headgear of the pit dominates the scene. Visitors came from all over to see these working locomotives and one such enthusiast was respected railway photographer Adrian Booth.
(Photo: courtesy of Adrian Booth)

On 29 May 1978 the washery at Waterside and locomotive No. 1 waits to deliver these wagons to Minnivey and Pennivenie whilst the steam from No. 24 shows that it is ready to work as banker. Waterside ironstone slag bing dominates the background and is a legacy of the Dalmellington Iron Companies work extracting ironstone to feed their furnaces at Waterside. The coal washing plant is to the right.
(Photo: Courtesy of Adrian Booth)

A rake of wagons head down from Waterside to Ayr around 1977 hauled by two British Railway locomotives.
(Photo: Courtesy of Adrian Booth)

With tender first locomotive No. 24, a great favourite with the drivers, delivers a load of empties up to Pennyvenie and is spotted just passing the bing on 27 May 1975. The houses of Broomknowe, Dalmellington, can just be seen in the background.
(Photo: Courtesy of Adrian Booth)

Waterside washery had a double-wagon tippler at the east end of the yard seen here on 29th May 1978 dealing with wagons of coal brought in from Minnivey and Pennyvenie.
(Photo: Courtesy of Adrian Booth)

A rake of wagons sit behind a British Railways locomotive at Waterside, waiting to be taken out through the Doon Valley. The chapel can be clearly seen in the background. This photo by Adrian Booth was taken in the early 1970s.
(Photo: Courtesy of Adrian Booth)

Waterside NCB in January 1969. A typical scene of the period with the steam engines working hard on the site. Barclay 0-6-0T No. 10 and 0-6-0T No 17 seen here. Waterside was one of the last locations where steam could be found working on a daily basis and steam enthusiasts came to this site from all over the United Kingdom.

A pug with a rake of wagons leaves Minnivey for Waterside in the 1960s.

Dalmellington Rangers football team in 1921.
Back row: Bob Hewitson, J Riggins and Joe Millar
Middle row: R Gault (trainer), B Dempsey, R Hill, H Cannon, J Findlay, T Stewart, A Orr and R Park.
Front row: R Blackwood, J Campbell, W Tyson, J Hainey, J Torbet.

Lethanhill School in 1956. The entire population of Lethanhill and Burnfoothill, known simply as the Hill, had been removed to Patna and Dalmellington by 1955, but strangely enough the school remained open and the pupils were bussed there until 1959. Little sign of the village remains except the lonely war memorial and trees cover the area where the rows formerly stood.
Back row: Billy Bryden, Jim Guthrie, Billy Brown, M Auld, Margaret Mullholland, Madge Bain, Charlotte McClymont, Ann Robertson, ?, Margaret McDermont, May McHattie, J Givens, Agnes Knox, Elizabeth Laughlan, John McLeod, Alex Kirk and Francie Bryce.
Second back row: Andrew Brown, Irene Gillespie, Elizabeth Murray, Margaret Johnstone, Mary Muir, Jean Grant, Mamie McCormack, Rita Wylie, Christine Coughtrie, Margaret Ferguson, Margaret Gillespie, Jessie Wilson, Ann Graham, Marjorie Fawcett, Helen Mitchell, William Walker and W Campbell.
Second front row: John Dunn, William Bryce, Betty Orr, Betty McCubbin, B Brown, S Ballantyne, Jean Findlater, Ella Knox, Helen Boyle, Mary McDougall, Jessie McLeod, Nancy Brolley, Janice Bradford, Marion Bryden, A McDougall, Agnes Fyvie, Annie Ferguson, Jim Stevenson, James Whiteford and James Spiers.
Front row: Billy McDermont, Jim Milligan, Tom Chalmers, Ian Wallace, Alistair Muir, J Lafferty, Alex Anderson, A Patterson, Wallace Lapslay, Robert McDermont, Andrew Currie, John Findlay, J McQuillan, Alec McCulloch and Joe Tinman.

Patna Public School in 1960. Many of those in this photo would have been among the last pupils at Lethanhill School which closed its doors in 1959
Back row (l to r): teacher unknown (3), A Kirwood, J Stewart, J Pettigrew, A Currie, R Law, J Cran, D Brown, ? Ashley, B Robertson, Billy Boyle, J Goodwin and D Robertson.
Second back row: Gordon Robertson (teacher), A Ballantyne, J Graham, unknown (2), Whiteford, unknown (2), A Lindsay, M Lafferty, A Graham, E Stevenson, unknown, Clark, J Smith, J McDougall, J Fitzsimmons, J Bradford, J Logan, M Finlay, H Lymburn and Mr May (teacher).
3rd back row: unknown, Graham, C McDonald, A Kennedy, M Knox, M Gillespie, M Torbet, J McWilliams, L Graham, I Johnstone, E Ferguson, E Dinwoodie, M McCallum, A Knox, A McDerment and teacher unknown
Second front row: S Lang, E Hamilton, M Tinman, E Thomson, M Murray, M Boyle, M Thomson, A Ballantyne, J Grant, J Kilpatrick, A Hainey, E Brown, J McGuigan and E Black.
Front row: G Graham, J Lynn, T McBride, unknown J Bryce, K Ferguson, unknown, unknown, G Peters, J Faulds, unknown, and J Graham.

Patna Amateurs Football team during 1959/60. This was the very successful team which won four cups that season. All the players held a reunion in 2000 in Patna Masonic Club with the exception of Tommy Campbell who died in Australia.

Back row (l to r): John Thomson, John Duncan, Duncan Robertson, John Pirrie (Ayr), George Ferguson, Tommy Walker, Willie Young and Andrew Beggs
Front row: Andrew Patterson, Tommy Campbell, Alex Kirkwood, Billy Campbell (Ayr), Billy Robertson, Andrew Black and Maxwell Murray.
(Photo: Courtesy of Duncan Robertson collection)

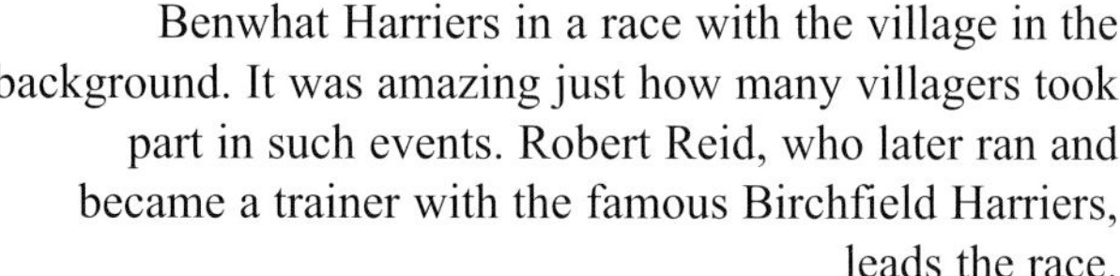

Benwhat Harriers in a race with the village in the background. It was amazing just how many villagers took part in such events. Robert Reid, who later ran and became a trainer with the famous Birchfield Harriers, leads the race.

Dunaskin Lads FC in 1907/08. This one was of a number of football teams in the area and was dominated by the Young and Grant families. Waterside was a busy little industrial village with a large population. This photo is taken outside what was the NCB wages office.
Back row (l to r): W Cord, S Fulton, J Young, J Young, T Grant, J Bingham, A Stevenson, J Denham (small man) and F Pollock.
Front row: J McMillan, Mr Young, W Reid, J Watson, W Henderson and A Grant.

Dalmellington Railway Station in the early 1900s showing the type of transport used to ferry passengers to places such as Loch Doon to enjoy the fishing. It might surprise young folk today, but Loch Doon and Ness Glen were very popular venues for tourists who came in large numbers to enjoy the countryside or to fish. Many stayed in local accommodation such as the Eglinton Hotel or Black Bull.

Dalmellington Bowling Green, pictured in the foreground, was established in 1875 while the open ground on the right became the King George V football park, used by local schoolboy and amateur teams. In the centre background above Dalmellington can be seen Benbraniachan with Chalmerston Pit just to the left in front.
(Photo: EAC DVM)

The village of Craigmark was built during the latter part of the nineteenth century. The village comprised of around 80 houses. There were six rows of houses, being Laigh Row (opposite the store), three single rows and two double rows which were back to back. Built by the Dalmellington Iron Company to house workers, most of the men who lived there worked in local pits such as Sillyhole, Chalmerston, Minnivey, Pennyvenie and Beoch.

Mr Brian Donohoe (left) with Mr Matt McLelland (teacher) at Lethanhill School around 1958.
(Photo: Courtesy of Anne McLean)

Waterside Reunion ticket 1959.

FIRST

WATERSIDE REUNION

HELD IN

Waterside Church Hall

Saturday 21st. March 1959

at 4p.m.

TICKETS 7/- EACH

Some of the industrial debris lying on the former Ayrshire Railway Preservation Group site at Minnivey in May 2015 (Photo: Donald L Reid)

Looking to what remains of Minnivey Colliery, Dalmellington in May 2015. (Photo: Donald L Reid)

May 2015 and an old steam crane which is lying abandoned and forlorn on the Minnivey site at Dalmellington. It is likely that the Ayrshire Railways Preservation Group will move this to Waterside in due course. (Photo: Donald L Reid)

The cairn at the entrance to Pennvenie Opencast site with a memorial to four miners who lost their lives - Brian Frencdh, Jim Griffin, Colin Ferguson and Neil Hodge. See appendice 1 in this book. (Photo: Donald L Reid)

Former Houldsworth Colliery near Patna in the 1950s.

Dalmellington: A Village in the Stars which relates to the star gazing observatory near Loch Doon.
(Photo: Donald L Reid)

A view across Dalmellington from Carspairn Road with the bowling green to the front and the parish church in the background.
(Photo: Donald L Reid)

Welcome to Dalmellington flower container on the Carsphairn Road, Dalmellington.
(Photo: Donald L Reid)

and over the page
Main Street, Dalmellington with Dalmellington House to the right.
(Photo: Donald L Reid)

WELCOME
TO
DALMELLINGTON

DALMELLINGTON
AREA CENTRE
East Ayrshire Council
Health Centre
Skills Development & Employability Service
Workspace Accommodation
Progress
Through
Partnership

Appendix 1

List of known Fatal Accidents in Doon Valley NCB Mines and Pits 1951 – 1971 (*apart from James Munn Hay)

Inevitably in compiling such a list of those who were fatally injured in mining accidents, there is always a danger that some individuals will have been overlooked during research. The aim, nevertheless, is simply to acknowledge those who lost their lives in coal mining.

These were ours in the days of their boyhood
And their names have become our heritage
(Recorded by Donald L Reid from a War Memorial in Knoydart)

*James Munn Hay, (22), 65 Burnton Dalmellington, died on 22 January 1943, following an earlier accident at Chalmerston Colliery, Dalmellington, from a roof fall. He later died of his injuries. He was buried on 25 January 1943 on what would have been his 23rd birthday.

Robert Findlay, (34) 67 Hopes Avenue, Dalmellington, died on 1 August 1951 at Ayr County Hospital as the result of a roof collapse at Pennyvenie 2/7 Colliery, on the same day.

Malcolm McPhail, 103 Park Crescent, Dalmellington, was killed in Pennyvenie No. 7 Colliery on 5 April 1952 when working at the pit bottom and the descending cage struck him.

William Barbour Carlyle, pan shifter, 30 Dalton Avenue, Dalmellington, Ayrshire, died on 2 November 1954 in the underground workings of Beoch Colliery, Ayrshire, when he was struck by a fall of stone from the roof.

Hugh Brown, beltman, 3 Clover Park Dunaskin, Ayrshire, died on 29 June 1954 at Ayr County Hospital, Ayr, from injuries sustained on the same day in the underground workings of Pennyvenie No. 7 Mine, Ayrshire, when the locomotive he was driving collided with a coal cutter haulage rope stretched across the railway track.

Arthur McGough, oncost worker, 14 Corserine Terrace, Dalmellington, Ayrshire, died on 10 February 1954 at Ayr County Council, Ayr, from injuries sustained on 8 February 1954 in the underground workings of Chalmerston Colliery, Ayrshire, when he was struck and knocked down by a runaway hutch loaded with coal.

Memorial to the miners of the Doon Valley located to the lower front of the Dalmellington war memorial. It was unveiled on Sunday 31 March 1996 which was the last day of Cumnock and Doon Valley District Council before it became East Ayrshire Council. Councillor Eric Ross the Convenor of The Council carried out his last official duty that day.

Robert Findlay of Hopes Avenue, Dalmellington, died on 1 August 1951 at Ayr County Hospital as the result of a roof collapse at Pennyvenie 2/7 Colliery, on the same day.
(L to r): Robert Findlay, wife Anne and daughters Ellen and Anne.
(Photo: Ellen McNee)

A group of miners enjoying a break at Pennyvenie prior to 1959. William Sloan Gault was killed as a result of a roof fall at Pennyvenie No. 4 on 12 February 1959.
Back: Francis Graham.
Middle: Alex 'Pale' Scally, William Gault, Duncan Gault, Robert McPhail
Front: Vincent Gault, John Kennedy, John Riley.
(Photo: Courtesy of Jeanie Cullen nee Gault)

Richard Armour, electrician, 4 Craigview, Pennyvenie, Dalmellington, Ayrshire, died on 2 November 1955 in the underground workings of Beoch Colliery, Dalmellington, beside a panel box carrying electric power.

John Steel McLarty, hutch clipper, 51 Auchenroy Crerscent, Dalmellington, died on 20 February 1956 in the underground workings at Beoch Colliery, Parish of Dalmellington, Ayrshire, when he was knocked down and run over by hutches.

Alexander Baird, developer, 25 Auchenroy Crescent, Dalmellington, Ayrshire, died on 6 November 1956 in the underground workings of Pennyvenie No. 7 Colliery, Dalmellington, Ayrshire, when he was struck by a fall of stone and other debris from the roof.

Allan Jackson, mine driver, 3 Gatefauldhead, Dalmellington, Ayrshire, died on 25 February 1957 in the underground workings at Beoch Colliery, Dalmellington, Ayrshire, when a large stone fell on him.

Jan Kowalewski, foreman mine driver, 90 Thornyflats Road, Ayr, died on 6 May 1957 at No. 4 Colliery Minnivey, Dalmellington, Ayrshire, when he was struck and knocked down by a bogie.

William Sloan Gault, coal miner, 5 Auchenroy Crescent, Bellsbank, Dalmellington, died on 12 February 1959 in an ambulance travelling on the Dalmellington to Ayr road near Hollybush Mains Farm, Hollybush, from injuries sustained on the same day in the underground workings known as Top Road, Splint Section, in Pennyvenie No. 4 Colliery, Dalmellington, when he was struck by a fall of stone from the wall.

John Paulin, Dalfarson Avenue, Dalmellington, died on 25 September 1959, aged 35 years having sustained injuries sometime previous at Pennyvenie No. 4 from a fall of stones.

John Waite Fisher, miner, aged 40 years of Park Crescent, Dalmellington, was founded dead under the conveyor belt underground at No. 7 Pennyvenie on 16 February 1962.

Joseph McCaskie Muir Timmins, coal miner, 4 Hopes Avenue, Dalmellington, died on 8 April 1963 at the County Hospital, Ayr, from injuries sustained on 1 April 1963 in No. 9 Left Section of Minnivey Colliery, Dalmellington, when he was struck by a fall of stone from the roof.

William Sloan Gault, coal miner, who died in a roof fall accident at Pennyvenie No. 4 on 12 February 1959. He was born in Lotta Cottage next to Gordon House, Dalmellington. He was one of eight children, five boys and three girls. One of the boys died in infancy and the other four became miners. William, was known as (Billy), Duncan, Tom known as Tarry and Vincent know as Vinnie. Their father, also William Gault, worked in the pit as an under manager at one time. (Photo: Courtesy of Jeanie Cullen nee Gault)

Daniel Wallace, coal miner, 53 Downieston Place, Patna, died on 13 March 1968 at Pennyvenie 2/7 Colliery, Dalmellington, when he was struck by a fall of stone from the roof.

William Kirkpatrick, colliery deputy, 28 Mossdale Terrace, Dalmellington, died on 27 May 1969 at Minnivey Colliery, Dalmellington, when a scraper-conveyor jammed, reared upwards and crushed him against the west wall.

Roger Muir, coal miner, Carnshalloch Avenue, Patna, died on 2 March 1971, aged 59 years, when he was in the process of removing pit props.

Doon Valley Opencast Mining Fatal Accidents 2000 - 2008

On 28 June 2000, Neil Hodge (30), truck driver, from Ochiltree, was on the back of a 35-tonne truck at Pennyvenie opencast site, Dalmellington, underneath the load carrier which had been hydraulically raised. It fell on him without warning, killing him instantly.

On 26 February 2007 about 1pm Colin Ferguson, (37), from Prestwick, and Brian French, (48), from Kelloholm, died on the opencast mining site at Pennyvenie, Dalmellington. The two men were in a Land Rover which was crushed by a dumper truck.

On 4 January 2008, Mr James Griffin, (40), died of massive crush injuries at Pennyvenie Open Cast site near Dalmellington, Ayrshire. The inquiry at Ayr Sheriff Court heard that Mr Griffin's 40 tonne truck had broken down and he had been given a jump start by a colleague's 35-tonner. Afterwards Mr Griffin, of Drongan, Ayrshire, was standing between the two massive vehicles, when his truck apparently rolled forward crushing him.

We read of disaster in some distant place,
And maybe we'll shed a silent tear:
But harder it seems when we do face
A disaster when it is here.

(anon)

Appendix 2

List of Players / Officials of Dalmellington Band who worked in Doon Valley Pits

Dalmellington Band members who were Doon Valley Mine Workers

Dalmellington Band was formed in 1864 and celebrated their sesquicentennial in 2014 – a proud record of 150 years of music making in a small former mining community with a population of some 3,200. This is really a quite remarkable achievement by one of Scotland's top concert bands.

The band from its inception has had miners as key members and committee members right up until Pennyvenie closed in 1978. In fact Hugh Johnstone MBE, aged 90, is the last former miner still active in the band.

The following is a list of Dalmellington Band members and officials who worked in the local coal pits and mines. This information was gleaned by Hugh Johnstone MBE from band photographs held in the band hall museum. The list shows the name of the mine worker and their role in the pits. It clearly highlights the central role of miners in playing roles, as well as supporting and sustaining the band over many years.

1922 photo of Dalmellington Band

Robert 'Beefy'Telfer, collier (also in 1932 photo); George English, collier; Jack Watson, blacksmith; George Hannah, coal washer manager (also in 1932 photo); Hugh Blackwood, coal washer manager; Hugh Blackwood, surface worker (also in 1932 photo); Jim Armour, collier; William Torbet, collier; James Hainey, collier (also in 1925 photo).

William McLelland, collier (also in 1932 photo); Robert McCreath, collier (also in 1932 photo); Robert Bell, surfaceman; Archie Kennedy, section oversman (also in 1932 photo); Robert 'Rabbie' Murray, hutch mender and canary keeper (also in 1932 photo); John McLelland, section oversman (also in 1932 photo); Jim McLelland, collier; John Kennedy, section oversman.

Jim Hill, shot firer; David Torbet, roadman (also in 1925 photo); Jim Torbet, woodman; Jim Dempsey, senior electrician; Robert Perry, hutch mender; James Armour, section oversman; Robert Mathieson, hutch member (also in 1932 photo); William Parker, railway maintenance (also in 1932 photo); James Orr, shot firer (also in 1932 photo); Jim Caddis (surface horseman).

1925 photo of Dalmellington Band

George Wallace, section oversman; William Blackwood, shot firer; Jackie Knox, collier and John Beck, woodman.

1932 photo of Dalmellington Band

George Park, railway union official; William Hainey, rail layer and maintenance; John Smith, road repairer; William Ireland, hutch mender; William Greig, haulage operator and David Scobie, collier; William Parker, collier.

1945 photo of Dalmellington Band

William Kennedy, engineer; John Paulin, collier; John Tylson, pit bottom banksman and Tom Park, road maintenance; Bill Hainey (also in 1932 photo); Ian Robb, senior underground survey team; Robert Gardiner, collier; Tom Telfer, chain runner; Tom Brown, hutch drawer; Robert Hill, woodman; Jim 'Jimsy' McPhail, hutch runner; Robert 'Beefy' Telfer, collier (also in 1922 photo); Tom Paulin, surfaceman; William Parker, collier; Hugh Johnstone (coal cutter operator).

1952 picture of Dalmellington Band

David Torbet, section oversman; William Currie, road maintenance; Jim Smith, collier (also 1932 photo); David Smith, collier; Edward Kerr, senior electrician; James Dick, electrician; Robert Boyd, weighman and surface worker; Robert Hill, woodman (also 1932 photo); Andrew Parker, shot firer; Tom Park, collier (also 1945 photo); James Graham, collier; Jim 'Jimsy' McPhail, collier (also 1945 photo); Tom Wilson, electrician; John Paulin, collier (also 1945 photo); John 'Jock' McLeod, surfaceman; William Greig, haulage operator (also 1932 photo); Jim Hose, surfaceman; Robert Peters, electrician.

1969 pictue of Dalmellington Band

John McCulloch (euphonium), collier, John 'Jubie' McCulloch (bass), general worker, Stephen Reid (collier), Lewis Uriarte (mine electrician), Roy Wright (engineer).